COMMUNITY LIBRARY

D0458934

PLAY IT AGAIN

PLAY IT AGAIN

AN AMATEUR AGAINST
THE IMPOSSIBLE

ALAN
RUSBRIDGER

FARRAR, STRAUS AND GIROUX

New York

Farrar, Straus and Giroux
18 West 18th Street, New York 10011

Copyright © 2013 by Alan Rusbridger
All rights reserved
Printed in the United States of America
Originally published in 2013 by Jonathan Cape, Great Britain
Published in the United States by Farrar, Straus and Giroux
First American edition, 2013

Grateful acknowledgment is made for permission to reprint the following material: Lines from *City Boy* by Edmund White, reproduced by kind permission of Edmund White and Bloomsbury Publishing. Ballade score © 1986 by Wiener Urtext Edition, Musikverlag Ges. m. b. H & Co., K. G., Wien/UT 50100, reproduced with permission.

Library of Congress Cataloging-in-Publication Data
Rusbridger, Alan.
    Play it again : an amateur against the impossible / Alan Rusbridger. — 1st edition.
        pages   cm
    Includes bibliographical references and index.
    ISBN 978-0-374-23291-7
    1. Rusbridger, Alan—Diaries.   2. Chopin, Frédéric, 1810–1849. Ballades, no. 1, op. 23, piano, G minor.   3. Pianists—Great Britain—Diaries.   4. Journalists—Great Britain—Diaries.   I. Title.

ML417.R798 A3 2013
786.2092—dc23
[B]

2013014884

www.fsgbooks.com
www.twitter.com/fsgbooks • www.facebook.com/fsgbooks

1   3   5   7   9   10   8   6   4   2

To my late mother, Barbara Rusbridger, who forced me to practise and who told me that music would lead to friendship. She was right.

CONTENTS

INTRODUCTION
1

PART ONE
9

PART TWO
35

PART THREE
105

PART FOUR
197

PART FIVE
221

PART SIX
249

PART SEVEN
277

PART EIGHT
303

EPILOGUE
351

SCORE AND COMMENTARY
355

ACKNOWLEDGEMENTS
389

FURTHER READING
391

INDEX
393

PLAY IT AGAIN

INTRODUCTION

This all began with Gary.

We were a group of strangers, who had come to the Lot Valley in central France to play the piano for a week; keen amateurs all. There was Stuart, the retired stockbroker; Liz from Manchester, who miraculously combined teaching, nursing and bringing up five kids; Fiona, the psychotherapist; John, the engineer; James, the paint company middle manager; Martin, the senior arts fund-raiser; Wendy, the clinical physiologist. And Gary.

Gary seemed the outsider – a little awkward, unfinished around the edges; at times distant, melancholy; troubled even. There had been hints about Gary's life – time spent as a Manchester cab driver; anecdotes about a pub he'd once run. And now, he'd produced business cards for his latest venture: a website for leather and PVC clothes. ('There's leather', he would say knowingly over dinner one night, 'and then there's . . . *leather*.')

A couple of days into the course, he'd broken off his masterclass – an overambitious attempt at some Liszt – saying he felt unwell. He was more than unusually withdrawn in the run-up to his final recital, when the nine of us played to each other. But then, on the last evening, he sat down and played Chopin's Ballade No. 1 in G minor, Op. 23.

In that bare stone-floored room in the Lot Valley, we were all transfixed. Gary's fingers seemed possessed. His customary sense of distraction had been replaced by complete absorption. He was playing one of the most complex and technically demanding pieces in the canon, and he was playing without the score, as if carrying the music inside him. All the hesitancy from earlier in the week had vanished. Something about this music had totally transformed Gary. As the piece picked up, moving into orgiastic furies of blurred finger-flying magic, Gary kept pace. Most of the notes were there and in the right place. The final Presto was both demonic and dramatic. The last converging octaves crashed out defiantly. He'd done it! An amateur pianist – no better than any of us – had just knocked off one of the most daunting

pieces in the piano repertoire. There was a moment of stunned silence. Gary turned round and looked a little sheepishly at us. And then the audience of eight burst into amazed applause.

A week or so later, I was packing for our annual August holiday in Italy, when at the last minute I found myself slipping a score of the Ballade into my suitcase. In our rented farmhouse, there was a cheap upright piano and, one day – the house was empty and with no danger of being overheard – I tentatively tried to pick my way through this formidable piece. I'd known the Chopin Ballades since university, but it had never before occurred to me to try to play any of them. In mountaineering terms, it would be akin to a middle-aged man deciding to climb the Matterhorn – something a few obsessive and foolhardy amateurs do, indeed, attempt, but fraught with peril.

I was the archetypal amateur who'd returned to the piano in middle age. My musical education had begun at the age of 6, when I joined the church choir. By 8, I was learning the piano. By 10, I had taken up the clarinet too, and then joined the cathedral choir at Guildford. For the next three years, I had a rather extraordinary immersion in music, with a rigid daily timetable of piano and clarinet practice, alongside choir rehearsals and church services.

I changed schools at 13, and arrived at Cranleigh School in Surrey – then a middle-of-the-road private school – where, for the next five years, singing and piano took a back seat to an intensive concentration on the clarinet. If, as the scientific consensus now apparently has it, it takes 10,000 hours to become expert in piano playing by the age of 18, I had missed the mark by a good 8,000 hours. I mucked around on the piano – often playing duets with friends – up to and including my days as a cub reporter on the *Cambridge Evening News*. Wherever I was living, I would enlist as a clarinettist in the local amateur orchestra, and seek out people who were up for piano duets. At Cambridge I rented pianos all through my undergraduate years. But I think I can safely say that I never seriously practised a single piano piece during my three years there. I certainly played a lot but I was, at best, a pianist endlessly replaying the few pieces I knew from school.

When I was about 19 I had a girlfriend, Ros, whose father was a slightly forbidding headmaster, a big gruff bear of a man, who seemed a rather nineteenth-century figure. Ros' parents had a grand piano in their sitting room and a few volumes of music, including some Chopin, which I would pick away at of an afternoon. To this day I remember her father challenging me on my opinion of Chopin. He demanded to know whether I took the fashionable view that Chopin was a sentimentalist.

I shifted uncomfortably on the sofa under his beady eye. And of course I denied it. Not at all. Chopin, sentimental? How ridiculous.

But, away from the head's study I realised that was exactly what I thought. Looking back now I guess it was purely a reaction against my parents' musical taste. A mild reaction, you might say, but a reaction nonetheless. Actually it wasn't precisely my parents' taste I was reacting against – Chopin was the sort of stuff my grandparents liked, and how on earth could you be drawn to anything like *that*?

Philip Feeney, one of my closest friends at Cambridge, a working-class boy who had won a musical scholarship to Winchester, eventually knocked this pretentiousness out of me. Philip's favourite piece of Chopin was the Nocturne No. 16 in E-flat major, Op. 55, No. 2. He'd play it repeatedly and I became enchanted by the way he performed the soaring leaps, the internal trills, the apparently endless melodies. So I'd found Chopin 'sentimental', but there was nothing sentimental about Philip, who was soon writing atonal music I couldn't begin to understand. That was a new prism for me: it was OK to be musically avant-garde and still like Chopin. Philip was the most unpretentious musician I knew. He almost physically prickled at the effete public-school atmosphere of Cambridge in whose midst he'd – reluctantly, it sometimes felt – arrived. He grew a shaggy beard, wore the same pair of unwashed jeans and T-shirt every day and would take me off to play darts every night in an attempt to knock some rough edges into me. If he liked Chopin, so could I.

My father – retired, no musical training, hobbies: newspapers and gardening – was also, improbably to me, falling in love with Chopin at the same time. He had been to hear the veteran French pianist Vlado Perlemuter play and something had gone pop in his brain. For the next twenty years he would buy his recordings and – right up to his last concerts (Perlemuter went on playing into his 80s) – would try to make it to hear him whenever he played in the UK. He travelled up to Cambridge to see the old man – who had a terrible musical memory – give a masterclass.

I started buying Chopin records and scores. The Etudes, the Nocturnes, the Preludes and concertos. And – in my second year at Cambridge – the Ballades. All I can remember of the cover of the Ballades LP was that it was sky blue. They were a revelation: almost a religious epiphany. Piano pieces on such a scale, of such intensity, with endless melodies; of such exquisite contrasts. This was sophisticated, large, elemental music of the heart. What on earth had I been thinking of – *sentimental*? Later I stumbled on the third sonata, which became a kind of anthem for me when I first moved to London until the tape wore out through constant repetition in my Renault 5's cassette player.

Which is not to say that I could play very much of it. I tried all the obvious pieces beginners try. I wasn't ready for the challenges of Chopin. I didn't learn these 'beginner' pieces properly; I just dabbled, as I did with all my piano playing for thirty years. It was only when I took a modest prelude to a teacher in my 40s that I realised what was involved in actually reading the notes; working out exactly where they fell; how to do legato fingering; how to pedal; how to bifurcate the brain so that the melody could float over a deep well of undulating harmony.

It was when I moved to London in 1979 to work as a journalist in Fleet Street that the real difficulties over keeping up with music began. I could never predictably be free for rehearsals or concerts: a reporter is always on the move, at the mercy of the news cycle. I moved from rented flat to rented flat – and, though I did buy an old upright piano somewhere along the way, it was always difficult to play in someone else's house. And then I moved to a flat too small for a piano.

By the time I got round to buying another old upright, it was the mid-1980s. I had married, Lindsay and I had two young daughters – Isabella and Lizzie – and my job involved long hours, foreign travel and, in 1986, six months abroad. My clarinets gathered dust. My piano repertoire dwindled to a handful of nursery rhymes. And then in my early 40s I became editor of the *Guardian* and had one of those jobs which expands infinitely to fill the time and then spill beyond it. An editor, particularly within a modern global media company, is never truly off duty. A news website churns away night and day, demanding constantly to be fed and refreshed. Emails gush in round the clock. Correspondents in far-flung parts find themselves in trouble; lawyers are threatening or suing; politicians are alternately cajoling or aggrieved. There's no time for a life, let alone a hobby. To be sure, some of my fellow editors would find time to go to the gym, or jog or play squash. They might even carve out a few hours at the weekend to play golf. But time to play the piano seriously? When?

Yet something in the creative DNA was stirring – a distant memory of that flourishing musical inner life that had been almost an obsession until my mid-20s.

'Creative DNA' is, obviously, not a precise statement of the science. Something I once read by Carl Jung best captured the sense of what was stirring within me. He wrote of how, as we approach the middle of life, we may well have succeeded 'socially'; that is, had children, become more comfortable materially, perhaps even gained status or modest recognition in our chosen field. But, at the same time, he said, we can 'overlook the essential fact that the social goal is attained only at the cost of a diminution of the personality'. 'Many – far too many – aspects of life which should have been experienced lie in the lumber-room among dusty memories,' he wrote. But all is not lost, because sometimes these memories 'are glowing coals under grey ashes'.

For Jung – and, please, I have Pass Notes Jung, not a PhD – middle age and the years that follow may in fact constitute our chance to do something about these 'glowing coals':

> A human being would certainly not grow to be 70 or 80 years old if this longevity had no meaning for the species to which he belongs. The afternoon of human life must also have a significance of its own and cannot be merely a pitiful appendage of life's morning. The significance of the morning undoubtedly lies in the development of the individual, our entrenchment in the outer world, the propagation of our kind and the care of our children. This is the obvious purpose of nature. But . . . whoever carries over into the afternoon the law of the morning must pay for so doing with damage to his soul. Moneymaking, social existence, family and posterity are nothing but plain

nature – not culture. Culture lies beyond the purpose of nature. Could by any chance culture be the meaning and purpose of the second half of life?

Whatever it was – DNA, psychology, a mundane need to have moments off the hamster wheel of editing – in my mid-40s, my 'afternoon', I felt this same instinct to wall off a small part of my life for creative expression, for 'culture'. Isabella and Lizzie were by now teenagers; they didn't need watching every minute. On the contrary, they would happily spend much of their daylight hours asleep – particularly at weekends or on holiday. At such moments I rediscovered time I'd forgotten I had. I wrote two children's books. I dusted off the watercolours and experienced again the feeling – lost since art lessons at 14 – of applying wet paint on paper. And I played the piano.

Of course, I discovered that, just as I couldn't paint, so I couldn't really play the piano. I generally picked up the same old pieces, with the mistakes as well-remembered as the notes, but occasionally now I tried to play with a little more focus. The thought did occur to me that I could try something new and challenging – the Mozart C minor sonata, for example. A Chopin nocturne, perhaps? And, for a few days, I would try . . . but then move on to something else.

I did, however, decide to take lessons. It was the first time since my early 20s that I had actually studied anything in any formal sense. I'd had a very clear determination on leaving university, after a dozen years of taking exams, that I never wanted to study anything again and, barring a patchy bash at mastering shorthand, I hadn't. But now I started lessons with Michael Shak, who lived three streets away in Kentish Town. Mild, earnest, gay, American, nervy, warm, exacting, he had at some point abandoned ambitions of playing professionally on account of 'performance issues', aka fear.

In the first couple of years with Michael, I more or less stuck to his very rigid way of working. He took me right back to some very short Schubert *Tänze* – each one only a few bars long and, apparently, simple stuff. But under Michael's regime, nothing was simple. He would sit at my elbow like a hawk, pouncing on any misplaced note. These were real lessons, with technique as the focus. But – to Michael's evident distaste – I was quickly acquiring a yen to try big, ambitious pieces and took him the first movement of Beethoven's Op. 110. We struggled with this for about three months before I retired hurt. For about the same time, we worked on the last movement of the Schumann Fantasie, a piece I had first messed around with at university. By the time Michael had finished with me, I could actually play every note in the right place, as written. I'm pretty sure this was the first time in my life I could say that of any piece. I was 50.

By then, playing piano had become a crucial part of my daily routine. Call it an escape, call it a compulsion, but it felt like a physical need. If I could spend twenty minutes at the piano before going to work, I had a powerful sense that the chemistry of my brain had been altered. On the days I played, my brain felt 'settled' and ready for whatever the next twelve hours would bring. Much later, I was to discover that it was not exactly a chemical reaction, but a literal rewiring of the neural circuitry.

And then, thanks to a former theatre critic of *The Times*, I discovered the Lot Music summer piano courses. Irving Wardle, by then nudging 80 but still playing, had read a piece I'd written for *Granta* about dabbling in the piano and he suggested I might find it fun to enrol. He sent me an article of his own, which included the memorable epigram: 'I am an excellent pianist. The only snag is that I don't play very well.'

And so it was that, each July for the following five years, I found myself at the home of Anne Brain, a Manchester-based plastic surgeon (and amateur pianist and flautist) who'd had the bright idea of using her French base – perched above the pretty little village of Prayssac – to house an annual piano camp for like-minded enthusiasts. And where this year Gary had astonished us with his performance of the Chopin Ballade. And now, three weeks later, here I was lying by the pool in Italy with the question still nagging at me: how on earth had Gary managed that?

In the league table of the amateur pianists on the course, he ranked somewhere in the middle. There had been one or two who could have had a professional career, had life dealt a different hand. And there were others who were simply madly enthusiastic hobbyists. Gary had a pretty good technique – better than mine – and was ambitious in his choice of repertoire. But, like me, there had been a gaping hole in his life as a pianist and, like me, it showed. He had an impressive ability to memorise music; I had none. I could sight-read pretty well; his sight-reading was not so good. We were playing in very roughly the same league. But here was a glaring difference: he could play Chopin's Ballade and I couldn't. Not in my dreams could I get near playing it. The thought niggled away. It wasn't (I think, I hope) a competitive thought – if he can, I must – so much as simple curiosity. How was it possible? If I could begin to comprehend that, I would have a much better understanding of how to play this instrument that had, if I was frank, really eluded me for the whole of my life.

And that's how, within that first week on holiday, I resolved to learn the piece and perform it. I would give myself a year. Day job or no day job, I'd carve out the time to practise the hell out of Chopin's Op. 23. I was three months short of my 57th birthday – quite late for a Damascene conversion to a musical rigour that I had so far shunned. Were my brain and fingers still capable of learning new tricks? I would have to acquire lashings of technique I knew about but had spent a life avoiding. I would have to coach my brain – hitherto incapable of memorising a single note of music – to retain a vast database of complex notation. I would have to un-learn a lifetime of bad habits – of sight-reading my way out of trouble; of playing pieces too fast too soon; of skating over tricky passages, pretending to myself that I would come back and tackle them later. In short, I would have to learn to play the piano properly.

Perhaps if I'd known then what else would soon be happening in my day job, I might have had second thoughts. For it would transpire that, at the same time, I would be steering the *Guardian* through one of the most dramatic years in its history: a year that began with WikiLeaks – the biggest dump of state secrets in history – and ended with the most powerful media organisation in the world reduced to abject apologies and corporate crisis-management over the *Guardian*'s revelations about widespread phone hacking – a story that would later see me immersed in the gargantuan Leveson Inquiry into the British press. In between, there were the Japanese tsunami, the Arab Spring, the English riots, the slow, teetering collapse of European finance mechanisms and the death of Osama Bin Laden. All of this in the midst of the biggest cultural, economic and technological changes newspapers had ever seen. The test would be to nibble out twenty minutes each day to do something that had nothing at all to do with any of the above.

I decided I would keep a diary of this year of the Ballade. I would find some time at weekends to interview pianists, amateur and professional, about the challenge I'd set myself. Over the course of eighteen months I met actors, sportsmen, taxi drivers, politicians, teachers and diplomats who, once they learned of the project, opened up about the gravitational pull of music in their own lives. I would quiz neuroscientists to try to unravel the workings of music on my brain.

And I would undertake to learn the piece that the great Murray Perahia was soon to warn me is 'one of the hardest pieces in the repertoire'.

PART ONE

Friday, 6 August 2010

The annual holiday begins. It's unadventurous of us, but for the past few years we've taken the same house on the La Foce estate in the Val d'Orcia in Italy. It's an old farmhouse with a pool and works fine for someone who, once they're on holiday, has no great inclination to move more than a hundred yards from the kitchen, a deckchair or a swim. The landscape all around is baked and agricultural – day after day a vast tractor ploughs the soil which breaks into such great boulders of heavy clay that it seems impossible that anything could grow in it. In the 1920s, the Anglo-American writer Iris Origo, who lived on the estate with her husband, Antonio, an Italian duke, described the area as marked by 'low clay hillocks' which are 'as bare and colourless as elephants' backs, as mountains of the moon'. The UNESCO World Heritage List calls it: 'an exceptional reflection of the way the landscape was rewritten in Renaissance times to reflect the ideals of good governance and to create an aesthetically pleasing picture'. The Renaissance flavour certainly hits you on rare sorties out of the house to the extraordinary hilltop town of Pienza, whose fifteenth-century cathedral and palaces tower over a valley with a view which can't have changed much over the past five centuries.

The holiday villa consists of four bedrooms above a ground floor which would once have been a winter shelter for animals and is now a very large ping-pong room with futons for spill-over guests. And, this year, a piano – quite unexpected and unasked for. It transpires the previous occupants had ordered it and the rental company has so far failed to collect it. So there it is: a shiny Yamaha upright in the corner of the downstairs room.

Saturday, 7 August

The La Foce estate is dotted with houses tucked away on hillsides or on the edges of forests. Mostly, you never discover who is staying in these houses: there is just the distant sight of a car kicking up dust along a winding white road, or the echoes of laughter. But there is a bush telegraph at work, with the occasional invitation to a drink or meal.

In the evening, Lindsay and I take a twenty-five-minute drive up a tortuous, rutted track to a hilltop house with spectacular views over the valley below. And there among the guests, sipping a glass of wine and gazing out over the volcanic valley, is none other than Alfred Brendel. He is looking good at eighty, and much more relaxed and easy-going since playing his last piano recital in Vienna, in December 2008 – I had reviewed the Musikverein concert in the *Guardian*. Over a drink Brendel says he's perfectly happy with his post-performance life. He didn't, he insists, live for applause or accolades. Lots of people may have shed tears when he gave up, but not him. Is he happy talking about the piano? It's difficult to tell, but he is extremely graceful in answering my questions, which I hope don't fall into the category of 'Where, as an editor, do you get all your stories from?'

He talks about the age in which he grew up – where you had to choose between the classical tradition (Haydn–Beethoven–Schubert) and Chopin (and, to a degree, Liszt). Brendel made one Chopin recording – and then, with some regrets now, decided not to play any more Chopin for the rest of his career. But he did play the G minor Ballade before the curtain came down on Chopin. I ask him about it. It is, objectively, not the hardest, he says, but it is very difficult to interpret. He tells me that the thing one has to realise about Chopin is that he was the only composer who wrote purely for the piano. The music grows out of the instrument. With all other composers you feel they have a symphonic side, or a choral side, which comes out in their piano music, but with Chopin it was all piano music.

Sunday, 8 August

Today, when the house is empty and there is no danger of being overheard, I decide it's time to begin. The girls will sleep in late. Lindsay is down at the pool. I have two hours to myself. I sit down at the shiny Yamaha and for the first time try sight-reading Chopin's G minor Ballade. I've known the piece since university, but it has never once, in the intervening years, occurred to me to try to play it. Turns out I was right to avoid it: it is surely an impossible piece for any amateur pianist to pull off. As I sit with my fingers fumbling their way laboriously over the notes at snail's pace, I am immediately overwhelmed with frustration. The technical challenges are so enormous. What if I'd not left it so late, if I'd kept up twenty minutes a day from the age of 30 instead of 50? Maybe then it wouldn't be so impossible.

The first of Chopin's four Ballades was probably composed around 1834–5. Chopin was about 24 and was living in Paris, having left Warsaw for an unsatisfactory nine-month stay in Vienna around the time of the 1830 uprising against Russian hegemony. Various musicologists think all these historical details help understand what's going on in the piece. A listener, they say, has to understand this is a work of exile. It's a piece composed during a revolutionary period when Polish nationalism found its way into culture – in the case of music, by virtue of folk songs or by drawing on folkloric forms from literature. Chopin, unable to return to Warsaw, wrote mazurkas and polonaises. He read the ballades of the Polish poet Adam Mickiewicz and moved away from many aspects of the classical tradition which arguably reached its peak with the late works of Beethoven. The Ballades were complex and revolutionary pieces in every way.

The Ballade lasts just under ten minutes – at least in the hands of professionals – and begins with a declamation. If this is a story, the storyteller is calling everyone to attention. For five bars there are only octaves, with no internal harmony or colouring. The starkness of the notes is compounded by confusion as to where they lead. It's not entirely clear what key the piece is in or where the tonal centre lies. The introduction ends with an extraordinary chord (bar 7) known as a Neapolitan sixth. This is an 'unstable'-sounding chord which has to be resolved – not straight to the key of the overall piece, G minor, but to the 'dominant' key of D *before* finally reaching G minor in bar 9.

By now we're into the first theme – theme A, which is certainly in G minor. But there's a little motif in that introduction which is worth noticing, a little 'sigh' in the second half of bar 3. We hear it again in bars 9/10 and across 13/14 – and then repeatedly and wistfully through the opening Moderato. Theme A is tender, yearning and built around a tentative two-bar phrase which Chopin keeps restating, each time with a slight harmonic or melodic variation. It's a lilting fragment of a tune at this stage, not quite a waltz, but with the hint, or echo, of one. There's also the suggestion of a heartbeat in the throb-throb pulse of the left-hand (LH) chords, the first maybe a tiny bit louder than the second. Only at bar 22 can we sink into a longer, more fluent statement. Then for a moment the music swells in confidence, only to become more hesitant again by bar 29.

From bar 36 we're into a linking passage – once more with a hint of the sighing motif from the introduction. At first the mood is still tender and wistful. But this four-bar phrase is repeated agitato and suddenly we're jolted out of a gentle, if sometimes edgy, world into something more menacing. The music is much faster now, more percussive and fragmentary. As before, there's a suggestion of a waltz, but a rather demotic one.

At bar 48 the mood changes again. Everything – at least in a professional performance – has been speeding up. Suddenly there's a torrent of sound – the left hand hammering and insistent over a cascade of right-hand (RH) notes with syncopated cross-rhythms. A series of rippling arpeggios and thundering LH octaves firmly establishes that we're rooted in G minor.

And then there's a simply magical transformation. The insistent hammering LH G minor chords in 56 and 60 become – in 64 – a far-off horn call. And then another and another. The music fades as the call becomes more distant. And we've changed key. Are we in F major now or F minor? Everything, within a bar, melts into E-flat major for the second tune – theme B. Once again, there is the lilt of a waltz to the tune, but this is the most exquisitely tender love music – sighs and all. Throughout the piece, Chopin never allows one mood to prevail for long. Within fifteen bars (at bar 82) there's an apparently new motif introduced – a little triplet ornament in the RH. In fact, it's a speeded-up variation on theme A, though not explicit enough for most ears to recognise it as such immediately.

At bar 92 the mood changes again. The temperature drops around 10 degrees in the space of a few notes, the harmonies wither away to a bleak and bare E. The throb-throb – so tender in the first hearing of theme A – is now a little menacing. The heartbeat is quickening a little as theme A returns in a much edgier way. The sigh has become anxious and, by bar 99, almost a question.

But then sunlight floods into the piece. At bar 106 theme B returns – by now not a whisper of love, but as something majestic or triumphant. It's large, expansive, grandiloquent music over grand fortissimo chords in the LH. Or is it? Pianists can't even agree over the key here – some think it's A major, some E major. And some urge you not to be seduced by the apparent grandeur. Listen more carefully: it's ironic, can't you see?

By 119 the grand mood, ironic or not, is dissipating. The LH chords become more dissonant, while the RH has ever more and insistent octave runs up to a dramatic fortississimo climax which lasts precisely one beat before it comes crashing down to something like pianissimo two bars later. Now the mood, with the goading LH interruptions and quickening tempo, is positively anxious. The clouds are once more casting a shadow of doubt.

But then what happens? Chopin – out of nowhere – gives us a real waltz (bar 138), not an implied or twisted or suggested one. We're back in a major key and the RH has a piece of filigree ornamentation over the elegant three-step LH. We could be in a Paris ballroom. But are we? Is this more irony? Is that the 'sigh' returning in the LH, with its feeling of regret and longing? Is the RH actually a distorted version of theme A?

In any case – and long before you have a chance to decide on any of that – the waltz is over as suddenly as it began. It's lasted precisely seven bars – in the middle of which (bar 141) Chopin subverts the whole thing by writing cross-rhythms into the RH which make the ear hear a bar in four time rather than three time.

Virtually throughout the piece the music is either falling or rising. Now, at bar 146, it starts rising chromatically and then in angular repeated patterns leading to another fortissimo one-beat climax – a second inversion (hence very 'unstable' F-sharp major chord) followed four bars later by a sforzando second inversion E-flat major chord at 158. The music rises again. And immediately, at 162, cascades down to another fortissimo restatement of theme B at 166. We're in B-flat major now – closely related to the original G minor. For some twenty-five bars the LH ripples away with an arpeggiated bass as the RH sings the theme . . . majestically? It certainly could be. But maybe by now the listener has learned to mistrust any of the surface moods of the music. It is never quite as tender, nor as sweet, nor grandiloquent, nor charming as it seems at first. Perhaps we simply suspend judgement and let the great heaving ocean waves of glory roll over us. By 180 the alert ear will pick up the double-speed variant of theme A that Chopin first introduced halfway through the first statement of theme B. Now (bar 180) it's a con forza – but soon melting.

By 194 it's melted. Precisely a hundred bars earlier the temperature dropped to a single note of doom. It does so again now, but a note lower. We're back with theme A, with the heartbeat LH. But no one could mistake this for tenderness now. It's an adrenaline heartbeat. There's worry, barely controlled panic in the sound. By 202 the RH sigh has been repeated three times. Theme A – remember how lilting, gentle and waltzlike it first sounded? – is turning to terror.

At 206 Chopin lays down an organ-like pedal in the dominant D and tells the pianist to play passionately and as loudly as possible. Something terrible is coming. In 207 he winds the spring to a pitch of unbearable tension which is only released with the arrival of G minor at the start of the coda.

The coda is the bit nearly every pianist fears, no matter how good they are, no matter how many hundreds of hours they've put into this piece. It explodes. It's presto con fuoco – extremely fast and fiery. The syncopated rhythms can throw and confuse the ear, the feet, the brain and the fingers. The RH is soon flying up and down the keyboard in trapeze-like leaps completely unrelated to the LH's own jumps. Something diabolic is happening – the listener must hear that – a sense of loss of control and a shattering of all earthly order. But how to convey that abandon without a loss of technical control?

By 230 the music is edging up chromatically, suggesting creeping horror. By 238 everything is falling to earth. Four bars later we're on our way back up – another chromatic sweep in the RH against a LH fanfare. And, at 246, the reverse – plunging from the top of the keyboard to the bottom, arriving on a knell of G minor. A moment of still. Then – whoosh – back up. A quiet chorale G minor chord. Theme A in its manic form breaks in. Silence. Again, another upward swoop – four octaves of G minor, this time in tenths. Silence. Chorale. Manic theme A. And – the most revolutionary ending to any piano piece ever written to that point? – a crashing convergence of octave chords. They start from opposite ends of the keyboard at first getting slower, then faster and faster. Sometimes harshly dissonant, sometimes not, they end with two octaves of a chromatic G minor scale. A final doom-laden knell of G minor.

So what's going to stop me being able to play this piece? I start to construct a list of the horrendous technical challenges which – at any other point in my life – would have deterred me from even trying. Here are a dozen immediately obvious reasons why the piece is unplayable . . . by me.

1.

This sort of stuff at bar 33 – squashed flies on a page – happens all over Chopin. One moment everything's calm, the next the right hand is fitting in millions of notes for every note in the LH. Well, not millions, but enough for the little black dots to blur in front of the eyes and beads of sweat to form on the forehead. Four per note for the first three beats. And then – count them – eighteen for the next three. Six a beat, strictly speaking, except that would sound rather mechanical. So perhaps split them six-eight-four? They have to sound effortless. But that means a long time with a pencil writing in exactly which finger is going to play which note and then memorising it all.

2.

The first bit of passage work which hits you three pages in. This is really hard. The LH starts in one octave and then plummets an octave. So does the RH, but exactly a bar later. The LH figure is a clumsy mixture of third fingers and fifth fingers – they'll have to find the leaps on their own because the eyes are going to be on the RH, which is darting all over the place – difficult fingerings, difficult leaps, twisty shapes. And the fact that the eyes are not going to be on the music means that every note must be memorised.

And the rhythm is disconcertingly syncopated. The RH looks and (without the LH) feels as if it's written in patterns of three, or even triplets. But add in the LH and the strong feeling is in two, not three.

3.

Same passagework a little later. Nearly ten bars of broken chords in the RH, over three octaves and in three different keys and far-from-obvious fingers. I haven't practised arpeggios for decades, or I would have a more instinctive idea of how these should be played. And, for added complication, Chopin's written in horn calls (in two different octaves) in the LH. Assuming eyes transfixed on RH fireworks (more memorising), how is the LH going to find its way to exactly the right spot for the horn calls?

4.

The big second tune – so sweet and melancholy in its first outing, now returns very grandly in A major or E major, depending on which pianist you talk to. Once again, as with much Chopin, the two hands have different problems to confront. The LH lays down a carpet of chords – changing key every bar, if not twice a bar and arcing over four octaves with each chord in a different inversion. So that, on its own, is an hour of fingering and a month of memorising. The RH is playing in large infilled octaves, trying to sing a triumphant melodic line over the LH, with some tricky triplet turns along the way.

5.

Just when you were getting the hang of the chords Chopin writes in three octave runs in the RH. But what on earth are they? Is the first B minor? But with an E sharp thrown in? The second C-sharp minor apart from an F double sharp? The third G-sharp minor? Even if I knew the vanilla version of these keys I'd still struggle because each scale is slightly 'wrong'. As it is I'll have to learn each one individually, together with the right fingerings. And memorise.

6.

I find this extremely tricky. The RH is a filigree moto perpetuo waltz – OK once you get the hang of it – but the LH has got big leaps (so that rules out looking at either the music or the RH, which is just going to have to play on autopilot) and these sighing chords, which don't fit naturally under my hand at all. Playable adagio – but anything faster than that sends shooting pains up my left arm.

7.

Passage work. Fingering. Notes. Memory. Coordination.

8.

Fairly horrible. A long descending scale which begins as one thing (?B-flat major, but with an E natural thrown in just in case that's too obvious). And then – with a large spread chord in the LH to distract you – it changes into something else. Nearly seven octaves in all.

9.

One of the most unnerving bars in the piece. Let me count the ways:

1) a trill on the first note in RH (with two weakest fingers, 4 and 5) while thumb holds the octave.
2) It's six beats in the bar. LH twelve notes. Outer part of RH seven notes. Inner part of RH seven notes. But a different seven. Middle part of RH two notes.
3) So get a pencil out and work out which note falls where. Draw lines on the score to show exactly where individual RH notes sound in relation to the LH. There's maths involved in working out the relation between a crotchet quadruplet (four single notes, or beats, in the time of three) versus a quaver triplet (three half-beats in the time of two) versus three quavers (three half-beats) versus two crotchets (two full beats).

4) Now you've marked it up, try to play it. And make the melody (in outer fingers of RH) sing over the musical quadratic equation going on underneath. With a bit of rubato please.

So this is where the real fun begins. The nightmare coda, which the best pianists in the world fear. It's presto con fuoco – demonically fast – and syncopated. The LH is making large leaps which confuse the expected rhythm. You're anticipating an oom-pah bass, whereas he's actually written a pah-oom bass. There's no time to catch breath or think – it's either there in the fingers or it isn't.

A nightmare for the RH, which is required to perform death-defying trapeze artist leaps in mid-air. The hand has to take off at the speed of sound, arriving precisely six and a half inches to the left, substituting a little finger for a thumb on a ridge of wood. This swoop down the piano is immediately followed by a swoop up – another leap of faith, with the thumb replacing the little finger, and then straight back down. The melody is essentially in the thumb, so everything else is decorative. But the thumb-melody is an octave apart. Once again, the eyes will be in two places at once (the LH is making its own octave leaps), so there's no possibility of looking at the score at the same time. More memorising.

12.

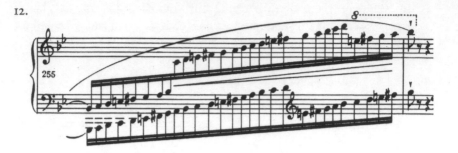

Having taken you right down to the bottom of the keyboard, Chopin races you back up again – twice. The first is a three-octave G minor scale, both hands in parallel. Too easy? OK, try this for size: two hands, four octaves and a tenth apart. So, each hand is playing a G minor scale, but starting on a different note.

At any other time in my life, I would quietly have closed the music and put it back on the shelf. The added fear overlaying the entire enterprise is that I have never memorised a note of music in my life. I can't remember poetry, dates, phone numbers, films, novels – or music. Given that half of the piece is unplayable unless the eyes are on the hands and not on the score, I have no idea how, in my late 50s, I am going to retrain my brain.

Tuesday, 10 August

Not only is there a piano in our villa, I've discovered there's a piano teacher on hand too. The people staying at the house next door have hired him from the local town of Sarteano. Would I like to share?

So a few days after our evening with the Dworkin/Brendels, I make my way across the little valley between the farmhouses to meet the teacher, Francesco Cioncoloni. Francesco speaks very little English and I speak very little Italian. He is in his mid-20s and, these days, primarily a church organist. His eyebrows arch at my holiday choice of piano music. He's never played the Ballade himself, but he knows it by reputation. He takes the first lesson gently – none of the really frightening stuff over the page, just the slightly easier first section. He wants me to think of it as bel canto – something beautifully sung. And, indeed, he sings it. Hearing him, I understand why people make the connection between Chopin and Vincenzo Bellini, the nineteenth-century opera composer.

Thursday, 12 August

Two days later, I cross the valley again for a second lesson. This time there's no avoiding the arpeggios. I've already spent hours over the holiday pencilling in how I intend to finger the piece, but now Francesco gets out his rubber and erases all my marks in these sections. Yes, it would normally be logical to have G minor arpeggios with the thumb on the G, but not in this passage. Here it makes more sense to have the thumb on the D, he says. I go back to the villa and play it very slowly, just the RH. One bar at a time. Trying to think of the notes in two groups of three – thumb, two, three; thumb, two, three – rather than in bars.

If I were truly disciplined I'd probably just stick with this passage for the time being, but I'm curious about the later bits – like the crashing chords around bar 106. My current bible on how to practise is a yellowing second-hand copy of *Playing the Piano for Pleasure*, a 1940s book by a former *New Yorker* writer, Charles Cooke, himself an amateur pianist. His technique was to identify the weakest moments in a piece (like my twelve horrors, above) and turn them into the strongest. He called these sections 'fractures'.

> I believe in marking off, in every piece we study, all passages that we find especially difficult, and then practising these passages patiently, concentratedly, intelligently, relentlessly until we have battered them down, knocked them out, surmounted them, dominated them, conquered them – until we have transformed them, thoroughly and permanently, from the weakest into the strongest passages in the piece.

I mark this section at bar 106, with its very large chords and octave reaches, as a 'fracture' in 6B pencil and then look again at the next passage – a series of rising octaves in the RH splattered in sharps and naturals. This is a whole new fingering feast. The thumb does all the work, playing all the lower notes. But Francesco has told me there are differing views about the right combination of fourth and fifth finger on the upper line, and just to make life more complicated he has suggested trying the odd third finger to get smoother runs – so 3–4–5 – but I've never played octaves with the third finger before, so that feels too strange for now. I look at other sections and they all contain myriad fingering complications. But they are a doddle compared with what happens at 130 – a four-bar passage with a little rising figure which repeats itself every sixteen notes. This is where music becomes maths. I count them: forty-eight notes in all, beginning on a second beat just to complicate matters. So how does this pattern work? There are eight notes – a mix of naturals, flats and sharps – starting on a B flat. And then, on the last beat of the bar, eight notes starting on an E natural and including a C flat. That means it's not in any recognisable key, so each note will have to be memorised and fingered separately, not in distinct patterns.

But by the end of the day I have managed to finger most of the piece bar the coda. The bareness of those pages makes the passage look even more frightening than it is already: there's something comforting about seeing lots of pencil marks above the notes. I begin to work out the patterns in the coda – a four-bar pattern which repeats itself; a two-bar repeating pattern. But the moment you look closer you see the ways in which Chopin constantly changes the pattern, subverts it, switches the beat, tweaks the harmonies. I am beginning to understand why he is so absorbing to listen to and so difficult to play: he keeps confounding the expectations of the ear. There are patterns here – God knows, I've just worked it out note by note – but it's almost deliberately written so that it would not be obvious to the listener.

There is, though, a kind of satisfying holiday rhythm in going through the piece with my 6B pencil working all of this out. Not the sort of thing you'd want to do back home in London with work pressing in, but pleasantly absorbing now. And I am beginning to grasp how I'll have to approach the piece. There's going to be no alternative to learning it inch by inch – you have to understand how it works and, once you understand, finally try to play it.

Thursday, 19 August

Our fortnight's holiday is almost over. Only a couple of days left, just as everything adjusts to the slower pace of life. But over the space of the last week – and with at least an hour a day of quite concentrated practice – I've gone from feeling that the Ballade is a completely unplayable piece to thinking it's just very, very, *very* difficult – and possibly, just possibly, within my grasp.

Last Friday, having spent the previous day sketching out the fingering, I tried to play some of the piece again. I started with the first six pages, which, with all kinds of qualifications, I could begin to play. Well, a bit. But not really. I still panic at the squashed flies at bar 33, and there are hideous wrenches of tempo as I slow down for the hard bits, and then (I hope no one's listening) speed up for the occasional easier bit. The big E major section has been a bit of a shambles – I still haven't remotely mastered the LH chords.

Instead of skimming over the panic moment of the squashed flies in bar 33, I went back to it to work out precisely what's going on. I spent fifteen minutes on the bar, working out the groups of six, practising them in different rhythms and experimenting with varied fingerings, questioning the marks I'd sketched out the day before. Would I ever have time to concentrate in this detail when I'm back at work?

But it's still holiday time, so I then apply the same concentration to the G minor arpeggios at bar 56, forcing myself to remember the new fingering with the thumb on the D not the G, and then trying consciously to remember (because otherwise it's total instinct) where exactly the left-hand horn calls come. The thumb-every-three-notes makes me think of the arpeggios as if they were triplets, but the LH breaks that into two notes, not three. So I forced my right hand to play in two, not three – ta-ta, not ta-ta-ta.

I then skipped forward and tried to work out the cross-rhythms in the little waltz. It's the LH that's the bugger here. There are huge leaps and, with the second trio of LH notes, a very awkward movement involving the weak little and fourth fingers – a shift which, for me, appears to involve a manoeuvre of the entire body. I seem to have to bend over rightwards in order to be able to move the two fingers. If I was a proper pianist, I would know how to angle the hand differently – I've been told that Russian pianists are taught to play with their hands at any angle to their arms – but for me, just getting that flexibility into my LH could take some weeks. Then at our final lesson, when I showed Francesco what I'm doing, with my rightwards tilt, he told me I should be moving my body out, not sideways.

I have also been confronting the coda. The last four pages of the Ballade must be the most exciting pages of piano music imaginable – if only one could play them. They involve a collision of so many technical challenges: enormous leaps in LH, very fast repeated chords RH, vast sweeping 'trapeze leaps' in RH, chromatic rising bass chords in RH with continued trapeze leaps, a three-octave chromatic scale RH, then an eight-octave swooping cascade of notes and G minor ascending scales in octaves and tenths. Each one of these elements is brutally hard. Put them together and play it presto and it becomes truly terrifying.

On all previous form I'd have somehow glossed over it, or simply given up, but with my new methodical approach I break it down. Three notes in one hand position. Then five in the next, then three. On their own they are playable – just at an embarrassingly slow speed. But I resolve to be patient about practising these individual clusters of notes. I can worry about putting them together later.

Friday, 20 August

Our final day in Italy, and I plunge into the coda once more. This time, I start with just the LH. Played slowly, it seems almost unrecognisable from the recordings, which – at presto – have a kind of forward momentum which makes the piece sound utterly different. I'm playing it at $\downarrow$ = 40 – which is slower than largo – and at this speed the music doesn't make sense at all.* It has no line or progression. So this is definitely going to be a nightmare passage. On the other hand, what had seemed completely unplayable a week ago, I can now play at paint-drying pace.

* Musicians dictate the speed of a piece by suggesting how many notes to the minute. It's complicated by American and English musicians using different language. So $\downarrow$ = 40 tells an English musician to play less than one crotchet per second. This is a very slow beat indeed. Americans call crotchets quarter-notes.

So much practice brings with it reminders that piano playing is an intensely physical business, one which has done actual harm to countless people who have overdone it, or started out with faulty technique. I've been putting off revisiting the broken chords at 166, because the big stretches in the LH required there are quite painful. If there is one bit of the piece where I am going to get some form of repetitive strain injury, it's going to be here. In fact, I have already started to get a burn in my arm muscles. This is probably the first warning sign about practising too intensively or too fast.

Over this final week of the holiday, I've also realised that it will be impossible to play some sections of the piece without first memorising them. It simply moves too fast to be able to switch attention from the notes on the page to the hands on the keyboard. This is making me anxious about the whole project, given the problems I've always had with remembering music.

And, of course, above all this, there remains my major worry. I've had the luxury of almost two weeks with the Ballade, and a week of really good, slow practice. Whenever the piece is really not clicking, it's because I'm playing too fast. Learning music is something like healing – something which takes time and can't be rushed. Back in London, as life speeds up, will I be able to transport myself back into this slow-music frame of mind? Is there any chance that I'll be able to carve out the time?

Saturday, 21 August

August is supposed to be the silly season, the period when there's no important news – though just as often it's the month when wars break out, famous people die and stock markets crash. Today I receive an immediate and startling reminder of the news cycle and its pressures within minutes of touching down at Heathrow: a text telling me that WikiLeaks founder Julian Assange has been arrested in Sweden on suspicion of rape.

We've been waiting for some kind of attempt to discredit him and this is surely it. Though it does seem remarkably crude. Part one of Wiki-Leaks – the publication of a ton of material about the war in Afghanistan – already feels like the distant past, though it was only a few weeks ago. At the *Guardian*, part two of the project, which will constitute the biggest leak of military and state secrets in history, has been poised and ready to go for a few weeks now. The plan has been to delay publication until September, but it has been such a complicated partnership to coordinate, with a German weekly, *Der Spiegel*, and the *New York Times*. Never mind Assange, the difficult, brilliant, elusive, slippery wizard behind it all. I email David Leigh, an investigative reporter at the paper, to find out what's up. He and our colleague Nick Davies have worked most closely with Assange and have more or less got on with him (though Nick's enthusiasm has been cooling of late). David – who has even had him sleeping in his flat for part of the collaboration – has nursed a theory that Assange is not quite of this planet. He emails me back: 'Apparently they have bad sexual manners on Alpha Centauri, where he comes from.' But Nick is worried. He has spoken to Assange's associates in Sweden, who insist this is not some kind of CIA smear – i.e. Assange hasn't been framed, but may well have done something problematical, which will need dealing with and explaining.

For a few hours we phone, text and email. We all agree we will have to report on whatever it is that's been going on. It would be fatal to the credibility of all involved if it looked as though the newspaper partners were protecting Assange simply because he had been a collaborator and/or source. In fact, it's even more complicated. He's both a collaborator and a source – but also *not* a source, in the sense he was not the original leaker. And he's a publisher in his own right – and an activist whose vision and aims will only partly coincide with ours.

Sunday, 22 August

From London, we head to Blockley for the final few days of our holiday. Blockley is a little village in North Gloucestershire halfway between Oxford and Stratford-upon-Avon and two hours from North London. We've had Fish Cottage, a little house there, for twenty-odd years. It acquired its name from a wooden gravestone to a fish, which now hangs in our dining room.

UNDER THE SOIL
THE OLD FISH, DO, LIE
20, YEARS HE, LIVED
AND THEN, DID, DIE
HE, WAS SO TAME
YOU, UNDERSTAND
HE, WOULD, COME, AND
EAT, OUT, OF, OUR, HAND
Died April the 20th 1855
Aged 20 YEARS

The cottage owes a very modest fame to this artefact, which is mentioned in one or two books about architectural oddities or follies. Once a fortnight in the summer a car or a rambler will arrive outside and demand to see the gravestone.

Blockley was built on numerous springs, around which grew a mill trade, with about a dozen mills recorded in the Domesday Book of 1086. In 1682, James Rushout, the son of a prosperous Flemish immigrant, came to the parish and built the first of the Blockley silk-throwing mills. This started a business supplying silk to the ribbon trade which would bring Blockley considerable wealth for the next two centuries – hence the rather imposing church at one end of the honey-coloured stone high street. It reached its peak in the 1820s when eight silk mills were operating along the brook and its tributary. But within fifty years the silk trade was on its knees – brought low by a free-trade battle won by the French. Two of the silk mills were turned into piano factories.

When we arrive at the cottage this morning there are two builders from Port Talbot in the garden driving piles twelve feet into the Cotswold clay where, only a month ago, there had been a tumbling down shed and garage. This needs a little diversion to explain . . .

Fish Cottage stopped being conventionally pretty the day it caught fire, maybe eighty or ninety years ago. Until that point it was a snug three- or four-roomed single-storey cottage with thick wattle and daub walls under a heavy thatch. Faded nineteenth- and early twentieth-century photos show it nestling in a bustling garden beneath a sparsely treed wood climbing up the hill behind it. The fire was an excuse for someone to build a second storey on, complete with a cantilevered balcony. The result is something between a Cotswold cottage and a tea planter's hill station. We bought the cottage from the late Mrs Dalrymple, who had, very aged, lived with the rats, the asbestos walls, the leaking asbestos roof tiles, the dry rot and the woodworm. We gutted and rebuilt the inside, running out of money before we could afford central heating. Over the years we did manage to add warmth, and built on one more bedroom and a small dining room. But swinging a cat in any of the rooms would not be advisable.

I did, however, contrive to squeeze a modern upright piano – a Danemann, once the official 'Harrods' piano – into the sitting room along with two armchairs. But that was it. Over the years, though, a fantasy grew that one day it would be nice to have a proper space to play music at Fish Cottage, not just alone, but with friends – an impossibility in the cramped confines. The dream had been fed some years before by visiting Benjamin Britten's Red House in Aldeburgh, with its own music room/library, built in a converted outhouse. This contained all the composer's music scores and was a place where, after dinner, he would retreat with friends to play chamber music.

And so perhaps I could construct something *outside* the cottage. But how? All we had was an enclosed cottage garden of about a third of an acre, bordered by a wood on one side and a brook on the other. And then one day, looking out of the bedroom window, I looked down on the tumbledown old wooden garage and wondered whether I couldn't simply knock that down and replace it with something a little larger.

It seemed a small enough matter to replace the garage – which sat on a concrete base – with a slightly larger room, enough for a baby grand, room for a string trio and three armchairs, perhaps. That was the theory. My father had died a couple of years previously, leaving some money to my brother and me. We found an architect based in nearby Moreton-in-Marsh – mild, soft-spoken Ed Tyack – and explained the vision. He agreed it was a plausible idea and thought it could easily be done within the modest legacy from my dad, with perhaps a little left over to buy a slightly better piano.

There are few things duller than other people's building stories. So here is the merest summary of the factors which we soon discovered complicated this otherwise straightforward fantasy.

Flood risk. The little brook running in front of the house had swelled to an overflowing torrent in the 2007 floods. So the Environment Agency had to sign off everything from the drainage, the roofing materials (for run-off), the bore size of the culverts, you name it. A few months to sort.

The water table. Blockley being a village of springs and streams, the moment we knocked down the garage and removed the concrete base on which it stood, we found nothing but rivulets and quagmires of mud. Thick cling-to-your-boots chunks of clay and mud. Sink-into-your-ankles mud. It may only be a music room, but it was going to need serious piledriving and water-piping to get the site remotely usable. Maybe a month's work just to prepare the ground.

Planners. Well, they were OK really. But they did change their minds very late in the day. One minute they were minded to approve Ed's original design with a pitch slate roof. The next they were minded to refuse. Back to the drawing board. Lower the height, curve it over and cover it in sedum. Better? Yes, much better in their view.

The hill behind the cottage. Which needed heavy-duty concrete retaining walls to stop it slipping down once we started levelling the site.

The trees. Over the years four or five pine trees in front of the cottage had tapped into the water and grown into straggly giants. They needed to go.

The dry stone wall in front of the house collapsed.

Which is to say that the fantasy was destined to be very earthbound indeed. And the estimate for the little room – so easy, so modest – soared. And then soared again. And my fantasy of throwing something up in weeks was punctured.

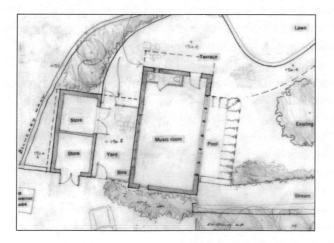

On the other hand we had a perfect local builder, Henry Goodrick Clarke – so calm, intelligent, cheerful, capable and such a generally all-round good guy that he has become known as the Messiah. Or, He who shall be called Wonderful. Or, as my friend Henry Porter dubbed him, Walk-on-Water. Which was just as well, as he had to do a fair amount of that.

Monday, 23 August

Now that the fantasy of the music room is beginning to take shape out of the mud, maybe it's time to start indulging the fantasy of what piano to put in it. I've sort of earmarked about £8,000–10,000 from my father's money for the piano, but I have no idea what this will buy, or indeed where to look. But today at Fish Cottage, I was flicking through *Pianist Magazine* and saw an advertisement for Shackell Pianos, in Witney, Oxfordshire – the heart of David Cameron's constituency and thirty-five minutes from Fish Cottage. I make an appointment and drive over. The address is 'Nimrod', redolent of rolling Malvern hills, tweed, pipe smoke, handlebar moustaches and sit-up-and-beg bicycles. But 'Nimrod' is in fact a modern prefab warehouse space of the sort that have been thrown up on the edges of most English towns.

Inside I find Jeff Shackell, the 50-ish mild-mannered owner of the business. His work overall covers a T-shirt and jeans. He's open, chatty, warm and a bit geeky. Downstairs he has a showroom of gleaming second-hand pianos – mainly Steinways. And upstairs a larger hangar with twenty or so piano hulks – some working but dishevelled, some in need of complete rebuilding. Downstairs the atmosphere is half showroom, half mausoleum – red carpet, respectful, hushed. Upstairs it's more like a factory – bare boards, metal walkways and dismembered parts of pianos in various stages of build. I have a sudden urge to cancel the rest of the day and work my way round both rooms, trying every single key of every single piano.

I tell Jeff my budget, which has already grown a bit fuzzy at the edges, as in '£7,000–15,000'. Jeff points me to an old Bechstein he sold the previous day for £5k. It has a very subdued tone, but is already several notches up on the Danemann piano currently residing in Fish Cottage. The skill of a piano dealer, like car dealers or estate agents, is presumably to get the client on the hook of a dream and then reel them gently in. And to do it imperceptibly. So the next thing Jeff does is encourage me to try a couple of Steinway Model A pianos in the showroom. There's a 1961 Model A, which is just beautiful – soft, quick, responsive, subtle. I move sideways to two Yamaha grands, one new at £17k, the other second-hand. They're both crisp and clear, but a touch soulless after the gorgeous Steinway. I'm on the hook already.

Jeff makes me a cup of tea and talks lovingly about how he plans to rebuild one particular 1930s piano with modern Steinway pianos. He touches on the way the actions have changed over the years and on the differences between the Hamburg Steinway and the New York version. He's straight into the detail. It's obvious he has an obsessive and loving knowledge of the mechanisms and engineering and knows how every part is produced, how they've changed over the decades and why. Mention other pianos, and his interest fades. Clearly, he's an out-and-out Steinway nut . . . and it is infectious. I leave thinking it's going to have to be a Steinway A. But I'm not entirely sure how I will afford that if Henry hits any further complications in putting up the music room.

Wednesday, 25 August

There's an email from Jeff:

> The 1961 Model A has been sold as the financial arrangements for my client have been approved and the 1984 Model A is also more or less sold. It is not

always like this but the fact remains that the Steinway is the most sought-after high-end piano.

So, whatever else is going on in the economy, the market for second-hand Steinways is pretty solid. Another email comes soon after:

There is a 1972 Model A coming up in an auction in early September, it is estimated at £12,000 to £18,000 depending on the condition of the piano and bidding competition. My company is hungry for stock at present and I am sure I will bid on this piano . . .

I don't know if you feel comfortable with auctions. Perhaps I could help take away some of the uncertainty by inspecting the piano with the option for you to then try it in more relaxed conditions in Witney if indeed I am successful in purchasing.

I realise that, in the space of three days, I have become resigned to the piano budget being twice where it started.

Sunday, 29 August

The holiday is now at an end, and this is the last day I can practise for some time. I play everything with a metronome so that I can judge progress. If I set it at $\downarrow$ = 63 – still painfully, unrecognisably slow – then I can get through most of the piece, but still with all those horrid tempo-wrenches and innumerable stumbles and pauses. Looking out of the window at Glan and his mate, the pilers from Port Talbot, I realise my musical endeavours are the equivalent of what they're doing – building the foundations. I'm not yet remotely ready to build the walls or roof. But, if this three weeks of fingering and slow working out has achieved anything, it ought to have established a solid platform on which to build. A thought strikes me: can I learn the Ballade in the time it takes Henry and his team to build the music room? They're estimating four to six months. Doable. Surely?

PART TWO

Sunday, 5 September 2010

The end of my first week back on the editing hamster wheel.

When I started editing the *Guardian* in 1995, it was a three-section newspaper. Even that, at around 200,000 words a day, was way too large for any one person to read everything in advance. I would guess the last time the editor of the *Guardian* could have aspired regularly to read every word ahead of publication would have been in the late 1950s or early 60s, when papers were far smaller. Now, though, the printed paper is just one of a number of platforms for reading the *Guardian*. In the fifteen years I've been editor, the circulation of the printed paper has, in step with most papers in the developed world, shrunk. But around 65 million browsers a month from every corner of the globe are reading guardian.co.uk via a computer or mobile device – a figure that's growing at about sixty per cent a year. The *Guardian* is now something you can read, watch or listen to. It tells stories in moving pictures, animated graphics, films and podcasts. It is something you can take part in, respond to, adapt, or mash up. It is a network and a platform as well as a publisher. And it is constantly updated, twenty-four hours a day, seven days a week.

So, of course, the job of editor has changed too. One hundred years ago the greatest of my predecessors, C. P. Scott, was largely preoccupied with the long daily leader – the main editorial pronouncement in which Scott and a small band of colleagues would offer judicious thoughts on the great events of the day. Now few editors of national newspapers would sit down to write editorials every day. Part of the job is, or should be, preparing for the seismic changes shaking the news business – i.e. much of the time will be spent learning about technology, with a reference frame far beyond newspapers – and working out how to adapt emerging ideas and incorporate digital developers (coders, engineers, product managers, search-engine optimisers, user interface designers, etc.) into a news media company (no longer a 'newspaper') in ways which best use their talents and imagination. The competition, which in 1995 was clearly understood and circumscribed (*The Times, Telegraph, FT* and *Independent*), now includes Google, Twitter, the Huffington Post, the Daily Beast, Reuters and Facebook as well as the *New York Times* and the BBC. And nagging away is the background existential question – how to pay for it? Today, the most common question most editors are asked is: 'What's the business model?' Which, in the minds of some, is framed in conventional terms of profit and loss, but which I suspect is a much more fundamental question about the changing nature of journalism itself.

So most editors now spend much more time with the commercial directors and managers trying to work out the new economic models of news media. I spend a great deal of time with colleagues and thinkers outside the immediate industry working out what journalism itself is becoming and how it is best integrated into the utterly changed world in which any individual can become a publisher. These are not simple questions, and they take a huge investment of time and group brain power to address. On top of this, the editor of the *Guardian* sits on the divisional and main boards, as well as that of the Scott Trust, which owns the *Guardian* – the paper has no proprietor as such. I am also legally and editorially responsible for all the content produced round the clock six days a week by the *Guardian* and, ultimately, by the *Observer*, the paper's Sunday sister, of which I am editor-in-chief.

Which boils down to this: a day which starts around 7.30 with the radio and the previous day's papers so that by the time I'm in the office I'm sufficiently up to speed. Two editorial conferences – post-mortem on yesterday and looking ahead a day – before 10.30. A leader writers' meeting before lunch. A working lunch (a sandwich at desk or with colleagues or politicians); then meetings and editing through to 8.30 or 9 p.m. most days. Two or three times a week, a breakfast meeting on top of this and three or four evening engagements (dinners, launches, events, speeches, etc.). The paper arrives at home sometime between 11 p.m. and 12.30 a.m. and I try to stay up to have a quick scan of it – or, if I have a breakfast the following morning, a more thorough read. So it's not uncommon for a day to end well after midnight. Most months there's a trip or two abroad to give a speech or sit on a panel – or simply to understand particular countries, regimes or leaders better, or to visit other news organisations to see how they're changing. We've recently expanded our US operation, which has taken me to New York every six to eight weeks. Saturdays and most Sundays tend to be quieter, though it's rare that I'm not making a few phone calls and it seems now to be everyone's assumption that we all read (and respond to) emails seven days a week. Most Sunday afternoons/evenings I do about six hours' work preparing for the week ahead.

Usually I know on a Monday morning how every quarter-hour slot until Friday evening could well be spent. But, of course, news (and its consequences) keeps intervening. One of the absolutely best things about being a journalist is not knowing at the start of the day what the job will entail – or even, as a reporter, where you'll sleep that night. A bomb, a big resignation, the unexpected end of a trial, a death, a riot, a leak, a kidnapping or a call from a whistleblower – all these can turn a day, or even a week, upside down. A global story like WikiLeaks – the sifting, editing, coordination, lawyering, publishing; the media, the aftermath – can eat up vast amounts of time over many months. And, all the while, the emails keep coming – probably sixty to eighty an hour. Not all of them require a response from me, but some do, and, buried in among them will be a legal time bomb, a reporter needing advice or help, or an advertiser or reader wanting an urgent response.

© Carmen Valino

What does all that add up to? A working week of sixty-five to eighty hours. Periods of routine, as in any job. Occasional highs as a campaign or investigation hits a particular note or target. A hum of low-level stress much of the time, with periodic eruptions of great tension. Above all, the sense of perpetual momentum that comes from the news itself. If you make your life the news business, the news will to some extent dictate your life.

*

Besides Assange and the WikiLeaks story, there is another long-term project bubbling away at the *Guardian* at the moment, with Nick Davies and others investigating the *News of the World* hacking phones in the UK. On Wednesday the *New York Times* finally published the result of its own months-long investigation into the same story. It's a very thorough, long (6,000 words) magazine piece with three bylines – seasoned reporters who have four Pulitzer Prizes between them. This article came about after I sent a long email to the *NYT*'s then executive editor, Bill Keller, back in March, setting out the background to the *Guardian*'s coverage of the story – the hacking itself and the subsequent cover-up. Around the same time, the story had got infinitely more complicated: we had learned of other private investigators who had been working for the *News of the World*, but, for legal reasons, we were unable to report some of the background we knew. Most glaringly, there was a very nasty and corrupt private investigator who had been hired back onto the *NotW* at the time that Andy Coulson was editing it, despite the fact that he had just spent a long time in prison and was now on remand charged with a violent crime. He is now on remand in prison charged with conspiracy to murder his former business partner by burying an axe in the back of his head. British contempt laws meant no UK-based title could publish this new line. But it seemed to me a significant piece of information that should be in the public domain before the probable next prime minister, David Cameron, appointed Coulson to be his press secretary.

Keller had responded swiftly to my email and dispatched three of his best reporters to London. We gave them a brief primer on the case – but they then went their separate ways, determined to verify everything for themselves . . . and to break new ground if they could. And they have broken some new ground with this piece – though, disappointingly, it doesn't actually go into the private investigator's case, which will, somewhere down the line, doubtless cause Cameron and News International a lot of problems. Like Nick Davies, the *NYT* team has found plenty of former *NotW* staff who will talk about how widespread and commonplace phone hacking was, but very few who will go on the record. But there is a new voice – a former reporter called Sean Hoare, who is quoted saying he used to play back tapes of voicemail messages and that he was 'actively encouraged' to do it.

The *New York Times* article is important for the way the story will play out. Essentially, it has independently verified every single thing we have been writing for well over a year. Until now News International has tried to dismiss our reporting – and others (including the police and the regulator, the Press Complaints Commission) have appeared perfectly willing to pretend the issue is not there. But here's the world's foremost English-language newspaper putting its weight behind the truth of everything the *Guardian* has reported – and to a large extent its own reputation on the line, given the fierce rivalry in the US between the *NYT* and the *Wall Street Journal*. Nobody can now doubt that the story the *Guardian* and *NYT* have independently investigated is bang on and that the NI 'one rotten apple' theory has been shot to pieces. Whether anyone's got the stomach to do something about it is a different matter.

But just a couple of days later, it seems the *NYT* piece is beginning to have an effect. On Friday, the Labour MP Alan Johnson said he wanted to go back into the Home Office – his right as a former Home Secretary – to inspect the files. Johnson revealed that as Home Secretary he had considered ordering Her Majesty's Inspectorate of Constabulary (HMIC), a body that inspects and publishes reports on police forces, to take over the investigation, but decided against it after discussions with Scotland Yard. Johnson thinks that there now may be a case for HMIC to investigate after reading in the *NYT* the unnamed detectives alleging they had cut short their investigation because of their close relationship with the *NotW*. This isn't going to go away.

So this first week back has been an intense one. I'm now very much immersed in the routine of work, and more aware than ever of just how hard it's going to be to get any meaningful practice in. The very best I can hope for is fifteen to twenty minutes a day.

This weekend, though, I've been able to get to Fish Cottage to have some concentrated music time. The builders are making steady progress. The music-room piling is now covered in at least a foot of concrete – topped by a mesh of iron ready for another two feet of concrete. Henry (who shall be called Wonderful) observed that they could build a skyscraper on this now, such are modern building regulations. So already the foundations of the room are quite a bit more advanced than my own foundations for the Ballade.

There is also the problem that I can't even work full-time on the Chopin for the time being, as I'm committed to arranging and performing in a charity concert in aid of the National Youth Orchestra of Great Britain, which I chair. This began as a joke, when my friend and occasional piano teacher

Lucy Parham agreed to curate a Schumann week at the beautiful new 420-seat, Dixon Jones–designed concert hall which shares the Kings Place building with the *Guardian*. 'I don't see myself on the bill,' I joked. The next thing I knew she had reserved a Saturday morning slot for me to rope in a bunch of amateur musicians to play a movement each of Schumann's *Kinderscenen* in aid of the NYO. I would play one of these myself, and precede the *Kinderscenen* movements with my friend and regular duet partner Martin Prendergast playing the rarely performed Schumann Canonic Etudes (arranged by Debussy for two pianos) – a little gem of a piece recently unearthed and championed by the American pianists Richard Goode and Jonathan Biss.

Without very much trouble I have found twelve other pianists willing to put their fingers on the line, including a peer of the realm, an archbishop and an actress. I have only ever heard three of them play before, so have no real idea of how this will work out when the time comes, which is now just over a month away. None of the Schumann pieces is anything like as complex as the Chopin. But playing anything in public demands a different level of concentration and engagement. It doesn't matter how 'amateur' you proclaim yourself to be: there's a big hurdle – not making a total idiot of yourself – you need to climb over. So, for the time being, this is going to suck up at least half my allotted twenty minutes a day.

But I have still been able to get some good time in with the Ballade this weekend, and I've spent the majority of it on the coda. Earlier in the week,

I happened to bump into Lucy Parham in the street outside Kings Place, where she has been preparing for the Schumann week. She couldn't resist a small laugh at the thought of me playing Op. 23. 'It's the hardest ballade, you know that?' She texted me later: 'I used to play it a lot so could help you with some of the tricks.' I'd like to take her up on the offer of lessons. I'm actually not taking any at the moment. On the other hand I'm now back in the straitjacket of editing, so any lessons will have to be squeezed into odd and unpredictable hours at the beginning and end of the day.

Lucy gave me a piece of advice: to obsess about the coda a) because it's easily the hardest bit, but also b) because, in any performance, it's psychologically important to believe the last three minutes are solid. The alternative is disastrous: the closer you get to the end the greater the sense of foreboding at what's to come.

So I've been working backwards, bar by bar from 236 – approximately the mid-point of the coda. I have tried to get my brain to remember the differences between 234 and 236, which look remarkably similar but, in that Chopin way, aren't. Then reading carefully the last beat of 232 – flats and double flats in the RH switching enharmonically to the same notes, but written out in sharps on the first beat of 233. Now try the whole of 232/233 together but so slowly you think you'll never get to the end of the second bar. Again, a page which, on first glance, is all a nightmare, can be broken down into stuff that's merely difficult and stuff that's unspeakably horrible.

I then moved further back, into the bars around 216, where there are fast octave leaps. They are really troubling me. The hand has to leave the keys in an act of faith, hoping it will land in the right place within a fraction of a second. The downward leap is the hardest, because it's the weak little finger of the left hand which has to arrive on the correct note. The landing area is a thin sliver of gleaming ebony less than a centimetre thick. To master this I'm going to have to improve two of my lesser abilities. First, the kind of motor skills which will enable me to judge, target and pinpoint these leaps. Then my memory, because you can't look at these leaps at the same time as looking at the sheet music.

At the end of the weekend's practice I decide to do a time trial. How fast can I play it, with, say, eighty per cent accuracy? Today I do manage roughly eight out of ten notes in the right place – but it takes me eighteen minutes. Most professional pianists take between nine and ten minutes. I suspect that if I tried to do it with every note right it would take me well over twenty minutes.

I think of the Matterhorn analogy. Looking at Matterhorn websites, it doesn't seem way off. Jerry R. Hobbs, an American computational linguistics expert and amateur climber, described the mountain as 'just about the hardest climb an ordinary person can do', which, apropos the G minor Ballade, sounds familiar. 'The climb is relentless. For the entire climb, there's never anything resembling a path. If you stop, you can only perch. You're always looking for handholds, and your average step would be like stepping onto a chair, if only the ledge were that big. Always up, up, up.' Which also sounds like a description of tackling Op. 23.

And this is Hobbs' evocation of the summit, which feels an apt metaphor for the high point of the Ballade – the ferocious coda, which induces night sweats in even professional pianists: 'one side is a sheer rock cliff and the other side is a steep slope of snow and the top itself is a track of footprints in the snow at the edge of the cliff. If your right foot slips, you end up in Switzerland. If your left foot slips, you end up in Italy.'

Another amateur who has written about trying the Matterhorn, Andrew Slough, described the mountain as a 'rite of passage' and trained for his climb with a weekly 150-mile bike ride and, twice a week, climbed 3,000 vertical feet in less than an hour.

That's the height of the mountain ahead. Hard enough with oxygen and aluminium ice picks. With my abilities, I feel more like George Mallory attempting Everest in 1924, in tweed jacket and puttees.

Monday, 6 September

A friend patiently points out my problem of fitting a passion around working life is not a new one, and sends me in the direction of Arnold Bennett. In 1910, Arnold Bennett – then a celebrated novelist, journalist and civil servant – published a short book, *How to Live on 24 Hours a Day*, in which he urged white-collar 'salarymen' to make better use of the hours not spent working or sleeping.

Bennett suspects his salaryman reader is 'constantly haunted by a suppressed dissatisfaction', which he thinks 'springs from a fixed idea that we ought to do something in addition to those things which we are loyally and morally obliged to do'. This reminds me of Jung. 'We are obliged', writes Bennett, 'by various codes written and unwritten, to maintain ourselves and our families (if any) in health and comfort, to pay our debts, to save, to increase our prosperity by increasing our efficiency. A task sufficiently difficult! . . . Yet, if we succeed in it, as we sometimes do, we are not satisfied; the skeleton is still with us.'

© Getty Images

The reader can dispel this dissatisfaction by finding 'something still further to do' – though he may think he's already overtaxed as it is. This activity can take any form. Bennett suspects that for the majority of readers it will take a literary shape, but this is 'not the only well'. It could be music, painting, running, model train sets, anything. But then comes the inevitable question: how can this be achieved, given the reader's pressed routine? Bennett's answer is a very simple one – 'a profound and neglected truth'. Essentially, you do have the time; you just don't realise it. 'We never shall have any more time. We have, and we have always had, all the time there is.' And so he takes his reader to task. He meets them as they emerge from their office:

> You are pale and tired. At any rate, your wife says you are pale, and you give her to understand that you are tired. During the journey home you have

been gradually working up the tired feeling. The tired feeling hangs heavy over the mighty suburbs of London like a virtuous and melancholy cloud, particularly in winter. You don't eat immediately on your arrival home. But in about an hour or so you feel as if you could sit up and take a little nourishment. And you do. Then you smoke, seriously; you see friends; you potter; you play cards; you flirt with a book; you note that old age is creeping on; you take a stroll; you caress the piano . . . By Jove! a quarter past eleven. You then devote quite forty minutes to thinking about going to bed; and it is conceivable that you are acquainted with a genuinely good whisky. At last you go to bed, exhausted by the day's work. Six hours, probably more, have gone since you left the office – gone like a dream, gone like magic, unaccountably gone!

He then shows his salaryman how to be more efficient with his time, and how ninety minutes can be carved out every other evening or more:

Briefly, get up earlier in the morning . . . Rise an hour, an hour and a half, or even two hours earlier.

This is roughly what I've been doing for some time now. Though my twenty-minute early morning practice may not amount to Bennett's recommended daily ninety minutes, it's something. And I take a little solace from his assertion that the morning is in fact the more productive period. He even promises 'you will accomplish as much in one morning hour as in two evening hours'.

All I'm lacking is a manservant. Bennett instructs his would-be pianist to ensure that the servants have made the correct preparations for their master's new routine – a tray holding 'two biscuits, a cup and saucer, a box of matches and a spirit-lamp' should be laid out in a 'suitable position' overnight, so that he can make his own tea in the morning.

As to the result: Bennett argues that the period spent with one's hobby or passion 'will quicken the whole life of the week, add zest to it, and increase the interest which you feel in even the most banal occupations'. Up to now, my sporadic sessions in the morning have certainly tended to make me feel more balanced throughout the working day. Will my new focus on the Ballade and its extreme demands change this? Will the zest remain? Might it even increase?

Friday, 10 September

So far this week, I've managed three twenty-minute morning sessions at the piano.

I get up half an hour earlier. I fit in ten minutes of yoga listening to the *Today* programme – not exactly meditative. Then breakfast and the papers with more *Today* programme all at the same time. Then I slip upstairs to the sitting room to play before driving into work.

It's a long room a little wider than the average nineteenth-century London semi. At one end sofas around an open fire, the other dominated by the piano – the greatest extravagance of my life, a Fazioli 212 bought with the proceeds of a television drama series I co-wrote some years ago. Next to it a Yamaha F01 Modus digital piano for two-piano playing. On both side walls fifty or more boxes of sheet music, very roughly catalogued and sorted by genre and composer. And a black-and-white picture of the incomparable Mitsuko Uchida taken by my *Guardian* colleague and friend Eamonn McCabe.

I sit at the piano blocking out any subconscious fear of being overheard by the commuters walking to work in the street beyond or by Lindsay downstairs, or by our neighbour Gill through the party wall. I know Gill can, in fact, hear very well what I'm practising – but then she, too, notches up the hours on her piano and cello and we're generally too polite to acknowledge that we've noticed. The light floods in at both ends of the quiet room. With luck the phone will stay silent for the next twenty minutes as I begin my little bubble of solitude before the day starts whirring away.

I recently read a profile of the actor and director Simon McBurney, who's living in a converted piano factory not far from where we live. During the nineteenth and early twentieth centuries Kentish Town became the base for many piano and organ manufacturers, partly because they could transport the heavy manufacturing materials up the Regent's Canal, which was connected both to the Thames and to the Midlands. Now the piano factories are all bijou flats like Simon's – though there is still one piano warehouse/ store a road down from where we live. I like it that Kentish Town – a little stretch of nondescript Victorian streets between the urban hip of Camden and the elevated elegance of Highgate – has strong connections with the piano trade. Just like Blockley.

I've continued to focus on the coda all week, playing it very slowly. Yesterday, though, I realised I'm going to have to go even slower. It's dawned on me I'm not playing the first four bars remotely as fast as I previously did. There are such big leaps in both RH and LH here and I'm doing my best to memorise the notes, I've slowed right down. So I'm actually going backwards. Maybe five years at this pace and I might crack this section.

I've also revisited the 'squashed flies' at bar 33, to see whether the fingers have remembered any of those notes. There is better news here. I can play it a bit faster than before, so some of it has definitely 'stuck', but there's still something in the middle that's causing me to trip up. I've spent a bit of time poring over the fingering here to see what the problem is. It's often the case that there is one finger out of place and once you find, identify and correct that then everything falls into place. That's the theory anyway.

I've been playing the Ballade for over a month now, so this morning I performed an experiment. I shut the music and tried to play the first page. I could sing you the first two pages. In fact I could sing you most of the piece. But, sitting at the piano without the music in front of my eyes, I have to feel my way through from the very first bar, with no confidence that I am going to judge the next interval right. It starts on a C, but I have no visual memory of anything after that. This almost complete inability to memorise any music must make me very unusual – though I've sort of known about it all my life, and so it's always seemed normal. In English classes I found I couldn't remember the titles, plots or characters, and in history classes I forgot the dates of crucial battles, and the names of kings, potentates and treaties. I have never learned more than a dozen lines of poetry in my life. And I have never memorised a note of music. I'm a good sight-reader, and can bluff my way semi-convincingly through all manner of music. But even after practising a piece for weeks, I'm helpless without the score. If I am ever going to play this piece, it does mean I have a big problem on my hands. Or in my head.

Sunday, 12 September

Last chance to play the piano for a while as I'm off to India next week. But – bingo! Yesterday morning I finally made a breakthrough on the Presto. The first four bars just suddenly flowed. That was really by taking the hands apart, playing it very slowly, as ever, and working out the hand positioning exactly. Even though I've been practising with more focus and patience than ever before, I realised I still hadn't really spent enough time just looking at the score, concentrating on what was going on. My instinct always just to play had still been getting in the way.

The troubling leaps and syncopated rhythms remain, though, with all the old problems of memory this will force me to grapple with. Of course, this is the same problem I've been having with the flying-trapeze notes at 216. I looked at Debussy's edition of that bar yesterday morning, and saw that he recommends landing on fingers 5 and 3, which I had before and which I'd crossed out and replaced with 5 and 2 when I was refingering on holiday. I'm now going to scrub this out and put it back to 5 and 3 to see if that helps with the landing. I found a self-help video on the web in which a young American pianist gives a lesson (in his sitting room, it seems) on how to play Op. 23. He advises trying to play the whole coda at largo, which I suppose I'm doing already. In the video, he has the pedal down and just plays it very gently and slowly, getting a sort of New Age music. I'll just keep repeating that pattern in order to try to get a sense of the geography. It's an almost geometrical piece of reckoning just working out the physical gaps. Mountain climbers must have the same kind of thing working out where to put their hands and feet.

All in all, though, it was my most positive morning so far, and I went off to Hampshire for the broadcaster Jon Snow's wedding in good spirits. But I must admit that after a moment of elation yesterday, I'm feeling a bit daunted by it all today. I went back to trying to do the Presto this morning, and while it is making more and more sense, I'm just not sure how quickly it's actually getting into the fingers. And while I'm thinking I might be mastering the RH (albeit very, very slowly), I realise with a sinking feeling how much work's going to be involved in getting the LH to behave itself over these four bars.

And I'm getting increasingly anxious about working exclusively on the coda and then losing the memory of the earlier parts. So this morning I looked back at earlier passages in the piece, which I'd classified as markedly easier. But, on closer inspection, it looks extremely tricky – it's the usual story of there being not quite regular patterns, so you can't remember things in any uniform way. How will I get the whole piece in the brain on just twenty minutes a day? This is doubtless why these pieces are played by professionals and not amateurs. There's simply not enough time to get it all memorised, even assuming you have anything like a normal brain. And in addition to a rotten memory, I have very limited mathematical skill, which I'm clearly going to need to find patterns in the piece. So today it feels as if there's a lot conspiring against me.

This evening, though, Lucy Parham made her way over to Kentish Town.

'Tricks': last week she promised me tricks. It's partly a joke between us. She's great as a performing teacher – someone who can tell the limitations of a pupil like me and who will get me through the notes with one or two corners cut if necessary. 'Any white tape so far?' she asks tonight. This is a reference to the time I came back from America with a roll or three of white tape, which I could tear off to cover up the occasional notes in a score that were particularly hard to play. She had never seen this done before, nor, I'm sure, would she ever consider it herself. But she went along with it for me when we practised Beethoven's Op. 110 together a few years ago. I pass it on as possibly my sole original contribution to the technique of amateur piano playing. If it's the difference between making a passable attempt at a passage – with ninety-eight per cent of people none the wiser – and not playing a piece at all, then why not? Some might try simply to block out the notes mentally. But the mind – well, mine at least – has a habit of trying to do what's written on the page. That fraction of a second in which your mind interprets the notes you've decided to miss out is a fatal distraction.

I have become more sparing with the white tape over time, though some of my early scores might, to a blind man, have felt like a 3-D relief map of the Cairngorms. It's a terrible habit, of course, and symptomatic of my general approach to playing and learning up to now.

I'm not going to resort to short cuts when it comes to the Ballade, at least not yet – so I ask Lucy for tips and insights rather than 'tricks'.

Lucy sits away from the piano, wine glass in hand – contrasted with Michael, who tends to sit by my right elbow. She's a proper grown-up concert pianist when not teaching. Her career was kick-started as a teenager by winning the piano section of the BBC Young Musician of the Year in the mid-1980s. Since then she's performed in most of the big British concert halls and with most of the main British symphony orchestras. So, in principle, a scary person to play for. But there's a sense of fun and mischief there which reduces the fear factor, at least for me. She starts by going over the coda for me. She is soon racing through the problems she says are faced by all pianists here. This is a comfort. The problems she identifies are exactly the ones I have been suffering. She advises:

- Bar 208. Those tricky LH leaps: aim for the thumb – imagine you are playing an octave note with your thumb. She actually writes in the thumb note in the score. You can stop playing it this way later but it will help you judge the distance. It's much easier to aim a thumb over a short leap than it is to aim a little finger. Over time the fifth finger will land automatically.

- Bar 16. Reduce the 'flying trapeze' here to just two notes. A flat and A/E flats. Try it in various keys by transposing the leaps up and down. Practise these leaps only. Stick close to keys on octave leaps. Change rhythms to half bar fast then the other half slow. Then switch to half bar slow, the last half fast. Then try the leap with just octaves – take out the third note. Then play with the third note and take out the octave.

- Bar 138. Emphasise the LH thumbs to bring out the tenor line.

- Bar 9. First tune, aim for the second chord to be slightly softer than the first. German word is '*Bebung*'. Strong/weak. The way you say 'mother'.

So that's a typical lesson with Lucy – for me at least. I'm sure with better pianists she gets stuck into a few bars and works on them in depth. But, with me, she dots around giving me half a dozen pointers to things I should work on or think about. In any case, I end the day a good deal less daunted.

Monday, 13 September

To India for a packed few days of speeches and panels in Delhi, Jaipur and Chennai and a chance to investigate their thriving newspaper market. I'll have no time to practise for almost a week now.

On the flight to Delhi I read Clay Shirky's new book, *Cognitive Surplus*. The book's (rather obscure) title refers to the amount of time that would be freed up if Americans used fewer mental hours passively consuming television – he estimates that they currently watch 'roughly two hundred billion hours of TV every year'. He then looks at what might instead be done with this time, and quotes the example of Wikipedia, where 'every edit made to every article, and every argument about those edits', amounts to 'something like one hundred million hours of human thought', just a fraction of that time spent in front of the box.

Shirky, now a professor at New York University, is one of those digital gurus sometimes dismissed as 'utopians', but his instincts coincide with my own about the pleasures, benefits and possibilities of amateurism and how new forms of publishing are shaping different ideas of authority and collaboration. He celebrates 'participatory culture' – though he laments having to use that term: 'The atomisation of social life in the twentieth century left us so far removed from participatory culture that when it came back, we needed the phrase "participatory culture" to describe it. Before the twentieth century, we didn't really have a phrase for participatory culture; in fact, it would have been something of a tautology. A significant chunk of culture was participatory – local gatherings, events, and performances – because where else could culture come from?' In his view, the rise of amateurism in the digital space – amateur journalists, film-makers, musicians, etc. who can now make their work as widely available as a 'professional' might – will only improve culture. This abundance of contributors might lead to an initial 'rapid fall in average quality', 'but over time experimentation pays off, diversity expands the range of the possible, and the best work becomes better than what went before'.

Where is all this leading with newspapers? The shorthand I use to explore this is by taking the example of the theatre critic. The *Guardian* has a wonderful critic, Michael Billington, who has been writing about the stage for the paper since 1971 and who has written the definitive book on post-war British theatre. So he is, by any definition, an 'expert', authority figure or professional. But ask anyone: is it conceivable that no one else in the 900-strong audience for the first night of a new production at the National Theatre in London has anything interesting to say about the performance? Of course, that's a silly idea. The theatre will be full of passionate and knowledgeable people. So the question is: should a newspaper create a forum for their views as well as giving Michael a pride-of-place platform? It seems to me the obvious answer is yes. You will, by definition, end up with a broader, more diverse range of views about the production. The sum of Billington plus the public will be better, editorially, than Billington alone. Conversely, if we don't do it, someone else will. Someone will create a platform for the amateurs – the people who will write out of their love of theatre.

And that's where the business argument kicks in. Suppose Billington is so good we score him nine out of ten. And score the best, most knowledge-able members of the audience six out of ten. So there's maybe a three-point gap between the collective best of the amateur and the professional when it comes to cultural criticism. No editor in his right mind would not continue to publish Michael, but it's a big risk to build a completely walled-off area where people would pay for that three-point difference. If all this is right then it's better to create a mutual space where the best of the 'amateurs'/readers and the best of the 'professionals'/journalists can coexist and, preferably, relate to each other. Indeed, it looks a little perverse to continue to think that publishing one view of one night is the best possible way of doing justice to any theatrical production. There remain two questions: how do you sort out the good stuff from the bad, the Brecht lover from the Broadway fan? That – in an age of publishing abundance – is a question facing any form of social media or business. Secondly, if the principle works for cultural criticism, does it work for other areas of newspaper life: investigative journalism; sports; fashion; foreign; science? The answer, in our experience, is nearly always 'yes'.

But how might the notion of the amateur enriching things be applied to music? It is wonderful to spend the evening with friends playing your way through the symphonic repertoire on one or two pianos, or playing and immersing yourself in the Brahms and Schumann piano quartets rather than having them on in the background or car radio. But besides the joy I get from playing, do my amateur efforts have any value?

There is the benefit of friendship, of course. 'The better you play,' writes Charles Cooke in *Playing the Piano for Pleasure*, 'the more your circle of friends will expand. You can count on this as confidently as you can count on the sun rising. Music is a powerful magnet which never fails to attract new, congenial, long-term friends.' My mother had a similar view of the social benefits of talents and was keen on me being sufficiently proficient in tennis, bridge and music precisely in order to attract friends in later life. Bridge I never mastered; tennis fell by the wayside. But music has remained – and it is, indeed, a very good way of making and keeping friends. For me, music is the easiest excuse in the world for inviting a comparative stranger into your house – and music groups are relatively easy to sustain over time, a natural cause for relatively regular meetings that ordinary friendships sometimes lack.

But do my amateur efforts provide any benefits for music itself? Is it possible that by playing I am somehow enriching the world of classical music? Am I perhaps helping to keep the music I love alive? And what do professional musicians make of amateur playing? Do these professional musicians value the amateur in the same way I, as a professional, value the amateur journalist? This is something to investigate.

Sunday, 19 September

As I'd expected, it's been impossible to get anywhere near a piano or to think about the Ballade this week – five cities in four days.

On Thursday evening, though, I had dinner in Delhi with N. Ram, the editor of the *Hindu*, and his wife, Mariam. There, I sat next to Praveen Swami, a senior correspondent on the *Hindu* who has just been appointed diplomatic editor of the *Telegraph* in London. As a young man, he had spent two years at a London conservatory studying the piano and flute – and he was good. But now he doesn't play at all. 'If you've once been quite good it is disheartening. It would take me so long to get back to where I was.' I've heard this so often from people who were once good players – people who could never settle for the inevitable disappointment of return. I always feel quietly pleased I was such a mediocre pianist when I was young.

On the flight back to London, I've been reading Prof. Regina Smendzianka on *How to Play Chopin*. She's very good on the Ballades, and on the difficulties of grasping the pieces. 'It takes a high-calibre artist to interpret Chopin's Ballades,' she writes. 'Neither careful phrasing, nor a careful showing of the regular structures of textural details, nor the allure of the episodes relieve the interpreter from taking in the entire piece.' It is reassuring to have this confirmed, and to see that she notes 'logical planning is needed' in approaching the pieces. This is certainly the direction I've been heading in, breaking it down bit by bit, slowing it down, separating hands.

There is also this wonderful analogy:

> One can compare listening to the Ballades to the aesthetic experience of looking at nineteenth-century masterpieces which convey the large canvas concept, where a multitude of carefully finished details does not obstruct the reception of the overall message.

All this reading is making me yearn to be at the piano and to get on with immersing myself in the challenge, but the reality is that the week to come in England will be as busy as my week in India. I've the Lib Dem conference and then a big away day with the paper – a chance for senior editorial, technical and commercial to step away from the daily production grind and look forward. And of course things haven't just stopped in London while I've been away. There's been a development in the hacking story. On Tuesday, I learned the police have begun another inquiry – at least their third – in the wake of the *NYT* piece. But, bizarrely, they want to interview the former *NotW* staff (including Sean Hoare and Paul McMullan) who are quoted in the *NYT* 'under caution' – i.e. they're being treated as suspects rather than witnesses or whistleblowers. So why would any of them talk on that basis? I was initially a little sceptical about Nick's theories about the police's behaviour in this case, but they seem so little interested in getting at the truth of this case that it is looking more and more like some form of cover-up. I'll now need to make sure that we're all up to speed with this aspect of the story.

So, reading is the closest contact I can hope to have with the Ballade for a little while yet.

Saturday, 25 September

We've managed to get to Blockley at the end of what's been a gruelling fortnight.

The away day on Wednesday was as intense as I'd thought it would be. We were working on what form the *Guardian* will take on the iPad. My personal journey to this moment began around sixteen years ago in America. Hints of what the internet was capable of doing to the news business had reached London, and the only way of checking them out was to fly over and find out. So a colleague and I arrived in Boulder, Colorado, where the Knight Ridder newspaper chain had set up a 'laboratory' to study the future of news. It was rumoured that they had built a 'tablet' – a portable screen on which people could read newspapers. And, indeed, there in the foothills of the Rockies was a team of a dozen or so working on the future under the leadership of a man called Roger Fidler. This is an extract of the memo I filed back to London:

> At present it consists only of an A4 block of wood, with a 'front page' stuck on it: the technology for creating Fidler's 'Flat Pad' is, he estimates, still a couple of years off. Fidler believes that the traditional horizontal computer screen is alien to non-computer readers, so his screen is vertical. He believes that it is impossible to convert a mass newspaper-reading public to an electronic version until you can produce something that you can read as easily in a bathroom or in bed as you can a paper. It must also look like a conventional paper document rather than rely on computer conventions.

And here, sixteen years later, it is. Not a block of wood – but the real thing. A handful of us from the paper spent the day working with some super-smart people, mainly called Matt, from a design consultancy, Berg, who have already built some early prototypes for European magazine publishers. Figuring out what the iPad can best do in terms of design, utility, journalism and commercially is clearly going to require more than this single day out of the office. By the end of it, there were too many questions and not enough answers – and I could have done with an ice pack on the forehead.

So, no practice this week, but I did do a little more reading. On the train up to Liverpool for the conference, I treated myself to more from Charles Cooke's *Playing the Piano for Pleasure*. There is so much to glean from Cooke. He is the most encouraging voice an amateur could hope for. For him, it's never too late to take up the piano ('the age of the student is immaterial'), and the amateur is in fact in an extremely privileged position:

> Remember, you are more fortunate in your playing than most professionals are in theirs. For you there is no grim grind of practising; no exhausting burden of responsibility; no fierce competition; no endless facing of audiences regardless of the condition of auditoriums, acoustics, or the state of your soul. For you the work is pleasure, as all hobby work is by its nature; the results a satisfaction to yourself, your fellow hobbyists, and such sympathetic listeners as you may find.

For Cooke the pleasure of playing is only ensured if it remains a hobby. 'Too many students study music with the view to becoming great virtuosi', but 'the place of music in the life of the amateur pianist should be, as I see it, important but not all-important: a source of pleasure in the work done and in the results achieved'.

He does, though, insist on 'one hour a day', and I'm currently falling well short of even my twenty minutes a morning. And I've little time to practise this weekend, as it's only a one-day visit to Fish Cottage before I head to Manchester for the Labour conference.

But there has been progress on the piano-purchasing front. This afternoon, I drove across Oxfordshire countryside bathed in warm fading sunlight to see Jeff Shackell. He had just returned from the North-East with a Steinway Model O he'd snapped up from a piano teacher who had died, and he wanted to show me two more Model Os he had recently bought in auction.

The first was a dark brown piano built in Hamburg in 1912. He opened it up and, in the mild yet excitable tones of an obsessive hobbyist rather than a salesman, gave me a running commentary. A Renaissance scholar describing a newly discovered Botticelli could not have matched his hushed reverence for the object in front of us. 'Gilded plate, restrung. Look at the soundboard, just perfect. Beautiful. They're not easy to find in that condition, no splits. That tells me it's been kept in good conditions. Original keys, the action needs doing up. There's quite a lot of moth damage – not so much the hammers, they seem to like the felts underneath the keys. It has been restrung, so it might be a candidate to leave alone, but there are no listings [strips of felt] there, which tells me it might have been restrung by someone who didn't know what they were doing.'

We moved to the next piano – the same model built four years earlier. But before he showed me the piano, he hauled out an older ledger book, almost hyperventilating with excitement. It had been bought by a friend in a Maidenhead bookshop and turned out to be a volume from Steinway Hall's archive of the pianos it sold and maintained. By sheer chance it was from 1908 – the same year as this Model O was made. 'Look – here's the Princess of Wales' piano,' he said, opening the book at random. 'And here's Mrs Asquith, with a note saying they moved her Petrof grand into Number 10 on 5 May. Look, they were going to charge her ten shillings and sixpence, but that's crossed out and she ended up paying twenty-one shillings. The cost of power!'

And there, a few pages back, was this very piano. 2 January 1908, the original order to send the piano to J. Locker-Lampson at Rowfant House in Crawley, Sussex. Jeff assumed J to be Jane, the wife of the poet Frederick Locker: the family was a mix of poets, soldiers and Tory MPs, he said. Jeff's wife had looked up the 1901 census to see who was living in the house at the time. I find myself quite caught up in Jeff's unique mixture of engineering, archaeology, genealogy . . . and encyclopaedic knowledge of anything and everything to do with Steinway pianos.

We move on to a 1924 Model M, and another from 1937. And then the 1978 Model O which Jeff had just brought back from the North-East. 'A little tight around the keys, but I think we can work on that.'

The light was fading and the pianos hadn't been tuned, but I sat down to try them all. The 1912 Hamburg piano sounded possible – but it would take months of rebuilding before I could be sure. The 1978 piano was a surer bet, but really out of my price range.

It was clear which piano Jeff wanted to guide me towards, even though he'd make more on the newer Model O. 'I can sell that three times over,' he said of it. 'It's fine, but the modern Steinways are factory-produced. You probably need one if you're young and are going to play it every day. But these older pianos,' he said, looking over at the 1912 Hamburg Model O, 'these older pianos, I just think they hark back to an age of hand craftsmanship. There's a soul there which the new pianos don't have. I could build you something really lovely from this piano. It would take a few months. I'm so busy, I can't tell you. We're looking at Easter 2011. But I'd love to have a crack.'

'First I've got to do that one over there' – he waved at another piano across the room. 'Similar idea. New set of hammers. They'll be Steinway hammers, but I have to shave them to get their weight down because the modern hammers are too heavy. That's from the 1920s. The question is, when does a Steinway die? I think the answer is, never.'

He promised to go away and play with some figures – though it might take a couple of days. Something tells me that 1912 Hamburg Steinway Model O is – at least in his thinking – destined to end up at Fish Cottage.

Monday, 27 September

I am in Manchester for the Labour Party conference. Last night I was up till 3 a.m. drinking with delegates bewildered by the turn of events which has just seen Ed Miliband installed as leader. This time last year the party was still in power, albeit creaking at the seams: this year they are in the wilderness.

The conference debates themselves are tame affairs these days – nothing like the smoke-filled intensity of the Blackpool Winter Gardens debates when I first reported party conferences in the late 1970s. Instead of lunch, I nip off for a cup of coffee with Gary, whose performance of the Ballade in the Lot Valley started me off on this journey. In the two-bedroomed flat he shares with his partner Wendy and a roomful of knee-length boots, corsets and high-heeled shoes, he told me an extraordinary story about the piece and its part in his life. He's about two or three years younger than me – in jeans, loose T-shirt and trainers, shortish grey hair, with a fleck of brown at the front. A long face, with a fine aquiline nose and good cheek-bones. The words tumble out in a Manchester accent, with a slight drawl and frequent punctuations of 'you know what I mean?'

Gary tells me his life story, drinking from a mug of tea on the sofa, sometimes jumping up to illustrate what he's talking about on the small Steinway in the corner. He first encountered the piano as a little boy at his grandmother's house. 'We used to go round on a Saturday afternoon and it was the usual "Three Blind Mice" and "Frère Jacques" and that kind of thing.' It wasn't until he was twelve that he started to take lessons. He had grown up in Manchester, his parents divorced; the family, which was in the rag trade, was still there when he was offered a scholarship to a school in Hampshire. When he arrived, he discovered a piano in the dining hall. 'I just phoned my mum up and said "Can I have lessons?"' But he didn't really enjoy playing that much at school, with the routine of lessons and exams it involved. And, as I'd suspected in the Lot Valley, we had been similarly average players as adolescents. 'I did up to Grade 7, but wasn't very good. I got passes but I didn't get any merits or distinctions.'

After he left school, Gary more or less forgot the piano. He studied accountancy. 'But then I realised I wanted to work for myself. At the age of 22, I came back from Australia after being there for a year, as you do, like a gap year after accountancy. I bought a newsagent's just across the road here.' After a while he left this behind, becoming a licensee in the pub trade for a few years. Then the 1990s recession hit and Gary got into financial difficulty. He soon needed to find new work that earned money fast. So he became a black-cab driver – 'Great money. Very simple.' And before he knew it almost ten years had passed. It was 2005 and he was 49.

'I worked hard, you know, I was able to go out, do twelve-hour shifts, six days a week and then, when you come in, you just crash out, you know what I mean? But I hated the cab, every morning going out, I hated it.'

The work took its toll and by 2005 there was no doubt in Gary's mind that he was depressed. 'It was like every morning was Groundhog Day. And the only way I knew of getting out of that is, at the time I tried to do it through artificial things like, go to the pub you know? Or maybe if the right girl comes along, you know what I mean?' He'd hit rock bottom – and at times felt suicidal. But then something happened.

Through the wall of his flat, Gary had become used to hearing a violinist practising. He made a decision. 'I was so depressed, I thought I needed – I knew I needed – something to divert my thoughts. So I thought "Well what about the piano?" because I hadn't touched it for years, never touched it. So I knocked on my neighbour next door and I said, "I hope you don't mind, but I can hear you playing the violin, I fancy taking up the piano again, can you point me in the direction?"

'He was a violinist with the BBC Philharmonic, and so he says, "There's the Alberti group that meet up in the city centre, at the Unitarian church on Cross Street. They meet up fortnightly, on a Wednesday."'

So Gary went to Cross Street Unitarian Chapel on a Wednesday evening in March 2005. (The chapel was, by coincidence, the church that C. P. Scott, the legendary editor and eventual owner of the *Manchester Guardian*, had attended.) The Alberti group consisted of amateurs, 'just people like us. They have other careers or are retired or whatever.' On that first evening, Gary played Beethoven's 'Für Elise' – the only piece he could remember from his schooldays. 'And that was it. I carried on going.'

He began to play frequently and found that the piano and these musical evenings with the group were having a wonderful effect on him. 'I used to find that to get myself out of myself, if I spent a couple of hours on the piano, bang, you know, I could sort of forget the depression.' And there was further happiness. After nearly a year with the group he met Wendy, asked her to play a duet with him, and fell in love.

A few months before he met Wendy, Gary had discovered the Ballade. He was watching Roman Polanski's *The Pianist*, the story of the Polish Jewish pianist Wladyslaw Szpilman. In the film, Szpilman suffers terribly in the Warsaw Ghetto, loses his whole family and, once the city has been razed and its population deported, finds himself more or less alone to wander the wreckage. In perhaps the most important scene in the film, Szpilman (played by Adrien Brody) is discovered by a *Wehrmacht* officer in the ruined city. This is possibly the end of the line for Szpilman, but first the officer forces him to play for him. Szpilman chooses the G minor Ballade.

Gary was spellbound. The piece spoke to him more deeply than any music he had ever heard. 'It was the combination of me, the film, the music, and the piano. It all sort of came together, like, in a bit of an equation and a little bell rang.' At first Gary struggles to explain the immediate appeal of the piece: 'If I was to put it on now for you . . . it's just majestic, it's sublime, it's . . .' But then he strikes on the thing that touched him so powerfully.

'To me, Chopin's telling a story of what he's going through in his life with the first Ballade. He composed it when he was in his early 20s and, like a lot of great minds, they suffer with depression, searching for happiness and, as you know, through the Ballade, it starts very morose and then he's trying to get himself out of this, and then it goes into that happy bit in the middle, and then it goes back into the depression, into that same theme, doesn't it? It's crying out for happiness. And then, right at the end, it's sort of like, "I'm determined not to let life get me down." It goes into this coda with a flourish right at the end saying, "I'm winning."

'The great thing with the Ballade, at the end it's like giving you hope, saying, "You know what, life is not that, it doesn't have to be that bad."'

Gary immediately decided to learn the piece. 'It didn't take me very long to remember the notes.'

'When you say it didn't take you very long . . .'

Gary goes on to tell me that for the next *two or three years*, he actually played the Ballade as many as six times a day *every single day*. But this wasn't enough. 'I hammered my way through it mainly on this digital piano. It has a tendency, because you can turn the volume down, to make you sound better than you really are.' Not only was the instrument deceptive, Gary was deceiving himself. 'The days and the weeks and the months tick by and, really, if I would be honest with myself, I was thinking "You're not doing this, Gary." You either give it up or play it very very slowly, or start again at the beginning.'

After these few years of obsessively playing the Ballade, but never *really* playing it, a moment came in early 2010, when Wendy asked, 'What are you going to play at Lot?' And from then on, for the seven months until piano camp, Gary put in an hour and a half a day of real practice – slow, methodical, repetitive, painstaking – the results of which were to have such an effect on me in that old French farmhouse.

I leave Gary feeling both uplifted and daunted. The story's an inspiring one – someone who had sunk low and was in something close to black despair who had found his way back to life through the associations of one ten-minute piece of music. I actually think of the piece very differently: far from the ending expressing hope, it seems to me to be about disintegration and despair. But it had, in the film, saved Szpilman's life and it had, in a way, saved Gary's. He found in the G minor Ballade a particular kind of redemptive power which drove him to play it obsessively. And then, when that didn't satisfy him, to begin all over again and learn how to *perform* it. Which was the daunting bit. Gary was my own beacon of hope: he gave me cause to believe that a modestly gifted amateur could, if determined enough, conquer the piece. But there was no way I could ever find the time to play it six times a day – and I am still pretty sceptical that I will manage to memorise more than a few bars.

I go back to the conference centre via Deansgate, one of the main streets in the city centre, where the *Guardian* kept its newsroom even after dropping 'Manchester' from its titlepiece. I nip into the piano showroom at Forsyth's, the grand 150-year-old music shop, almost as old as the *Guardian* itself. Another showroom – warmer in atmosphere than Jeff's rather austere hangar – and more serried ranks of pianos, their lids up, beckoning the passer-by to have a go. I'm still on a very steep learning curve about trying out pianos – getting used to the infinite variations of touch, sonority, pedal, etc. I only have twenty minutes to spare, but I am quite struck – both in tone and touch – by the Schimmels. I tried one with Lucy Parham earlier this year. But that was when I assumed my budget was half what it seems to be now, at least if Jeff has his way in persuading me to abandon all restraint. It strikes me that it's impossible to compare these Schimmels against Jeff's Steinways unless they are all in the same place at the same time, and that's not going to happen. But I take a catalogue in any case, and a friendly middle-aged woman assistant promises to send me a brown paper cut-out of the six-foot piano so I can tell how it would fit into the music room.

Saturday, 2 October

It's time for the charity Schumann concert at Kings Place, the concert hall underneath the offices of the *Guardian*. When I first visited the site – trying to decide where the paper's new home should be – there was a giant hole in the ground next to the old Regent's Canal round the back of King's

Cross Station, one of the bleakest quarters in north-central London. The developer was Peter Milican, a mop-haired former optician from the North-East who was intent on putting a concert hall at the bottom of this cavernous hole. All things being equal, he would run it. And so it all turned out. The architect, Jeremy Dixon, designed a 420-seat hall which sat on giant shock absorbers to shield off the noise of the streets and trains, and lined it all with oak veneer. And then the two of them jaunted off to Hamburg to buy a stable of Steinways to populate the halls and rehearsal rooms – with an extra one for Jeremy himself since, late in life, he'd got the piano bug, too.

Today Kings Place is a buzzing arts and conference venue and the derelict land opposite is a teeming building site, soon to be a huge area of parks, art colleges, restaurants, offices, streets and houses.

This is the line-up I'd managed to bring together: Cardinal Cormac Murphy O'Connor (former Archbishop of Westminster), Edward Fox (*Day of the Jackal* actor), Oliver Condy (editor of *BBC Music Magazine*), Sue Perkins (comedienne and writer, who won the BBC conducting competition, *Maestro*), David Pickard (general director of Glyndebourne Opera House), Michael Foyle (former leader of the National Youth Orchestra), Katie Derham (broadcaster and presenter of the BBC Proms), Lord (Claus) Moser (former head of government statistics under Harold Wilson and former chairman of the Royal Opera House), Kit Hesketh-Harvey (writer and one-half of Kit and the Widow, the musical comedy act), Conrad Williams (film agent and author), Sarah Walker (Radio 3 presenter), Richard Ingrams (former editor of *Private Eye)*, and me.

The pianists arrive in varying states of nerves and excitement this morning. The calmest may well be the shaggy-haired Richard Ingrams. If you've had as many writs as he has in his life, you doubtless develop a carapace of external calm. The most nervous is Sue Perkins, despite spending her entire life as a performer. It turns out that she had given up the piano at 17 after a mortifying experience of freezing mid-performance. And in the morning run-through she freezes again. Her fingers turn to jelly, her legs shaking with terror.

On stage, we have two pianos, back to back, so that each player is able to slink onto the stage while the previous pianist is still playing, meaning there is no pause between each of the *Kinderscenen* movements. I've no idea if *Kinderscenen* has ever been done like this before. Schumann labelled the pieces '*Leichte Stücke*' – easy pieces. And they are certainly not in the class of his major works for piano (the Fantasie, *Carnaval*, *Etudes symphoniques*). But there are still tricky turns in many of them – and when I first mentioned the project to the participants, it was interesting to see who 'grabbed' which piece on the first-come-first-served basis.

Last night I tweeted the event. '13 amateurs play Schumann . . .' A tweet came by return: 'Poor Schumann.' But in fact Schumann is served rather well – and, to my amazement, there are 350-odd people here to witness the eccentric event. The cardinal leads off with a fluent, quite jaunty account of 'Of Foreign Lands'. He has played only a little since his school days (though he told me he unsuccessfully tried to inveigle the Holy Father into a duet on his recent trip to the UK). Then Edward Fox crouches over the keyboard to play the slowest version of 'A Curious Story' anyone in the hall had ever heard. The piece is normally brisk, but he plays it lento, at least, with some of the phrases actually slowing down as he nears the end.* It takes about a third of the piece to get over the shock of the playing and to take it on its own terms. Few would have the nerve to play it like Edward. But this is, after all, a world-famous actor taking the stage, and he is determined to take all the time he wants. ('Of course,' he said drily afterwards. 'That's how I act. Once you're on the stage they can't throw you off.') It is an entirely different piece in his hands, but by the end it is almost as convincing as the faster conventional versions.

Next up is Oliver Condy, who whisks through 'Blind Man's Buff' with the feather-fingered dexterity you might expect of someone who regularly plays the organ in public. Then comes Sue Perkins. She might be sick with nerves, but she manages to get through 'Pleading Child' with calm grace, nearly all the notes in place, and with a lovely tender slow ending. David Pickard is next with 'Happy Enough'. I've played with him before and know him to be a very good sight-reader, a skill which he uses to cajole visiting opera conductors to share duets in the Sussex countryside. He audibly grows in confidence as he plays today, with some elegant changes of harmony. Then it's our youngest player, Michael Foyle, who is in his late teens. His piano teacher, the rather famous Julian Jacobson, professor of piano at the Royal College of Music, is, unnervingly, in the audience. But Michael still plays like the professional he will undoubtedly become.

Then it is time for the very composed Katie Derham followed by the

---

* Conrad Williams later wrote that it sounded 'like an impression of a 300-year-old Rumpelstiltskin having a bad dream and a heart attack at the same time'. But he conceded it was nevertheless riveting.

87-year-old Claus Moser, who plays 'At the Fireside'. The presenter of the concert, Radio 3's Petroc Trelawny, had earlier, in the green room, asked Moser to name the pianist who had most impressed him during his long life. Moser said it was Edwin Fisher, whom he had heard play before the war, when he was a child in Berlin. At his home in Camden Town, Claus still plays on the Bechstein his family smuggled out when they fled the city in 1936. His playing today is elegiac – a singing line of melody over carefully placed chords. Again, slower than any professional pianist would take this piece, but overwhelmingly wistful, as if this might be the last time he'll play in public. Kit Hesketh-Harvey is next up, playing 'Knight of the Hobbyhorse'. He takes it at a steady lick, with a nicely rocking motion. At the end he brings out the left hand in a way which suggests some years of practice or tuition – even if he scrambles to the end, improvising a last triumphant chord, not quite as written.

The Radio 3 presenter Sarah Walker is particularly polished – understandably so, as she read music at university and then studied performance at music college. She handles 'Frightening' with note-perfect ease – the only one of the thirteen (young Michael excepted) who might have made some sort of living from keyboard-playing. Richard Ingrams brings up the rear with a version of 'The Poet Speaking' which is quite unsentimental, but full of intensity and feeling. Anyone who has suffered his bitingly satiric pen over the years might wonder at this glimpse of another side of his personality – and the image of a white-haired figure, lost in sensitive concentration in this music.

And me? I hadn't listened to any recordings while learning my movement, 'Child Falling Asleep', so just before leaving the house this morning I played myself Barenboim's and Horowitz's recordings. Both play it quite briskly – very clearly two beats a bar – and not exactly gently. So the child is not so much falling asleep as lying there refusing to go to sleep. I realised as I played today that I hear the piece differently. To me there's something so hushed and tender about a child falling asleep – every parent learns the art of imperceptibly moving out from under a child so as not to wake her, and tiptoeing from the room. I have done that a thousand times with our daughters. The piece graphically describes that feeling – with the magical, velvet moment when the piece arrives in E major, and the ever-slowing breathing of the last few bars as sleep finally settles. So – judging by the interpretations of the two great virtuosi – I hear and play the movement 'wrong'. But I think my slower version corresponds with the moment I think Schumann was describing so vividly. And playing a Steinway in Jeremy Dixon's wonderful airy hall is just a delight. I feel no nerves at all – I've no idea why not.

Before the *Kinderscenen*, Martin Prendergast and I played the Canonic Etudes as planned. They went just fine as well. And again I felt no nerves at all – though this was perhaps the result of being so well prepared. Martin and I have played the piece maybe twenty times on Sunday nights over the course of more than a year. A few years ago I would never have had the nerve or inclination to play the piano in public. When it became unavoidable – because I was attending masterclasses or courses – I had the most extraordinary physical reaction. It would begin with uncontrollable shaking in the feet – nightmarish if trying to pedal – and would spread to the arms and hands. But here I am able to play in front of an audience of hundreds and feel no fear. The context is everything. Today's concert is all about amateurs – people literally doing it out of love of music. And the audience respond with generosity: they aren't sitting there, their ears cocked for the slightest slip; on the contrary they are willing us on. Which is just the loveliest feeling – of giving and receiving.

Conrad Williams made a similar point in his own account of the event in *Pianist Magazine*. 'There is a very simple truth,' he wrote, 'which amateurs should mark. People like to hear music played live and will tolerate different standards if the context is right. It's only really music critics and piano teachers who can't abide the imperfect. We amateurs will never touch the pros, but just conceivably we might touch an audience. Preparation, a bit of courage and a love for the music can take you a long way, because music is better than it can be played anyway and something always comes over if a pianist puts everything on the line.' Here then is another crucial value of amateur playing – that, through our playing, we might just occasionally touch an audience.

Sunday, 3 October

This morning in the front room at Kentish Town, I am at last able to spend a little time at the piano with the Ballade. Still working on the coda and still stuck on $\quad = 63$. What I've done today is just practise with separate hands. (I've found a book that actually advises cutting the music up and sticking down the LH and RH separately and doing no other sort of practice until each hand is mastered.) I try first with just LH alone. In some ways it is more difficult than the RH, but I got it up to ♩ = 80. I then did the same with the RH, and was eventually able to get it up to the same speed. I went on to play the coda through another three times with each hand, and then put the hands together at ♩ = 63. The result was that things now feel much more solid. So maybe the foundations are getting there after all. I also practised the G minor scales at the end, again at ♩ = 63, doing one octave – i.e. playing just eight notes – waiting, and doing another one, and so on. But when I tried it with the hands a tenth apart (so ten notes rather than eight) – the LH starting on a G, the RH starting on a B flat – the LH falls apart. That suggests to me that I can't really play a G minor scale with my left hand. That's a legacy of giving up piano when I was 16 – it's exactly the kind of stuff that you have to do repeatedly in order to progress up the grades. So if I'd persisted back then, I could actually have built up a proper technique. But what would I tell a 16-year-old today? 'Take one passage and work on it every day for ten weeks, repeating it endlessly, incredibly slowly.' How many 16-year-olds would see the point?

How am I doing in the Ballade/music-room race? We were able to muster a brief escape to Fish Cottage last weekend. There was complete chaos on the building site – with trenches and pipes and cables and half-built walls rising out of the mud. Musically, my main area of concentration at the moment is the coda but as with the building site, you feel you have to attend to many other areas: if you don't get the wires in now, then you won't be able to put the floors down, and so on. There are some earlier passages that I know are going to be problematic later on and that, if I don't start working on them now – a bit like the drains and plumbing and wiring – then they are not going to be ready by the time the walls are going up. (['That's enough building-site metaphors for now – Ed'] as Richard Ingrams would say.) But tomorrow it is the Conservative conference, so that means another forty-eight hours away from the piano, and another delay in any progress.

There have been non-musical developments today. This evening C4 *Dispatches* was investigating the phone-hacking story. The programme had two MPs on the media select committee, which last year investigated phone hacking, confessing they were too intimidated by News International to look into things properly. Adam Price, one of the MPs, said 'I was told by a senior Conservative member of the committee, who I knew was in direct contact with executives at News International, that if we went for her [Rebekah Brooks], they would go for us – effectively that they would delve into our personal lives in order to punish us'.

Labour MP Tom Watson also gave an account of how he was threatened in 2006 after he called for Tony Blair to resign at a time when News International was supporting him: 'A very senior News International journalist told me that Rebekah would never forgive me for what I did and that she would pursue me through Parliament for the rest of my time as an MP . . . It led me to seriously consider leaving Parliament, because the pressure and the stress were so great.'

Watson claims there are senior politicians who are frightened to pursue evidence that their own voicemail was intercepted: 'There are former ministers that I know, because they've told me, who believe that their phones were hacked and they're not prepared to go public because, at the moment, they feel frightened and intimidated by News International. I'm obviously trying to convince them that it's their duty to do so.'

Just as I suspected: that Parliament itself was cowed from doing its job of holding people accountable out of simple fear of what those people could do to them.

It will be interesting to see what effect the show has.

Sunday, 17 October

A weekend at Fish Cottage, and a pause after two very hectic weeks. Work is advancing on the WikiLeaks cables front, and we've decided to publish the second instalment, which will consist of the Pentagon's Iraq War log, this Friday. But all the partners are becoming increasingly anxious about timings and communications from Assange, who returned to London from Sweden last month with the rape allegations still hanging over him. We've worked out that the total extent of the leaked material we've handled since July is roughly 300 million words. That's a hell of a lot of stuff to search through, find connections and supply context for. For two months David

Leigh has been focusing on the State Department cables with the help of a system editor, Harold Frayman. He's discovering extraordinary material about nuclear proliferation, military exports, Saudi sex parties, and Prince Andrew's questionable trade dealings. We'll publish this material in a separate instalment later in the year. Well, that's the plan. But now we're picking up hints that another journalist – the London-based writer Heather Brooke – is also on the trail of the cables and may even have a copy. If so, that makes the whole existing collaboration between Assange and the partners (which, he insists, should not include the *NYT* this time round) even more fragile and complex. It seems likely that Daniel Ellsberg, of Pentagon Papers fame, may also have a copy of the State Department cables. It's all getting very frayed.

And the US government now knows what we are about to do with the Iraq War log. This is increasing tension among the partners. Someone writing as '@WikiLeaks' – probably Assange himself – has tweeted, 'Pentagon appears to pre-empt alleged WikiLeaks Iraq leak with FOIA release.' But this doesn't look too significant. We're still heading for simultaneous publication on Friday. The *NYT* – assuming we iron out all the wrinkles with Assange – will go at 5 p.m. NY time, the *Guardian* 10 p.m. UK time and *Der Spiegel* at 11 p.m. in Hamburg. It's a crazy time for us to be publishing – late on a Friday evening – but it's the only time that makes sense in terms of *Der Spiegel*'s weekly deadlines.

In the middle of all this I've been away at the Tory conference – more meetings, endless late-night drinks, early breakfasts, snatched sandwiches – and then back to a draining daily schedule at the office. What's happening at the moment is there are just days full of meetings. Then, somehow, towards the end of the day, when you've had all the meetings, which are essentially all about the changing economics and techniques of newspapers, you have to somehow find time to immerse yourself in the journalism itself. By which time there are usually thirty, forty, fifty emails that have accumulated during the course of the day. And so you can find yourself just trying to keep up with that deluge, and working most evenings until at least ten o'clock.

All of which means I've missed the chance to play the piano on all but two mornings this week – so just forty minutes' practice. Next week is even worse, with a trip to Berlin midweek and then two nights in some soulless conference hotel near the M25, for a crucial away day, looking at financial and editorial options for the paper. Work seems to speed up and allow no time for anything else at the moment. But the Ballade is my one chance to do something that slows down the general non-stop whirring of the editorial running machine.

This weekend I put in a couple of solid hours to try to make up for the lost practice. I could feel a tugging urge to start speeding up. And, in odd bars, the speed was beginning to get there, but my new mantra must always kick in: slow down, slow down, slow down. I tried something out, though: breaking down the 'fractures' in the coda and notching up the speed by playing very small bits of it – maybe ten notes at a time at something like ♩ = 90 in the RH and then putting it together at ♩ = 80, which was seventeen notches faster than I was playing it before. By just concentrating on tiny little bits, I realised that it was beginning to come together. However, let's not overstate the progress on the piece as a whole. For weeks I've been worrying about having neglected other parts of the piece given my focus on the coda – and I was right to do so. I thought I at least knew what the notes were in the waltz section, but now I realise I don't. Ditto bar 33 – the first 'squashed flies' bar.

I'm wondering about whether there are two forms of parallel practice, two different types of learning that go on simultaneously. One is about speed – about getting the fingers to fly around quickly – and the other is about memory. Of course, you can't get the speed without memorising the notes. But you also have to play some sections *very* fast, and the purely motor mechanics of that need work on their own. I remember one teacher even giving me a book of exercise – Czerny's *School of Velocity* – which was purely about speeding up the fingers.

Meanwhile at Fish Cottage, the builders are now winning hands down, and there's little chance I'll have the Ballade done by the time they finish. The ex-garage behind the music shed now has four breeze-block walls, a floor and a roof – and there's about twenty metres of walling gone up (essentially shoring up the wooded hill above the cottage). The builders have encountered several springs since doing the earth-moving works, and there have been quite a few unanticipated problems in laying down additional drainage to pipe the water underground into the stream at the end of the garden. But there is still barely any hope of my catching them up. The hubris of ever thinking I could manage this in the time it took them to build a music room . . .

There has been one memorable evening off this week. On Thursday, I went to see the Teresa Carreno Youth Orchestra of Venezuela at the Festival Hall – another one of the extraordinary young bands to have come out of that country's El Sistema, the music project which is as much a social venture as a musical one. The Venezuelan experiment is now the stuff of legend, with great western conductors making pilgrimages to Caracas to see their young conductor Gustavo Dudamel at work with the poorest of children, brought up to treat music as essential a part of their lives as food and drink. Dudamel was credited by the Berlin Philharmonic maestro Simon Rattle with single-handedly rescuing the tradition of western classical music out of the barrios of South America. It's proof that great music has universal power to move, regardless of background, wealth or culture. So that explained the edge of anticipation as the full house settled down to hear these kids get stuck into Tchaikovsky's Fifth Symphony.

As I listened to the piece, my mind went back to a piece my friend Ed Vulliamy wrote in the *Guardian* describing a trip to see the Simón Bolívar Orchestra in action in 2007. He spent a day with a 22-year-old bassoonist, following him home from rehearsal to the ramshackle barrio of San Andrews on the outskirts of Caracas – a jostle of mud, breeze blocks and corrugated iron. On days with late rehearsals he stayed in town rather than risk the journey home – and he didn't keep his instrument at home out of fear it would be nicked.

At the Festival Hall, I watched the bassoon entry of the second subject in the first movement, played effortlessly by a young woman, and wondered about her own life story, and the journey which had taken her from a similar background to playing in front of this audience on the South Bank. She played it perfectly, with poise and feeling. What would become of her? Of the rest of the orchestra, concentrating on every note of the unrolling symphony? She was good, but – to be ruthlessly honest – her tone was a bit throaty. Set her against a hundred other bassoonists of her age, would she be the one who made it through to a professional orchestral career? And if not, what, then, of all the thousands of hours that had brought her this far? The same for all of them. The whole point of El Sistema is that it produces hundreds, thousands of young people with an extraordinary talent for orchestral playing – but only a fraction will presumably ever make their living from it.

But then this experience of playing in an orchestra to this standard will have given the bassoonist two things. The first is an incalculable sense of discipline, confidence, self-worth, of working in teams, of listening to others, of her own value. The second is the music itself – the making of it, but also the sound, shape and passion of it. That won't go away, whatever she does in life.

On Friday, Jeff Shackell emailed to update me on a couple of the Model Os he'd shown me last month. The 1908 – the one recorded in the Steinway ledger he'd produced – needs a lot more work, but he is clearly still very excited by it and keen for me to consider it. He also mentions the 1978 Hamburg O, which he'd just brought back from the North-East when I saw him last. 'The O grand has cleaned up very well,' he said in his email.

> The action works much better now after servicing. However I have identified that the action rails are split and I will need to fit a new action frame before selling. The part is on order from Steinway. So what you feel and hear now will be replicated after the work, but with a complete new action frame in place. Other than that the piano is in lovely condition. The asking price is £25,000.

I had left 'Nimrod' in September thinking that the 1912 Model O was destined to be mine, but even though the 1908 would be a shot in the dark and the asking price of the 1978 is eye-watering, I was tantalised by Jeff's email. Knowing how quickly his pianos sell, I was anxious to get over to Witney to reconsider things. Jeff wasn't available this afternoon – when he's not dismantling pianos he takes steam engines apart. His Facebook page is a scrapbook of open-top vintage cars, steam engines and old flying machines. His profile picture shows him, not peering into the belly of a Bösendorfer, but with flying goggles in the seat of a 1920s sports car. Same kind of idea, just different machinery. Anyway, his priorities for this Sunday were clear: 'the boiler washout & cleaning down of firebox is something I do need to attend to & I don't get too many weekend chances to do it'. So his wife Anna was minding the shop. I was the second pianist in this morning. A woman had just left, having bought a Steinway A for the thick end of £40k. They seem to be flying out of the warehouse.

Anna left me the key to lock up after she'd gone. I was alone in the deserted hangar and gave myself an hour to decide whether to buy the 1978 or the 1908 piano. The 1912 Model O had a wonderfully romantic back-story – but I have no idea how it would shape up into something for daily use. I know the 1978 instrument doesn't warm Jeff's heart quite as much as the old 1908 Hamburg instrument sitting upstairs. On the other hand, I know what the newer one sounds like, while the 1908 piano would be a leap of faith into whatever emerges from Jeff's loving hands next Easter.

I started playing the Ballade on the 1978 piano. The action was clean and responsive, and the tone a little softer than some Steinways. The bass is not as fully throated as other pianos I've tried – doubtless because the instrument is, at 5' 10", a bit shorter. The middle bloomed. There was a slight dead patch in the upper middle, but the top was crystal clear.

Whichever piano I buy, it will end up being the most expensive thing I've bought apart from my house and the Fazioli. With only thirty minutes left, I wandered over to a much longer (seven feet) Steinway B that caught my eye on the other side of the showroom. I expected to be beguiled by its punch and resonance. But the touch was less subtle and the fuller sound a little unsettling. I moved down the row to another Steinway B – one I'd tried three weeks earlier and much admired. Today it was full-sounding and deep, but also big – like a turbocharged BMW Series 7 or a very large Mercedes.

How does anyone ever make up his mind about a piano? Three months ago I dismissed a second-hand Schimmel in the Steinway Hall because it seemed too solid and Germanic. But the Schimmel I tried at Forsyth's in Manchester seemed to have an entirely different quality – much more yielding and not at all stolid. I'd happily buy Anne Brain's Yamaha on which we play each piano course in Lot. But all the Yamahas I've tried since didn't have much soul.

I go back to the 1978 Model O and find I am rather enjoying its more restrained quality. It's a more intimate instrument – not for making a grand statement or performing so much as having a quiet moment of contemplation, or conversation. That's in keeping with the space that's being built for it – no audience, but, hopefully, one or two collaborators in the form of chamber musicians or singers.

By the time I'd locked up and slipped the key through the front door, I had resolved to buy it.

All this agonising about pianos makes me remember the time, a few years ago, when Alfred Brendel came to dinner in Kentish Town and spent a few minutes running his fingers over the Fazioli in our front room – possibly just out of curiosity, since they were then not so common. He walked straight over to the piano and played two-thirds of the Schubert G flat impromptu. He stopped and said nothing. Then he started singling notes out, one at a time, running his fingers up and down scales. He tried the soft pedal and then played a little more Schubert.

For a few minutes I basked in the glow of the velvety sounds filling the room – but a bask tinged with apprehension as to his verdict. Finally he pronounced: 'The piano is lovely, but not yet perfect.' There were areas which did not match, he said. The bass was too dominant: there were ugly notes in the treble. He played them: it was obvious the moment he pointed them out. And the carpet must go. Of course. He would send his technician round to sort it out.

A couple of weeks later his technician, Peter Salisbury, arrived. He came by motorbike, dressed head to toes in black leather, with a case full of tools in his hand like a plumber, or – in the days when they made house calls – a doctor. He had his own Fazioli, he said. A beautiful instrument – the only competitor to Steinway. At their best, better.

He talked about working with Brendel, one of only three pianists he could name who truly understood the piano and how it worked and should be voiced. With Brendel, he said, it used to be all about context – the relationship of one note on a particular piano to all the others, so-called 'voicing'. He'd voice the instrument, and then Brendel would sit at it and find, invariably, a 'wrong' note. At first it mystified Peter. He began to watch Brendel's fingers while he was playing. Eventually he appreciated how he bent the final joint of his finger as he touched the key – it was how he got the perfect pianissimo. Once he'd worked out this was how Brendel played the piano, he voiced it accordingly. Eventually there came a day when Brendel could find no 'wrong note' and Salisbury punched the air to himself with a private 'Yesss!'

But no two pianists can agree what sound a piano should make. Peter told me he'd tuned three pianos at the South Bank for a piano week featuring many of the great contemporary players. Murray Perahia had rejected the first two and settled on the third. Brendel had followed, rejected the third and gone for the first. 'You can't leave pianos in the hands of pianists,' was Peter's view.

He asked me to play my Fazioli, stopping me after a few minutes. 'I know all I need to know now.' I didn't know what he had divined from my playing. But he then sat down to work – and was still there twelve hours later, during which time we'd driven down to Blockley and back. He'd stripped off his jacket, but was still in the leather motorcycle trousers he'd arrived in and hadn't taken a break for food or drink. 'It's been a very difficult job,' he said when we found him still at work. 'Fazioli do "factory voicing". It's the only bit of the process that's not handmade.' The whole piano needed adjusting. Every time he did it at one end, he had to start at the other – softening some hammers, injecting others to firm them up. He finally finished work at nearly 10 p.m. The piano did sound different – but then Peter warned me that it would take several weeks of the hammers settling down before I could really judge how it would sound.

A few months later I met the equally legendary pianist Daniel Barenboim at a strange evening organised by M&C Saatchi as part of their programme to promote the arts and hence, I suppose, their brand. There was a mixed audience of clients and journalists, plus the pianist Evgeny Kissin and the playwright David Hare. We all stood with drinks in our hands as Barenboim played an utterly magical performance of the slow movement from Schubert's last piano sonata in B flat, D960.

Over dinner that evening I told Barenboim about my Fazioli, Brendel's visit and Peter's work on the piano. He started rolling his eyes. 'Alfred is so prescriptive about pianos. I love and admire him. He's a great, great pianist, a towering intellect and a wonderful humanist. But he fucks up pianos!' He looked quite aghast that anyone would voluntarily entrust their piano to the tender mercies of Alfred Brendel.

Monday, 18 October

I've decided I'm going to need regular lessons if the Ballade is going to be playable. Lucy is the wrong side of town. More important, she is, with me at least, a performance teacher – in lessons with her, we jump around and even think about short cuts for tricky moments. At this stage I need detailed attention to make me continue to focus on the intricacies of the score. There's only one man for the job. So I'm going back to Michael Shak. He lives just round the corner and if we start at 8.30 – some lessons will have to be at eight – then most weeks I should be able to find one morning where I can squeeze in an hour before work. It's been four or five years since I had regular lessons with him in his neat semi, where he lives with his partner, Stefan. And here I am again on his doorstep waiting for him to break off his early morning practice to greet me.

Michael had asked in advance what piece I was planning to bring him. His first words today were not encouraging.

'Alan, I've been thinking. There are some technical things which even I maybe can't help you with. You might want to see another teacher to build on what I'm telling you.'

'It's difficult?'

'It's difficult.'

He knew the piece, of course, but not to play. Today, he wanted to start at the beginning, since he'd been looking at that. Typically methodical, he'd worked out all the fingerings for the first three pages. Lessons with Michael always begin with the fingerings.

It's been some time since I played the opening pages. I have just finished breakfast and my brain is still not really engaged. I falter over the opening notes of the Largo – probably the easiest bars of the entire piece. His pencil is immediately out. 'The problem is the left hand,' he says. 'I think if you use the fourth on the E flat and then the thumb on the B flat that might help. Otherwise it's just too much of a stretch.'

Inwardly I groan. Now I'm going to have to relearn this passage from scratch – drum into the fingers this new shape. But the fact that I stumbled indicates it wasn't secure in the first place. That's what Michael's great at: he is a kind of heat-seeking device for working out what's shaky, and why.

We move on through the opening Moderato section. By now I am concentrating fiercely and get through to the squashed-fly passage at bar 33 without too many mistakes. He stops me at the black flies. The fingerings, he approves of. But, he asks, how am I breaking down the eighteen notes there and dividing them between the three crotchets? Blimey. My only thought up to now has been to get them down in roughly the right order. Eighteen between three equals six. So, how about six a beat?

'Hmm, I think it's more interesting if you do four notes on the last beat. That will give the impression of slowing down. And then, in the middle beat why not eight? Which leaves six for the first beat.' He carries on: 'Initially I thought you should try and make the top D coincide with the second beat because it would accentuate the dissonant notes.'

My head is spinning.

'But I think 6/8/4 makes kind of sense. It's easier.'

Oh good. He then takes me back to the beginning and talks about pedalling. His pencil is skidding across the page showing me where to depress and release the pedal. Next he asks me to replay various bars and questions why I am changing fingers on a particular note.

'To get a smoother legato line?' (It's an invisible trick of pianists to make a fluid, singing melodic line – no sooner has a finger struck a note than you replace it with another, freeing up the finger to play the next.)

'Hmm, I don't think that's necessary. Oh and here' – he starts to scribble – 'you can take those notes in the left hand in order to free up the right hand and get a better melodic line.'

Then he looks at the trill in bar 25.

'Are you starting that on the beat?'

I am.

'Good, I think that's right. But your grace notes in bar 27 and 29 were a little fast. Oh, and in bar 33, this is going to sound crazy, but why not two thumbs on the G sharp and the A. That's just my little trick.'

I reel out an hour later. It had been super-intense. In the end, we had looked at thirty-five bars in minute detail. And these are the easiest bars in the piece, technically. God knows what it will be like when we try the really hard stuff.

Friday, 22 October

Back from Berlin into King's Cross for morning conference. Then a hurried meeting to discuss the kidnap risks of a reporter in Afghanistan. Then I drive around the M25 for the away day to discuss future business models and whether or not we should be expanding more aggressively into America. And in a few hours we break the next WikiLeaks story.

I haven't touched a piano since Tuesday morning. Not good, and it affects me at work. The great Spanish cellist Pablo Casals couldn't start the day until he'd played a Bach prelude or fugue on the piano. He called it 'a benediction on the house'. Maybe scientists will one day be able to show the minute changes in brain chemistry that explain it. With other people it's yoga, or a run or a burst in the gym. Twenty minutes on the piano has the same effect for me. Once it's in the bank I'm ready for more or less anything the day can throw at me. Without it, things are harder.

Sunday, 24 October

Publication of the Iraq War logs (just about) went to plan on Friday – though everyone jumped the gun when it turned out that Al Jazeera (brought in at a late stage by Assange) published some of the material they had a little in advance of what we'd all thought was the agreed schedule. After months of really harmonious collaboration a misunderstanding over the difference in publication time of minutes, or even seconds, has the potential to badly spoil relationships. But this was soon forgotten as, once again, we saw a story ripple around the world.

Internally, there are some bruised feelings among colleagues who would have liked to contribute and who knew nothing about the project until the last minute. The whole WikiLeaks project has been very tightly guarded in the building – with a small dedicated team working on a different floor in an anonymous project room. Our deputy editor Ian Katz emails one wounded colleague: 'You're probably right that we should have thought earlier about trying to do something ambitious . . . The fact that we didn't was largely down to the extraordinary sensitivity of the logs and our determination to keep the knowledge of the project to the smallest possible group. For the first few weeks that meant only Nick, David and Alan and as late as a week before we published the Afghan material no one on the newsdesk bar [assistant news editor] Stuart [Millar] had any knowledge of it. We felt we had to keep it so tight because any sniff of it outside the building might have led to an attempt to prevent publication.'

But already our minds are on the richest material – the State Department cables, which we plan to publish at the end of next month. Because of the Heather Brooke leak (now confirmed: it seems to have come via Iceland, where Assange was briefly based) none of us is very keen to be sitting on this material for too long. However, relations between the *NYT* and Assange are really terrible now – he has said he doesn't want to have anything more to do with them. And today it looks like this might be an impossible situation to remedy: the *NYT* has published a profile of Assange and he's not going to like it. The authors – the London correspondent, John F. Burns, and Raavi Somaiya – obviously feel no great chemistry with him. They quote one source as saying 'he is not in his right mind' and quote Assange as dismissing their questions as 'cretinous and facile'. This breakdown in a crucial relationship means the whole project could now get very ragged indeed. David Leigh's heading off to Washington at the end of the week to meet up with the *NYT* team, along with the guys from *Der Spiegel*, even though we can now be sure that Assange will be trying to find an alternative partner in the US. Very messy.

But we've been able to get to Blockley for the weekend, and so yesterday I decided to drive over to Witney to photograph the Steinway Hall logbook from 1908 before Jeff gives it back to the piano tuner, Gill Green, who discovered it in the second-hand bookshop in Maidenhead. I found Jeff having a tea break with his colleague Clive Ackroyd – grey hair, V-neck jumper and jeans – who is head piano technician at the Royal Academy of Music. They were discussing the relative merits of Steinways versus other pianos: both agree no other piano can compare. Why? For Clive it begins with the trees in the Steinway forest, from which they choose the soundboards.

'Steinway has its own forest?'

He looked at me quizzically, as if wondering how this could possibly be news to anyone. Yes, it has its own forest and it takes the wood from the centre of the forest, where the trees have to grow taller in order to reach the light. The trees are therefore straighter, which means you get a superior cut of wood for the soundboard. Other, lesser, piano manufacturers presumably have to make do with the punier spruce trees at the edge of whichever plantation serves as their source.

Jeff said he once asked a Steinway technician for the secret of the Steinway sound. 'He said, "Think of two pebbles dropping in two ponds. One has a muddy edge, the other a concrete edge. With the former the ripples blur into the mud. With concrete, they hit it with force. That's the Steinway."' The casework, Clive explained, is made out of a continuous rock-hard maple rim, whereas lesser pianos not only use lesser wood; they aren't built in one piece.

Then they started discussing the difference between Hamburg- and New York–built Steinways. Mine's a Hamburg. Which is better? It seems to come down to a matter of taste. Jeff implies the New York factory has still got more of a handmade feel about it – but he conceded that when European pianists go to play in America they sometimes struggle to adjust to the differences, with the New York pianos a bit brighter and more immediate in tone. He said the English pianist John Lill had recently gone to the States, where he found the Steinways 'horrible' compared with their Hamburg counterparts.

When the conversation paused at last, Jeff took me upstairs for a last semi-longing look at his 1908 piano. The 1978 piano is lovely, but Jeff doesn't sigh when he looks at it, as he does gazing at the battered old case of the 102-year-old instrument. I can tell he still wishes I'd gone for it and there's a definite tinge of disappointment in me.

He's got to do one thing to mine before he can release it – replace a split in the brass rails which holds together the action. A common problem in 1970s Steinways, apparently. Easily fixed. The music room's not remotely ready yet, so I'm relaxed that it will be a few months before he's ready with the instrument.

I photographed the pages from the Jan–June 1908 Steinway Hall order book, and was able to study them in more detail than when I last saw them. They are redolent of Edwardian middle- and upper-class England, where no respectable household could be without a boudoir or drawing-room grand. Here is the Princess of Wales at Marlborough House, with her Halle piano stool. And, as Jeff described, here is Mrs Asquith moving her Petrof grand from 20 Cavendish Square to 10 Downing Street. Here's a whole page devoted to the upkeep of Baron (in pencil) Alfred de Rothschild of Tring. And there is the piano I didn't buy – then sold to the Locker-Lampson family of Crawley, Sussex.

The coda has been inching along this weekend. An inch forward, half an inch back – but definitely moving in the right direction. Just v.e.r.y slowly. But yet again, whenever I look around the rest of the piece I frighten myself with how much else there is to do. It's taken me a solid six weeks of work on the coda to feel remotely confident about the notes – and when I say confident, I mean confident I absolutely know what they *should* be and have a feeling that my fingers will find them automatically at a given pace. I don't mean I can play it with any confidence, let alone proficiency or musicality.

I have been making some progress with memorising things, though. I've been trying to do this a bar or two at a time. And yesterday, I could very, very gradually sense connections being made between fingers and brain – a strange sense of new, untested ducts and previously unforged connections between synapses. Or rather, not new. It's almost like walking down an echoing old underground tunnel, long deserted. I remember exploring the tunnel under Kingsway in central London, now used to store old railings, discarded road signs and building material, but which still has traces of the old Holborn tram station. This experiment with my memory has a similar feel of abandoned corridors of the mind.

And there was another strange 'memory' discovery on Saturday. If I try to play with the music closed in front of me, that slams the memory door closed. If I open the book, and play without looking . . . the notes flow. Explain that.

There was a sneery little newspaper diary paragraph about me playing the piano today, suggesting that editors have no business having any interests outside work. Or, no cultural interests anyway. The editor of this particular newspaper I know to be fanatical about keeping fit – I sometimes see his fine athletic frame pounding the pavements of North London. Editor goes to gym: not news. Editor plays golf: not news. Editor plays piano: news. I know – from the many friends who run/work out/play football/squash/ tennis – how central exercise is to their lives. How they couldn't work as effectively without it. How an hour of sweat and burn blasts away the stress and sets them up for the day. Well, the piano's the same.

As a side note, great editors are often quite obsessional. A few of them manage to remain reasonably sane and keep some sense of proportion about what they do, and what they ask of others. But many of them burn out quite quickly, or find it difficult to keep the obsessional aspects of the job in check. In this respect I don't suppose much has changed in a hundred years. George Bernard Shaw had it about right: 'Lighthouse keepers with wireless sets know far more of what is going on in the world than editors,' he wrote. 'A daily paper should have at least three editors, each one having one day on and two days off. At present the papers are twenty years behind the times because the editors are recluses.'

Saturday, 30 October

I went to see Claus Moser today. His short interview on stage before the charity Schumann concert intrigued me, and I wanted to hear in more detail his memories of amateur music-making before his family fled Germany. He is a few weeks short of his 88th birthday and is of the last of the generation of Jews who fled Germany before the war and who were old enough at the time to remember their 'German' life. In his time in Britain he seems to have had a hand in running everything – from music academies to banks to Oxford colleges, museums and the Royal Opera House. But it is being an amateur pianist that is perhaps the central obsession of his long life. I found him in an armchair in his upstairs sitting room just off Regent's Park – an L-shaped room with the family Bechstein which also escaped Hitler in one wing of the L: 'It's not fantastic,' he says, 'but I can't get rid of it, it's too emotional.'

Outside the trees are golden brown in the late October sun, which adds to the autumnal air as we talk about some his of earliest memories. I begin by asking him about *Hausmusik*, the predominantly German tradition of amateur music-making in the family home. He answers in a still-firm and resonant voice, with an impeccable English upper-middle-class modulation:

> *Hausmusik*, as we call it, was absolutely the centre of life in the sort of home in which I grew up. What I can describe as *Hausmusik*, I think even Hitler couldn't disturb. In any middle-class family, not to mention upper-class family, which I suppose we were, the chances are nine out of ten that somebody in the family plays something. I mean, it's just more natural than not. It would be sort of very unusual if a Berlin family didn't have anybody who played and that can be a piano or it can be any other instrument.
>
> My family . . . well, they were musical. My father played, my mother played, my brother played, I played. My brother was a violinist, the others were all pianists. It would be absolutely normal and expected that, certainly once a month, but probably more, there would be a chamber-music evening in the house. I think that goes back to Bach and Handel and so on, I mean *Hausmusik* was just part of life, much more common than going out to supper or having dinner parties.
>
> Two nights ago we had dinner and the 81-year-old Dutch conductor Bernard Haitink and his wife were there. They're old friends. And I got Bernard to talk a bit about amateur music when he was a kid in Holland and it was very similar. I think it's the Continent really.

In Moser's experience there was not much distinction between the amateur and the professional world. Through *Hausmusik*, the two commingled:

If the family was well off enough, as happily we were in Germany, then amateurs would be joined by professionals. That's the other point. It wasn't just amateurs, it wasn't just family making music. It was quite common that we'd have first-rate professionals making music with us and we'd practise like mad. So amateurs like me grew up trying to be as good as the professionals in a way. Not that we were, but we were never a separate clique in that sense. So high standards were aimed at, were there, from the beginning and it was all enriched in those years until Hitler came to power.

Later, after leaving Moser, I wonder what effect this interaction had on the professionals. As Moser said, the amateur world was enriched by this contact and standards rose; but did it enrich the world of the professional players? Did Clay Shirky's model of the amateur contribution improving the 'professional' world apply here? Was there an infectious charge from contact with a simple amateurish love for music, which sometimes seems to fade in some (especially orchestral) professional musicians?

Moser also had an interesting note of caution to raise regarding his early experience as an amateur:

> We were very traditional. We really were absolutely fully into Mozart, Beethoven, Schubert, Schumann, etc. We were steeped in German and Austrian tradition above all, which I had no complaints about at all, but I think is one of the reasons why I've certainly grown up too conventional really. I mean Benjamin Britten is fine but I find playing contemporary music quite tricky. I think this is a criticism in a way of becoming an amateur musician. If one perhaps gets too hooked on what one can possibly play.

However, while he may have failed to test himself against the challenges of contemporary pieces as a young amateur, Moser's contact with the professional world and the general standard to which he was playing meant that a dangerous ambition took hold. He told me the story of the teacher who intervened to ensure that Moser lived a happier life than he might have otherwise:

> I was absolutely determined when I was 5 to become the world's greatest pianist. Then when I came to England, in '36, went to Frensham Heights [a school in Surrey], had a very nice piano teacher who I was devoted to. When I was leaving school, I said, 'Mr Rice, I'm going to become a pianist,'

and he said, 'Well, don't.' He said, 'I've enjoyed teaching you for four years. I think you're talented. You're not talented enough to become one of the great pianists and, if you're not one of the great pianists, it's a lousy life. Much better,' he said, 'to be an amateur pianist and earn your money doing something else.' That's what he said. That changed my career. He told me later, 'You probably could have mastered the techniques necessary because it's not all that difficult and there are dozens of great technical pianists but to be one of the great pianists, you've got to have the sort of personality confidence to be up on the platform for two and a half hours and just be so lost in your music that it's not a problem. I don't think you've got the nerves.' And he was dead right because whenever I've played in concerts, I've been so nervous for months beforehand that it practically killed me. So he judged my nature, rightly, and he judged rightly that, unless one had all that, as well as the ability to play the fast stuff, and so on, you're not going to be one of the greats. But, he said: 'You will have much more joy.'

And Moser found that he did have much more joy as an amateur pianist. But while he began his career – initially as a banker – he began to get worse as a pianist. There was a very obvious reason for this, he was told:

When I was something like 23, 24 I made the terrible mistake of stopping lessons. I played a lot. I played chamber music more than ever, until one day someone I was playing with said that she thought I ought to have lessons again. Did I understand that if one didn't have lessons one inevitably gets worse?

But why were lessons so important?

Because you cannot listen to yourself as other people would listen to you . . . The difficult thing is listening to oneself. I don't think I was ever quite good enough at really hearing what music I was making . . . I had got too casual in being satisfied with my technical command of a particular work without really asking myself 'Am I playing this the way I would like to hear it being played?'

So he went back to having lessons. And not just any lessons. The friend who'd noticed his decline in the chamber group introduced him to the formidable Louis Kentner, the Hungarian Liszt and Chopin specialist, who had moved to England. Kentner agreed to take Moser on as a pupil.

When I went to see him I was terrified, rightly terrified, because he was a terrifying sort of person. He was a great Liszt pianist above all and he was [celebrated violinist and conductor Yehudi] Menuhin's brother-in-law. He was very well known but he wasn't the success he thought he ought to be. But anyway, he asked me to play to him and I said, 'I'm sorry Mr Kentner but I'm too nervous to play to you,' and he said, 'If you're too nervous to play to me, you're not really a pianist. I mean, you're not playing at the Albert Hall, you're playing to me.' He was very, very angry with me, but I wasn't prepared to play to him. He had two pianos, so I said 'Mr Kentner, could we possibly play the Mozart two-piano sonata together?' and he said, 'I've never been asked by an amateur pianist to play that with him.' . . . We played the first movement and he got up. He said, 'Not very satisfactory really.' He said, 'Have you had any lessons recently?' I said, 'No,' and he said, 'Well there are so many things wrong. Let me just tell you ten of the things that are wrong.' So he told me ten things that were wrong. He then said, 'Now let's try again.' So we played it again and when we finished he got up and he said, 'Of course I'll teach you.' He was suddenly very pleased.

Then he said, 'I think I want you to learn the César Franck Prelude, Chorale and Fugue?' I said, 'That's too difficult for me, Mr Kentner.' He said, 'I am going to judge what is too difficult for you, not you.' He was a terrifying chap really, a real Hungarian. And he said, 'When I've taught you for five weeks you will find it very easy to play. At that point, I will start to see whether you can make music out of it.' And I've never forgotten that set of remarks because it was incredible. All his teaching related to pedalling, to fingering and to certain bits of technique. And believe it or not I could play it . . . Then when he finally said, 'I'm now happy with the fact that you can play it. Now can we make music out of it?' – that's when the real lessons began.

So it's fair to say that I've got it somewhat easier with Michael as a teacher. Though he, too, was a pupil of Kentner. I wonder how Moser made the time for what sounds like such demanding practice. He was a banker at Rothschilds, which must have been unforgiving, and also warden of Wadham College, Oxford. His answer is reassuring. Like me, he practised in the morning – and like me, he was convinced he didn't practise enough.

Finally, I asked him how the experience of piano playing changes as one gets older. It's interesting that he highlights the two parallel paths I know I need to work on with the Ballade: finger speed and dexterity, then memory.

It's not, on the whole, good news. My fingers are not . . . I've had four operations – Dupuytren's, you know; two on each hand, over the years – and my fingers are now straight. So I honestly cannot pretend that my fingers are getting less supple or anything like that, so that's the fingers . . . no excuse there really. Memory? Appalling in every sphere . . . It means I take longer to learn a piece. No, that's not a major problem. What is a major problem is that sight-reading has become much more difficult. I used to be rather good at sight-reading. So, on the whole, it's not good news, but it's not very bad news, the ageing.

Monday, 1 November

Last week it was decided we had to have a clear-the-air meeting with Assange. We – that's *Der Spiegel* and the *Guardian*, but not, at this stage, the *New York Times* – need to sit down face to face. Assange is so nomadic and (with reason) paranoid that there's been no meaningful day-to-day contact for very long periods. There are, it seems, at least three other copies of the State Department cables circulating now and it could all end in tears.

Assange was supposed to join the *Guardian* and *Spiegel* teams at the *Guardian* around 6 p.m. this evening. Around 7.30 Mark Stephens, a London libel lawyer I've known for years, bursts through the door of my office, followed by Assange and a young female lawyer, later introduced as a junior solicitor in Stephens' office, Jennifer Robinson. It looks and feels like an ambush.

Assange has barely sat down before he starts passionately denouncing the *Guardian*. Do the *NYT* have the cables? How do they have them? Who has given it to them? This was a breach of trust – voice raised and angry. He doesn't look well – pale and sweating and a hacking cough. There's half an hour or more of further denunciations before I persuade him to bring the others present (including the editor of *Der Spiegel*, Georg Mascolo) into the conversation. We then have another argument about whether or not he can have lawyers in the room: if he has lawyers, we need lawyers. So I set off to try to raise a lawyer.

I return lawyerless, so it's agreed that we should proceed without Mark and Jennifer, who sit outside the room. Then Assange spends some more time denouncing the *NYT* and, in particular, the 'sleazy' John F. Burns profile of a week or so ago. 'They actually have to be actively hostile towards us and demonstrate that on the front page, lest they be accused of being some kind of sympathiser.' His language becomes oddly old-fashioned the angrier he gets. At times he sounds positively Dickensian in his circumlocutions.

He demands to know who now has the cables. I explain the changed circumstances – including the fact that we have a second source for the cables, in the form of Heather Brooke, and that we're now negotiating with her to join the *Guardian* team. Otherwise, I explain (as if he couldn't work it out) she'd be free to take the cables to any paper – which would mean we would all lose control of the story. This makes him furious. She wasn't a second source – Brooke had *stolen* the cables. It had been done 'by theft, by deception . . . certainly unethical means'. [Brooke, needless to say, completely denies this version of events]. He claims he knows sufficient about the way she has operated to destroy her. It's angry stuff. Generally, when people become angry my instinct is to be very un-angry. I concentrate on being very, very calm.

Assange – the arch anti-Establishment information anarchist and hacker – keeps referring to how 'a gentleman' would behave: 'People who aren't behaving like gentlemen should start behaving like one.' He would prefer to deal with people who behaved like gentlemen – and he mentions the *Washington Post*. 'The strategy that the *New York Times* engaged in was not very gentlemanly. It's an organisation whose modus operandi is to protect itself by destroying us . . . The *Times* has defiled the relationship.' His voice has become loud, declamatory, intense.

I propose a time-out. When we reassemble, still without lawyers, the temperature has lowered a bit. I suggest we look at some of the issues around the sequencing and timing of stories – which subject should run in which order? Suddenly there's a different Assange. He becomes calm, attentive and focused. He's now the CEO – planning with strategic intelligence how to play out the stories, how they will be received, which stories are best kept until later. The ordering has to be arranged so that it doesn't appear simply anti-American, he says. The aggression's gone. As if a switch has been flicked. He's now rather impressive.

But he's very unhappy to be releasing the material soon: his ideal is early in 2011. He says, 'We have woken a giant by wounding one of its legs and the release of this material will cause the other leg to stand up. We are taking as much fire as we can, but we can't take any more.'

He then announces that he wants to involve newspapers from the 'Romance languages' – he mentions *El País* and *Le Monde* – which will certainly complicate the logistics. But at least we're now having a negotiation about modus operandi. By this time it's nearly 10 p.m. and I produce a couple of bottles of Chablis. Everyone thinks we could settle the outstanding issues over some food at the Rotunda restaurant downstairs at Kings Place.

But over dinner Assange reverts to Mr Angry. He will only consider working with the *NYT* again if the paper a) agrees to run no more negative material about him, and b) offers him a right to reply to the Burns piece with equal prominence – i.e. on the front page. By midnight it's apparent this was the deal-breaker. I am deputed to go and ring [*NYT* executive editor] Bill Keller while the others relocate – taking the wine with them – to another meeting room in the *Guardian*.

I know in advance what Bill's going to say. Which he does. And so I take back the message – that Assange can certainly write a letter but Keller has no intention of publishing any kind of apology. This changes nothing for Assange. All bets are off, he says. Both the *NYT* and *Guardian* are now out. Then Georg Mascolo interrupts, speaking deliberately and seriously: the three papers are tied together. If Assange is cutting the other two papers then *Der Spiegel* is out, too. It is nearly 1.30 a.m.

The discussion is going nowhere, so I do my best to summarise Assange's options, as I see them:

'One, we reach no deal. Two, you try and substitute the *Washington Post* for the *NYT*. Three, you do a deal with us three. One and Two don't work because you've lost control of the material. So that's just going to result in chaos. So I can't see that you have any option but Three.'

I can see Assange's mind coldly weighing up the options. But it's also clear that he's not going to do a deal tonight so we all go our different ways. As Assange heads off coughing into the night, he shakes hands with David Leigh, shooting him a meaningful look and urging him: 'Be careful.'

It's now 2.30, and I'm exhausted after seven hours of a bizarre concoction of tense confrontation, negotiation and collaboration.

Wednesday, 3 November

I had my third lesson with Michael today. We'd had another lesson last week, focusing on the coda. He hadn't looked at the coda himself, so I played it to him – slowly, but all the way through. It wasn't too bad, even under the added pressure of Michael hawkishly looking for the tiniest slip. He made a couple of fairly crushing observations. The first was that my pedalling was all wrong. He wanted two pedals a bar, on the beat – apparently I had been pedalling off the beat. Second, the death trapeze. Maybe I should be using a second finger in the RH chord on the second and third beats of bar 212, not a third? They're the 'hinge' chords as the hand flips up and down the keyboard. My heart sank. Two months of prac-tising with a third and now he wanted me to switch. I made an argument for keeping it as it was. He had four editions of the score on his piano and compared all the fingerings. Then he sat down at the piano and played it with second and then third and, thankfully, relented. So I'm still allowed to use the third.

But then as he pushed me to show I could land accurately with the third, I began fluffing it repeatedly. So he advised 'blocking' the chord – playing it in chords and shifting position between them rather than trying to pivot over the thumb – which is the natural motion if trying to play at speed. This was a completely different approach – requiring a rapid shift ten inches to the left between notes. But it seemed to work. He recommended a week of playing it slowly – not with metronome even. Just making sure the notes are in the fingers.

So when I turn up today I expect more coda. But Michael wants to move on. We've only just started on it, I protest. 'I know, but I think we need to get an overview of the whole piece before we concentrate on that section.' I ask him: 'How do I keep the coda in my memory while looking at the rest?' He smiles sympathetically but doesn't answer.

So we spend some time refingering the runs at 246 – one of the killer passages on my secret list of reasons why I'll never be able to play the piece – and examining the repeating patterns within the runs, trying to work out how to shape the phrase. We also look at the octaves in the last seven bars of the coda. I have been playing all the outer notes with consecutive fifth fingers, bouncing down from key to key, whereas Michael wants fourth fingers on the black notes and fifth fingers on the whites.

Michael has been playing the Ballade between lessons and locating some of the trickiest bars in terms of which notes fall where in terms of RH–LH. Bar 179 is a classic example (and another on my own list of nasties). In the second half of the bar the RH plays four-against-three, i.e. four notes in the time of three. This has to fit in with six LH notes. And at the same time the inner fingers of the RH have to 'detach' themselves and play in different rhythms from the outer fingers (which, just to be complicated, have three-against-two on the last beat). In all, therefore, six, four and three beats all in the same time, with an additional tied triplet. It's the musical equivalent of making circles on your head while tapping your stomach, and simultaneously knocking out a different rhythm with your feet.

My mind wanders in the middle of all this musical arithmetic. I was in the office until 2 a.m. on Monday helping to orchestrate the biggest leak in history. The previous night I was out all evening trying to sign up an interesting Dutch journalist for a column. I'm about to concentrate on our coverage of the US midterm elections while at the same time jostling with the intricate negotiations that will be necessary to keep the *NYT*, Assange and *Der Spiegel* on the same page, and it seems I'm going to have to get to know the teams at *Le Monde* and *El País* and bring them up to speed on months of work on the State Department cables. And here I am at breakfast time spending fifteen minutes peering at bar 179 of the Chopin G minor Ballade, examining the notes in the Henle edition and trying to work out Michael's scribbles on a Post-it note indicating where particular notes fall in relation to others. I need all my powers of concentration to make sure I continue to focus on the notes and nothing but the notes.

Michael ends the lesson by saying: 'To begin with I didn't think we could continue this for six months, but now I realise there's so much to do. Six months may not be long enough.' Back in the summer, the builders estimated their work would take six months – so that's it confirmed: I'll never have the Ballade down by the time they've finished. I have to reassess the deadline I've given myself.

Thursday, 4 November

We have dinner at our friends Henry and Liz Porter's tonight, at which I met Ronnie Harwood, the writer of *The Pianist*, the film in which the Ballade so inspired Gary. I tell Ronnie Gary's story, which pleases him. As Gary had reminded me when we met, in his memoir Wladyslaw Szpilman doesn't actually play the Ballade to the German officer, but Chopin's posthumous nocturne. So, I ask Ronnie, whose idea was it to have the Ballade instead? 'It was mine,' he says, his voice husky through a life of chain-smoking. 'It's the most important scene in the film and it had to work emotionally. I listened to so much Chopin at the time to get exactly the right piece.'

At work today I received an email from Michael:

Alan
    Looked at the coda again after you left.
    From bar 246 – the long descending scale – try playing the B natural with the second finger. It's easier to get to at speed and makes the subsequent 5–4–3 a little easier. See what you think.

I make a mental note to try it the following morning.

The rest of the day is taken up fine-tuning the agreement with Assange and the other partners. We eventually settle on ten points:

1. Publish on 29 Nov in a staggered form.
2. Run over two weeks or more up to just before Xmas.
3. Exclusive to *G*, *NYT*, *DS* (with the possible addition of *El País* and *Le Monde*).
4. Subject matter to be coordinated between partners and to stay off certain issues initially. No veto to anyone over subjects covered over whole course of series. WikiLeaks to publish cited documents at same time.
5. After Xmas the exclusivity continues for one more week, starting around 3/4 Jan.
6. Thereafter WikiLeaks will start to share stories on a regional basis among forty serious newspapers around the world, who will be given access to 'bags' of material relating to their own regions.
7. *Guardian* to hire Heather Brooke on an exclusive basis.

8. If there is a 'critical' attack on WikiLeaks – by the US government, for instance – WikiLeaks will publish everything immediately.

9. If material is leaked to/shared with any other news organisation in breach of this understanding all bets are off.

10. If all of the above is agreed, the team will commence work on a grid of stories for the first phase of the State Department cables leak.

So, we're on. The next few days/weeks are going to be intensive and, probably, quite bumpy. Little moments of musical escape are going to be vital– forced interludes where my brain is required temporarily to empty itself of everything else, where manual skills and emotional sensibilities are pulled into the foreground and made to perform or engage.

Friday, 5 November

We're on the way to Angus in the north of Scotland so see Lindsay's father, George, a former farmer, much-decorated Bomber Command navigator, Liberal MP and peer, now 91 and living in retirement. This means the train to Edinburgh; and as with many of my long journeys of late, I spend some of it reading around the Ballade. All Claus Moser's talk about his old teacher – and Michael's – has inspired me to also track down Louis Kentner's book *Piano*.

In it Kentner says that the Ballades 'show a diversity of character, ranging from the lyrical to the dramatic, even to the sunny and gracious, which, in the hands of a lesser composer, might have threatened the unity of form'. In Chopin, though, 'this unity is triumphantly upheld'. In the G minor Ballade itself, Kentner sees a piece which is 'personal in feeling and technique', but which, in its 'roundness and inevitability', is like a 'natural event, and not a note could be changed, added or left out'. I feel quite relieved not to be studying the work with Kentner.

As Moser said, Kentner was a Chopin specialist, and in *Piano* he credits Chopin with changing music for ever: 'when you look at his brave new world made accessible to the old world by Chopin, you wonder what was left to do by others who came after him'. But this new world was a complex one – as I'm learning only too well – a 'bewildering mass of pianistic discovery', a vertiginous new universe of 'widely spaced arpeggios, double thirds, sixths and octaves in every possible combination'. I'm glad to see that a pianist of Kentner's quality acknowledged this inherent difficulty – that it was hard even for him, perhaps. Indeed, he says that to play the 'end of each piece' – the coda in the G minor Ballade, for instance – 'the greatest effort is required of the performer . . . Leaps, novel chord formations, double notes, octave tremolos mixed with chromaticism, and much else . . . are thrown at the player at breathtaking speed.' But while he admits this complexity, I can see why Kentner was the unforgiving teacher Moser described. Not only is it implied that the player should learn to surmount these challenges; they must do so with seeming nonchalance. There should be no trace of 'effort' in the playing, 'for perfect art must be effortless'.

There's a very interesting passage later on in the book, when Kentner discusses the 'spectacular invasion' by the piano 'into drawing rooms all over the world'. This invasion which 'lasted for over a century' was, by the time Kentner wrote the book in 1976, being 'partially replaced by another invasion, that of radio and television, to which it is gradually giving way'. Clay Shirky territory. Kentner thought the emergence of the gramophone had aided 'this subsidence of the once all-powerful pianoforte as an integral part of every self-respecting household'. It had deflected 'so many music lovers not only from the pleasures of the concert hall . . . but also from the once highly popular pastime of making one's own music, however badly, in one's own home, with one's own hands'. I can't help but wonder what Kentner would have made of the prospects for amateur playing today, in the world of Spotify and YouTube, where just about any recording or televised performance ever made is obtainable in an instant. At school we had a small record library – maybe a hundred discs – and very limited access to the record player. Radio 3 was a lifeline to any music student, though it required advance planning with the *Radio Times* to see what was upcoming. For the rest, there was no alternative to reading through orchestral scores at the piano. Of course I prefer the near universal access of today – but I still learn more about any piece from picking my way through it, bar by bar, to see how it's been made.

Sunday, 14 November

We get down to Fish Cottage on Friday. The shed seems to be more or less complete, and the music room now has the framework up for the walls. It's just waiting for cladding and a roof. The floor is two inches deep in water and surrounded by mud; where the piano will sit is just a puddle and old bits of wood; there's a lot of dangling pipework and cables – but it's still as clear as day that the builders are going to manage to have built the two buildings – with all the electrics, plumbing, carpentry and stonework – months before I've mastered my 264 bars of music. The music room does need a big window, though. Perhaps this is my one chance of catching up, since there's a ten-week lead time on them?

This has been an amazingly packed few days at work – one of those weeks where everything has combined. On Wednesday there was an all-day Guardian Media Group away day, in the evening a Scott Trust dinner and on Thursday morning the Scott Trust board meeting. Both the board meeting and away day demanded lots of preparatory work, which inevitably happens once the regular day is done. Then between two o'clock on Thursday, when the Scott Trust meeting ended, and eleven o'clock in the evening, there was a nine-hour meeting of the *Guardian*, *Der Spiegel*, *Le Monde*, *El País*, the *New York Times*, Assange and his lawyer, in which we tried to fine-tune the publication grid for the State Department cables. Ian Katz, the *Guardian*'s deputy editor, is masterminding this grid. It's a vital document and will help us agree all our redactions, ensuring that we don't start firing off in different directions and scooping each other. *Le Monde* and *El País*, who are now full partners, have been working furiously to catch up with the rest of us. Coordinating web and paper publications schedules across time zones is complicated in the extreme, and having a weekly magazine in the form of *Der Spiegel* involved makes things even more complex.

We're still working with a self-contained group within the office, and have recalled to London our correspondents from Moscow, Brussels, Nairobi, Delhi and Caracas so that they can sift through the relevant cables for material on their own patches. There are now more than twenty-five editors and reporters involved, with the heaviest burden in many ways falling on the small team whose job it is to read every cable we're citing and, where necessary, redacting them to make sure no harm will befall any named source or informants. From there, everything is going through a legal filter to make sure we won't end up with an undefendable libel action. All the legal marks then have to go back through the redaction team – and all the redactions have to be adopted by all publishers to avoid the possibility of 'jigsaw' identification.

Though Assange was on his best behaviour on Thursday, communications with him and his team remain difficult; he's decamped to his own 'bunker' – location currently unknown – and is increasingly paranoid about using conventional communication methods. So we now find ourselves communicating through the encrypted instant-messaging systems on which he insists. The paranoia is contagious. Now nobody involved is using phone or email when talking about specific cables. Despite these complications and obstacles, we are still managing to process around 200 cables a day.

But the upshot of all this is that by working fourteen- or fifteen-hour days I've managed to get just an hour this week for practice. I did make time for a lesson on Wednesday morning, though. We had to start fifteen minutes early so I could get to the GMG group meeting on time. Michael was anxious this was too early for the neighbours, so we began by talking about some of the fingering. Once again, Michael had been looking at the piece between lessons and wanted to share his thoughts on how to divide the falling figures in bars 124–5 – a tumbling and unusual arpeggio in the RH while also catching the last three B naturals in the LH. Then he warned me that he finds the rest of that page rather tricky. As if I didn't have enough to worry about.

But we made good progress during the lesson. We got as far as doing the second theme, which I had imagined was fairly straightforward but, of course, I haven't worked on it properly and trying to get the complete legato pace made me realise yet again that even the so-called easy bits in this piece require a hell of a lot of work.

At the end of the lesson, I told Michael I'd been flicking through Kentner's book and had heard much about him from Claus Moser. Was Michael as terrified of him as Claus had been?

'No. He could be very commanding, but he was diminutive and physically unintimidating. I didn't find him frightening. Except when he played, because it all seemed so easy, with the whole repertoire in his fingers. He was very human, even though you were greeted for a lesson by a butler.

When his butler was arrested for having gay sex in a public garden, Louis and his wife were bemused, tolerant and supportive.'

The weekend has been taken up with writing a lecture which I have to give in Australia next week, and I've only managed forty minutes' practice over the two days. That means for the whole week I'm averaging just over ten minutes a day, and that's not the kind of time commitment that is going to get me over the finish line on this piece. The weekend practice has been spent on the 'passage work', which – as I'd suspected in the ping-pong room in Italy last summer – contains some of the most demanding technical challenges in the piece. The first bit of passage work starts at bar 37, and I make this my focus. Again, this is a passage that I can't imagine you could play while reading the music at the same time. So, while keeping in my mind the coda at the end, I am trying to memorise it. From here to bar 45, the LH chords are subtly different. Yet again, you can't just take it for granted that this is a four-bar passage that repeats itself. It's Chopin, so things are always subtly different. And the passage gets faster and faster – by the time you get to bar 45, it's a blur of fingers.

But of course it's nothing like a blur of fingers at the moment – it's a rather sedentary stroll by digits feeling their way around. As the passage goes on, there should be a sense of just flying free and launching yourself at the notes, but I'm just fumbling towards the end of each bar. It's the same old story: very, very slow work and finding it impossible to imagine ever playing this at anything near the correct speed. Once more, I've been caught out by the fact that I didn't practise G minor arpeggios when I should have done in my teens.

I've also been working on the waltz in the middle and I think I've made a little progress here this week. I've already learned the tune and have been breaking it down into three lines. The first is the RH tune. The second is the main emphasis, or anchor, of the left hand so I'm playing the tune just with the first and fourth beats (the oom beats in the oom-pah-pah of a waltz), the E flat and the B, the E flat and the B, the E flat and the A flat and so on (a waltz is usually written in three beats per bar: this one is in six, but should sound in three). Then, thirdly, I'm just playing the tune with the inner parts – the 'pah-pah' beats where the left hand leaps to the middle of the piano to play a series of wistful sighs. I can now play that with both versions and that's been tremendously clarifying.

Monday, 15 November

On the flight to Sydney. I am going to be in the air for twenty-one hours, and so it's another chance to get some Ballade reading done. I read somewhere that studying a score on a plane is an effective way of cementing the work into the visual memory – as opposed to aural or finger memory. And the pianist Artur Pizarro once told me he managed to learn the Brahms second piano concerto on a flight to the Far East. He barely knew the piece when he took off. By the time he arrived he'd memorised it.

Lucy Parham has given me a little advice on how to approach this score-reading. She suggests looking at clusters and chord positions in the Ballade – especially in the E major restatement of the second tune after bar 100. So this is what I do as others settle down for their inflight movies. It's a surprisingly helpful process. For example, I had never quite understood how the (apparently repeated) four-bar pattern at bar 150 worked. But reading it now, I see that it's a pattern repeated three times, rising a tone each time. The first time there are (RH) two B flats separated by one D and a similar pattern in the LH; next it starts on C, but this time there are two notes separating the 'pegs'; and then again with two Ds separated by two notes. And in between each repeated pattern, two other rising notes of semitones. It's kind of obvious, really. But twenty minutes of practice a day neither allows you the time to stand back and see the bigger picture, nor to burrow into the detail.

Friday, 19 November

Back in Sydney after a day at the Australian Parliament in Canberra meeting with assorted politicians in the company of the director general of the Australian Broadcasting Corporation, Mark Scott. We sit in on the interminable prime minister's questions. It must be more than twenty-five years since I was last in Canberra and it's still a very strange, detached place. Of course it feels even more detached today, as I struggle across time zones to keep track of developments over the State Department cables taking final shape on the other side of the world.

This evening I gave the Andrew Olle Lecture – the main media lecture of the Australian year in a grand hotel ballroom before 200–300 movers and shakers of the Australian media scene. I deliberately included a passage attacking Murdoch over phone hacking and calling for the BSkyB bid [in which News Corp wants to take full control of the British satellite broadcaster] to be blocked. It won't have any effect, but needs saying in a country with not very much plurality of ownership. It's listened to in respectful silence by his former compatriots, many of whom work for him. The bit everyone talked about at the end (and which is now bouncing its way virally around the world) is a small section when I gave fifteen reasons why Twitter is such an astonishing medium for journalists – for information generally – and why senior executives in media companies who don't 'get it' shouldn't be in a job.

Back in mid-October I set my TweetDeck to surface anyone in the world using 'Chopin' and 'Ballade' in the same 140-character tweet. Instantly someone from Long Beach in California popped up: 'Having a hard time getting my Chopin ballade down: my brain and hands are not cooperating.' You, too, eh? Since then there's been a daily crop, from people just expressing their love of the piece ('I hope they play Chopin's Ballade No. 1 in G minor all the time in Heaven . . . I never grow tired of it! Absolute. Perfection. Period.'), sharing opinions on who they think were the finest Chopin pianists of all time, or just tweeting links to pianists playing the Ballade – in schools, in warehouses, in their own homes, in concert halls all over the world. A large number of them appear to live in Japan, China and Korea. It's a tiny illustration of two of my Twitter rules:

—It creates communities. Or, rather communities form themselves around particular issues, people, events, artefacts, cultures, ideas, subjects or geographies. They may be temporary communities, or long-term ones, strong ones or weak ones. But I think they are recognisably communities.

—It has a long attention span. The opposite is usually argued – that Twitter is simply an instant, highly condensed stream of consciousness. The perfect medium for goldfish. But set your TweetDeck to follow a particular keyword or issue or subject and you may well find that the attention span of Twitterers puts newspapers to shame. They will be ferreting out and aggregating information on the issues that concern them long after the caravan of professional journalists has moved on.

Sunday, 21 November

I'm now flying back to London, having spent *six* days completely away from the piano. Again, I'm looking at the Ballade score on the plane, this time trying to work out the harmonic structure. This has always been a blind spot for me musically. In choir I had to train myself to 'hear' how big an interval was, which I couldn't do without my own set of aural mnemonics. The interval between the first note of a scale and the second would be the same as that between the first two 'notes' in a fire engine's siren. The interval between first and third, the same as a doorbell's ding-dong ('Avon calling') or a cuckoo; fourth – the two opening notes of 'Away in a Manger' fifth – the opening of *The Flying Dutchman*; sixth – 'The Holly and the Ivy'.

In harmony lessons as a 13-year-old choirboy, I was told to listen to the bass line to work out where the keys were going – but that was immediately complicated when, the following week, we learned about chord inversions – the fact that any chord can be structured at least three ways, so that the bass note, as printed on the page, might actually be a third or a fifth harmonically. With time I learned to hear the 'second inversion' (with the fifth in the bass) as a 'weak' chord. But I never developed the ability that others had of being able to hear naturally when a piece had modulated into the subdominant or associated minor key. The notion of a French or Neopolitan sixth still eludes me, even though the latter is crucial to the first page of the first Ballade and Michael has patiently explained it twice. So I've a struggle on my hands trying to grasp and remember the key structures of different passages.

Before getting on the plane, I saw that someone had tweeted a YouTube clip of the French-Canadian virtuoso Marc-André Hamelin playing the fastest coda I've ever heard – recorded in 1997. And then another tweet linked to what looked like a piano in a workshed, with a balding man in glasses working his way through the Ballade. It's been viewed more than 3,000 times – that's six times the audience at Wigmore Hall in London.

Meanwhile, in Washington, the *NYT* is approaching the White House today to discuss the release of the State Department cables. All the European partners have mixed feelings about this. I think it mainly reflects different legal systems. In the UK we would be very unwilling to approach the government in advance, because, on all past form, we'd expect to be injuncted, if not actually prosecuted. Bill Keller has evidently got less fear of any form of legal gag and thinks there may be positive benefits from establishing a dialogue in advance with the Administration. He's probably right. The ability to harness the WikiLeaks revelations about despotic regimes to the American First Amendment was one of the reasons we originally approached the *NYT* to see if they'd collaborate with us.

Saturday, 27 November

I have felt rising stress levels all this week, as we prepare to break the State Department cables. Yesterday, just two days before we publish, there's a particularly tense, hour-long conference call with the State Department, the CIA and Defense Intelligence Agency, the National Security Council, the Pentagon and Hillary Clinton's chief of staff. The State Department's spokesman, P. J. Crowley, begins by stating that, from the US government's perspective, these are 'stolen documents'. They want the numbers of all the cables we're intending to use. I demur. They press. I refuse. I do tell them the general areas we'll be writing about, and on which day we'll cover which subject. In the end, we exchange email addresses and phone numbers. 'Will you be working this weekend?' I ask. 'Oh yes, sir,' says one of the disembodied intelligence chiefs from the speakerphone. 'We'll be working all right.'

On Wednesday, a colleague who has been out of the loop on the cables picks up a whiff of what's going on and sends me a long email asking if I'm entirely sure that what we're doing is right. Of course, this kind of internal challenge is essential in any newspaper, where, all too often, a small group can get carried away by the apparent rectitude of their own group-think. So I ask Simon Jenkins, *Guardian* columnist and former editor of *The Times*, to come in and nose around the cables by way of a reality check on my own judgement. Simon is no part of the *Guardian* liberal consensus – that's why I hired him – and I know he'll give me a straight opinion on the ethical balance between publication and US and, to a much lesser extent, UK national interests. After a couple of hours he comes back with a brief injunction: publish!

So it's been a fraught week, but still I've managed my twenty minutes a day most mornings. And I've really felt the benefits – playing each morning has given me a small period where I'm walled off from all the fracas, and focused only on the challenge of the score. On Tuesday, I have an 'earworm' all day long after my morning's lesson with Michael – the waltz. During a couple of meetings I find myself tracing it out on the table, my RH repetitively playing in loop. I'm sure close colleagues suspect it's piano practice. I hope it didn't look like impatient drumming of fingers.

Just over three months into this project, how am I doing? The headline news is that I have committed at least half the coda to memory. This to me is astonishing; it's a funny thing to discover about yourself in your mid-50s – that you spent the previous forty years not doing something on the assumption that you couldn't do it, when all along you could. Maybe I can now learn German, or how to become a Java programmer or do algebra.

But I can only play this half of the coda from memory very slowly, mind. I have a feeling it is going to take twenty or more hours to get it even up to half the speed most professionals take it at. Other major progress is that the G minor scales at the end now look manageable. Even the one in tenths. And the first two pages – i.e. the first theme – is almost there, apart from the black squashed-fly notes at bar 33, which I still cannot play up to speed. I've made inroads into the first piece of 'passage work', and I can now understand the shape of the arpeggios in a way I couldn't to begin with. But I am still miles off memorising this section, and I'm particularly bad at coordinating left and right hands from bars 54 to 65. In the second theme, I still have to work on the legato and haven't worked out the left-hand chords. Then there's the passage work from 121 to 136, which isn't remotely there yet and very uncertain on the octave passages in RH, the LH in the waltz which seems trickier each time I try to revisit it. And it seems incredible that I've been working on it for the best part of three and a half months and still haven't finalised the fingerings of everything, but there you go. Looking ahead there are still two very tricky pages of unfingered territory to go. In fact, the list of problems could go on indefinitely. So, way to go.

The builders have won. I'm going to have to find a new deadline, and force myself to stick to it. July seems doable – and there'd be a satisfying symmetry in being able to play it at piano camp next summer, exactly a year after watching Gary pull it off. When I suggested July as a target to Michael this week, his immediate reaction was: 'Not long enough.' I'll see if I can prove him wrong.

But enough piano talk for now. Tomorrow we publish the biggest leak of state secrets in history.

PART THREE

Sunday, 28 November

At precisely 21.30 we were supposed to release the first tranche of the State Department cables. But things have not gone quite to plan. The day, which started in Blockley, nearly unravels with flashes of slapstick. I get a call mid-morning from the *Spiegel* editor Georg Mascolo telling me there's been an embarrassing leak at their end. A solitary newspaper vendor at Basel station has started selling early copies of his magazine, and Georg wants to warn me that a pseudonymous tweeter calling himself 'Freelance_09' has begun to tweet the highlights of the magazine's coverage. At that point Freelance_09 has only forty followers, but this clearly has the potential to disrupt the carefully laid intercontinental plans for a simultaneous publication this evening. Georg is beside himself with embarrassment, but something like this was inevitable. I jump in the car to drive back to London. By the time we reach the M25 junction Freelance_09 has 150 followers; word is obviously spreading fast. Lindsay's driving: I'm monitoring Twitter, calling assorted partners and colleagues about revising the launch time. By early afternoon I'm in the office and our tweeting friend has found a scanner and has begun to feed in pages of *Der Spiegel*. And then, accidentally, a *Spiegel* developer 'lives' an extract from the magazine. In New York, the *NYT* sees the leak, and by 6 p.m. any idea of a later embargo is in shreds as we all stampede to publish our versions of the material. The best-laid plans . . .

The *Guardian*'s version, based on all that work by the team painstakingly picking their way through 250,000 cables, kicks off with the revelation that Arab leaders have been privately urging an air strike on Iran. We later learn the State Department has assembled a team of 120 staff to sift through all the cables being released by the five partners and Assange himself (who is still hidden away in a 'bunker' somewhere in England). The Italian foreign minister was one of the first to grasp the significance of what was happening. 'It's the 9/11 of world diplomacy,' he says.

Friday, 3 December

The week begins with a Tube strike paralysing London, which complicates a journey across town to White City to do the *Today* programme on BBC radio. By dawn the story has gone completely global. Monday and Tuesday are a total blur as we're besieged with media requests and enquiries from newspapers all over the world wanting us to share material with them; but we have to keep our heads down and focus on producing the following day's revelations according to the schedules the partners have spent so long agreeing.

It is going to be like this right up to Christmas, I suspect. I can't remember any story quite like it: each day – actually twice a day, since we're launching stories in the morning and late at night – the partner newspapers are setting something off that ends up being discussed simultaneously in the White House, the Pentagon, the Kremlin, the Elysée Palace, in Delhi, Caracas and Canberra. It's the first prolonged rolling, real-time global scoop – a vast spillage of information seeping out across the world.

Somehow I'm managing to keep playing my twenty minutes a day most days, and on Wednesday – in the middle of all this – I have precisely fifty-nine minutes with Michael. It feels slightly surrealistic to be plunged straight back into fingering discussions while the WikiLeaks story is pinging round the chancelries and parliaments of the world. But I'm back into the scrum of the story within a blink, so I do my best to shut out all other thoughts for an hour.

We pick up at the precise spot we left off last Wednesday – looking at the problem of how to tackle the octaves at bar 119. First the turn on the second beat. I find that difficult: it's enough to stretch an octave without having to execute a twiddle using the weakest fingers (4 and 5) while holding down the thumb at the same time. Michael's suggestion seems even worse: using the third finger – a real stretch – and going 3-5-3. I'm not sure that will feel right, but it's the sort of thing that can only be settled on my own during practice.

If I'd thought this was going to be fifty-nine minutes of respite or retreat, I was wrong. The Wiener Urtext score has two alternative suggestions for how to finger the octave scales here. But first, what are the notes? Michael says it's in 'B minor – apart from the E sharp', which might be a help if I'd ever learned my B minor scales. And, to complicate things, he doesn't agree with either of my suggested fingerings. Again, he wants me to use my third finger for an octave reach – which I've never done before – on the basis that using the third finger on the first F sharp will help make sense of the beginning of the scale. He fingers it 3-4-5-5-4-5-5-4. But I can't – at that time of the morning anyway – work out the logic for why he's made some of those choices, or how I'll remember them.

The next scale in the octaves is 'C-sharp minor, apart from the F double sharp', which is of equally limited use to my brain at this time in the morning (or, if I'm honest, ever). This time he wants two third fingers in the mix. The final scale is – *mainly* – G-sharp minor, and again, I am going to have to learn it note by note, never having previously considered playing G-sharp minor scales to be an essential life skill. This section is rapidly creeping up as being one of the most difficult in the piece – a fact that had escaped me because it's not the best or most memorable music in the Ballade.

We then discuss – not for the first time – how to split the falling arpeggios at bars 124–5 between the hands. In the past, Lucy has suggested splitting the falling figures two per hand; on Wednesday, Michael suggests three in RH and one in LH – and we aren't able to resolve the problem during the lesson. Next, we spend some time peering at the really fiddly rising figures in the right hand beginning at bar 130, which are extraordinarily difficult to finger – a tangle of different digits in a phrase which (we work out) repeats itself after sixteen notes over four bars. We agree that one way to think of this passage is to parcel up the separate progression of lower and upper notes to see what pattern there is in each.

Then we're on to the waltz, where the fingering is pretty straightforward. So instead Michael is worried about the pedals – whether the apparent score-marking to lift the pedal every three beats is right, or whether it's better to clear the sound after two notes in view of all the notes tumbling out of the right hand. By the end, we get right through to bar 153, with Michael instructing me on which notes to bring out in the rising octave figures in 150–3.

It's 9.29 when we stop. For a few seconds – as I come blinking out into the Kentish Town daylight – my mind remains lost in Chopin and Michael's convoluted technical challenges. But it is only seconds. I'm immediately checking emails and within fifteen minutes I'm back at my desk, the morning conference about to start. There's a brief post-mortem on Tuesday's WikiLeaks releases – encompassing Pakistani, British and French politics – and then a look ahead to Wednesday's, with all its myriad complications. How, for example, can we negotiate the legal rapids around the accusations that Putin runs a mafia state and the stream of details about his relationship with Berlusconi? There's also damning material scheduled on Sri Lankan politics, EU energy supplies and how Britain colluded to evade a ban on cluster bombs. I really need to keep across the redaction process, and so by 11 a.m. I have had separate discussions with the head of news, the web editor, the head of legal and the chief investigations editor. The problem of how to finger an octave C-sharp minor scale was receding. But the fifty-nine minutes of non-WikiLeaks has, as ever, helped clear the head and reset the mental clock.

Saturday, 4 December

This morning we get down to Fish Cottage in three inches of snow, which has produced an elegant arc on the curved roof of the ghostly shell of the music room. There's sheet plastic where the windows will be – so now, for the first time, the room is enclosed. And the brown paper piano template has finally arrived from Forsyth's in Manchester. I lay it down on the concrete screed – tracing the shape of its outline like a chalked body at the scene of a crime. For the first time I can clearly imagine how a piano will fit into the room and feel in the space.

I spend part of today trying to escape the stresses of the past weeks by reading George Bernard Shaw. I read his review of a new Chopin biography (published in November 1892) by one Charles Willeby. He thinks it 'supplies a want', but there's a marvellous put-down of Willeby at the end: 'a few slips in the critical analyses may very well be condoned for the sake of a readable biography of Chopin which is not nine-tenths a work of pure imagination'.

This evening I lie in the bath wondering why on earth I have so spectacularly exceeded my own budget for a piano. Can I justify it on an amortised basis? A free iPad app has calculated my life expectancy at another thirty-nine years – on what actuarial basis, I don't know. So one way of looking at the extra £15k is to say that it's going to cost me another £7.50 a week for the rest of my life. I almost feel better.

Monday, 6 December

What can I do about my terrible memory? What goes on between the eyes reading the notes on the page and the fingers moving across the keys? Who can explain it all to me? A few months back I tried these questions on Clive Coen, a professor of neuroscience at King's College London, who plays in a quartet I sometimes hook up with. Clive pointed me in the direction of Ray Dolan, FRS, professor of neuropsychiatry at UCL, and one of the pioneers of modern neurobehavioural research – he's also a hiking partner and scientific muse to the novelist Ian McEwan. And so today I nipped out for a lunchtime coffee in his office overlooking Queen Square in central London, where he works at the neurological hospital.

I find a 50-something, warm, loquacious Irishman with endless patience to explain the intricacies of the brain to an arts graduate whose last exposure to the biological sciences was in O-level classes forty-odd years previously. I begin by explaining the nature of my problem: that I can sight-read music perfectly well, but the moment the sheet of music is taken away from me I really struggle – in fact, until recently I couldn't play a note without sheet music in front of me. Dolan immediately reassures me. 'You have a memory,' he says firmly, 'and the fact is that, at the end of that first month on the foothills, you were better at playing the Ballade. So something has gone in, something has happened. What the sheet is, essentially, is a cue and a lot of us need a cue to remember things, just something that will elicit the memory. So the music for you, as it's written and in front of you, is clearly a guide, it's a script, but it's a cue as well. It's eliciting memories that have been laid down.'

He proceeds to give me a lesson in memory. Broadly speaking, there are two types. 'The first is what's called explicit memory: and then there's implicit memory. Explicit memory is what I bring to mind and declare in some way. So the fact that yesterday morning I was in Potsdam. I can remember what I had for breakfast. I can remember waiting for the taxi to pick me up, going to the airport. So that's declarative memory.'

I'm already struggling. This sounds like three types of memory – implicit, explicit, declarative. Not two.

'Well, there's two types of explicit memory, so let me unpack it a little bit better. The memory I'm describing is what's called an episodic declarative memory. In other words, I can retrieve the actual "me" embedded in the memory. There's another type of memory which doesn't require the "me" but which I can make explicit, which is "I know that Angela Merkel is the chancellor; I know that Joe Biden is the vice president of the US". So I don't have to think of "me" in that memory but I can bring it to consciousness.

'So that's two types of explicit, one is episodic, the other is semantic. You can bring them to your mind. I would say that that is a small component of the brain's memory ability. The vast majority of your memory is implicit. It cannot be brought to consciousness, but it is there and we know it's there for the following reasons. Based upon prior experience, the fluency with which you can do things is enhanced, and that goes for everything from walking, to riding a bicycle, to writing. These are all what's called procedural memories, procedural skills. And the vast majority of memories are of that ilk. They're acquired, you acquire a fluency in your behaviour consequent upon that prior experience and this enables you to do things that you would not otherwise be able to do. There are many examples, things like skiing, for example. And all you need is to be back in the context for the memory to be elicited.'

One of the characteristics of implicit memory, he explains, is that it is not flexible. For example, 'my [explicit] memory of being in Potsdam and knowing where the bridge is that once divided east from west might be useful to me in the future, in some other context. If I was there and there was suddenly an outbreak of war, I'd know how to get across a bridge. So it is flexible, it can be deployed in other contexts. Procedural memories tend to be context-specific. So knowing how to ski or knowing how to play piano has no other application that we know of in other domains. It's very domain-specific.'

Playing piano is a skill that falls under procedural memory. But Dolan makes it clear that 'it's not just the skill of playing the chords that's procedural. The piece itself will be remembered, I think, largely as a procedural memory.'

I ask Dolan if these two different kinds of memory are located in different parts of the brain.

Explicit memory, he says, involves a part of the brain called the hippocampus, which is in the temporal lobe and plays an absolutely crucial role in helping us lay down day-to-day memories, such as recalling the specific instance of getting that phone call, of meeting that person, or seeing this thing on the street. How do we know this?

'Well we know this because of a famous man called HM. He was a patient who suffered with epilepsy and he was operated upon in Montreal in the 1950s by somebody called Penfield. After he had the operation to relieve epilepsy, he seemed intellectually intact except that he could not remember a thing that happened to him outside a temporal window of one minute. In other words, he lived in a permanent one-minute here and now. What happened three minutes ago, five minutes ago, was gone, but what happened to him before he had the operation was preserved. He died, in fact, last year and he still thought Eisenhower was US president, and that TV was black and white.

'Indeed, there is a famous musician, Clive Wearing, who has herpes simplex encephalitis, a rare viral infection that can affect your brain, which tends to take out this very part of the brain [the hippocampus]. Now the interesting thing is that, if I studied Clive Wearing or HM, I could, in principle, teach them a new piece if they were both musicians, assuming they have the basic skills. If you exposed them to a new piece of music and taught them to play it repetitively, over an extended period of time, you could then set them down at the piano and say, "Well could you play that new piece?" and they'd say, "No, I never heard it before." But if you gave them a cue, it is likely to be the case that they could just roll it all out because it is present as a procedural memory. So that tells you that procedural memory is a distinct type of memory, distinct from episodic memory – recall that patients like HM do not remember anything outside a one-minute here-and-now time-frame – and it tells you that this type of memory is dependent on a different part of the brain from that needed for episodic memory.'

So where is procedural skill located? Dolan says that the striatum – a grouping of nuclei deep in the middle of your brain – and a structure at the back of the brain called the cerebellum are critical for procedural skills. 'We know that from the type of work that people like me do, using non-invasive imaging to track how activity in the brain changes as you acquire a skill. But we also know it from pathologies in the brain, of which the most dramatic and tragic is Huntington's disease.'

We then move on to discuss why some pianists can infuse a piece of music with emotion when they play, but others can't. He mentions he'd met the pianist Angela Hewitt about six months ago. She told him that she taught some kids in China. It was a kind of a masterclass and she said some of them had trained since they were tiny, but that while they could play note perfect, they were unable to conjure emotion in the listener. 'Why do you think that is?' Dolan asks me.

I say that, in layman's terms, I'd put it down to the life experiences and feelings for which we somehow manage to find an equivalence in music, a way of musically expressing accumulated experiences and emotions. A less individualistic culture might well create musicians who felt and expressed music differently.

Dolan introduces another way of thinking about this. First, though, he has to lay out a global picture as to how the brain works.

'Your brain has to assimilate all the sensory information that is coming in from the visual world around you, the noises outside, the dog barking in the park there. It's a sensory bombardment and it's continuous. So the amount of information is overwhelming. There is no computer in the world that could possibly process that. It's just too rich. And how does your brain do it?

'It does it by using a simple trick, a trick interestingly enough used by Alan Turing in decoding the German Enigma machines. It turned out this involved having hunches which could put some sort of bound on the potential solutions to an enciphered code. Your brain is also predicting the sensory input at each moment in time, and these predictions help reduce the processing demands of the brain. These predictions are not random but rest on lived experience, including childhood experiences. It included such mundane predictions as surfaces tend to be hard and hot surfaces tend to burn. This has given rise to the idea that the brain is a predictive machine that exploits mathematical principles that were first articulated by a dissenting Anglican minister at the end of the eighteenth century, called Thomas Bayes. In fact, he is buried not too far from here in the City of London. Thomas Bayes only published a single paper during his lifetime and another that was posthumous. The latter was picked up after his death by French mathematician Pierre-Simon Laplace. Bayes, and the whole tradition he spawned, now provides a principal intellectual basis for how we think the brain handles complex information. His influence in fact suffuses much of biology, including about how the machinery of the brain works, and the formation of the synaptic connections that are the core of stable memories.'

I've lost the starting point of all this – the China question. My own brain is working hard to digest this absorbing personal seminar. I'm beginning to understand Ian McEwan's fascination with the man and their habit of going off on hikes together, sometimes lasting days. But how, I ask Dolan, does all this help us to understand what might allow one pianist to move us when another can't?

'Well, when you acquire a skill, that skill is enacted out by you making predictions about the consequences of your actions. A lot of motor skills are also of that ilk. You're making predictions of the consequences of your actions. And those predictions, they perfectly line up with the consequences so you don't notice anything. It's only when there's a deviation that you notice. And that deviation in mathematical terms is called "surprise". But I think that's one of the things that good musicians do. They're not aware of this in any technical sense, but a crucial thing is to bring elements of surprise into how you play it. It is my intuition that this element of surprise, or a nuancing of expectations, provides a skilled musician with the core algorithm that is exploited to evoke emotion in an audience.'

So a good pianist has this ability to provide 'surprise' and so stimulate emotion in the listener. But is there anything that distinguishes the brain of a great pianist from a mediocre one?

'If you have to do a neuroscience dissection of great musicians,' Ray says, 'the one thing that they would have is great memories, and probably for-midable procedural memories.' This allows them to learn a vast canon of music and then recall it easily when at the piano. What is crucial, though, is that they have the ability not to corrupt their procedural memory, so that 'people who become the finest musicians are the people who can just let the procedural memory unfold without the anxiety and worry of trying to recall it explicitly. I guess a lot of jazz musicians must operate at this level. They've learned scales over and over again and they get a cue from the context provided by the other musicians with whom they are interacting.'

Dolan also thinks it very unlikely that a successful pianist would be able to recall any piece explicitly; that is, they might be able to play it, even without the music, but without the cue of the keyboard itself, they could not just sit down with pen and paper and tell you 'that note follows that note, follows that note'. Indeed, according to Dolan, taking any procedural skill and trying to access it as an explicit memory can have problematic effects. He explains this with a story of his own.

'I had somebody staying at my house and they called me up here [at the office] and they said, "Listen we're going out. Do we have to put the alarm on?" I said, "Yes" and they asked, "What's the code?" Now every night I would simply tap in the code. This started off as an episodic memory the first few times I had a new alarm fitted. With practice it was transformed into a procedural skill. On the occasion I was asked for the code over the phone I could of course not consciously recall what was now procedural, even though this was the very thing I did, without thinking, every night. In other words, it was only there as a procedural skill. I struggled and struggled but it wouldn't come. Now, I am usually the last person in my house to go to bed. But when I tried to enter the code that night, to set the alarm, I simply could not as I was still trying to recall it as an episodic memory. I had to go upstairs to my wife and embarrassingly say, "I'm really losing it, the old buffer can't remember the alarm code." So that's just an example of how they can occasionally corrupt. They can interfere with each other.'

At this point I mention the Artur Pizarro story – learning the Brahms second piano concerto on a long-haul flight to the Far East. What was going on there? Dolan isn't sure the story can be literally true; but if it is, it presents a very interesting proposition. 'Because if you read a piece on the plane for four, five, six hours, that's not a procedural skill, unless as they are reading it, they are actually imagining themselves motorically playing the piece. I think you could show that this imaginative act is transforming a semantic input (reading the score) into a procedural skill. Some people are very good at that. People will offer you coaching for tennis where you do it in your mind first, or they'd offer it for skiing where you didn't have to go onto the slopes. There is in fact evidence that you can become more skilled by just enacting motor acts in your imagination.'

I ask him what he understood by the term 'muscle memory'. He says there is no such thing. 'Your muscles have no memory at all. That's the first thing I'd say to you. If somebody has used that as a description of what they experience, I would say it's procedural memory. It is the elicitation of this memory that is not available to consciousness laid down as a pattern of activity.'

'So, I'm sitting there repeatedly playing the same arpeggios, drumming, as I think of it, patterns into my fingers. But that's a complete misunderstanding of what's going on?'

'Yes, it's [only being drummed] into your brain. So when you play the first note of an arpeggio, the second note you've set up. That is the cue for you to complete it. It's the cue that elicits that procedural skill. A lot of language acquisition is really of this ilk as well. So as a child, I learned Gaelic, and I learned an awful lot of it. I can say prayers in Gaelic and, occasionally, I can't say them until I get a start. I might sometimes go on the internet and look up how to say the Our Father in Gaelic. But if I get the start of it I can just reel it off as a procedural skill. So a lot of it is getting those first elements, which is a bit like what is provided to you by having the music laid out in front of you.'

'So the act of doing exercises might just be about improving your muscles?'

'Yes. Your muscles can atrophy from lack of use and they can hypertrophy, get bigger and stronger, but they never acquire memory.'

'Is there a bit of the brain that relates to your fingers?'

He has a model of a brain in his office and holds it up to illustrate what he's saying.

'An important part of the cortex is the motor cortex and, behind it, the sensory cortex, responsible for motor output and sensory input respectively. A trivial fact is that we are much more dependent on our hand, because of the dexterity it affords, than we are on our shoulder. This has the consequence that the representation of the hand takes up more geographical space in the cortex. The dimensions of this space can actually expand at the edges. If, for example, you acquire a new skill with your hand, then the hand representation expands a little bit and the surrounding areas, which represent adjacent structures, are squashed a bit. Some kind of Darwinian principle of selection is at work here, so that the size of the representation for any bodily part enlarges if that body part is used to a greater degree than another body part.'

'Is that both in childhood and in adulthood?'

'More in childhood. The plasticity of the brain is greater in childhood.'

'But the hand bit of my brain could still grow a bit now if I played every day?'

'Yes, it could happen in adulthood as well. It's not too late for you.'

I am encouraged by this exchange. My brain is still capable of stretching to these new challenges – 'it's not too late for you': I'll remember that. Dolan fleshes it out with an example.

'Let's suppose we now decided we will get somebody who's aged 50, never played the piano. You're going to just lock them up in a castle somewhere. They're told: "Only come out when you can play a very complex bit of Liszt." That was their goal, to Grade 8 standard. We measured their brain before they went in. Now the skill that they would be acquiring would be a procedural skill primarily. It would be expressed via the hands because they're playing the piano. We measure the structure of their brain in an MRI scanner. If you acquire new skills, you can't grow more neurons (nerve cells). Instead, what happens is that the neuron sprouts more tentacles, or what are technically referred to as dendrites. Because of the sprouting of dendrites and the connections they make with other cells, at junctions called synapses, we could show at the end of a year's training a change in the configuration restricted to that part of the brain representing the organ that has acquired new skills. In this case the hand representation would be larger and the associated cortex would be thicker.'

Finally, I tell Dolan about why I feel my piano time helps my professional time. I hesitate to describe what it feels like – how it seems as if I'm using a different part of my brain when I'm doing my daily twenty minutes, and in some way it sets me up for the day. The chemistry has been altered. Does that make sense to him?

'One of the things I do with my kids in half term,' he tells me, 'is to go skiing with them. When I ski, I notice that I don't think about other things – all my anxieties are gone out of the window. So what I think is that when you are in that mode, using procedural memory, it probably suppresses activity in other memory systems, for example the episodic memory system that gives content to your anxieties. I am sure that in your case, when you are playing the piano, that it is very difficult for you to be worried about whatever a *Guardian* editor worries about. You're liberated from the tyranny of your explicit, you know, over-representational mind.'

And, he adds, it is not just the brain that benefits from this 'suspension' while I'm playing. He thinks it relaxes me in other ways, gives my *body* a break. 'Because although you might have anxieties, that's not just something that exists in your head; it exists in your body. Your blood pressure is going up, your stress ions are going up, and playing music is a great way of suspending it. My wife, who usually plays the piano for an hour a day, does it, she tells me, for that very reason: she's just in another world. She works as a breast radiologist, so in everyday life she has to deal with the tragic situation of diagnosing women with breast cancer and then breaking this news to them. For her, playing the piano helps suspend the memory systems that embody this distressing experience, and sees her through to the end of the day in a much calmer state.'

I'm charmed by the man and heartened by his description of how it all works and what it does for the spirit, soul and body – three words I'm sure he would never dream of using in such a context. In particular, the notion that the 56-year-old brain can certainly learn new tricks. I can almost feel the neurons and dendrites sprouting as I trip out of his office and head back to the tyranny of my explicit, over-representational day job.

Monday, 13 December

The WikiLeaks disclosures are finally settling into some sort of routine, with the redaction and publication coordination running smoothly and continued radio silence – barring the occasional appearance on encrypted channels – of Assange.

Meanwhile, it's time for me to start talking to proper pianists who have played this piece and who know it inside out. I begin with Ronan O'Hora, head of keyboards at Guildhall School of Music, who has been the course tutor at Lot a couple of times. He's played around the world, recorded more than thirty CDs (including the Ballade) and is one of those pianists who, in a 'blind tasting', would be indistinguishable from the top flight of internationally known pianists to ninety-nine per cent of the population. We carve out a little time for a sandwich lunch in my office on a day when WikiLeaks is relatively quiet.

We first met at Lot maybe five years ago. Ronan – a large, avuncular, gentle figure – was there with his wife, Hannah, a good amateur soprano. In addition to being a thoughtful and generous teacher, he was up for fun, thinking little of returning to the house after a decent dinner and a few armagnacs to knock off an unprecious sight-reading of the four-handed arrangement of a Sibelius symphony while the rest of the crew took a midnight dip. He has a quiet erudition acquired over twenty or more years of playing and teaching at a high level. And stamina. After our first Lot course he was straight off to do all five Beethoven concertos in two nights in Germany. The prospect didn't seem to be keeping him awake at night.

He knows about my Ballade project and so we begin by talking about the piece in a very general way. Ronan thinks the Ballade is representative of Chopin in the way it hides a very sophisticated structure 'under a facade of seemingly pure elemental improvisation'. What sets the Ballade apart for him, though, is that its 'visceral qualities' – the diabolic outburst of the coda, for example – are such that the piece marks 'a particular sort of end point . . . a particular kind of expression in Chopin that he never went quite back to. It's probably one of those pieces that you can imagine alarming its own creator and uncovering things that, to some extent, they step away from – like Richard Strauss with *Elektra*.'

Ronan first played the Ballade when he was about 14, and it was the 'visceral qualities' that drew him to the piece. As he puts it, there is 'some sort of adolescent hormonal attraction to a piece like that'. But he found the piece difficult, and is convinced that even the greatest pianists struggle with it. He tells me that lots of people find Rachmaninov 3 impossible, or Brahms 2 – though he is somehow able to get his fingers around that one – but almost every pianist feels 'total fear' playing the Ballade. 'There's something about it which just doesn't fit in their fingers and which is always unpredictable. Even if you play it once, you can't be sure that you'll play it right another time.' He says you could line up a lot of concert pianists and ask them which is the piece they would least like to play cold before an audience or on camera, and an awful lot of them would say the G minor Ballade.

I tried to pin him down on the reason for this. He thinks the broadest problem is that visceral quality of the piece. When young people play it, for instance, they tend to give 'a kind of hysterical performance, probably in several senses of the word, but literally too'. The heightened drama of the coda can become 'almost comic or grotesque'. The key is to find the balance in the piece's dual identity – the calm sophistication versus the elemental outbursts. 'It's a very fine line to tread,' he says, and few pianists are capable of it.

We also touch on the complexity of the structures, keys and proportions of the harmonic language, and the challenge they set the player. These 'very, very, very daring' innovations of Chopin's are, in Ronan's opinion, what makes him so great. As he points out, 'The difference with talent and genius is that genius takes things and just pushes them one degree further, one degree off centre. And with Chopin the big difference is the harmony. Even Chopin's melodies, when you take away the harmony, are not so extraordinary. It's the harmony which provokes a lot of the emotion in the music.' In his opinion, this means it's 'absolutely essential' that students studying the Ballade work out which key they are in at any point. I kept quiet about my own struggles with this up to now.

At one point, Ronan compares Chopin with Brahms, and touches on something I've been noticing. 'It's very interesting,' he says, 'that in terms of the actual amount and distribution of notes in each hand, very often a passage of Chopin is not that different from a passage of Brahms. But with Brahms there is a centre of gravity, which relates also to his psychological view of music and art.' In Chopin, though, this 'centre of gravity' is absent.

As I've discovered, the notes, though not spread too far apart, do not return or repeat in any clear pattern. 'Those more intense textures,' he says, 'are representations of a heightened psychological state.'

He also talks about the need for there to be a kind of 'struggle' within the music. For instance, when we speak about the coda, he says it is 'closer to the feeling of playing Beethoven, which is unusual for Chopin'. I ask him to explain what he means. 'Very often the physical feeling of playing Beethoven is, as you know, trying to get your hands round something that won't be quite encompassed. If there isn't some sense of that feeling, there'll be something missing. That's why it's very difficult, I think, for hyper-virtuosi to play Beethoven convincingly, because you actually need some sense of struggling with one's own kind of limitation. That's actually part of the central utterance of Beethoven.' The Ballade, he thinks, is the nearest you get to this in Chopin – 'where you actually need to feel a player at the edge of their powers'.

I'd certainly pass that test as things stand. I wonder, though, if such tension really can be heard in the great recordings. Ronan is convinced that there has never been a definitive recording of the Ballade, which suggests not. 'You hear wonderful and incredible performances but not conclusive. Of course, that's true for everything, but it's truer for some pieces.' And he thinks the current 'age of great perfection', where there are so many technically perfect pianists, means it's unlikely there will be a 'conclusive' recording any time soon. He thinks these great technical players struggle to definitively capture the piece because they don't 'risk sufficiently', when 'the nature of the dramatic demands' in the piece means that to be too restrained is 'likely to leave you out of touch with the whole central strand of the piece'.

We move on to talk about my own problems with the Ballade. Fresh from my chat with Ray Dolan, I touch on my concerns about memorising the piece. Ronan tries to reassure me, telling me I probably don't have a problem with memorising, just an anxiety about forgetting. I tell him that learning just six bars of the coda has required enormous effort, practice and concentration over a long period. Surely this isn't the case for professionals. I read that someone like Walter Gieseking could look only once at a passage like the coda and he'd be able to play it. 'You hear about Gieseking,' Ronan replies, 'you hear about Barenboim – it's obviously true that they have a remarkably accelerated gift. But it's not accidental that they also have a remarkably heightened *confidence* in their gift. I think that's a very crucial thing. I don't think it's necessarily always that they have memories beyond human imagining, except their capacity to look and think, yep, OK, I've got it, and walk away and believe they've got it.'

But it must still be true that the absorption rate is quicker for professional pianists? 'Of course. That passage you're struggling to remember, most pianists would look at something like that and work out the patterns quite quickly. I think most of the time the looking, I suppose memorising, is subconsciously looking for patterns, looking for connections.' Has he found that his own memory has changed with age? 'You do find – this is why most pianists will learn the vast bulk of their repertoire in their teens or 20s – there is an age at which you are just sponge-like and absorb a lot of things, like languages, and your initial intake of them is very easy and open. Certainly that is true for me and I think it's true for most people. I'd like to think I learn better now, but I learn slower, there's no question about it.' So perhaps I don't have to worry if I'm not learning the Ballade at lightning speed; perhaps I am just learning it *well*. I hope so.

Ronan also mentions Liszt while we're discussing memory, suggesting he'd introduced the idea of 'the visible need for memorisation as an act of performing authority'. In Ronan's view this 'mystique of memorisation' was no more than 'a kind of sales technique, a statement of charismatic authority about music'. But he does warn me that with any extremely demanding piece, such as the Ballade, you have to be 'very clear' as to how you're going to use the score, 'because you won't be able to truly read it, except as an aide-memoire or psychological support'.

Next, I ask Ronan about fingering. I take out a score and show him an example of my fingering – bar 68, the soft second tune, where I have pencilled in fingers 1 and 3 in the RH. 'You see, I can't imagine myself ever using that fingering within the context. Not because there's anything neces- sarily wrong. It's a perfectly workable fingering. It's just that I would rarely put the two most powerful fingers in a context like that particularly if, say, you had a piano that was very bright.' Because the tune should be soft, he'd be more likely to use weaker fingers, 'something like 5 and 2'. I learn that Ronan has a wonderful flexibility when it comes to fingering, and can ac- tually change fingerings on the day of a concert to suit the kind of piano he'll have to play. A lot of his students struggle with fingering Chopin, he says – especially the earlier Viennese music, which was not composed for the 'modern instrument with its sustaining power'.

I tell him that my problems are perhaps more basic – the fingerings just aren't obvious to me; it's not a question of considering the instrument or anything like that. I reveal to him how long it is taking me to work out how to finger the 'G minor' arpeggios at bar 56, for example, because the fingerings don't seem to follow the key: you're fingering it in a way that goes against the normal approach to a G minor arpeggio. This makes sense to Ronan, as there are benefits to this alternative approach to the arpeggio. 'I mean there are times in Beethoven where you'll deliberately use a more difficult fingering because of the *musical effect*.' He gives, by example, the opening of the 'Hammerklavier', which you can easily play with two hands, but the musical effect here requires audible challenge, he says, so the pianist needs to look for a riskier fingering.

I also ask him about the opening pages of the piece. In a way it's the easiest passage, but I'm finding it difficult to bring off, and I'm trying to work out why this is. In Ronan's experience, this is common. 'If somebody plays it to you in a masterclass, it's often going to be the opening pages that are the least successful.' To his mind, the biggest problem here is that the chords are very powerful, especially when augmented by the force of a modern piano – which he likens to handling a sports car. On a piano of the period, these chords would not be shouting over the melody, but balanced within and around it. Nowadays, they often sound 'too large for the melody – they literally obscure it'. Even Ronan's most talented students find the opening difficult. 'They develop fingers and get round the instrument, they've got a sort of confidence in the instrument.' But the opening pages of the Ballade force them to go further into the modern instrument and coax the correct internal balance and textures of the piece from the piano. 'And that's what's very, very exposing.'

We look at the score again. I point to the trapeze leaps at bars 216–17. This currently strikes me as the single most difficult leap in the piece. 'The thing to take comfort in,' Ronan says, 'is it's always easier to leap to black notes than to white notes.'

'Why?'

'Well, because the black notes stand out, as it were. If the black notes came out as far as the white notes do, it might be different, but any pianist will agree that anything that goes to a black note or from a black note will be easier . . . It's interesting, this point about the black notes and the white notes. The last scale Chopin would teach in his routine of the scales to his students was C major. C major is by far the hardest scale and, in many respects, C major is the hardest key to play because you just don't have the ballast of the black notes.'

Feeling a little more positive, I then tell Ronan about my experience a few weeks ago when I played the three or four bars just before the coda and it sort of possessed me – this despairing cry before the release of the coda. It's all based in the dominant – so the ear is waiting for it to resolve to the tonic. Chopin urges the pianist to play 'il più forte possibile' – as loudly as possible. And he deliberately plays with the rhythm of the notes – a mixture of quavers, triplets and quintuplets in a way which ratchets up the emotional pitch. 'I suppose if you're really caught up in it when you're performing it that can suddenly happen to you in a way which just carries you away.'

'It can, and particularly when you learn to develop more trust in riding the wave of the thing, rather than feeling you've got to grip it. One of the biggest problems for a young performer is feeling you've got to create energy whereas, in fact, you know, you have to connect with energy. It's a different thing. So, I think, what you're experiencing there, what you were realising, was that if you connect with the tension, then the release will come naturally, as it were.'

Before he leaves, Ronan gives me a very interesting piece of advice. 'If you think of the time it takes to produce a note on the clarinet, it's a physical act of natural preparation and release.' With the piano, things are different. The piano, he says, has an 'unnatural speed of utterance', which means this 'natural preparation' can be sidestepped. In Ronan's opinion, this means that 'often you haven't really played a note, you've just struck it'. His advice is to avoid this temptation, and to be led by your ear, so that 'you literally don't play the next note along until you've heard it internally'. This translation of hearing to playing is something he encourages in all his students and he swears by it. I'll have to try it out.

Saturday, 18 December

WikiLeaks is now winding down. Of course there's boundless material, but the team are near the limit of what they can process. Christmas is coming up – and we can't keep going over the holiday period. And Assange is being so mercurial and elusive that none of us wants to be surprised by anything that might happen while our offices are shuttered. So we agree between the publishing partners that we'll bring down the curtain on the exercise in the next few days.

Really unsatisfactory piano practice today. It's all going too slowly. I can't feel any progress. And I am back to practising like I did when I was a teenager. Instead of concentrating on one passage and working on it repeatedly, I'm skimming through numerous passages. I'm going to need a surge of willpower to force me back onto the straight and narrow.

Sunday, 19 December

I spend this evening at Richard Sennett's house, playing chamber music. Richard, a writer and professor of sociology at LSE and NYU, has just returned from three months in New York. He is a New Yorker, and thirty or so years ago, he kept a kind of open house there – and, periodically, he re-creates the same kind of salon in the Clerkenwell loft apartment he shares with his wife, the academic Saskia Sassens. The London groups never quite live up to the vivid description of Richard's New York open evenings in Edmund White's memoir *City Boy*:

> Dick mainly liked to entertain, but not just anyone. At his house on the mews you could meet Isaiah Berlin or Michel Foucault or Susan Sontag or Jürgen Habermas or Alfred Brendel. Like most intellectuals, these men and the occasional woman didn't want to make engagements far in advance – not in the usual busy-busy New York fashion. They never knew when inspiration might strike . . . But since they were apt to get lonely like anyone else, especially after dark on a cold February night, they could always drift over to Dick's house, where it was okay just to ring the bell . . . Dick was always available. He was at home downstairs cooking in his modern, roomy kitchen or upstairs entertaining in his atelier-like living room with its skylights and vast airy ceilings and its grand piano. He might be scraping away at his cello while Brendel played the piano part. Or people of every sort, many of them Europeans, might be sitting on the big, deep couch and in the comfy armchairs, chatting away.

London is not New York, and Richard's a little older now, but he's retained the endearing habit of opening his house to any passing musician, and there's still the same sense of not knowing who will turn up, or who's been invited. He doesn't care whether the resulting combination of musicians is matched in ability, or whether any music in fact exists for the combination of musicians available on any given evening. And as with Claus Moser's Berlin *Hausmusik*, there is often a commingling of professional and amateur musicians. I once had to endure the exquisite embarrassment of being forced to sight-read through Schumann's *Dichterliebe* with a visiting professional German tenor. I still have night sweats thinking about it. Belated apologies, whoever you were that night. (Again, my memory fails me.)

Richard has developed at least two chamber groups while living in London; there may be others I'm not aware of. Tonight's what I think of as the B group – not in quality, just because they came after the other group. They include Clive Coen, the neuroscience professor who'd recommended I meet Ray Dolan; Charlotte Higgins, the *Guardian*'s chief arts writer; Susanna Eastburn, who runs music at the Arts Council; and Mark Prescott, who runs his own arts consultancy. Outside it's blanket white and perilously frosty, nothing much moving. There's the usual fug inside, since Richard's one of the few remaining people in London to smoke a pipe. There's wine, mince pies, warmth. I pick up the clarinet for the first time since the summer and plunge into the Mozart quintet. But my concentration's wandering and I miss an entry. Am I just tired and ready for Christmas? And is this what's been affecting my Ballade practice too? Even though we're winding it down, the weekend has been dominated by WikiLeaks – legal queries, quarrelsome exchanges with Assange, emails, phone calls – and it's difficult to push it all out of the mind, even with Mozart.

I remember two times when I have performed this piece and had a similar wandering mind: once at school in front of 300 parents, when I suspected I had just set fire to an armchair in my shared boarding room by forgetting to turn off an illegal toaster (this turned out to be true); and once, about ten years ago, when I played it in a concert in Putney. That time I held on the long notes in the Adagio wondering a) if I would split one, and b) why on earth I was putting myself through this torture of playing in public.

But there's no torture tonight. The embouchure was a bit loose and the tonguing not as sharp as it should be, but otherwise it could have been a lot worse, given the four-month gap since I last played. The procedural memory for clarinet playing is obviously not totally extinct. And I noticed when I played tonight that while I was a technically better clarinettist at 18, I couldn't 'feel' the piece in the way I can now. I can impose myself on the music, and give it shape. When I was 18 it shaped me. I used to whisk through this piece. But now I think I listen to myself more carefully and have a better sense of line and flow.

After the Mozart, we take a break for supper and then play three movements of the Brahms quintet before rolling into the crisp, silent, pre-Christmas streets. Playing tonight instilled me with a little more musical confidence. Just before bed, though, I see a Ballade tweet. I followed the link and saw a doll-like 13-year-old girl knocking off Op. 23 pretty proficiently. I don't know whether to be inspired or depressed.

Tuesday, 28 December

Thursday was my last day in the office, and we brought the curtain down on WikiLeaks. It's been a scratchy few weeks, but we achieved what we set out to do – to publish a vast quantity of material safely (at least as far as we know – and you can be sure the US government would have told us by now if we'd endangered lives).

The tensions of the past few weeks have been aggravated by not being able to talk to the Assange camp. And I'm not sure that Assange has been helped by some of his advisers and supporters, who have been pretty wild in the way they have smeared the Swedish women with whom he was involved. Some of his friends/supporters have privately spoken to me, expressing anxieties about the way the case is being handled. My deputy on news, Ian, and reporter Luke Harding spent Thursday with Assange in his country-house retreat – it turns out he's been in Norfolk all along – trying to re-establish a rapport. The impression is it went well-ish, despite an initial coolness and after a rehearsal of old grievances.

After leaving work, I set off by train for Blockley with the girls – Lindsay has gone on ahead. We passed through snow-covered field after snow-covered field, but then stopped at Oxford and couldn't get any further. So we travelled the last forty miles by taxi, and skidded our way down Blockley high street. There was silence as we emerged from the taxi into fourteen inches of snow.

On Christmas Eve morning I peeked inside the music room. It's now completely empty, with what looks like bubble wrap on the floor – which is in fact part of the underfloor heating (it does a body swerve around where the piano will sit). More and more, I can imagine the space as it will be.

Yesterday, I drove across the whited-out countryside to 'Nimrod', where Jeff was waiting to show me the Model O. He's replaced the action frame and begun to voice it; and he produced the old action – split in two places, a common problem on Steinways of that vintage, he says. It's been a good Christmas period for Jeff: he says he now has eighteen months' worth of orders for reconditioned Steinways ahead of him.

And then he left me alone with the piano . . . but also with half a dozen other Steinways, most of them larger Model As and Bs. I played 'my' O, and could immediately hear that Jeff's work has generally evened out the sound so that the 'dull' patch in the middle-upper register is now brighter. The F ten notes above middle C still doesn't quite sing as the other notes do, but otherwise its action is crisp and it has a really dulcet tone – a soft, gentle lullaby sound. I don't know if Jeff has deliberately left all the other pianos open for me. Even at this stage he must be used to clients upgrading as they hear the superior clarity of the Model A or the sheer oomph of the Model B. For a moment I wavered. But I controlled myself in time. I tried the first page of the Brahms Op. 117 intermezzo on the Model O. It was sweet, responsive, yielding. Lovely.

Afterwards, I raise the question of the 'dull' F with Jeff. He shrugged. 'I can try to brighten it a bit,' he says, 'but sometimes these things are just in the piano.' He pulled out the action to show me the new frame and ran his fingers across the hammers. 'It's got a good ten years before you'll have to replace those. It's been gently treated.' He says he is sometimes called into music colleges where pianos are subjected to the most astonishing forces. 'The young players today play with such strength. They regularly break strings. Something has changed about the way people play the piano these days. I watch them play to try and work out what we can do about it.'

Finally, we shake hands on the deal and Jeff produces the piano's original paperwork from 1978 – showing that the owner had paid just over £7,000 for it. They now sell for £52k, he says.

So I have the piano, and the music room is there, but for the floor and windows. If only the Ballade itself were that easy. I practise today, but am continuing to lose confidence. I had earmarked the Christmas holidays as a time when I would make a giant leap forward. But here I am halfway through them and I have played the piano much less than I'd planned – a combination of flu, friends and general tiredness after the weeks of frantic WikiLeaking and much else. I'm trying to work on the coda. I think I'm doing all the right things – playing slowly, repeated patterns, different groupings and rhythms, etc. – but the more I slow down and concentrate, the more I realise how much there is to memorise. I also realise that often where I thought I was making progress, I've still only hazily learned large sections, while positively mislearning other bits.

Wednesday, 29 December

My 57th birthday. Spend an hour playing the coda on a now very out-of-tune Danemann upright looking out at the snow-bound Cotswolds. At lunchtime Twitter sends me to www.joshwrightpianotv.com, where Josh Wright, a 22-year-old pianist from Utah University, has filmed a nine-minute tutorial in his sitting room in Salt Lake City. The subject is the coda of the G minor Ballade. How about that for synchronicity? He's even playing on a 5' 11" Hamburg Steinway, like my Model O. He tells me nothing I haven't been told already – play slowly, find the musical line, etc. – but it is helpful to see him talk as he plays. And it makes me wonder all over again at the world of virtual communities. This – people who are studying Chopin's Op. 23 – must be one of the more obscure ones, but it's real enough and thriving. And, today, useful.

On my birthday I've been floating back in my mind, reconstructing my relationship with the music and the piano. I've been doing this with the aid of a fading folder of old school reports and examination papers which my mother carefully preserved over the years and which I discovered on clearing out my parents' old house on the death of my father four years ago.

1958-ish. My earliest memory: sitting under our old upright – a Rud Ibach – while my mother played Debussy's 'Clair de Lune'. It must have been in the London flat we moved to after returning to London from Africa, where my father had been an educational civil servant. My grandmother had played it when she was feeling sad; it has associations with her husband walking out when my mother was a young girl. So the piece made me feel sad too.

1958. Longacre School, near Guildford. Aged 4½. School report. Singing and Music. 'Appears to enjoy this subject . . . When he listens more carefully his sense of rhythm will improve.'

1959. Camden House School, Gloucester Place, W1. Aged 5. 'Percussion playing good and rhythmical.'

1961. Aged 7. Music: 'He is very responsive and imaginative in his movement and has a good ear for listening games and singing.'

1962. Aged 8. Recorder. 'Most promising.'

1963. Guildford Cathedral Choir. Aged 10. 'He could do very well and I shall look for great things from him.' (This is from Barry Rose, the slightly terrifying master of choristers.)

1963. Grade 1 piano – distinction. (This is the year I started the clarinet.)

1964. Grade 2 piano – merit. 'Promising.' Scales: 'sound'. It seems the examiner was impressed by my sight-reading, but only moderately impressed by my piano playing. The shape of things to come, alas.

1965. Aged 11. 'Alan is showing us some very disturbing signs of complacency – and from the musical side he has nothing to be complacent about!' (Barry Rose again.)

1958 to 1967. Piano lessons with Miss Dunn Davies in Guildford. She lived with another woman – 'spinster' was, I think, the term then – in a detached Edwardian house. I cannot now remember anything I learned with Miss

Dunn Davies. She was stern, but kindly, perhaps not very inspiring. She was the one that got me through the grades, though.

Then at some point my mother sold the upright piano we had and bought a Challen baby grand. I think it cost about £300 and she was immensely proud of the purchase and really quite upset when a visiting piano teacher was later rather dismissive of it. It sat in the corner of the sitting room. My father – who had no musical learning at all, but later in life fell surprisingly in love with the playing of Perlemuter – would sometimes sit down and play one chord, which he would repeat up and down the keyboard, with a churchy cadence at the end. He was old enough to have remembered hand-pumping the bellows in the Devon church of which his father was minister during the First World War.

1966. Aged 12. I sometimes accompanied the morning assembly. My music teacher, Mr Cork, showed me a useful trick when playing hymns, which was to miss out the tenor line, it being the least important line in the harmony. It was a valuable, if dangerous lesson, because it was my first instruction in getting by, in not playing the notes exactly as they were. It set me on that road of always being a very good sight-reader, but probably holed below the water line any ambitions of being a rigorous pianist faithful to a given score.

1967. I change schools and leave Longacre for Cranleigh on a music exhibition, presumably based on my triple experience of piano, singing in choirs and playing in orchestras.

My new piano teacher was Jean Bourgeois, who was actually a violinist. She was extremely glamorous and fun – the opposite of Miss Dunn Davies. Her husband, the composer Derek Bourgeois, taught me composition and harmony. They were both in their early 20s and would invite the music scholars to dinner once a year, for curry and lager. I learned so many pieces with Jean. We started with Schumann's *Kinderscenen*, and then Beethoven's easy G major sonata. Next it was Beethoven's 'Pathétique' Sonata (the slow second movement followed by the first, then a stab at the third). Then Mozart's C minor fantasy, before Grieg's *Holberg Suite*. And, mixed in with that, some Bach preludes and fugues.

Summer 1968. Report from Jean Bourgeois: 'He must try to learn his pieces more accurately right from the beginning now.' So the rot has definitely set in . . .

Lent 1969. Jean again: 'He has done good work this term but must try to learn his notes more carefully as we spend a long time during each lesson correcting mistakes.'

Michaelmas 1969. 'He tries hard and does good work between the lessons. He likes to play loudly the entire time, and sometimes a combination of this . . . and his fondness for the sustaining pedal, results in rather a muddy noise. He has to try to achieve greater clarity in his playing.'

Summer 1970. 'Very good work and attitude throughout the term. He tries hard during his lessons and works well between them.'

In the summer of 1971 – when I was 17 – Derek and Jean left to go and live in Bristol. A new piano teacher arrived: Enloc Wu, who, I now discover from the internet, had been brought up in Hong Kong and has since taught at the Royal College of Music. She was a much better pianist than Jean – and much more serious about piano playing in general. I played Enloc Wu the Mozart fantasy: she told me I wasn't emotionally mature enough to do it justice, which was crushing, but probably true. We then learned the companion C minor sonata, which has some very tricky corners. I played it in a very solid way but was already deep into the habit of learning the notes approximately.

But by this time I was increasingly drawn to the clarinet and the opportunities it offered for playing with others. I performed the Mozart clarinet quintet and trio, and, with the school orchestra, the first movement of the Mozart concerto. Every term we put on ambitious concerts, with 'stiffening' by professional players. I got to play Tchaikovsky, Brahms, Beethoven and Schubert symphonies, the Verdi, Berlioz and Brahms requiems, Orff's *Carmina burana*, Vaughan Williams' *A Sea Symphony* and Walton's *Belshazzar's Feast*, as well as musicals and chamber music. I found it quite intoxicating to sit in the middle of an orchestra and chorus, surrounded by sound, nervous tension and excitement. So the piano palled a bit by comparison. It was a solitary occupation. And, compared with my clarinet playing, I was not really that good.

I sat one more grade – and scraped through by one point.

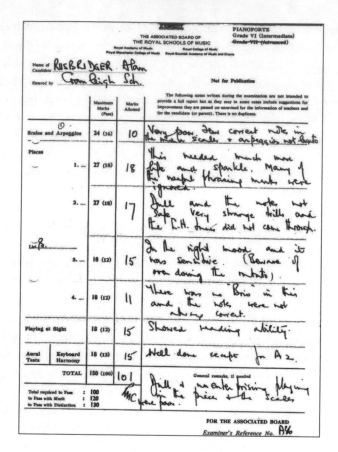

December 1971. Aged 17. Grade 6. Good mark for sight-reading, terrible marks for everything else. 'Dull and unenterprising playing in the pieces and the scales were poor.' In fact, the scales were 'very poor. Few correct notes in the minor scales and arpeggios not legato.'

I turned up at piano lessons with Miss Wu, hoping to bluff my way through. I avoided all scales and arpeggios. I don't remember paying much attention to fingering, or pedalling or trying to achieve a legato line. I realised such joy as I'd ever had from playing the piano was draining out of me – particularly after my miserable showing in Grade 6 – and so I gave up altogether.

I picked it up again a year or so later, by which time I was at Cambridge. My three best friends there were all very good musicians. One, Philip Feeney, went on to compose lush ballet scores for Northern Ballet. Another, Richard

Morrison, became the *Times* music critic. The third, Robert White, later had a spell as a music agent.

I didn't play with any real focus or determination, and certainly never practised properly, but Philip and I played a lot of duets on the Magdalene College grand. He was a much, much better pianist than I was, but he didn't seem to mind sharing the music with me as we read our way through Schubert duets or Beethoven symphonies. The night the news came through (in October 1974) that the IRA had blown up the Horse and Groom pub in Guildford, where I had often drunk while doing work experience at the *Surrey Advertiser*, we played our way through the slow movement of Beethoven's Ninth.

Philip inspired me to try to learn two new pieces – the last movement of Schumann's Fantasie Op. 17 and Chopin's Nocturne No. 16 in E-flat major, Op. 55, No. 2. Though he was at that stage a very modernist composer, Philip was transported by these two pieces and was constantly chivvying me to play them. I tried, but by now I had no concept of how you 'learned' or practised a piece, never mind memorised it.

After graduating, I worked as a local newspaper reporter in Cambridge. I had hired pianos while at university and I went on hiring them now, until eventually I bought a rackety old second-hand piano. But I was still just replaying the same pieces, with little focus.

1979. Moved to share a rented house in London. The second-hand piano comes too, but I play it even less as I try to learn how to become a reporter on the *Guardian*.

1982. Marry Lindsay. We buy a house in North London. The upright follows. Isabella and Lizzie are born within the next three years, and I play them nursery rhymes. Both have lessons, but never really take to it. I am very un-pushy about it, fearing that I'll put them off. The opposite of my mother. But if I'd insisted, would it have made any difference to the outcome?

Around 1990 we inherited the Challen baby grand. This sparked a new interest in me. And maybe this new interest coincided with a subconscious awareness of the foreshortening of life. I was bordering on the outskirts of middle age, but, even then, as life continued to get busier and busier, I had begun to establish a compartment in my mind of things I would do once retired. I had seen my dad forced to retire early, about 60, through ill health (though he lived in pretty robust spirit to the age of 96), so I had a model for a long retirement. There would be time later to read all the works of Dickens, George Eliot, Proust, Trollope and Tolstoy that I had somehow managed not to read so far. I even bought and stored up copies of all the books I intended to read later in life.

I had begun to apply this to piano playing too. I'm pretty sure that when I was around 40 I planned to learn the Beethoven sonatas and all of the forty-eight Bach Preludes and Fugues at some unspecified moment in later life. Not to mention the better Schubert sonatas and much of Debussy, Ravel and the best of Billy Mayerl. But then at some point the penny dropped that a) this dream of a culture-packed retirement was almost certainly a fantasy, and that b) I was missing out on an awful lot of life today by saving things up for a mythical period of contemplation and learning later. Anyway, by the time I was 65 I might well be arthritic. And I would have missed twenty years of recovering some sort of technique, not to mention the discovery of the pieces themselves. In other words, some inklings of mortality began to twitch. It's possible that the death of a parent has a role, too. My mother died in 1995 – when I was around 41. I'm sure Jung would have seen a connection.

So I decided to take lessons again, instead of putting things off till I was old. And that's when I met Michael. I remember my first lesson with him. I took a Mozart piece I had been toying with most of my adult life – the Mozart Fantasy in C Minor, K475 (the same one I had trotted out for Enloc Wu) – and expected an hour of work on phrasing and general musicality awareness. But Michael didn't work like that. It was like calling in the builders to do a bit of wallpapering only to be confronted with – *ahem* – the matter of dry rot. Within minutes he had stuck his metaphorical penknife in, and the structures were crumbling into dust.

And of course, that's what separates a teenage pianist from an adult. My 15-year-old self would have reacted badly to Michael's insistence on stripping everything back to the bare wood and bricks (end of metaphor!). My 40-something self swallowed his pride and resolved to do things differently. I wouldn't just play pieces in future: I would learn them.

So this was the beginning of the path that later led, at the age of 51, to my attending the Lot camp from 2005. For the first couple of years I brought solo piano music. But then I met Alex Knox, a very talented young singer, then at Manchester University, who was later to study at Guildhall before turning professional. Neither of us really knew the great song cycles of Schubert and Schumann. So, over three years, we prepared *Winterreise*, *Dichterliebe* and *Die schöne Müllerin* together.

Five years previously I would never have attempted these mammoth song cycles. Each of them has many numbers that are eminently playable – but there were simply too many songs that required a real technique to even get close to them. How on earth to bring off four pages of rippling without the right hand seizing up in 'Wohin'? Or to prevent total paralysis of the muscles in 'Ungeduld'? Or develop the stamina to keep ploughing on through 'Das ist ein Flöten und Geigen' in *Dichterliebe*? I still didn't have the various techniques to play some of this, but I had acquired the habit of taking a long time – up to a year – to learn a single song cycle. And I knew, much better than when I was young, how to practise. I had better powers of concentration and more motivation.

So I was, in fact, becoming a much better pianist in my early 50s than I had ever been before. I very rarely felt discouraged by my progress – quite the opposite. There was, I concluded, much to be said for acquiring the basis of a musical technique in youth while remaining defiantly mediocre. Because the only way from there is up. The challenge now is to apply that same optimism to the Ballade, and to summon once more those powers of concentration and motivation which in recent weeks I've felt slip away.

Sunday, 2 January 2011

We spent New Year's Eve in our customary way, by holding a dinner at Kentish Town. I sat next to the composer George Benjamin, who has been coming to New Year's dinners with his partner, Michael Waldman, for a few years. We've developed a little annual ritual after these dinners: we go upstairs and play middle-of-the-night New Year piano duets. George loves four-hand music and said he's in the middle of writing a piece for the medium. He talked about how four-hand playing was, for many people, the only way of getting to know the orchestral repertoire until the mid-twentieth century. 'Composers then earned their royalty from selling arrangements of the music, not from recording.'

After supper I again managed to tempt him up to the sitting room. This time, though, we were joined by two others from the assembled company and so 2011 began with an eight-hand two-piano performance of Tchaikovsky's Fifth Symphony, in an 1892 Hamburg arrangement I'd picked up in a music shop in Amsterdam earlier in the year. On piano two (my Yamaha Fo1 Modus digital piano): myself and my friend Mark Prescott; George and the concert pianist Imogen Cooper on the other. We'd all had a drink or three, which led to some terrifying tempi. But it was a really skilful arrangement – satisfying for all four parts – and Imogen made a memorably beautiful fist of the horn solo at the start of the slow movement.

George and Mark – who are both fantastic sight-readers – followed this up with a two-piano *Meistersinger* prelude. It was quite fascinating to see George, as a composer, getting to grips with such a piece. 'I thought I knew it so well, but I'd never realised there was so much going on internally. It's much more complicated and layered than I appreciated.' It fell to Imogen to be the sensible one, when, at around 2 a.m., she vetoed an enthusiastic attempt by George to launch into an eight-hand version of Beethoven 9. 'That's just sacrilege,' she announced firmly, walking away from the piano. So instead we ended with Pomp and Circumstance 1. Which, after Tchaik 5, was another kind of sacrilege.

On New Year's Day, Twitter was full of resolutions, and people recording their achievements over the past twelve months. Here, for instance, was Christian Oliver, a digital strategist at CNN and a keen runner: 'Last year

I ran 245 times, totaling 261:37 h:m 1,848.84 miles and burned 181,587 calories. Want to run more in 2011 :-)'

This made me wonder about my own work rate – and any possible health benefit. I very crudely estimate that last year I played the piano around 250 times, totalling about 150 hours, including weekends, the time equivalent, perhaps, of fortnightly golf. There are websites (of course) which calculate how much energy is consumed by piano playing. According to www.fitday .com, I might have burned 14,976 calories in that 150 hours. Another website estimates 164 calories per hour for an average 145-pound person, which would amount to almost twice the 'fitday' figure. It says: 'playing the piano engages small muscle groups in the upper body as you push down on each key to create notes and music . . . More intense, fast-paced music that requires more energy and stamina may burn extra calories.' So the Ballade must be at the upper end of the calorie-burners.

I guess that since August I've probably spent about seventy hours exclusively on the Ballade. If I increase my work rate this year, I might be able to fit in about a hundred hours of practice before piano camp in July. It's daunting to think that I'm not yet halfway there. And in any case, will that even be enough time to get the piece right?

Monday, 3 January

Today is the last day before I go back to work. I've spent the majority of it at Radley College, Oxfordshire, watching the National Youth Orchestra rehearsals of the Janáček Sinfonietta. I've chaired the orchestra for six years – having failed to get in as a teenage clarinettist. Driving down from London with my brother Richard and nephew Charlie, we spoke about the origins of the NYO, that amazing, brief period of idealism at the end of the war, which saw the Butler Education Act, the creation of the welfare state and, in 1948, the formation of a national orchestra for outstanding young would-be musicians. The current orchestra is getting together for the first time – half of them are new this year, all of them under 18 – but the technique and cohesion is dazzling, as always. No one even gets an audition for the orchestra unless they get distinction in Grade 8, but even so, the technical assurance of the young players is always stunning. Afterwards, the three of us walk through the long corridors of the school's art department, with hundreds of wonderful pictures and sculptures by former pupils. Where are they now, these Old Radleians? In the law, the City and business? What do they do with that creativity that flowered in youth? How many of them paint now at weekends, or play music?

Back at home, and inspired by our New Year's eight-hand extravaganza, I spend this evening looking at the astonishing amounts of free music online – particularly at the Petrucci International Music Score Library Project, a miraculous kind of Wikipedia of out-of-copyright music, which has further eight-hand arrangements of Tchaikovsky symphonies and much else. There's a new feature – Performers' Editions – which will bind the music up and ship it.

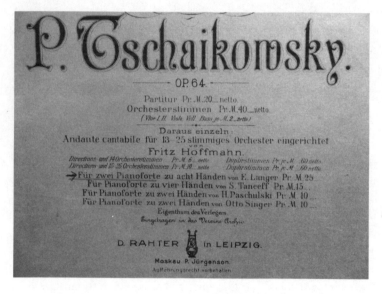

So I ordered: *Sleeping Beauty*; Tchaik 1; Capriccio Italien and the 1812 Overture – all for eight hands. Then Mozart's Requiem (arranged by Czerny); Elgar's *Serenade for Strings* and Berlioz's *Symphonie fantastique*, for four hands. The whole lot cost less than one score in the second-hand bookshop in Amsterdam where I found the Tchaikovsky 5.

And there, at three more clicks of the mouse, were first editions of Chopin online. I think back to the time I studied music at school, and the small library of scores and LPs we had, and I wish I'd had access to all this four-hand and eight-hand music when a teenager. I could really have got to grips with the complexity of the music I was studying in a way recorded music just can't do. It's interesting how the twenty-first century opening up of digital libraries has enabled a return to this nineteenth-century method of learning.

I also managed to get a little practice in today. I keep repeating the coda. Things are better. I can play it very slowly, but play it nonetheless. Today's problem, though, is one of holding my nerve. Should I now be speeding it up, or just hold fast and continue at this speed, embedding it in the procedural memory? Of course, this dilemma doesn't just apply to the coda, but to the whole piece. Should I really just keep repeating, even if it feels in the end a bit mindless? It might begin to feel not even a particularly 'musical' act, but more a 'manual' act of simple repetition – like learning how to plane wood or machine metal or swing a tennis racquet. Have I got the true confidence that this endless repetition will lead to the piece embedding itself in fingers and brain? And will I be able to then just 'add musicality' later?

There is another concern about this repetitive approach. I have a definite feeling of weakness and strain in my left arm. I Google 'weakness in left arm'. Answer: heart attack. Surely it's just some form of RSI. I don't want that. But it's better than a heart attack.

Sunday, 9 January

It's been a frantic first week back, full of exhaustingly long days. On Friday I had a meeting with Mark Porter, the *Guardian*'s design consultant, who is developing thoughts on how the *Guardian*'s look and feel might have to change in print. But the demands of the week were such that I just haven't had time to prepare – so I found myself having to stay up till 1.30 a.m. on Thursday night ripping out various tear sheets of assorted European newspapers and magazines as last-minute preparation.

The big news of the week, though, is that the *News of the World* has suspended Ian Edmondson, its news editor. This is really significant. After months – even years – when very little has happened on the hacking story, it's now evident that things are beginning to move fast behind the scenes. And the story is lapping closer and closer to the highest echelons within

News Corp and Downing Street. But, as luck would have it, Nick Davies, who has been working on the story for three years now, is on sabbatical in Kenya and determinedly not answering his phone.

But I was able to have a lesson with Michael – our first of the year, and in fact the first for about three weeks. I play him the coda and it's not too bad. Of course, he has his usual unerring ear for the bits that still aren't yet soundly in the fingers – especially the rising chromatic passage from 228 onwards, which I always fumble; in fact we spend most of the hour on that passage and the next ten bars. He tries one or two different fingerings before we revert to the original choices. It's slow going, but eventually we pinpoint the 'troublesome' moment here – the third beat of 232. A big pencil circle goes round it. Towards the end of the lesson, he produces a book on pedalling he's just found. This leads to a ten-minute discussion about pedalling the coda . . . But then our time is suddenly up, and it is back to the office to get to grips with the assassination of Salman Taseer, the liberal governor of Punjab province in Pakistan.

On Friday night, Lindsay and I go to see the NYO concert at the Barbican, the 1970s London housing scheme clustered around a thriving arts centre. I'm seated next to Cherie Blair; she's brought along her son Leo, who proudly tells me he's learning the violin, piano and trombone. I have an extraordinary physical reaction to the concert – a tingling in the scalp at the Bach chorale and, at the thrilling brass sound in the Janáček Sinfonietta, a tightening of the skin at the back of the neck, which then spreads up and over the head. Music's capacity to affect you in this physical way is an incredible thing; I'm sure Ray Dolan could explain it for me. Over the weekend, I manage to dig out a *Nature* article which illustrates what was going on at the concert. It is all to do with the release of the chemical dopamine at peak moments of enjoyment, according to the researchers from McGill University. 'Dopamine is pivotal for establishing and maintaining behavior', reads the abstract. 'If music-induced emotional states can lead to dopamine release, as our findings indicate, it may begin to explain why musical experiences are so valued. These results further speak to why music can be effectively used in rituals, marketing or film to manipulate hedonic states. Our findings provide neuro-chemical evidence that intense emotional responses to music involve ancient reward circuitry and serve as a starting point for more detailed investigations of the biological substrates that underlie abstract forms of pleasure.'

After the concert – dopamine now subsiding – I have dinner with the two soloists, both (unusually for classical music) black. The first is Tai Murray, who has just played a magical Berg Violin Concerto. She's from Chicago, one of six children brought up by a single mother, and none of the siblings is musical. The other is Stewart Goodyear, who played Liszt's formidable *Totentanz*. He tells me he played the G minor Ballade when he was 13. He gives the impression of not finding it unduly difficult. I try very hard not to dislike him for it.

The weekend has been spent in London, and has been notable for the number of Twitter links to prodigious young Ballade players which have been popping up on my screen. There's a YouTube video of an 11-year-old Canadian, Annie Zhou, performing the Ballade rather well, followed by one Tiffany Poon (13) doing the same. And then there's 10-year-old Szuyu 'Rachel' Su (b. 1998) who lives in Tainan City, Taiwan. I see that an astonishing 3.2 million people have downloaded videos of her since September 2006. Forty-six thousand people have looked at a video of her performance of the Ballade in her sitting room in 2008. That's the equivalent of twenty-five or so sell-out performances at the Royal Festival Hall. Her feet can hardly reach the pedals. And her head is barely six inches above the top of the piano lid. The thread of comments underneath is a mixture of astonishment and viciousness:

Oh come on. You're obviously very talented, but this doesn't work . . . No 10 year old in the world has the emotion it takes to play this piece. Your teacher can give you pieces that suit you a lot more, which not only develop technique, as this one. I suggest you try smaller pieces, like Chopin's nocturnes, at first, before you go with his ballades.

Unfortunately she does have the emotional depth of a twig . . . but that's because she's only 10. What she must realise to become a true musician is that notes is one thing . . . beauty is another. This piece is beyond her by a couple of years and I mean that nicely . . . no one's doubting that she's talented . . . but to try and pull off Chopin's Ballade No. 1 at 10 years of age is just painful . . . to the student trying to master it, and the teacher realising that she's got a long way to go.

The more difficult and demanding works she plays, the more there'd be people here trashing her endeavors. So I guess there's a huge problem with her which is that she CAN play this. I would suggest she make a video swearing that she'll lock herself in a room and not do anything for the rest of her life and THAT would REALLY satisfy those sophisticated people on youtube . . .

> Even tho she makes lots of mistakes here, I think she is very brave to just
> take on this very difficult piece. Bravo to Rachel.

On Saturday, Lucy Parham rings to offer a lesson in the afternoon, so I beetle
round to her flat at the Barbican. I tell her that my new plan is to have the
piece ready for music camp in July as I've no chance of ever matching the
builders. She wants to know what my plan is for getting it ready in time.
I'm managing about three hours a week at the moment, I tell her, which is
twelve hours a month, or seventy-two hours by July. She wrinkles her nose
to imply 'not enough'. A professional pianist doing eight-hour days of practice would pack seventy-two hours into less than two weeks. So she's not
very impressed by that amount of work spread over six months.

Have I got a plan for how to get it all into the fingers, she asks. Er, not
really – I'm just endlessly repeating the coda at the moment. She suggests
a grid – literally, make a plan now for which bit you're planning to play in
which weeks. But – very important, she says – I must play the whole piece
at least once a week. Otherwise it's just disconnected bits and I'll never
develop a sense of the overall shape and how the pieces fit together. I'm not
sure about the grid, but I'll try it. She also advises me to play the coda every
single day, no matter what else I'm working on. It's the hardest bit, and –
she reiterates the maxim she gave me months ago – you must always make
sure you can play the end of any piece solidly.

I try the coda for her. It was OK with Michael in the week, but with Lucy
it just falls apart. Wrong notes spraying around, and everything suddenly complicated by my uncertainty whether to play from memory or look at the music.
She stops me and does her usual thing of picking out little tricks for finding
hand positions – particularly when large octave leaps are involved. Later, when
we get to bar 250 – the low G at the end of the long downward swoop – she's
horrified I'm playing it with my 'weak' fifth finger. She shows me how to make
a 'wedge' with my thumb tucked in behind the third finger to hit the note
firmly. This is like Ronan's dislike of my chosen fingering for the start of the
second theme. My approach is not 'wrong' exactly. But not right either.

We spend the rest of our time flitting around the piece, finding trouble
spots to work on. The big left-hand chords at 106: play them in dotted
rhythms – so-called 'dotted practice' – to embed the chords more firmly.
The tricky upward run at 130. How to remember the notes and the fingers of this repeating sixteen-note phrase? Answer: just play four of them
and stop. That's the task for one day. Play them first as chords, then as

written. Tomorrow do the next four. And then four on the third day. Four notes a day to remember, how hard is that? And so on.

She has one final tip: to remember notes and keys by mnemonics. So, in the waltz section, remember E and B as the base notes. 'I would remember that by a friend's name,' she says.

'Like Emily Bell?' I offer, thinking of the head of digital at the paper.

'Precisely. I find that easier than remembering key structures. I don't have time to think about all that when I'm on stage. So I will remember friends' names to recall which keys I'm in or which notes to play.'

'Is this how you spend your days?' I ask as I leave. 'Breaking down pieces into small chunks and then endless repetition until it embeds itself?'

'Pretty much.'

She says she sometimes wonders what on earth she's doing and whether she shouldn't get a proper job.

Tonight I end the weekend by playing duets with my regular piano partner Martin Prendergast in Kentish Town. He has just come back from Vienna and has made a visit to the little second-hand music room at Doblingers, which we discovered in December 2008 when we made our pilgrimage to hear Brendel's last concert. We read our way through Milhaud's *Scaramouche* and Saint-Saëns' *Variations on a Theme of Beethoven*. Both pretty hard pieces I don't think I'd have dreamed of playing a couple of years ago. And I'm not ready to play them yet. But after the Ballade, I'll probably be ready for anything. This two hours of music-making late afternoon or early evening on a Sunday night is now becoming a habit. It's invariably followed by two or three hours of work, but it's a satisfying bookend to the week – both an end and a start.

Tuesday, 11 January

Ray Dolan has recommended that I see a neuroscientist with a more specialised interest in music than him. So today I have a sandwich lunch with Lauren Stewart, a 30-something amateur violinist who has specialised in music and the mind at Goldsmiths College in London. She's shyer than Dolan, and less used, I suspect, to addressing a general audience. But she clearly knows her subject and arrives with both her instrument case and a laptop, which she uses throughout our conversation to find references and illustrations.

Almost her opening words are 'the big thing is plasticity', which is an encouraging message for middle-aged amateur pianists. 'We used to think that people who've got special skills had different brains to start off with. Now we know that that's not the case. It's the other way round – learning these special skills actually gives you a different kind of brain. It sculpts the brain in particular ways that you need.'

As an example, she talks about the brains of violinists, who have been shown to develop a larger area of somatosensory cortex, particularly in the right lobe. This makes sense. As Dolan explained, geographical representation in the brain is 'flipped': the right lobe represents the left of the body, the left lobe the right. A violinist's left hand does the more complex job of stopping on the instrument, whereas the right hand merely holds the bow – hence the violinist's asymmetry – a big bulge on the right. Pianists, who engage both hands in equal measure, have more of a 'bilateral bulge'. I wonder about the size of this 'musical bulge'. Is it visible with a microscope? Stewart says it's much bigger than that. On an MRI scan you can pick up the differences with the naked eye.

I wonder if these developments took years, and if it was crucial that you started learning before the age of 7, say? Not at all, according to Stewart. The change can be rapid, occurring over the course of just a few weeks, even. She tells me there have been arguments that if you don't begin learning before an early age, you'll never have perfect pitch, but she thinks perfect pitch is 'over-hyped' in any case, and that most musicians don't really want it. But no, learning from an early age isn't necessary in allowing these neurological developments.

Stewart goes over some of the same territory as Dolan, explaining about neurons, axons and dendrites. I get her to show me the areas of the brain on a medical illustration of grey matter I've downloaded from the web. She talks excitedly about all the recent research which shows what's going on inside the brain when music is being created. We look at the corpus callosum, the flat bundle of neurons that connects the two hemispheres of the brain. 'The research has shown that in musicians the corpus callosum is enlarged, not throughout, but just in the large anterior portion, so probably this bit' – she points to an area of the brain on my illustration. 'They think this is probably due to the requirement that musicians have to essentially coordinate between their hands and their feet. Again, that is something that is sculpted through intense training.'

We then move on to talk about the work she'd done for her PhD, which has originally involved trying to find people who were illiterate and then scanning them progressively using functional MRI as they learned to read. By giving them the same set of word stimuli over time and comparing how the brain's response changed, she would be able to see which brain areas or networks of brain areas were being altered through learning. 'But we couldn't find these people because they don't really exist – everybody has got a certain level of literacy and, if they haven't, there's normally a good reason why they haven't. So I said: "Well, why don't we look at people who are musically illiterate because there's definitely loads of them and I would be able to teach people to read music and play the piano in a way that I wouldn't really be able to teach people how to read language."'

So she recruited fifteen adults who had never read music or played an instrument but who were really keen to do so, bought a set of Casio keyboards and then, every week, she would teach them in groups of four to read music and to play keyboard. She taught them music theory as well and, after three months, they reached Grade 1 standard. By this stage they could play with two hands and manage basic things such as scales.

'The important thing was that we scanned them both before and after the training and we also scanned a group of similar people before and after. These control people had never read music but also didn't learn it either so that was a control.'

Stewart discovered two particularly interesting things. The first was that she saw changes in the superior parietal lobe. 'This is an area that's involved in spatial transformations, when you have to plan your actions based on the position of something in space. I always think of playing tennis, you are actually planning the trajectory of the ball and you have to think, "Right, where do I need to be?" so you have to use spatial coordinates to plan your actions. That's really what you're doing if you're a pianist. If we just think about pitch, because of pitch being organised vertically and the keyboard being organised horizontally, you're pretty much doing a spatial rotation.'

The second insight related to an area of the brain called the supramarginal gyrus. 'This area has been associated with *intention to act*.' What this suggested to Stewart was that once you've become an expert in decoding musical notation, even if you're, relatively speaking, a novice, you automatically prepare to act when you see that notation, 'even when you're told not to'. 'In fact,' she says, 'you have to inhibit the learned action.'

She talks a little more about the technicalities of her work, and I begin to get lost. I try to drag things back down to my level, and ask if she's learned any basic principles as to how memory works in relation to music. She tells me about the concept of 'chunking'. 'Think of people who can remember pi to hundreds or thousands of decimal places: it just seems like a superhuman feat. You think, "Well, these must be very unusual people." But they have a special trick to do it, which is that they essentially break a very long number up. Instead of, for instance, having to remember a hundred individual items, they might break that into ten items of ten where those ten – that is, the composition of one chunk of ten items – is meaningful to them. Chess grandmasters can do this very, very well. Perfectly, in fact.'

This 'chunking' is applied by the brain in music reading, especially when you're first trying to make sense of a piece of music. 'You've got two staves and there might be several notes per stave. So the way you do that is by thinking, "Well, that's a chord of C major and that moves to F major and there's an arpeggio." So you can turn something that looks like a whole bundle of confusing notes into a meaningful digested thing by drawing on your knowledge of music and also by using what we call "top-down expectations" about what's going to come next.'

This sounds very similar to Ray Dolan's concept of the brain working on a principle of prediction. Indeed, Stewart tells me 'there have been studies where you get people to sight-read a piece of piano music and then you whip the music away from them at a particular point and you see how many more notes they can bang out that are correct. Some people are really good sight-readers and that means that they are looking further ahead and planning further ahead. That kind of thing happens also if you're doing touch-typing; if you're transcribing from a written text you're planning well ahead of where you actually are.' So as a good sight-reader, I must be a good 'chunker'. But am I going to be able to use this ability to learn the Ballade note by note?

Stewart finishes by talking about what happens 'when plasticity goes bad'. The result is focal dystonia, in which misfiring neurons cause involuntary muscle contractions. 'When you're learning you might get cortical expansion of the territory. Well, if you get too much of that you start to lose the individual representation of each digit, so that you can no longer exercise them independently, which is a disaster for any high-level musician.' But this also seems to involve personality factors like anxiety and stress, she says. She tells me the story of the pianist Leon Fleisher, who developed focal dystonia just as he was about to become a total star. For many years he couldn't play with both hands. 'But he relearned, he went to see a neurologist. They managed to rehabilitate him.'

Again, I'm encouraged by our conversation, and especially Stewart's focus on plasticity. I was quite prepared for the scientists I was meeting to take me aside and gently dissuade me from trying to coach my 57-year-old brain to attempt new skills. On the contrary . . .

Sunday, 16 January

Fish Cottage for the first time in two weeks. The snow has gone, revealing the sedum roof of the music room, which is like a russet lawn on top of the building. It helps blend the room with the woods and the fields around. And there's now a door on it, a very stout oak door. And since we last visited, the garden has been remoulded around the room and lots of work has been done in cutting down trees and beginning to lay paths. Within the music room itself, the builders have put down a concrete floor over the underfloor heating and done quite a lot of plastering. So it's really taking shape.

Yesterday, I had to work on one of the chapters for the instant WikiLeaks book that we're producing, out in a fortnight, on 3 February. I then sat down in the evening to do an hour of practice. I've managed a fair bit of practice this week, mostly struggling with the impenetrable octave runs in bars 119, 121 and 123. I've also been working on the big chords around bar 106, and I'm anxious that this in particular has led to what feels like RSI in my left arm.

Anyway, I take it very slowly – trying to remember the key structure which I find difficult. I'm forcing myself not to play the next chord until I can visualise it (or rather, given Ronan's tip, hear it). I practise ten minutes left hand alone, ten minutes right hand alone and then put it together – again very, very slowly – but in the end that is as much as I could do without becoming anxious about injury.

Then I go back to the coda. I would have once marked the whole section as a 'fracture'. But of course there are mini fractures within the whole fracture. Some bits of it I'm now fairly competent on but just can't play very fast; and then there are other bits where I'm still kidding myself if I think I know the notes exactly. I'm now using coloured Post-it notes to set up a traffic-light system – green, amber and red. Green = nearly there. Red = way to go.

When we return to Kentish Town this evening, the music I ordered from the Petrucci International Score Library Project has arrived. I celebrate by immediately ordering another $200 worth of eight-hand music, including the Brahms and Schumann symphonies. Since my orchestral playing days are probably over, this eight-hand playing is going to be the nearest I'll ever get to sitting in a band and experiencing the thrill of ensemble playing with these great nineteenth-century masterpieces.

Later this evening I checked my TweetDeck and see another Japanese pianist has popped up saying she's working on the Ballade. I email her to find out what motivated her to pick this particular piece. 'Suzie K' quickly replies with her reasons, apologising for her English:

Last year was Chopin's 200th birth anniversary. I listened to a lot of his pieces. This is one of the pieces chosen from among that. I am self-study now. Therefore, I play my favorite pieces only.

Not only this piece but many classical music lovers in Japan love Chopin. I think that his dramatic, melodious pieces are close to our sense. People not so interested in the classical music know Minute Waltz (Op. 64, No. 1), Revolutionary Etude (Op. 10, No. 12), and Fantaisie-Impromptu, etc.

I read 'Always Chopin in the pocket', a Japanese cartoon. There is a scene where the boy for whom the heroine is yearning plays this piece. And she also plays this piece.

I think this piece to be liked by people who play the piano well. I saw the first stage of the 'International Chopin piano competition in ASIA' (Tokyo area: amateur B category) several contestants selected this piece . . . I have played easy waltzes and nocturnes before. It was not enough to playing the piece. I felt that I need more training. Long scales, arpeggios and other fast passages, etc. If I cannot clear these problems, this piece cannot be expressed.

Zen-On, a music publishing company in Japan, ranked each scores. 'Ballades' ranked high category. Same as 'Etudes'. I Know. But I wanted to try. I want to try again. I will practise long time.

I am fascinated by the thought of a Japanese cartoon book devoted to Chopin. Suzie scans in this particular issue and emails it to me. I'll show it to Noriko Ogawa (who taught the most recent piano camp in the Lot Valley) when I see her shortly and ask her to translate it for me. It is exactly as Suzie describes – a mass-market manga cartoon book devoted to Chopin, with this episode all about a love relationship of a teenager learning the G minor Ballade. It's a long away from the *Beano*.

Friday, 21 January

It's been another hectic week. The big news is that today Andy Coulson – editor of the *News of the World* for four years (2003–7) – resigned as Downing Street press secretary. He was one of the new breed of showbiz writers who rose to edit national papers in the UK and, arguably, the most successful. But all the evidence suggests that phone hacking was endemic within his newsroom and it was a piece of staggeringly bad judgement by David Cameron to hire him as press adviser, still less to take him into government with him. This has been building up, but I don't quite understand the timing, unless it was in the hope that Tony Blair appearing before the Chilcot Inquiry into the Iraq War would drown out the coverage.

On Tuesday, I met with one of the lawyers working for the victims of phone hacking. He was frustratingly discreet, but it's definitely going to be useful to keep in touch with this network. They are all loners, small firms, plugging away in a rather tenacious way. Things are being made harder by the fact that Nick Davies is still on his Kenyan retreat and refusing to break off, despite a bombardment of texts and emails from me. I feel like Walter Matthau to his Jack Lemmon. My Walter Burns to his Hildy Johnson in the remake of *The Front Page*.

I write a leader as soon as I hear the Coulson news, then dash off to appear on *Channel 4 News*. Supposedly, that marks the end of the working week, and so I head off to dinner with Richard Morrison, the *Times* arts columnist, whom I've known since university days, and his partner, the pianist Anna Tilbrook. Before supper Anna and I tinker through the *Magic Flute* overture in the little studio at the back of their North London flat.

She's the most effortless sight-reader I know (or, as Lauren Stewart might put it, a good 'chunker'). Later she tells me she's currently recording all nine Beethoven symphonies for piano duet, conducted by the 85-year-old George Hurst, who wants to commit his version of the symphonies to record before he dies.* She never looks at the scores before recording sessions – she simply turns up and plays. 'I just see the notes and have perfect pitch, so I can work out keys. There seems to be nothing between seeing and playing. I never have to think at all.'

She first tried the Ballade around the age of 13, but she tells me she has been frightened of the piece throughout her life. 'It's very hard,' she says over dinner. 'There's something powerful and intimidating about it. I've never played it in public for that reason, but often played it in private. I just love playing it. Sometimes when I'm trying something else at the piano I'll just break off and play that coda, it's such amazing stuff to play.'

She makes me particularly jealous when she tells me she has never had problems memorising anything. It just goes in and stays. 'Sometimes I am playing and I realise that about eight seconds on I can't visualise at all where the music is going. Sometimes I get within a couple of seconds, but the unconscious then takes over. On a couple of occasions I've just found myself playing something – the right notes – but it's as if the fingers have remembered rather than me.' I don't tell her what Ray Dolan told me: the fingers remember nothing; it's all in the brain. And besides, I know exactly what she means.

As well as some steady practice in the mornings this week, and the usual lesson with Michael, I managed to carve out time on Tuesday for a sandwich lunch in my office with Noriko Ogawa, who divides her life between London and Tokyo. She's 40-ish, striking-looking and – once the initial Japanese reserve has melted – a bundle of energy, gossip and laughter. She spent the first eighteen years of her life in Japan, then had a rather miserable few years at the Juilliard school of music in New York before meeting an English piano teacher, Benjamin Kaplan, who managed to rekindle her enthusiasm for music in a way the Juilliard professors had failed. She came third in the 1987 Leeds International Piano Competition and worked a lot with the Japanese composer Takemitsu, whose pieces she still performs. I ask her why – to judge from Twitter – Chopin is so amazingly popular in Japan. 'Well,' she says, 'even if you play Chopin like a dead duck, you can tell it is

* He died in September 2012.

Chopin. If you pick up a piece by Schumann, for example, and play like a dead duck, it does not sound like Schumann, unless you really know his music very well. So for a country like Japan, where, relatively speaking, classical music is new, Chopin is very easy to get into. For Japanese people it is very easy to say, "Oh that's Chopin." Even the four Ballades, which are so different – but if you played Number 2 somebody who only knows Number 1 will say, "Oh yes that's another Chopin, isn't it?"' She tells me that during the first ten years of her career, whenever she went back to Japan, people repeatedly asked her to play Chopin. 'They were probably looking for very stereotypical, sentimental Chopin – somebody who is very ill, might-die-tomorrow type of music.'

We then speak about the G minor Ballade itself. She first played it at the age of 13. Unlike Ronan O'Hora, who also played it at that age and was attracted to its visceral qualities, the pull of the Ballade was different for Noriko. In her opinion, teenagers are drawn to the piece because 'very simply, it's a very, very famous piece. If you play the piano you want to pick it up.' There is also the lure of its difficulty: 'It has got very challenging technical parts. So for teenagers, or young pianists, it is a quite definite challenge.'

I ask Noriko if she could remember how long it took her to learn the Ballade back then.

'Maybe about one week.'

'A week!'

'Yes, yes, to memorise, but to play it properly probably took a couple of months.'

She tells me the story of how she learned the piece, taking it to her piano teacher one day. As Ronan suggested is the case with most young students, Noriko found it particularly hard to play the opening bars in a way that her teacher found satisfactory. 'When I first took it to my lesson, my piano teacher went on and on and on and on about the very first notes. That became such an issue and I remember myself feeling so intimidated.'

It's interesting that while Ronan's students struggle with the opening because they are so used to the force of the modern piano and have to learn ways to coax a new delicacy from it, Noriko thinks the problem for her was one of emotional maturity. 'I was a kid, so I couldn't quite get the rubato properly. I had never been abroad. I didn't know what my teachers were going on about if they said that, no, it's not natural enough, that it's not romantic enough, you're not singing. As a person I'm pretty realistic, not very dreamy, so my first seven bars sounded very strong. I just wanted to get on with it but my teacher wouldn't let me so we got stuck.'

Although Noriko thinks the fourth Ballade is the 'fiddly one' – that is, the piece that's 'technically' hardest – the first Ballade is still the most difficult, 'to shape it nicely, to play it convincingly'. And like everybody else she zeroed in on the difficulties of the coda when we spoke. 'It's hell for every pianist. Right from the beginning, everybody is worried about that part. You breathe in, and then off you go. If you're too excited, you blow up. So every pianist is so scared right from the beginning. It's notorious.' I think back to my chat with Ronan again, and his thinking that many pianists slip into making the coda 'grotesque'. Noriko went one better: 'Everybody goes berserk,' she says.

Noriko still plays the Ballade. She played it a few times in the north last spring and is due to play it a few times in Japan later this year. But she still isn't satisfied she has it mastered, especially the coda – 'I still think technically the final bit is terrible!' Nowadays, she tells me, her interpretation of the piece relies on calmness. 'You have to be pretty excited, but I think it's very important to secretly work out what kind of point you are going to get to every eight bars. In Schumann's music you can really get drowned. Chopin, I don't think so. You have to be pretty cool all the way through. Schumann's different. Beethoven, oh gosh! I'm practising late Beethoven now and it's really so personal: he is really asking us to understand his pain and his sorrow and it's really, like, in my face all the time, whereas Chopin, no. It's a very beautifully finished product and he didn't want us to know what kind of pain he has. Everything is so sophisticated, it's all filtered already.'

I was interested in whether the piece stayed in her fingers, even though she'd first learned it as a young girl. Or did she have to more or less relearn it every time she revisited the piece? 'Yes, it was always there. But I'm not a great sight-reader and I am not a kind of pianist who can just play after one day of brushing up. I have to go over it quite a few times before I can actually present it in public. But in terms of whether I can remember from the beginning to the end, yes, it was there.' I wonder if the fact that I'm a good sight-reader means that I won't ever develop this skill in the way Noriko has.

Over the past fortnight or so there's been a lot of press for a controversial book called *Battle Hymn of the Tiger Mother*. In it, the author, Amy Chua, records the upbringing of her two children, whom she raised in the fiercest, most disciplined manner. Her kids could never attend a sleepover, be in a school play, watch TV or play computer games. They couldn't choose their own extracurricular activities, or get any grade less than an A. They had to be the number one student in every subject except gym and drama, had to play the violin and piano and weren't allowed to play any other instrument. In Chua's view western parents are failing their kids by not adhering to this model. A fierce debate has been raging online and in the papers ever since. I wondered if Noriko was similarly pushed in Japan.

'Oh, yes. I did have a very strict teacher and I had a very strict mother. Even today my mother says that she was just so strict because she couldn't bear watching me being told off by my teachers, so she just wanted to prepare me all right, sort of thing. But then it became a lot of pressure not only for my family but, you know, my teacher. Yes it was pretty tough.' When she first came to England and was living with this English family, the family read all the school reports aloud, including hers. 'The mother would say, "Isn't it good? We're so proud of her." Japanese language would not sit well like that. We would say something different. Behind closed doors, maybe between Mum and Dad. It's not in our culture to say, "Isn't she doing well, we're so proud." We just don't do it, it doesn't exist. Grammatically, yes; but culturally, no.'

For Noriko, this meant it took her some time until she was able to enjoy her playing. 'Even after I started performing, I used to think, "I am going to be told off." Finally, my western friends said: "You play concerts and you're giving people pleasure. They are not there trying to criticise, they just want to come and have a nice evening out." That really turned the table for me: I didn't see it like that until I was 30-something. I just realised, "Ah, I could go out and give some kind of pleasure." So when I go to teach now I see very few young pianists who are completely tired and burnt out, whereas I come across some students in Japan, even today, whose energy has gone, it is all used up.'

As we're talking about cultural differences, I thought it the right moment to produce the manga strip I'd been sent by Suzie K on Sunday. Noriko looked at 'Always Chopin in My Pocket' and began to translate a few panels of the story for me. A little girl is practising the Op. No. 23. Her teacher is very strict and always criticises her staccato for being too strong. The girl is in love with a boy, and every time she plays the piece she thinks of him. The girl is told by her teacher to go away and study the first Ballade for an upcoming masterclass or exam. The day of the exam comes and the boy is there! 'Do your best,' he says, and she begins the piece and continues to think of him and the playing gets better and better. Eventually she plays it at a concert and everybody praises her rendition. 'It's very soap opera,' says Noriko.

This kind of manga is a genre in itself, according to Noriko. 'There are several manga comics talking about classical music students. There is another one which eventually became a film and TV programme. So if I play some repertoire which happens to come from that programme, a lot of people will recognise the tune.' They're not just read by teenagers, but adults too.

I try to imagine hundreds of thousands of Londoners sitting on the Circle Line reading a graphic novel about Chopin's Op. 23 masterpiece. If only.

And I think of our own girls. Should I have been a bit more Tiger Dad–ish over their musical development? Both had piano lessons for a couple of years or more: neither really clicked. Should we have pushed? My fear at the time was of alienating them – of driving them so hard they'd develop a lifelong loathing of the piano and classical music. Both are now in their mid to late 20s: neither seems to bear a burning resentment or to feel the lack of instrumental ability to be a yawning gap in their lives. Isabella has eclectic tastes. Lizzie has an almost enclyclopaedic knowledge of all popular music from the birth of the blues through to Adele. Neither has shut themselves off from classical music, nor have they sought it out. Just occasionally they find themselves enchanted by an accidental discovery – Isabella stumbles on Elgar, Lizzie on a Schubert sonata or a Bruckner symphony. For a moment they're dazzled. But not – yet – enough to immerse themselves in more.

Monday, 31 January

Another lesson with Michael today. Apart from a break imposed by forty-eight hours in Munich for a digital conference I've practised every morning of the past week, and have spent every session trying to make progress on the same four bars – the little figures in the run-up to the waltz. I can see what the pattern is here, but there's no easy way of remembering the dissonant pairings of notes as they tumble upwards, nor of instantly sensing the shape of the sixteen-note repeating template.

We spend some time on these today without making too much progress. Then we move on to the waltz. I'm conscious that Michael is gazing intently at my feet, which is very off-putting. I know what's coming. 'Alan, we have a problem with your pedalling,' he sighs at the end. 'It used to be the fingering. Now it's the pedals.'

He's right. I have been sinning with the pedals. Time to slow down. Again. And work something out from scratch. Again.

Friday, 4 February

I'm in New York to launch the *Guardian*'s book on WikiLeaks. Yesterday, I took part in a symposium at the Columbia School of Journalism with Bill Keller and Jack Goldsmith, a professor at Harvard Law School and former assistant Attorney General. Some of it was bogged down by a strangely old-fashioned discussion about whether what WikiLeaks does can be called journalism. It matters legally: the US government's enthusiasm for prosecuting Julian Assange may depend on whether he is seen as a 'journalist'. But otherwise not much hangs on it. As one blogger – Mathew Ingram – writes about the discussion: 'the tools of journalism have been set loose from the control of entities like the *New York Times* or the *Guardian*. Anyone can effectively become a publisher now, and that includes WikiLeaks and OpenLeaks and anyone who makes use of similar tools – just as people who find themselves in the central square in Cairo or Tunisia can behave as journalists if they wish to. That's an important phenomenon.'

Yes, indeed. It's the amateurising of journalism – with all that's good and bad about that.

I've extended my trip by twenty-four hours, so that this morning I could go to see Charles Rosen, the writer and pianist, who's lived in the same flat in the Upper West Side since he was 6 – i.e. since the early 1930s. There must have been some confusion over email, because he comes to the door at 10 a.m. in pyjamas and dressing gown looking old and frail and surprised to see me. Worse still, he announces that he has just come back from hospital having had a pacemaker fitted. I hesitate on the doorstep – torn between retiring and taking probably my only chance to see the great man, surely the only person alive to have studied with a pupil of Liszt – which means I'd be just three handshakes from Chopin himself. Fortunately, he asks me in – and we sit in the little kitchen off his sitting room, two yards from the 1930s Steinway which has stood in the same spot for decades, its lid bearing the repeated impact of Rosen's gouging fingers, the odd missing ivory. 'My piano dates from 1939,' he tells me. 'It has quite a beautiful cantabile sound. It is true that today the German Steinways have a better standard than the American ones and I prefer them.'

I need not have worried about his health. He pours himself a strong cup of coffee and then launches into a twenty-minute peroration about the unity of keys in Mozart operas. But of course I want to get him on Chopin, about whom he has written so eloquently – particularly in his books *The Classical Style* and *On Romanticism in Music*.

Next, though, he talks about his teacher Moriz Rosenthal, the man who had studied under Liszt. Rosen explains how they met. 'In 1939, after the *Anschluss* in Austria, all these great German musicians came here. Moriz Rosenthal came here and we had the same dentist so I was introduced to him and he offered to teach me. He was 75 years old. Very funny. He never said to me that I was wrong. He said, politely, I have a different idea of this piece, he would say, and go to the piano and show me. He was a very nice man. He was also famous for being extremely nasty about other pianists, largely because he couldn't resist a joke.' But Rosenthal never told Rosen about lessons with Liszt, 'except for the fact that it was difficult to get Liszt out of the café and back to the studio to get a lesson. That's all I know about Liszt's teaching habits.'

Rosenthal had not only been a star pupil of Liszt's; he'd also met Brahms. 'Rosenthal was 25 years old,' Rosen tells me. 'He was playing the most difficult of all the Liszt pieces, the *Réminiscences de Don Juan*. It was in a place in Vienna where they had tables with people sitting around the tables drinking beer. Brahms had his back to the stage and all Rosenthal could think about was making him turn around. So when he got to page five, where there's a huge passage with thirds up and down the piano in the right hand, he played chromatic thirds on both hands. Brahms not only turned around but came backstage and asked Rosenthal if he would play the Paganini Variations, which he did.'

At this time in Germany, there was a schism – 'a full fight', as Rosen puts it – between the Wagner and Liszt devotees on the one hand and disciples of Brahms and Joachim on the other. 'It's very funny because Brahms was actually stealing the great Liszt pianist for himself . . . Rosenthal told me a lot about Brahms, whom he got to know quite well.'

I tell Rosen how fascinating it is to be in a room with someone who has this direct connection with those great nineteenth-century titans. In fact the chain of connections goes even further back: Rosen studied under Rosenthal, Rosenthal studied with Liszt, Liszt studied with Czerny, Czerny studied with Beethoven, Beethoven studied with Haydn. 'But remember,' Rosen says, 'that between generations there's always a big reaction. I mean, at the time when I was studying with Rosenthal, I had been listening to Arthur Rubinstein and Rudolf Serkin so I didn't want to play like Rosenthal, he was very old-fashioned. He never wanted me to play that way. Actually, I do a little more now but at that time he never tried to make me play in the way he played.'

Occasionally, Rosen gets up from his breakfast table as we speak and illustrates some point or other at the piano, warning me that he couldn't play too energetically because of the advice from his doctor not to do too much with his left arm following the operation.

He knows I am keen to discuss the Ballade, but before any talk of that, he insists on me listening to the playing of Josef Hofmann, who, he thinks, was probably the greatest piano player of all time and whom he first heard when he was 6. So we go through into the sitting room above the snowy streets of the Upper West Side and he puts on a crackly 1920s recording of Hofmann. We listen to him play Scarlatti and Chopin, with Rosen's face transported, not by the memory, just by the playing itself – by the variations of tones, the control and the musicality. 'Hofmann actually had a very small hand,' Rosen tells me. 'He could only reach an octave; he couldn't reach a ninth. Steinway built him a special keyboard, so he could just reach the ninth key.'

At last, we get to the Ballade. Rosen first played it in this very room, as a teenager in the early 1940s. He was able to memorise it very quickly, as he was most pieces as a young man – things are slightly different in his 80s, though: 'Now I have to play it over many times in memorising. I just keep playing until I have it in memory.' But because he learned the Ballade at such a young age, he finds it is a piece that's still 'in his fingers'. 'I've never forgotten it,' he says. I ask how he went about learning the Ballade. When he learns a piece, does he think in terms of structures and patterns, or approach things more instinctively? 'I try to find a good fingering, that's basically what I do. I have prejudices about fingering.' A man after Michael Shak's heart.

In Rosen's view, the Ballade is one of the great pieces. 'I think it was [the music critic] Gerald Abraham who said, "Nobody would think that the first Ballade was a masterpiece." Well I do. It's a very extraordinary invention.' Why does he think it so great? 'Well, I mean it has the completely dramatic narrative worked out. It's not a sonata. You know, there's a small resemblance to a sonata form, it does have two main themes with a closing theme. But it works it out into a very complex relationship in harmony, the most radical of its time.'

Rosen goes into a little digression about so-called Romantic composers and their reactions against classical forms. A classical sonata 'always resolved into the tonic between two-thirds and three-quarters of the way through the movement'. The Romantic composer, on the other hand, 'wanted to keep the tension going until the end'. 'Basically,' he says, 'Chopin decided to cut the recapitulation into the smallest possible space towards the end. The first Ballade is the one where he experiments the most radically.'

I put it to Rosen that some people say the generation after Beethoven had to wait until Beethoven's death in order to be able to write music like the Ballade. 'Well, that's what they say but . . . it's not quite true. Schubert is really experimenting before the death of Beethoven. I mean, he doesn't go *that* far from the Beethoven form, but Schumann does, for example, in his piano sonatas.'

We then touch on the technical difficulties raised by these innovations. Like everybody else I've spoken to, Rosen admits there are serious challenges in the piece, and like everybody else he singles out the coda. In his opinion, a lot of the challenges in the piece are caused by the different tempi and the fact that 'you have to make a kind of unity out of it'. But Rosen offers insights into the piece that I've not heard before. For example, when we discussed how the Ballade was related to Italian opera – the opening bars resembling bel canto; the distinct ending recalling a cabaletta, the quick final section of an aria – Rosen raises the question of theft. People often talk about the influence of Bellini in Chopin's work, but Rosen thinks Bellini's presence goes beyond influence in the Ballade.

'He actually steals something from Bellini . . . It begins with a cello melody that was written after Bellini had come to Paris.'

And then it's back to pedalling. Rosen points to bar 73 of the score. 'The most interesting thing is that all editions have the wrong pedalling. In bar 73 you bring out the tenor voice, you don't put the pedal on the bass.'

'So it's a two-beat pedal here rather than a three-beat?'

'That's right. The pedal goes opposite to the rhythm of the harmony. Your right hand is in three beats.'

This is known as hemiola – that is, the ratio of 3:2; the hand in three beats, while the pedal is in two – and it's something I've discussed with Michael in relation to this passage. Rosen thinks this shows the influence of Bach, and the crucial role of 'counterpoint' in his compositions. 'Chopin studied Bach all his life,' he says, 'and he thought of music as actually always in counterpoint.'

I leave Rosen's apartment, making a mental note to try this counterpoint pedalling, and head in the direction of the midtown offices of the *New Yorker*. I have booked coffee with its music critic, Alex Ross, whose stunning history of the twentieth century in music, *The Rest Is Noise*, caused such a sensation when it came out in 2007. He's more recently been writing about how professional playing was changed by the advent of recorded sound – and how that changed the relationship between professional and amateur music-making. This was what I was keen to quiz him about. We meet in his cramped office, stacked from floor to ceiling with books and

CDs, with a tiny space in which to work – by the low glow of a Philippe Starck light.

To begin with I ask him to sketch out his thoughts on the impact of recording. 'I guess it's a sort of complicated series of transformations that took place at the end of the nineteenth century. Obviously, there was at that point much less of a distinction between professional musician and passive listener. I mean, so many of the listeners played themselves, in their homes.' He thinks that if we were able to hear professional music-making from that period, it would probably strike us as very 'amateurish'. 'I think if we heard performances, perhaps even by some of the most famous virtuosos of the day, we might instinctively hear them now as sloppy, as less controlled than so much of what we hear nowadays.'

Ross says he isn't trying to make this case himself – 'I only read in the field' (citing, in particular, Robert Philip and Mark Katz) – but a number of commentators believe that the advent of recording at the end of the nineteenth century changed not just how people played, but how they listened. 'It was a sort of a mirror moment. Certainly, musicians became much more conscious of how they actually sounded. It was quite jarring and frightening to a lot of people that they could hear these mistakes or approximations or, I think, expressive gestures in their playing. Even if the musician was, in fact, totally in control of what he was doing, you could suddenly hear a slide or a portamento in a string section, rolling chords at the piano, or an effect where the right hand was maybe moving a little ahead, or a little behind, the left. I think all these kinds of gestures were done deliberately for expressive reasons, but, after recording came in, there was just increasingly this emphasis on precision, on togetherness, on technical control.'

And how exactly did recording change the listening audience? 'Well, people became accustomed to listening to multi-movement symphonies or quartets in the silence of one's living room.' This silent atmosphere was then echoed in the concert halls. Before recording there was sometimes applause *during* the pieces, not just after, and there were far more calls for encores. With the advent of recordings, as Ross put it, things started 'quieting down'.

Recording also brought about an increasing distinction between composers and performers. Prior to recording, this distinction didn't exist. 'Until the latter part of the nineteenth century there were very few pianists at least, or conductors, who weren't also composers themselves.' This meant there had been a culture where the performer gave a more 'creative element' to the piece. 'A movement of a multi-movement piece might be repeated; pianists would introduce works with an improvisatory episode – "preluding" it was called – then as they finished they might add something of their own to sort of link up with the next piece.' As recording accelerated what Ross refers to as 'the cult of precision', these flourishes vanished and the composer-performer was replaced by the pure, and more technically proficient, performer.

The 'cult of precision' reached a climax, Ross thinks, during 'the golden age of the LP, maybe stretching into the early CD era' – so from the late 1960s through to the early 1980s. By this point things had almost become artificial. Behind the scenes, the precise and perfect recorded performance 'was to some extent the creation of a great deal of splicing together of takes and retakes'. This would create almost impossible pressures for the pianists, the orchestra or the string quartet that would have to live up to these semi-artificial creations and sustain that level of technical control in the live performance. It created a culture in the conservatories of endless practising in pursuit of this 'perfect performance'.

However, Ross thinks that things have been changing. He tells me that 'it seems as though then we've been moving into an age more recently where, though that conservatoire culture is still very much present, I do feel as though there has been a certain loosening up. There certainly are performers now who are investigating improvisation – a soloist writing his or her own cadenzas for a concerto. They are cultivating again the more creative end of performance.'

Is this just a result of frustration with how things have been? 'Quite a bit of this is rooted in the early music movement,' Ross says. 'Early music we think of in its early days as highly antiquarian and academic in its sensibility. But then, after a certain stage, performers began studying the manuals for performance, accounts of how music was really made in the seventeenth, eighteenth centuries especially. They decided, "We need to begin ornamenting in the fashion of those days and perhaps even improvising and just to bring a lot more spontaneity to the performance." So now you have these sometimes shockingly, wonderfully rambunctious, performances of Vivaldi concertos or the "Brandenburg" Concertos or other Baroque pieces.'

But has this trend begun to infiltrate the core Romantic repertory, the performance of nineteenth-century music which up to now has seemed almost sacrosanct? 'I haven't really seen this happening yet – but we may get to a point where some of that same mentality comes into it. But we've heard these pieces done more or less the same way for so long that for an interpreter to come along and decide to improvise something at the beginning of the "Hammerklavier" Sonata leading into the opening chords would be just unimaginably shocking whereas, with a relatively obscure Vivaldi opera, people take this kind of experimentation a lot more easily.'

We finish our conversation discussing how the digital revolution has affected the world of classical music today. It certainly seems to be the case that the technology which allowed recording to reach that high point of precision and perfection has now started to destroy the economic basis of the recording industry. 'Absolutely,' agrees Ross. This means that studio recordings, though still made, are no longer the goal of a performing career. 'The young conductor doesn't imagine now, "I'm going to go and do a studio one day and record my complete Mahler symphonies cycle, or the Ring cycle." No one is thinking that way any more and the recordings are emanating from live performances more often.' The result is that imperfections, or rather 'expressive gestures', are coming back into the recordings.

But then there is the question of distribution. As Ross puts it, 'So many performances now are streamed on the internet or go out on internet radio or even on high-quality video transmission. So there's actually a lot more music just accumulating, being preserved now, sort of building up all over the internet and finding its way onto people's hard drives, whether legally released or not.' I tell Ross about the number of Ballade performances I'd discovered through Twitter, each one of which might have anything from a hundred viewers to 20,000 viewers or 200,000 viewers depending on whether it's a cute little 11-year-old, or a rising star. I put it to him this is a return to a form of music sharing that has more in common with the nineteenth century – breaking down the barriers between the professional and amateur – only on a much more significant scale.

'Yeah, and it feels absolutely healthy. The complaint that I've had about classical performance culture for a while, is that we're surrounded by this highly specialised, highly professionalised, proficient culture of performance which yields, generally, excellent performances night after night in concert halls. I seldom go to a performance in any leading concert hall that goes below a certain base level of technical proficiency, but it doesn't so often rise far above that level. There are thousands of very good performances and rather few really great ones. So I think this moment in which everything is starting to seem much more chaotic and a sort of a partial breakdown in the filters that have controlled who becomes known, in a sense, who finds an audience, [is healthy] . . . In a way it does feel like a return to the culture of the eighteenth and nineteenth centuries, except now on a global scale as opposed to a much more local scale. I think it's just fundamentally healthy for this system, this rather monolithic and highly routinised classical system – the agencies, the orchestras, the conservatories (above all, the conservatories) are at the heart of this system, the publishers for composers, record labels. You know, it is being shaken up in an interesting way. Critics as well, of course. We now have so many voices outside of newspapers and magazines on the internet and I think that's healthy too.'

After leaving Ross, I check my phone and email. There's been a call from Steven Spielberg's company, DreamWorks, asking for a copy of the *Guardian* WikiLeaks book. But less promising news comes through on Twitter. @Wikileaks, which means Julian Assange, has tweeted that WikiLeaks 'will be taking action' over 'malicious libels' in our book. For several reasons, that might be the most entertaining court case imaginable. But I hope, and suspect, it will never happen.

Sunday, 6 February

Back in London for the weekend, and realising that my pianists are bunching up a little. Today it's the turn of Murray Perahia, who asks me over to his new house in St John's Wood, North London. He's recently moved from Ealing, which was his and his wife Ninette's home for many years. We start with tea and chocolate cake, the three of us sitting in their light, airy kitchen/dining room. He says he has not played piano since July – he's had a recurrence of a thumb problem – though he is convinced, as of yesterday, that he has finally sorted it out. We didn't discuss how. He uses his 'down' time to think and study. He has recently been trying to get to grips with Wagner, whom he has always disliked, but now that he's listened to most of the operas in different versions, his opinion has softened.

His new home is not far from the old house of the British pianist Myra Hess, famous for her wartime National Gallery concerts: his face lights up at the thought of her playing. He's also pleased to hear that I live in

Kentish Town and tells me that I would have had my own august pianist neighbour years ago: Clifford Curzon lived there, and Peràhia used to visit a lot.

© Felix Broede

Eventually he leads the way into his sitting room and sits at his gleaming Steinway B and begins to talk about the Ballade. 'The first thing is to understand the structure of the whole piece.' Like Charles Rosen, he sees it as similar to a sonata form, but agrees that eventually the resemblance breaks down. Where he deviates from everybody else I've spoken to is the big restatement of the second tune at bar 106. 'The textbooks will tell you this is in A major. I don't think it's in A major. I think it's in E major.' He plays the passage through to show me what he means. The section certainly arrives emphatically on a chord of A major at bar 107 and again at 115. But in his playing he's more drawn to the giant E major chords at 109 and 117. I'm not sure quite what hangs on this, though; both keys are a very long way from the tonal centre of the piece in G minor, and also from the first statement of the second theme.

Perahia moves on, telling me 'we have to get to the emotional message of the piece first, because that affects the tone, it affects the way one plays it'. 'The connection between technique and musicality and feelings is very strong; all colours in music come from emotional states. They're not put on by themselves, so to speak, they demonstrate emotional turmoil or emotional moods, peace, or whatever. I very often use a story, a metaphor, for what's going on in the tones. It's not an exact story.'

He then asks if I have a 'story' for the piece.

'Only when I get to the second theme – but it's not so much a story as a kind of image of something incredibly soft, bathed in soft light.'

This isn't sufficient for Perahia. I need a story that connects each passage of the piece with the next and allows me to understand it as a whole. So he sets out the story he has for the Ballade (influenced, he says, by an academic friend, Karol Berger). Very often, he says, musicologists think of Chopin's pieces as exodus stories, and his interpretation of the Ballade fits into this. He tells me the Ballade story is split into three basic parts: 'a sense of enslavement, present exile, future rebirth'. [He emails me the next day to say he relies on other sources for this narrative.] And in there, he says, there's 'an additional thing, the second theme – the love. It could be transmitted love of a person even, but basically the love is of the people, of, let's say, Poland which is part and parcel of Chopin.'

He then takes me through the score, showing how the music connects with this interpretation. The beginning, he thinks, establishes the theme of enslavement. Perahia detects sadness, for example, in the sighing descents in the opening bars, 'the sadness about losing; about Poland being under the grip of, at that time . . . I think it was three powers'. In fact, when Chopin started composing the piece in 1831, it was just a few months after the Cadet Revolution, when the military academy in partitioned Poland led an uprising against the Russian Empire. 'I don't know enough about it,' says Perahia, 'but I do know that this was an undercurrent in all of the exiles' life' – including Chopin's, who at this time was in Paris.

Perahia tracks the complex emotions of this enslavement for me as the piece goes on. At bar 56, for example, he sees a pining for revolution – 'suddenly, there's hope, but the hope is in turbulence, the hope is in martial activity . . . war'. This then fades away. At bar 68, 'the pedal goes off, you make a diminuendo and you're in pianissimo for the first time in the piece'. In Perahia's 'story' this pianissimo is 'very personal and, therefore, it's a feeling of love; maybe love to a Polish girl, maybe love to Poland, but it's still love'. Then at bar 94, which is the first restatement of the motif from the piece's first theme, there's a 'big difference'. 'There's this pedal point, which is somewhat menacing . . . an ascent, for the first time ever in this theme . . . It's going to constantly go higher and higher and higher, with all of these octave runs from 119 until the triple fortissimo in 124. Triple fortissimo!' And for Perahia this dramatic ascent constitutes the 'yearning to cut the yoke of the sadness that started the piece', so the yoke of enslavement. 'Notice at 126 he says "più animato" – faster, faster,' noted Perahia. 'It has stirred something quite wild.'

With the intricate emotions of enslavement now firmly established, Perahia thinks the piece moves into a representation of Chopin's exile in France with the playful scherzando middle section. 'This for me,' he explains, 'is *personal*: it's the present exile in Paris, in the society of Paris, with all the fineries, the bourgeois sophistication.' And he tells me to pay attention to the accompanying descents in this section – 'the sighs, the little sighs, which come from the theme'. Might this hint at regret with his present distance for his homeland? When the big second tune comes back at bar 166, Perahia certainly hears something that is 'all for Poland, all for this love that he has'.

And then, finally, comes the representation of rebirth, according to Perahia. This is the 'unleashed' coda. In it Perahia says he hears 'the end of the world and everybody in horror. And then, finally the end of the regime.' Of bar 246 he says, 'I can't help but be reminded of the idea of the tombs opening up, you know, at the end of the world' – might this, then, be the suppressed Polish at last rising up, reborn?

So there it was: an exodus story for the Ballade. Does Perahia construct stories like this for all the pieces he plays? 'All pieces,' he replies. 'It shouldn't be too specific. I think if you only know three basic things, like I say, enslavement, exile, future birth, that's enough. It doesn't need a big story.'

And is he conscious of these stories when he's performing the piece?

'I forget all of that. First of all, it's simple, so it'll be there anyway, I only think of line when I'm playing. Where's the phrase going to? Where's the end of this line? How does it get there?' But he emphasises it's essential that the story informs the playing. 'It's a story about, as I said, the deepest feelings that the composer has, of his hopes, of his dreams, of his suffering. That has to be in the playing somehow.'

We move on from his Ballade story, to talk about his experiences of learning the piece. He managed to play it earlier than anybody else I've spoken to up to now – he was 8! '8, yeah. I still have somewhere my teacher's copy of it with big letters: SING.'

'Did it speak to you at that point?'

'I always loved it. It's a piece I've always loved, my whole life. But it's a piece I went back to many times. I left it, went back to it. I was there when Horowitz made his comeback and he played that Ballade and it was staggering. I've heard it since on YouTube, that performance, it's an amazing performance. So it's a piece I've kept in touch with, so to speak.'

'And how hard is it for you?'

'It's very hard. I think it's one of the hardest pieces in the repertoire. It's what, about ten minutes of music, and in ten minutes of music you have to express a world, and a continuous world. That's a difficulty because it can get segmented, it can get "this little bit is like this" and "that little bit is like that".'

'Well, now I have to play it.'

'How much time do you get to practise it? You probably don't get any time.'

'I practise twenty minutes in the morning and then at the weekends if I can . . . I'm aiming for July. It will have taken me a year.'

That won't do for Perahia. 'You need two hours a day for anything to stick. Twenty minutes is not enough.'

'For anything to stick in the mind?'

'Yeah, because you'll get many ideas and they have to sort of crystallise and focus on something. I'm not excessive over practice, but you do need two hours.'

I quickly change the subject, and tell him what Alex Ross has been saying about recorded music leading to a quest for perfection – and how that has widened the gap between professional and amateur.

'I completely agree with that,' he says.

'And he thinks this has fed into the conservatoires.'

'Well said.'

'And then at some point the recording industry hit the buffers because of everything we understand about digital?'

'Yes, I completely agree – up to a point. I think that's a good point, and we do strive for perfection. But I think it comes from a deeper reason, not just recording. Popular music and classical music was one thing up until around 1920. Let's put it more concretely: 1911, when atonality started. And then you have wonderful pop composers that were still steeped in a classical tradition, people like Gershwin, Cole Porter. Cole Porter, wonderful composer. I love Cole Porter.

'And then classical music became impossible to understand, with the twelve tones, and with the set theories and all of this . . . the layman couldn't understand it. And pop music became, on the other extreme, too simple, no counterpoint; no involved melodies. And I think this relationship between the pop and the classical is very important because it's the memories. You get your memories not only from the great music but from the simple pop tunes. Schubert wrote waltzes, which are gorgeous melodies, and they somehow stay with you. Or Cole Porter's and Gershwin's, Frank Loesser. And I think when that went . . . You get two extremes and separation.'

'And a separation between professional and amateur as well?'

'That's right, exactly. So the amateur can't pick out the tune in any modern music, so they feel lost from the contemporary scene. Even the professional musician can't, and so there's a disparateness. When you try to play classical music you get into a ghetto. Some solutions people have suggested, like a performer should wear a lounge suit, they're superficial. The problem is the language . . . I don't know if it can be fixed, but we've broken down the language between pop and classical. And this has resulted in a rigidness; there's become a metronomisation instead of free tempi – a kind of rigid aspect to classical music that, I think, is destructive to it. This idea of perfection that comes with recording is a very annoying one, but it's a deeper thing.

'You know on YouTube, I was listening to the Horowitz performance of the Ballade, and there's all these idiots writing in, "Oh there's so many mistakes." I don't hear them, I really don't hear them. We're listening so clinically to things now that it's . . . as far as I'm concerned it's a perfect performance. I don't hear those wrong notes that everybody hears. Yes, of course, if I clinically listen – but I'm not listening that way . . . and I'm not struck with, "Oh yeah, well maybe he rubbed his finger against that." I don't hear those things. All these nuts, you know, they write into YouTube, they say, "I can play better than that," so I say, "Well, post it then, let's hear it."'

Our time comes to an end and I head home. When I get in – Perahia's words still ringing in my ears – I sit down and plan to play for two hours. At the end of ninety minutes I've developed a searing pain in my neck. Ten minutes later I actually have to lie on the floor with arms outstretched to get rid of the burning shoots of pain.

Sunday, 13 February

On Tuesday a letter arrives from the Yehudi Menuhin School, the academy set up by the late violinist in 1963 to educate prodigies. It's an invitation to take part in a piano day for adult learners on 6 March. I've been considering this all week. Should I? Could I? I'm not remotely ready yet to perform the entire Ballade in public. But the letter promises coaching from Ruth Nye, the head of keyboards at the school. She's a redoubtable Australian concert pianist who studied with, and was close to, the Chilean pianist Claudio Arrau. This is one of the most terrifying offers I could have imagined – but maybe I need to accept just to make me focus more on my practising.

Another small moment on Wednesday: DreamWorks are definitely optioning the WikiLeaks book, and they want me and others involved in the saga to sign a contract which enables them to 'creatively establish' my character before, during and after WikiLeaks. Literally signing your life away to Steven Spielberg is, er, quite something. And probably one for the lawyers.

Earlier on Wednesday I have time for a morning lesson with Michael. We spend most of the session on the arpeggiated section from bar 166. I'm still really struggling with these big spread broken chords in the LH, as I always knew I would. Over the years, I have grown accustomed to playing with a rigid wrist – but these big spreads require the wrist to rotate through at least 45 degrees. 'We'll come back to this next week,' says Michael, ominously.

Yesterday, with the week over, we get down to Fish Cottage – to find the glass is in! So the external building is now done: walls, windows, doors, the lot. The underfloor heating is working too, and I can really feel how the room will relate to the outside garden and sheep-dotted hill beyond. I spend a happy moment sunk in the builder's chair savouring it.

As I sit there, a couple – I assume they're retired – walk past wanting to know the name of the dry-stone waller who has been working on the project. 'And what's the room for?' they ask. I tell them about the music. The man's face brightened. 'Oh, I used to play the double bass. All kinds of groups and bands. Then, you know, life takes over.'

After my happy moment of contemplation in the builder's chair, I'm jerked back to reality when strange things start happening to my email.

Normally I don't get too paranoid about such stuff, but with WikiLeaks and the hacking story we're currently making a lot of enemies of people who would have the means and motive. I get in touch with the office. The *Guardian* security people can't understand what was happening, so I end up awake till 2 a.m. this morning talking to Google HQ at Cupertino. They agree something odd's happened, but they can't explain it.

In the midst of those strange goings-on, I try to practise. It doesn't go well. I'm back to all the bad old habits of just playing random bits of the whole work, playing it too fast, and then just getting more and more depressed as I realise I'm still miles and miles *and miles* away from playing this piece. After a while I take myself off to the pub, thinking I'm really a bit crap and that this whole thing might be unmanageable.

This morning, though, I go back to it with more focus and resolve, concentrating on the arpeggiated section I'd looked at with Michael on Wednesday. Besides the twisting of the wrists, I realise today that my problem with this section really comes at bar 170, where there is a tricky five-against-six in the RH. I also realise that the problems in the piece are a bit like referred pain. Just as pain sometimes appears in an area far removed from the actual source of the problem, so I find myself thinking I'm struggling with one part of a passage when the real problem actually lies a few notes away.

I'm also learning that progress isn't linear. I have to accept that just because you can play a section one day doesn't mean that you will be able to play it better, or faster, the next day. Reminding myself of that should keep me from the kind of mood I got into during yesterday's practice. Sometimes you have to go back and play things even more slowly. Sometimes you get worse before you get better. I also need to remember the paradox that velocity comes about through slow playing; so I may get frustrated repeatedly practising something slowly, feeling I'm getting nowhere, but I should keep faith that the moment will come when I suddenly make the breakthrough into playing it really fast. Besides, if you try to inch up the speed each day, it's not necessarily guaranteed to get something 'embedded in the fingers'. As I'm learning not to call it.

Also, I receive an email today which snaps me out of yesterday's torpor. It's from a former girlfriend: she says the breast cancer she had five or so years ago has returned. She's optimistic, but dreading the renewed treatment. A few hours later I find myself talking to our next-door neighbour in Blockley. He's been receiving chemotherapy for a year or more now and thinks he'll be on some form of similar regime for the rest of his life. Two

Guardian columnists are undergoing treatment for breast cancer (one is learning the piano at the same time) and another *Guardian* colleague is dealing with a brain tumour diagnosed earlier this year. My friend Jeff Jarvis, whom I saw in Munich two weeks ago, has dealt with treatment of prostate and thyroid cancers. They are all my age or thereabouts. I suppose this is probably no more than the average in terms of anyone's experience of friends and family. But, in terms of getting on with one's life ambitions, I'm hit by more than a tinge of *carpe diem*.

I find twenty minutes this evening for a telephone call with the American pianist Richard Goode. I've met him once – he's a friend of Richard Sennett (as is Perahia) and a thoughtful, down-to-earth musician just reaching his prime in his mid to late 60s. He takes the phone to his piano room as he talks, interrupting his thoughts with the occasional musical illustration.

The Ballade was one of the first major Chopin pieces he played. He doesn't remember learning it, but thinks he must have been a teenager. He chimes with others I've spoken to when I ask why he thinks it might appeal to that age group. 'Passion, Baroque, tragedy, all spelled out very dramatically,' he says. 'It's a very wonderfully written piece but it's also, emotionally speaking, very direct and somewhat simple because it doesn't have the convolutions of some of the pieces like the Polonaise-Fantaisie or the fourth Ballade. I think in a certain way the emotions are very stark, enormous contrasts and great tenderness. There's a sense of doom and then, of course, the scene of destruction at the end. It was very attractive to me at that age certainly.'

But Goode then spent many years away from the Ballade. 'I had difficulty identifying myself as a Chopin player for all kinds of reasons,' he explains. 'I do think that Chopin is a special kind of composer; and the style of Chopin is a special kind of style, not necessarily always harmonious and compatible with playing some of the German classic composers' – that is, the likes of Mozart, Beethoven and Schubert, whom Goode naturally gravitates towards in his repertoire. 'But in recent years I've moved much nearer to Chopin and feel much more identification to Chopin.' When he did come back to the Ballade, 'the outlines remained very clear'. Distance and a more experienced eye gave him a fresh perspective on the piece. 'I might have seen a little more about the craft of it because it's remarkably written, and just looking at it a little bit now I see that the intertwining of motifs, I think, is more remarkable than I probably saw when I was much younger. That's one of the things I think that makes the piece so wonderful: the intricacy of the craft.'

'Can you give me an example of that?'

'I mean throughout . . . the way the first phrase in bar 8 reappears at the end of the second theme [bar 82], so beautifully interwoven. So that after a while you begin to feel the unity of the whole, no matter how disparate emotionally things are. Somehow everything is tied up with every-thing else. At the same time you have this taking fire and bravura and virtuosity, and so forth, but still you have the connection with the motific working which I think deepens the whole thing.'

But his admiration of the piece is not without reservations. 'I love the ending, but I think that it is maybe a little, for me, a little too unrelated to what was before.'

'It feels a bit grafted on rather than growing out of it?'

'A little bit. You feel in a piece like the Polonaise-Fantaisie and the Barcarolle and, for that matter, the third Ballade, complete integration of the end to the beginning. But then that's part of the poetic idea probably, that these are codas of which there is a sort of disassociation because every-thing goes up in flames.'

I ask Goode if – like Murray Perahia – he ever approached pieces in terms of a kind of story or a narrative.

'I don't,' he replies. 'In various pieces of Chopin I have certain moments where certain things are happening which I can't avoid the feeling of story, I can't avoid certain moments for example in the Polonaise-Fantaisie where the time seems to shift and where you seem to be going back into the past. And there are always moments like that in these pieces, but as far as a consistent story, I don't do that. I feel that the music implies all kinds of things but I don't feel the need to put a definite story to it. You feel the story is taking you to different regions, different realms and of course that's where the music and the narrative come together. The music implies the different regions of the narrative.'

I then put to the test Perahia's theory about the big restatement of the second tune. Does Goode think it's in A major or E major?

'A major, or E major? It's all in A major. It comes in A major, doesn't it? I'm looking at it here, the big fortissimo statement? It's unambiguously A major. Can it be otherwise?'

'Well, Murray Perahia says it's E major.'

'I'll give him a call! E major?'

'He says everyone says it's an A major but he's convinced it's an E major because, for him—'

'I see what he means. It's maybe something to think about.'

'He says it affects the way he thinks about the tonal structure.'

'Of course, it eventually gets to an E flat later on. That's true. Very interesting.'

To conclude, I ask Goode to give me his take on the gap between amateur and professional, and the extent to which the recording has affected it. He is of the same mind as Perahia and Alex Ross on this – that the cult of precision precipitated by recording is generally restrictive. Goode underlines the importance of recordings made before the onset of the drive for perfection, because in them 'we hear styles of playing from the early part of the century and realise how different they are from what we do nowadays and, in a certain way, how much broader the possibilities are. I think that can be liberating for people who are a little bit raised too much on the styles of the last ten years, for example, or fifteen years, to go back and listen to other styles and realise how many more things were possible at a time when, after all, the players were closer to the time of the composers.' He tells me that at the music festival he co-directs – Marlboro Music, held in the southern foothills of Vermont – they have some sessions where the participants listen to CDs 'of early recordings of the late Beethoven quartets and so forth' and people 'are quite astonished at how different they sound'.

Friday, 18 February

Another lesson with Michael on Wednesday. We don't go back to the arpeggiated chords, but focus on the bits I might play if I do go to the YM school in March. This means looking at the opening, which isn't remotely there yet, and then the coda. We do just the first four bars of the coda, and I can actually play them – though I still can't get the pedals on the right beat. It's that pah-oom structure again, and I'm still pedalling the oom instead of the pah – I've got to learn to bring the pedal down on the first and third beats of the bar rather than (as feels more natural to me) the second and fourth. So Michael slows this right down: we probably spend thirty minutes on just those four bars. I've also had time to practise most mornings this week.

Throughout the week at work, I've been ensuring that all parties are prepared for when the phone-hacking story blows up in earnest, as it looks like it surely will at some point. On Thursday I have lunch with Jemima Khan, one of the hacking victims. It's important that the beleaguered phone-hacking sorority/fraternity stay together and in good spirits. She hints that Hugh Grant might be willing to play a higher-profile role as the story develops.

Saturday, 19 February

I'll be away from the piano for a couple of days this week as I'm going to Madrid for a debate hosted by *El País*. So I'm trying to practise with complete focus today. The central heating isn't working at Fish Cottage, and nor is the broadband. No email, no distractions. I've just been sitting at the piano trying the Charles Cooke–recommended technique of playing with my eyes shut. Especially the coda, because so much of this is about spatial awareness, trying to work out where the fingers are going to land without much time to think about it. You've got to be sure of distances.

And playing with your eyes shut forces you to slow down – obviously. You're thinking very carefully what the next notes or chords are. It takes me about ten minutes to play through the coda with my eyes shut, and though that's painfully slow and is littered with long pauses as I try to remember just what comes next, I do, in fact, remember most of it. I then play it with my eyes open, and it feels like the exercise has been instantly helpful. Perhaps the exercise is allowing me to develop a spatial awareness that I don't have naturally.

Thursday, 23 February

I'm in Madrid for the WikiLeaks debate with the editors of *Le Monde*, *NYT*, *Der Spiegel* and *El País* and some of the reporters involved in the story. It's followed by a private dinner cooked by the most exclusive chef in the world, Ferran Adrià, the head of El Bulli. But our hosts at *El País* have surpassed even that, arranging for their guests to have a pre-dinner private viewing of *Guernica* and an hour in the Museo del Prado, where we stood alone in front of Bosch's *Garden of Earthly Delights*. Extraordinary to have this private intimate moment with one of the great cultural artefacts of western art. Which, as I thought about it later, made me want to see the original autographed manuscript of the Ballade – just to look for myself at the scratched pen strokes on paper that gave birth to 180 years of performances. And pain.

Where is it? I remember a book saying it was in the ownership of Gregor Piatigorsky, the American cellist. A couple of weeks ago I looked online to see if I could uncover any other leads as to its whereabouts. My search led me to Horowitz's website, where I got distracted by the comprehensive list of his every recital, which regularly ended with the G minor Ballade. He often played the Ballades in reverse order, presumably to end on the impact of those final crashing octaves.

This page also confirmed that Horowitz played the piece on his return – after an absence of thirty-one years – to the London stage. I was there. It was 22 May 1982, and I had the job of interviewing him in his suite at the Connaught Hotel.

This is what I wrote:

> He plays for an hour each morning; each evening he slips into a taxi to eat out with friends. He is 77, which gives him the excuse, in the nicest possible way, to pass over the questions which bore him. He can remember all 630 Scarlatti sonatas, but not a thing about London. Famous premieres? 'Oh there was the Prokofiev sonata, the Barber sonata . . . I don't even remember them now.' He has not been here since 1951 because he was bored of travel, bored of changing hotel beds every night, bored of playing concerts five nights a week. Now he never plays from November to February (too cold) and when he does give concerts he gives them on Saturday afternoons. This is so he can go to sleep afterwards; so that New York audiences don't get mugged and so that his audiences don't fall asleep in mid-sonata. The modern style of piano playing is, he says 'more notes than spirit. They play a little bit more like a typewriter than with spirit.'

So I definitely heard the great Horowitz play the Chopin G minor Ballade. But I don't remember it at all. Surely not everyone's memory is *that* bad.

Sunday, 26 February

Yesterday afternoon there was chamber music at Richard Sennett's. As usual, it's impossible to pin him down on who will be there, and with which combination of instruments. I email him to see what music to bring, but to no avail. In the end, it's a collection of regulars: Clive; Charlotte; Susanna; Mark. To which Richard has added two more violins – Stuart, a research student, and Michelle, a former professional violinist.

I've brought the Bach Double Violin Concerto with me – which is just piano and violins. But, after five minutes on the Petrucci Library (that wonderful Wikipedia of sheet music), we find viola and cello parts, print them off and are away. We do the same for the Mozart Sinfonia Concertante, which somebody else has brought along. After playing those two, we end up with some Dvořák and Shostakovich before sitting down for a plate of food. And then we head off to hear Maurizio Pollini at the Festival Hall. The only living man, according to some, who can actually play the G minor Ballade exactly as written.

It's packed to the rafters – nearly 3,000 people there to hear the maestro playing the three last Schubert sonatas. Sitting there, waiting for Pollini to come on stage, I try to visualise the Ballade, but realise I can't 'see' even the first bar. I have no pictorial memory of what it looks like, no intrinsic visual sense of what key it's in or what the notes are. I feel slightly depressed, so do my best to recall Ray Dolan's words about procedural memory.

As we arrived, we'd met Richard's friend Rafael Viñoly, the Uruguyan architect, who turns out to be both a friend of Pollini and himself a keen pianist. I tell him about my Ballade project. 'Oh you must talk to the *New York Times* art critic, Michael Kimmelman. He's obsessed with the Ballade. Plays it all the time.'

Then the main event. Pollini – the man who many think has made *the* great recording of the Ballade – plays with an incredible light touch. But though the performance was smooth, it also felt somewhat contained and a bit no-nonsense. I wasn't convinced it ever quite hit the heights.

The next day Rafael emails me with Kimmelman's contact details. Cc-ing Richard, he also mentioned that Pollini is giving up smoking. Richard emails back to say that explains why his performance was a bit subdued.

I Google Kimmelman and find a magazine piece he wrote in 1999 about entering an amateur piano-playing competition in Fort Worth in which he played the G minor Ballade. He is evidently a much more accomplished pianist than I could ever hope to be. He nearly went to conservatoire instead of university, but decided against it. He then put the piano aside until he was around 40. Like me. But when he came back to it he was good enough to start giving concerts in public again quite soon thereafter. So there the similarity ends. But we must meet.

Wednesday, 2 March

I've now resolved to go to the YM piano day – in just three days' time – and I think I'm going to play either the first two or the last four pages. At this morning's lesson with Michael, I try a run-out of both again. The first two pages were much improved on my last attempt in front of Michael. They are of course the easiest technically, but it felt as if, at last, I am dealing with a passage on a musical, rather than a purely technical, level. The coda's a different matter. A fortnight ago with Michael, I made a very decent fist of its first four bars. Today, I played twenty bars, and I merely scramble through them. Michael drily 'reassures' me, remarking that I must remember this is to be a masterclass, not a performance.

Later in the day, there's a BBC report that the government has decided to give the BSkyB deal the green light. If the phone-hacking story ever explodes, I wonder if they'll feel the same way.

Saturday, 5 March

It's the YM piano day tomorrow. Apprehension increasing by the hour. But tonight I have the perfect distraction, dinner at Claus Moser's. Two other great figures of his generation are there – David Attenborough and the former high court judge Nicholas Browne-Wilkinson. And Murray and Ninette Perahia. And David and Louise Miliband.

Perahia is about to try his first concert after the seven-month lay-off from his hand injury. 'After meeting you I nearly played the G minor Ballade to come back,' he says. 'But maybe I need to ease myself in a little more gently.' I ask him again about the trapeze leaps in the coda. He says he has been thinking about Chopin and realises that so much of what he writes requires a movement like a bird beak opening. He demonstrates with his hand, closing the fingers and thumb and then stretching his hand back open. That was the movement needed in those leaps as you come down. As he speaks I'm trying to imagine what he means. I guess that he plays the first A flat on the second beat of bar 216 with a relaxed, or closed hand, which then opens like a bird beak to hit the top two notes before closing again. 'These things you discover so late!'

It's not the right moment to take him over to Claus' old piano for a demonstration, alas. Over dinner, Perahia tells of how he got started on the piano as a 3½-year-old living in the Bronx. His father had encouraged him, though he knew nothing about music. His mother still hates music. So no one really pushed him. He says that when he was 17, he was offered lessons by Horowitz – but the old rascal wanted $100 a lesson, paid two years in advance. There was no way Perahia or his family could afford that, and he wasn't sure he wanted it anyway. Much later in life – when he was about 40 – Horowitz did end up giving him some lessons, but this time for free.

There is much more piano talk. Claus – now 88 – says he wonders when he will give up. The other evening, he tells us, he sat down and played so badly it gave him no pleasure. And it turns out that David Attenborough, himself 84, is also a keen amateur pianist – he is evidently in awe of Perahia, and there is more than a little bit of awe in return. In the middle of a discussion about music and memory, he tells us, 'I was at the piano the other day and found myself playing a piece I hadn't touched for fifty years. It was in there somewhere.' So the procedural memory at work again, refusing to go away.

Sunday, 6 March

Drive down to woody Surrey countryside – with the M25 a not-too-distant background hum – for the adult 'piano clinic'. It's been billed as a day for '5–85-year-olds'. There are about 150 people there, not all of them playing, split into five groups.

Before things get under way, I bump into Malcolm Singer, whom I last saw at university in the mid-1970s, and who is now the music director of the Menuhin School. He is wearing a bright bow tie – the first person I've met for many years to wear one in the hours of daylight. He says I have a treat in store – the concert Fazioli they have bought for the school. 'We tried ten Steinways and eventually found one. Then we flew to Sacile [the home of the Fazioli], where there were two pianos. One was beautiful and the other even more beautiful.'

If this is a 'clinic', then the top consultant is Ruth Nye, as promised in the letter I received in February. Her bio says she grew up in Australia and was invited to New York to be a pupil of Claudio Arrau by the man himself after he heard her play in Australia. 'After settling in the UK Nye travelled with Arrau on various concert tours both in the UK and abroad covering a period of thirty years up until his death in 1991.' She tells me later that her biography is coming out soon – mainly covering the years with Arrau.

The participants – around thirty or so of us – are organised into two groups, the aim being to allow each of us one session with Ruth or one of the other professors. The day kicks off in the little concert hall with a 6-year-old playing the last movement of a Haydn sonata – a questionable motivational introduction for a bunch of adult learners wondering if they've left it too late.

Confidence sinks further with the first pianist up, William Corke, a 40-ish digital marketing man, who polishes off an extremely accomplished performance of Debussy's 'Homage à Rameau' from *Images*, followed by a little teaching from Ruth. It's obviously unnecessary to compare your own skills with others on such occasions. But it's not so much competitive – more the fear of being completely shown up. I don't want to be better than William Corke, just not really, utterly, embarrassingly worse.

But, in these terms alone, there is comfort in the next pianist up, Frank

Watson, a snowy-haired 80-year-old retired research chemist (crystallography and protein structures) who started learning seriously when he was 78. 'I'm just a beginner,' he tells the audience before he embarks on the first movement of Schumann's *Kinderscenen*. 'I'd never even seen a piano until I was 15 and tried to teach myself over the years. But it was only eighteen months ago that I got serious and made any progress.' If you've never seen a grown man shaking like a leaf you've never attended an amateur piano day. Poor Frank was trembling with nerves, so much so it was astonishing his hands could make any contact with the keys at all. Ruth Nye rather brilliantly calmed him down, soothed him into concentrating on a small section of the piece – and, before you knew it, he'd played it all.

Then it was me. I stare into the audience, which, besides the adults, has a sprinkling of young prodigies staring back. 'How many of you have tried this piece?' asks Ruth before I embark on anything. To my horror several hands go up. My mouth goes dry.

My masterplan is simple: play the opening two pages and then start on the coda at a very steady tempo . . . and beg for advice. But immediately, the opening of the first tune throws me. Chopin's fingering asks for the use of consecutive little fingers (5-5) as you come down the descending first phrase, and that's exactly what I've played every time I've practised. But today I use 5-3. Why? 5-4 would at least be a plausible alternative, but 5-3 makes no sense at all. I'm sure no one in the audience notices, but I can feel Ruth's eyes piercing into the back of my hand. Somehow the mind has to blot out the immediate self-questioning – *Why did that happen? Am I about to make another mistake? Can I play any of it?* – and press on. Which I do, plausibly enough, ending firmly at the end of page 2.

'Carry on.'

Ah. But page 3 is not ready.

There's clearly no point in arguing, though . . . so I play page 3. Ruth then says she wants the audience to understand the structure of the piece, so would I mind playing all the versions of the second tune that occur throughout the piece? I mind very much since that means having to play the devilish big crashing chords and the LH arpeggios at bar 166.

And then she wants me to play all the statements of the first theme . . . And then the beginning of the coda. It starts confidently, but about twenty bars in I'm struck by fatal indecision as to whether to look at the music or the hands. The mind goes blank. I pause and look helplessly at the music for a microsecond – though it feels like a slow-motion frame-by-frame disaster movie – and recover. Mouth parched once more. Ruth makes some kindly comments, but my main instinct is to get off the stage as fast as humanly possible.

We take a break. William, the impressive Debussy player, tells me he plays for ten minutes every day and then again in the evenings. His is a familiar pattern – he learned the piano at school, dropped it in his 20s and then started missing it in his 30s. Like me, if he doesn't play in the mornings he now feels quite differently about the day ahead – we share that feeling of the brain being settled for the day by whatever it is that happens when you are forced to concentrate on music for a bit.

After the break two women (Diane and someone billed as D, or Dee, Major – can that really be her name?) play a Mozart duet. A woman called Caroline plays a Grade 5 piece by Walter Caroll. And Terry Lewis, the general manager at Fazioli pianos, plays a very passable and limpid 'Un sospiro' by Liszt.

Then I'm back up and trying the coda again. 'It is fiendishly difficult,' Ruth tells the others, before asking me to play the flying-trapeze section. I do this, and like all piano teachers she has the unerring ability to spot the point of greatest weakness. The problem, she correctly states, is that my hand is spending too much time in mid-air between the notes as I make my octave leaps. I have to be far more 'sticky' and close to the keys or I'll never land accurately. She shows me a hand movement that is identical to the Murray Perahia bird beak – the hand extending and then crouching.

She then grasps my wrist and pushes it down into the keys. But I'm confused as the only way to do this bird-beak rotation seems to be to elevate the wrist. She seizes my arm and shakes it around. I can see what she's driving at. I'd been fooling myself that I was making progress on these leaps.

After the masterclass, I stay for the concert by pupils. The star was Rosalind Phang from Malaysia with a really beautifully done 'Moonlight' Sonata. I drive back round the M25 feeling sober. The Lot piano course is only four months away and, on today's evidence, the piece is nowhere near ready for a public outing. But the thought of Frank, starting the piano at 78, and taking a bow on stage after his debut recital at 80, cheers me up.

Sunday, 13 March

A weekend at Fish Cottage. The news cycle has been extraordinary and relentless over the past few days, particularly for the foreign desk, which is trying to stretch its resources to covering the Arab Spring and, since Friday, this terrible tsunami. The Japanese disaster coincided with the decision that we were finally free to name the corrupt private investigator who had been working for the *News of the World* despite having served a jail sentence for corruption and being accused of a violent crime. But the timing means that a story that would have broken onto front pages is barely noticed.

But the sun is out at Fish Cottage, and so are a few daffodils. The music room is all but done. The inside space is light and feels linked to the garden and the water. I still can't quite believe it's there – more or less how I imagined it. In a couple of weeks there will be cherry blossom, the ground will have been turfed over and the building will begin to settle into its surroundings, an arc of trees behind it and a gentle grassy sheep-specked hill in front of it.

I'm delighted with the room, but much of the weekend has been spent trying to find the whereabouts of our star Middle Eastern reporter, Ghaith Abdul-Ahad. Ghaith is a charismatic, handsome, brave Iraqi who has been writing for the *Guardian* for several years now, having originally trained as an architect in his native Baghdad. He is fascinated by all the conflicts in his region and has a relentless thirst to report on all of them – but never from the 'official' point of view. He has no interest in being embedded with the US or British armies; he'd much rather trek for a week across hostile mountain terrain in search of the Taliban or Somali pirates. Which makes for unique, wonderfully informative writing (and pictures). But it does land him in trouble – and he appears to be in trouble again. He's disappeared from radar, after trying to enter Libya from the Tunisian border, travelling with tribesmen.

The first time he disappeared (three years ago, kidnapped in the mountains of NE Afghanistan) a week of my life disappeared too. We set up a kidnap office in the *Guardian*, bought a number of air mattresses to sleep on, and took it in turns to keep the operation going twenty-four hours a day. It became a kind of war room, with giant maps and security specialists on tap as we tried to find someone to drive up to the mountains after dark – probably the most dangerous valley on the face of the globe – to discuss his release terms. After one failed attempt (involving the relations of Afghan holy men who happened to be living in Wembley) we pulled it off. Next time he vanished it was north of Kabul. He was off to meet a Taliban commander and (it later transpired) became caught up in a firefight with the Americans.

Ghaith always suspects that his mobile phone is being tracked – he is probably right about that – and so his instinct is always to turn it off, and never to use it. But that makes us all very uneasy back in London since we have no idea at all where he is. We've heard nothing for several days now. I've been sitting in Blockley ringing every contact I can think of – especially highest-level people in the Turkish government. Around lunchtime I manage to get through to Gaddafi's son Saif al-Islam, probably the most influential person in the country barring the old man himself. He says he knows nothing about Ghaith, but will get back to me. I doubt either part of this is true. It occurs to me I might have to go to Libya myself if nothing else turns up – though I'm actually due to fly to Austin, Texas, tomorrow to take part in the SXSW festival of music and technology, which has got a major *Guardian* presence this year.

Despite all this, I have time over the weekend to fit in another interview with a pianist. This time it is Emanuel Ax, the great American pianist whom I've long admired. Like Richard Goode, he only has time for an interview on the phone. So – in between the calls to Libya and to the spooks – I ring the 62-year-old Ax from Fish Cottage.

We dive straight into discussing the Ballade. Like so many of the others I've spoken to, Ax first picked it up as a teenager. I tell him what people have said about the appeal of the 'visceral' elements of the piece to a teenage sensibility. He sees something of this in his own case, of course, but like Noriko Ogawa thinks that perhaps the main appeal at that age, for somebody who is beginning to think of themselves as a 'serious pianist', is the difficulty of the piece. 'First of all, it's a real hurdle,' he tells me. 'It's obviously, on the face of it, incredibly challenging, so if you want to be a pianist you think, "Well, maybe I'll try this piece."'

Ax says that though he first played it at 15, he certainly hadn't mastered it by that age, and he didn't think it was at a performable standard until he was in his early 20s. His problems with the piece have persisted. 'I don't think I ever played the coda accurately and I think I still don't play the coda accurately, to be honest. You know, it's a very, very hard thing.' When he has played it accurately, he says, 'it's been mostly a matter of luck'. And he thinks that everyone has a similar experience to this. 'It's impossible for most of us actually. I can tell you that I heard Pollini play it impeccably. Well, he plays everything impeccably. I used to hear him so much when I was young and he just, he never did anything wrong, ever. That was staggering.'

Thinking of Murray Perahia, I ask Ax if he thinks the Ballade tells a story. He does, but says that it's not the kind of story that can be easily expressed, or at least put into words. He quotes Mendelssohn, who says 'it's not that music is too vague to put into words, it's too specific to put into words'. Ax thinks this principle can be applied to stories in music. 'I'm one of the people that believe that there's always some kind of story in music, that it's about something, but I think everybody has his own story and there's nothing distinct, there's nothing I could put into words about any of it. I think you definitely feel a narrative in this piece, as you do in all the others, but I think this one is so multifaceted.'

We go through the narrative as he sees it. 'The very beginning – it's like, how "The Rime of the Ancient Mariner" starts? "He stoppeth one of three." He grabs the guy by, basically, by his shirt and says, "You're going to listen to this story." That's for me the same thing when Chopin hits that C, you know, it means "stop and listen to what I'm going to tell you". But then what Chopin has to say is hard to define; you can only track the shifting moods in the story he's telling: the A major section is so triumphant. Then the E flat, the waltz stuff, you know, is so brilliant and light and elegant. Then you have, right after that, this ecstatic burst in E-flat major. The coda is totally terrifying, ending up with those jagged . . . that violent dissonance, coming together, I don't know, it's scary.'

I then want to talk about memory. Does Ax find that after a break from the piece he can return to it and find it is still there 'in the fingers'? As I expected, he absolutely can. But this has its disadvantages, 'because what you would like sometimes is maybe a new way of doing it. I don't mean in conception; I just mean physically. Sometimes it would be great to find a different approach, move your hand a different way or use a different fingering or something that might make things sound better. And sometimes if it stays with you all the time you have a hard time cutting off what you learned before. You know, unlearning the bad.'

Ax starts to talk about the standard of contemporary professional playing.

© J. Henry Fair

'I have to tell you,' he says, 'that these days the level of pianistic prowess is so phenomenal that I think none of this is difficult for any of the young kids. It's all easy. I don't know if you've heard Yuja Wang and Lang Lang and people like that? I mean nothing is difficult. This becomes a kind of, "Yeah, fine, what the heck, the G minor Ballade!"' He agrees with Alex Ross that this has come about 'because of recordings, because availability to everybody of the best piano playing, of the highest level, has changed what kids strive for. The whole idea of having records which are beautifully engineered and fixed up has changed all of music.' And, like Alex, he doesn't think this is an entirely positive trend. 'There's hardly any room to play a messy performance. That used to be the norm, that used to be perfectly OK, and musicians were able to come to a concert and actually relax and not worry about detail sometimes and let go and play inspired performances in spite of a couple of lapses and I think that doesn't happen any longer.'

But Ax doesn't agree with Ross' theory that the digital revolution might bring about a loosening up in the cult of precision. 'No, that aspect won't change because now we have people who literally don't play any wrong notes – it's as simple as that. I thank goodness that I'm a very old guy now and, you know, in another couple of years people will expect me to play very, very badly, and that's good. I'm very relieved, you know. I just think it's a phenomenon that won't go back now.'

He agrees, though, that 'the unfortunate part of this development' is the widening gap between professional musicians and amateurs. 'Everybody who wants to,' he says, 'should play the piano.' People should remember the enjoyment of playing just for themselves and not worrying about holding themselves up against the daunting standards of modern professionals. Ax is dedicated to bridging the gap between the two worlds and getting this message across, he tells me. 'I try to play chamber music with people I know from every corner of life. I've got lawyer friends I play with; I've got doctor friends I play with. Wherever I go I try to arrange things like that and I think that would be a great loss if people stopped doing that. It's very akin to tennis for me, just because my wife doesn't play like Kuznetsova she still goes out and plays, you know, it's fun to do it. And I think we need the same attitude in music.'

So (he finishes by saying) he's very pleased that I'm attempting the Ballade, and promises I'll get an 'incredible satisfaction out of it' in the end. He signs off with some wonderfully upbeat advice: 'Look, you won't play the piece like Pollini, but neither will I, so we're both distant from the ideal. That's fine, nothing wrong with that.'

Monday, 14 March

It's confirmed overnight that Ghaith is being held in prison somewhere in Libya. The outlook is not good for him as he has an Iraqi passport rather than a British one – and even if he had a British one, the embassy in Libya is long closed. The international tensions surrounding Libya are heightening by the hour. The French and British have both been talking about imposing a no-fly zone and there's a lot of talk about military strikes. So I head down to the Libyan consulate this morning – a rather run-down building in a very posh part of London which was hardly teeming with people trying to get into Libya. I wanted to see if I could get a visa to go to Tripoli. If yes, I'll fly to Libya. If no, I'll set off for Texas.

While I'm at the consulate, the conductor Daniel Harding emails from Tokyo for advice on radiation risk from the nuclear reactors in the north of the country which are imploding post-earthquake (such are the demands for information on editors). I ping his email to our science editor, and forward the (partially reassuring) response to Daniel. Daniel emails back: 'People here amazing and determined. Mahler 5, just after quake, was an unforgettable experience.'

The upshot of my trip to the consulate is that by 3 p.m. I am on a flight to Cairo instead of Dallas. I arrive at the hotel at 11 p.m., just in time to whisk into the city centre to see (a now deserted) Tahrir Square. There are plenty of tanks and armoured cars around, but the square itself is back to its rather unremarkable pre-revolutionary state. I'm travelling with Ian Black, the veteran Middle East editor of the *Guardian*, who speaks fluent Hebrew and Arabic and has been visiting the region for nearly forty years. Together we've been keeping a log of our attempts, over many days now, to pull all possible strings to get Ghaith out. Looking at it today, Ian remarked on how a newspaper like the *Guardian* has the most extraordinary ability to tap into such a wide net of contacts at such a time. He's right. Between us we've managed to mobilise prime ministers, foreign ministries, spies, presidents, international humanitarian organisations, CEOs and even premiership footballers (one of Gaddafi's sons being madly keen on the sport).

Ian is a man completely absorbed in the politics and culture of the region. In the taxi back from Tahrir Square, knowing of my musical interests, he says he's heard that the distinguished Foreign Office diplomat Robert Cooper is married to 'some sort of pianist'. I realise there is only a very small group of people – i.e. foreign-policy wonks – who would approach the marriage of Cooper and the world-famous Mitsuko Uchida from that particular end of the telescope.

Tuesday, 15 March

We are up at six to catch a (deserted) Egyptair flight to Libya. I am nearly refused exit from Egypt on account of my Libyan visa not having been translated into Arabic – a common scam, according to Ian. I am able to resolve this by purchasing a return flight, which seems to satisfy the authorities – though, increasingly, there's no certainty there will be any flights out of Libya any time soon. We are met off the plane by Libyan officials, who take us off through a VIP exit and into a waiting black Audi 6. The airport has become an enormous makeshift camp, thronged with the tents of the thousands of Africans trying to escape Libya.

We are driven to the Corinthia Hotel – avoiding the Rixos, where the main body of journalists are camped out, in order to keep low-profile. It's a huge new hotel, with maybe 800 bedrooms, but barely any guests. Echoing marble halls, red carpets and gilt. There's a skeleton service at best: almost all the staff have fled. We are warned by the officials that all our conversations will be listened to: spooks will monitor everything. There is no phone signal and no internet, so, for the first time in years, I'm completely out of touch with home or the office. Our colleague Peter Beaumont has been in Libya for two weeks and is staying at the hotel. He is edgy and wired. And it's catching. Within minutes, Ian and I are both feeling uncomfortable. Peter's been picked up two or three times already and detained, once for seven hours. The *Telegraph* correspondent has been picked up four times. An Al Jazeera correspondent has been shot dead; three BBC staff badly beaten up. Peter has a satphone he can rig up later and which can download emails very slowly. Otherwise he has one Libyan mobile phone with a dead battery and not much credit – the spooks follow westerners on every trip out of the hotel, so it's extraordinarily difficult to get top-up credit or new SIM cards for the mobile – and only Libyan SIM cards will work. It's totalitarian control of all means of communication.

It is very eerie walking down the deserted corridors, past empty bedrooms to my own. There's a latch on the door, but there are dents and missing paint by this. It's the same on every bedroom door, suggesting all have been broken into at some stage. In the echoing downstairs lobby there's a Czech-made Petrof grand piano that has seen better days. I run my fingers over the keys, several of which are stuck.

The three of us take a walk around the Medina, opposite the hotel. This is forbidden: no journalists are supposed to leave the hotel without informing their minders, but we risk it. We go through endless narrow alleyways, glimpsing barber shops, workshops, food shops, more workshops. No one stops to talk or hassle. We end up at Green Square, the scene of the various attempted rebel rallies, which is now full of Gaddafi counter-rallies. It is only here that dark-glassed men ask who we are. Just forty-eight hours ago I was sitting in our Blockley garden.

Such is the life of a foreign correspondent – now distant in my own past. I am transported back to covering the Iran–Iraq War years ago and how one day you're living in the civilised norms of North London, the next literally walking through minefields, looking for signs of chemical weapons and dead bodies. Then two days later, you're enjoying a bowl of pasta during a three-hour stopover in Rome, on your way back to North London family life.

As we walk there is a phone call on Peter's mobile from Saif's chief of staff, Mohammed Ismail. He wants to meet. We then receive another from a woman called Jackie, an American PR from LA who is, incongruously enough, acting for another of Gaddafi's sons, Saadi. Back at the hotel, Jackie arrives first: 31, blonde, smart. It is bizarre stuff as she launches into slick West Coast PR shtick on behalf of 'my boss'. 'I don't do politics,' she says. 'I represent the business interests.' But she then does a very smooth job explaining away the politics: she talks of 'the family'. 'This has drawn them together, they are working together.' She sounds for all the world as if this were a Midwestern American clan coping with an errant teenage son who has gone off the rails.

Then Mohammed Ismail arrives with Mr Abdulmajeed Ramadan El-Dursi, the chairman of the Foreign Media Authority, Great Socialist People's Libyan Arab Jamahiriya – aka head of their foreign press operation. I assume this means the message has got through that an editor-in-chief is in town. We sit in armchairs in the empty marble lobby. Dursi is in his late 60s, tweed jacket, immaculate manners, gentle voice, urbane, quizzical, exhausted. But I suspect Mohammed Ismail will be the key figure in the next twenty-four hours. He is a different proposition – two-day stubble, handsome, intelligent eyes, but overweight – in jeans, a blue blazer with four brass buttons. And four mobile phones, which he lays out on the table in front of us. All Nokias, two black, one grey, one white. Over the next two hours they keep bursting into life in turn – each with different ringtones. Every time one goes off he stares at the number, rarely answering.

We talk business. Mohammed Ismail promises to return at 10.45 tomorrow and take us to meet Ghaith at eleven. He is fine, he says. We can then leave by a flight to Cairo or Casablanca. But we know it's too late for Cairo. The situation is escalating so rapidly that there are now virtually no Egyptian flights in or out of Libya. So it will have to be Casablanca – though that creates its own problems, given Ghaith's Iraqi passport. Peter disappears to start fixing the flight.

We then talk about Ghaith in different terms. I sketch him as a human being – irrepressible, human, messy, brilliant. I joke he is as much a problem to us as to them. I want to make them realise they are dealing with flesh and blood. Jackie cuts in: 'Gentlemen, what sort of coverage are you planning to give this?' Now that's an LA publicist speaking. I answer honestly:

'Ghaith has never been one to write about himself. It's not his style. He doesn't put himself at the heart of the story.' I tell them he had been in scrapes twice before and didn't write self-glorifying accounts. Ismail asks, 'When?' I have a heart-sinking feeling he is going to Google Ghaith to see if I'm telling the truth.

Jackie says she's keen that everything remains low-key, and Ismail agrees. He evidently wants Ghaith out of the country, problem solved, not hanging around in Tripoli. After an hour it becomes apparent the business is done, but Ismail and Jackie, who are, currently, as close as you can get to the Gaddafi family, stay and keep talking, reasonably openly: they do not, one suspects, want needlessly to make an enemy of the *Guardian*. Peter is now back in the room, so he goes about pumping them for all the information he can. But we end up somewhere between small talk and bonding. Ismail's kids go to prep school in Hampshire, it transpires. He has been in the habit of visiting London every weekend.

After another half-hour or so, they leave. The three of us then go for supper in the empty hotel restaurant, with skeleton staff again. There is distant gunfire. Peter thinks it is probably just 'celebrations' in Green Square. The government troops have just taken (we discovered in our meeting) the key town of Ajdabiya. A waiter whispers it is all wrong. 'They should not be celebrating killing fellow Libyans.'

After eating we go up to the roof, where there are a handful of other journalists trying to get satphone connections. We stand on the hotel's incongruous artificial grass lawn listening to the sirens, tracer bullets, automatic fire. Peter pulls us inside: 'I've seen these guys shooting. They have no idea where they're aiming.'

Just before I turn in there is a call from Ismail. If we're struggling with finding flights, he thinks the prime minister of Turkey may lay on a private jet. The trip has just become even more surreal. So we could be in Turkey this time tomorrow evening or Casablanca. If it's Casablanca, movie-loving tradition dictates I must find a piano there and play it.

Should I ever make a book out of my endeavour with the Ballade, I resolve, I've at least got the title: *Play It Again*. It has two associations apart from the possibility that I might be sitting in front of an old upright piano in Casablanca this time tomorrow night: returning to the piano as an adult, and the fact that it's only by endless repetition that any progress is made. The journalist in me also likes the fact that it's a misquote. Bogart never said it.

It's midnight when I get to bed. Gaddafi is live on TV ranting to a crowd of loyalists.

Wednesday, 16 March

Today the Steinway is due to arrive at Fish Cottage, and I wake to find myself still 1,500 miles from home. I have breakfast with Peter and Ian. There are maybe half a dozen other hotel guests there. As we eat, I spy another hotel Petrof, up on the internal balcony overlooking the restaurant. I have packed the Ballade score in my bag, we've two hours to kill before Ismail is due to take us to Ghaith, and I have no wish to risk leaving the hotel. I ask a waiter if I can practise on the piano. He seems baffled to be asked, but readily agrees. And so I sit down in Tripoli, in the middle of a civil war, on a ledge above an echoing and virtually deserted restaurant – with just the faintest hint of Frank Sinatra over the muzak system – and play the first few pages of the Chopin Ballade. I see a few faces craning up at me, but soon they go back to their scrambled eggs and grilled tomatoes. This is hardly the craziest thing happening in Tripoli at the moment.

At first I am self-conscious. The Petrof is pretty ropey. But soon I forget any company and concentrate on the music, the piano echoing out over the chandeliers into the cavernous space above the restaurant. I remember Murray Perahia telling me the piece is all about revolution and exile, and here I am playing it on a trip all about captivity (Ghaith's) and counter-revolution. My playing, once I relax, has a kind of heightened intensity about it. As at home, the concentration kicks in and I am suddenly conscious only of the narrow corridor between my eyes and my hands. For the first time since landing in Tripoli I can find a form of escape. And not just escape, but immersion. The G minor Ballade is, for all its technical challenges, not simply an exercise. It's impossible to play it without being pulled – physically and soulfully – into the vortex of the emotions it describes and creates. The surroundings may be incongruous, but then Harwood and Polanski sensed how the piece would work in a far more extreme version of dislocation – an abandoned house in the middle of total war. This is a not-quite-abandoned hotel on the eve of war. For a few minutes, though, the notes have that same gravitational traction away from the immediate surroundings and into a very different place.

Ismail arrives, only fifteen minutes late, dressed today in washed-out khaki top and black denim trousers. There is a ten-minute drive into the city centre, round windy streets. We draw up at an anonymous building behind a half-built concrete hotel. Where are we? I ask.

'A security building.'

We are shown into a waiting room. There are black leather sofas and a trophy cabinet all along one side of the wall. I spot a white porcelain plate from New Scotland Yard and another wooden plinth with an inscription from the British Joint Council for the Analysis of Terrorism, JCAT. Waiting for us here is another middle-aged government official, who announces himself as a friend of the British broadcaster Kate Adie – another of the contacts we've rung in the hunt for Ghaith. He tells me he used to be an English professor before he became involved in Libyan government security and foreign relations, and says he has had a hip operation at King Edward VII's Hospital near Harley Street. Who are his favourite English writers? I ask. 'Blake,' he answers, unhesitatingly. 'The more you read, the more complex it is. And Yeats, he's also very complex.' He starts quoting passages, to the evident distaste of a shaven-haired unsmiling Libyan beside him. 'What do you do?' I ask this second man. Unsmiling answer: 'I'm not a journalist.'

We are soon moved to another room, where we all sit in silence. Then, suddenly, there is Ghaith in the doorway. He is in a cream top, full beard and jeans, a leather bag over his shoulder, as if he'd just been out for a stroll round the market. But he lets out an involuntary gasp when he sees me. Much hugging follows. Then – soft-spoken, commanding, firm – he thanks everyone. He has been very well treated, he says. No one has laid a finger on him. The assembled Libyans – there are by now maybe ten of them – look relieved. This is going well; he is saying what they want to hear.*

I have to sign a release form. Then Ismail suggests we go to his office in another part of town. Of course, we actually want to drive straight to the airport, but for the time being we are the guests of the Libyan state, so this is an offer we cannot politely refuse – and, in any event, we still have no

---

* A little while later Ghaith was to write a piece telling of how, during his fortnight in a jail outside Tripoli, he had been interrogated for hours, blindfold and handcuffed, and fell asleep each night in a filthy cell to the sound of his fellow prisoners being beaten and tortured. Still later he would track down one of his captors to interview him. But, for now, he shared the same aim of getting out of this room – and out of Libya before the shooting started.

knowledge of how we are supposed to be leaving the country, far less where we would be going: Peter still hasn't been able to finalise any flight details.

So we drive across the city to Ismail's office. There is a huge TV screen, black sofas, smoothies and flunkies. We are getting impatient, time burning away. Ismail – now playing the expansive host – is insistent we have to wait for the plane to be ready. We have no idea which plane this is, but it can't be the Morocco flight Ian's been trying to arrange. It seems we are not going to Casablanca, then. Ghaith is glued to the television, which is replaying scenes of devastation from the tsunami five days earlier. This is the first he's heard of it.

Ismail seems oblivious to our growing impatience and keeps talking. He claims that Saif Gaddafi paid Sarkozy €5 million in backhanders for his election funds. They have documents, he says, receipts – waving in the general direction of filing cabinets in the corner of the room. [Sarkozy later described the claims as 'grotesque'.] 'What do they take us for?' he spits out, denouncing the French as the only country to have recognised the rebels. Peter's phone is out of credit, so I borrow Ismail's to pass on this intelligence, reliable or not, to the foreign desk. The desk responds with the news that some *NYT* journalists have now been taken. I immediately ring Bill Keller (it must be 5 a.m. or so in NY) and hand the phone to Ismail, so they can begin the negotiation.*

Eventually our patience – and nerves – run out. Surely the plane is ready now? 'Yes it was here last night,' says Ismail, who suddenly waves his hand and dismisses us. 'You can go.' Was he bored of us? Was he keeping us there simply to feed us the line about Sarko? Another black Audi is laid on to take us to the airport. We are waved through every checkpoint, and pass a huge wall mural of Berlusconi and Gaddafi beaming together in solidarity. At the airport, we are left in a deserted and windowless VIP lounge, anxious, with still no idea of what, if any, arrangements have been made to get us out of the country. We wait for another couple of hours: the whole airport empty and noiseless until the arrival of a platoon of troops under our room, apparently on their way to Benghazi, shouting, 'We will die for Gaddafi!'

Eventually we are taken out of the lounge by armed guards and straight onto the runway, on which sits a solitary plane – a private jet. We climb on board and settle into the plush leather seats – yet another layer of incongruity. But just as the engines start, two suited figures climb into the plane and sit

---

* They were freed a few days later.

down opposite us – one a crop-haired figure and tough-looking, the other overweight and vaguely sinister. Military intelligence, surely. My heart sinks. But no. As the plane door is closed, they introduce themselves. These are the Turks who, at the request of their prime minister, have come to rescue us.

Two hours later and we are in Istanbul's airport, and three of the more surreal days in my life are over.*

* The next day, 17 March, the UN Security Council imposed a no-fly zone over Libya. Air strikes began on 19 March.

PART FOUR

Saturday, 19 March

It's been the most gorgeous Gloucestershire day. Vivid colours all around. The landscape gardeners have laid very green turf where, until two weeks ago, there was builder's mud. Blue skies. Yellow daffodils. Sparkling clear water in the stream. And the music room: it has floors, doors, heating, windows . . . and a piano! Two pianos, in fact, as I have kept the old Danemann.

The Steinway is sitting there at the end of the room: it looks quite small in overall proportion to the space. Jeff has left the original brochure ('See one, touch one, play one, own one'), which the previous owner had evidently kept with the piano. On page 14 the owner has written in red biro 'Purchased March 1978'. Exactly thirty-three years ago – when I was living in Cambridge with a £150 upright piano for company. On another page is written £7,532 – underlined twice in red.

This morning, I sit down at the piano for the first time, braced for disappointment. But it's beautiful . . . And echoey. Have I got the acoustics right? Friends kept asking that question during the building, as if we'd have consulted a professional acoustic engineer over our modest little garden room. I experiment with an old tartan rug underneath the soundboard. I move the piano around, pointing it at the window to try different angles. Eventually the echoey sound is softened into one which is just a bit blossomy. But that will all deaden down further when the room gets its curtains and a chair or two, so no point fretting too much now. The keys feel so light. I try the coda and find myself whisking through it, fingers skating over keys. It's very different from the Fazioli – and a world away from the beaten-up old brute I recently played in Tripoli. And so I sit in our new room staring out over the garden and the dimpled field beyond thinking England's a pretty good place all in all.

Friday, 25 March

Lunch with Noriko Ogawa today. She's just flown from Japan and looks emotional and sombre. I suggested a couple of weeks back that she might give a Kings Place concert in aid of the Japanese tsunami relief appeal. She immediately agreed – and promised to play the G minor Ballade. After a single course we steal off for a very quick lesson in one of the rehearsal rooms in Kings Place. She begins by playing the piece to me. I realise that this is the first time since I started on this journey that I have heard the piece live and played by a 'proper' pianist. I've of course sampled numerous recordings on YouTube and iTunes, but nothing in the flesh. She plays it with incredible power and certainty – especially given the inner turbulence she must be feeling after such personal exposure to the tsunami, which has wrecked the concert hall where she most regularly plays. The piece today has an extra dimension – the sheer elemental feeling of some of the passages, that sense of being almost out of control, or rather in the control of wilder external forces. At the end, she seems shocked by what's just happened. We both sit there in silence for a few moments. Noriko then asks me to play. I struggle – even though it's a new Steinway O – to make the piano sing, to tease a delicate sound out of it. On Saturday at Fish Cottage I was flying on my newly arrived Steinway. Further evidence that progress is not linear.

Noriko says I was better than she'd expected. What can she have been anticipating? She homes in on bar 48 – the first bit of passage work – and says she thinks I may be hearing the top line in triplets and thus becoming confused by the cross-rhythms. I must instead hear the crotchet beat in LH and make the right hand feel it too, she says. But she's not too fussed by how I finger it. The main thing, she says, is just to decide – and stick with it.

It's then back to the demands of work and meetings this afternoon, but the evening brings more piano, this time in the form of Michael Kimmelman – the *NYT* art critic and amateur pianist whom Richard's friend Rafael Viñoly mentioned to me at the Pollini concert – who drops in at the end of the day. He's in his late 40s, dressed in chinos, and in a Manhattan drawl launches into the story of his relationship with the piano, which began when he was a 5-year-old in New York.

He was a very promising student and soon hooked up with a teacher named Simon Bernstein. For all his promise, though, he wasn't a *good* pupil. 'I suppose I had enough skill at it that I could get away with not practising very much for a long time, so I was a perpetually disappointing student to Simon.' But he was still good enough, when the time came, to be encouraged to opt for music conservatory over university. This wasn't for him, though, and so he went off to Yale.

He graduated and began a career as an academic, writer and journalist, and while he continued to play for a little while and was entered into various prestigious competitions, he eventually stopped playing altogether. Part of the reason, he thinks, is that he had begun to write music criticism for a living, 'which was a poisonous thing for my own playing'. The 'sheer routine of it', having to attend concert after concert and think of the music critically rather than emotionally, 'just gave a drudgery to something that had been the closest thing to my heart'.

This break from playing lasted ten years. Then, when Michael was in his early 30s, he saw his childhood teacher, Simon, again. Simon made a suggestion. 'He asked me: "Look, this is crazy. You're a pianist, this is a whole life. Why don't you just come over and we'll work together a little bit, just for fun?"' For Michael this was a way to renew a relationship. 'He was like my surrogate father. I loved him very much and I felt always that I had disappointed him, so I felt this would be good.' Simon insisted there would be no obligations or expectations. 'If I couldn't practise, I didn't have to practise. It was just getting together.' But, as Michael puts it, this was 'very sneaky' of Simon, who knew what would happen once Michael started any kind of practice again. 'You know,' Michael says, 'if you've played seriously before, and you start to work on things, an inevitable outcome of this is that you want to work it up.'

The result was that after a few months of 'getting together', Simon suggested Michael choose a couple of pieces, invite some people over and play for them. Michael went for it. 'I asked a bunch of people, some of whom were music people from the *Times*. They were my colleagues. I remember vividly that, because they had no idea that I had been a pianist, it was really like being asked by your dentist, while he has some drill in your mouth, whether you would come to see him perform in *The Fantasticks*, or something. I could see them clutch their chairs and think, oh my God, what the hell is this? Actually it was very useful, because this set the bar so low that I almost couldn't disappoint them.

'That was an extremely interesting and profound experience for me, as, I suspect, it will be for you playing the Chopin Ballade.' I ask him to elaborate. 'First of all, it was fun and I enjoyed it enormously and I was reminded how this was something that was so irreproducible in my life, something so deep and extraordinary. But, more than that, what was really surprising was to be reminded of what it was like to play for people whom you loved; and friends and others, many of whom had never actually been in a situation where they were in a room with someone, whom they knew, performing something at least competently. You know, the whole amateur world, the whole way in which people used to make music for each other, is gone. So the experience of going to somebody's house, or sitting in a studio ten feet away from somebody who you actually know, who is playing something, is . . . I was very moved by how moving this was for them. I don't mean this in an egocentric way. I mean the general experience of having music as an intimate thing shared between people who know each other and love music, this was really extraordinary for me to see.'

A little while after he'd started to play for friends in this way, Michael's editor at the *New York Times* put it to him that he might want to enter the Van Cliburn competition for amateur pianists, held in Fort Worth. The idea was that he'd then write about the experience. Michael was wary of combining his professional life with his amateur passion in this way, but he reluctantly agreed. He played the G minor Ballade and made it to the final. In the initial stages, the competition was a friendly affair of like-minded amateurs cheering each other on, and openly sharing their passion for the music with one another. Michael tells me, 'I had a couple of friends who were in the competition, and the joy, the incredible sense of satisfaction and pride, when they would pass through a round. I remember there was a group photograph of people just beaming with pleasure and a sense of pure satisfaction.'

When he reached the final, though, he found the atmosphere among the remaining contestants changed. 'Moving from this sort of wonderful atmosphere of just having worked towards playing something just for the sake of playing for strangers, you get to this group. Same thing, same room, and there were five of us, I think. I remember we walked in the room and the first thing one of them said was, "I only can give you five minutes, I have to go to sleep tonight, and we have this tomorrow, and, by the way, I'm not going to take the first practice time on the piano tomorrow. I don't need that. I want a later time." And another one said, "Well I'm not going to take the first time either and also I need you to give me another practice room and I need my own piano.'''

So these finalists took on an attitude more closely associated with the professional world, perhaps. He concludes that the terms 'amateur' and 'professional' are 'very shaky'. He goes on: 'It's a question of, I think, how one sees oneself and the terms bother me because "amateur" now means "incompetent"; and, yet, "professional" just means someone who declares it's what they consider themselves.' What he means by amateur is 'what Charles Cooke was talking about'. It turns out we have a mutual bond in Cooke's book, a new edition of which he has just edited, and both agree with his definition of amateurism, which is – as Michael put it – 'you have another life, it's a full and interesting life, but you decide to add this life as well because music gives you something that you can't get from this other life. It isn't about having a career and making a living from it, it's about something that only music-making will give you.'

After the competition, Michael kept playing to friends and soon his reputation grew. Eventually, he began to receive requests to play public concerts, which he has been doing for some years now. He only plays a handful a year, and makes sure that it remains an amateur hobby distinct from his professional life – he didn't want to be the 'art critic who played the piano'. He thinks that public performance has a very positive effect on his approach to the piano, and allows a deeper connection with the music. As he puts it tonight, 'It happens both in the way you prepare and think through a piece and it also happens in the way the piece is performed. There are certain edge-of-the-seat things, certain ways in which your mind works, certain feelings you have that cannot be reproduced when you're just doing it for yourself in a room. So, for me, having the concerts as a goal is very important and I believe it really is the deepest commitment one makes to music.'

We then backtrack a little. We're both journalists, and I want to know how Michael thinks his playing has affected his work. To him, it is only beneficial. He finds his work, being at a desk, writing or thinking, 'gruelling and painful'. When he gets up from the desk and walks to the piano, on the other hand, he says he knows he's 'going to get somewhere'. 'Whereas when I sit down to write, I never really believe that I'll actually get to the end of this thing, it's very difficult for me.' It's the other way round for me, I think. Work is certainly 'gruelling', but I don't go to the piano thinking I'm going to get anywhere. In fact, I'd say at the moment I find the challenge of learning the Ballade just as gruelling as, and perhaps even more 'painful' than, work.

But as we speak further, Michael strikes on the juxtaposition between the nature of journalism and the nature of learning a piece for piano which I find so rewarding. 'What we do,' he says, 'or anyway, what I do, involves a lot of learning something very quickly and trying to produce something: the cycle is extremely quick. The sense of accomplishment comes from being able to master something quickly and move on. Once I started to go back to music and pieces like the G minor Ballade or the F minor Ballade or the Op. 110, or whatever it was that I was working on – these were pieces that just, it sounds a little stupid, and I don't know how to say it, but just infinite complexity, there was no end to the learning process. And the sense of slowness, the slow incremental process by which I physically learned them, and began to understand them intellectually, was very beautiful to me, exactly the opposite of what was happening at work. I'm sure you understand, but I can't even put it into words – how beautiful it is to be able to see this slow thing evolving in your hands physically.'

I do see what he means, and feel the same about the benefits of this contrast. But whether I'm yet at a stage where I find the pace of learning the Ballade 'beautiful' rather than frustrating is very much up for debate . . .

Sunday, 27 March

The musical event of the week has been a little impromptu affair at the office. Radiohead announce they are publishing a newspaper, so Janine Gibson, our head of digital, has the bright idea of collecting the musical talent within the *Guardian* to record a Radiohead song. Within a couple of hours there are half a dozen of us in one of the upstairs studios doing a cover of the Radiohead classic 'Creep'. As the scratch band tunes up and starts playing – all of them without music – I can't hear the electric piano over the sound of drums and bass guitar. There are only four chords in the song, but I have a real problem even 'hearing' these right. My colleagues can hear pitches. I can't. There are many different kinds of musical ability and intelligence on show. The *Guardian* columnist Tim Dowling turns out to be a mean banjo player, and veteran *Observer* writer Ed Vulliamy has a voice that reeks of a thousand Gauloises and Jack Daniel's. Not sure he smokes or drinks either – but that's his singing voice. Who knew?

Radiohead's Colin Greenwood pens a very funny damn-with-faint-praise review of our performance on the *Guardian*'s website. It ends: 'My favourite performance of the lot was the unshowy yet commanding piano work by Alan – he held it all together and led the way for the others to follow. Without his obvious musical gifts it might have all fallen apart. I'd say he certainly has a future in live music, and I would happily ask to go on a guest list to see him play again.'

I email to tell him it was no worse than his 'newspaper'.

Richard Sennett and his wife, Saskia, come to stay at Fish Cottage on Saturday night. Before supper we head to the music room to play a couple of Bach cello sonatas, and read our way (in my case, very approximately) through the Fauré sonata. After supper we try Beethoven Op. 5, No. 2. I'm loving the piano more and more – delicate, clean touch, lovely singing sound. And the experience of playing with someone else in the room is fantastic as we exchange sounds in this vibrant, vibrating, resonant space. We experiment for a while, moving the piano around the room to get the acoustic exactly right. The sound projects well, so that music-making becomes much more intimate: there's less pressure to force the sound from the keys; there's a floating sense of it almost happening by itself.

Then back in London on Sunday evening, my brother Richard (a Kleinian psychoanalyst four years older than me) and I go around the corner to neuro-scientist Bryan Youl's house for another eight-hand evening. (I'm now referring to these eight-hand get-togethers as 'Spider Club'.) Bryan has two concert grands side by side – entirely occupying his front room. One is a Steinway, which Bryan bought from the Conway Hall meeting rooms; the other a Bechstein. We play two enormous slabs of orchestral writing, Beethoven 5 and Schubert 9. Then supper, followed by a crack at the *Meistersinger* overture.

Sunday, 3 April

On Saturday I spend a couple of hours on the Ballade, and things don't go well. It is one of those days when I'm convinced everything is slipping backwards, the bits I thought I could play I'm no longer sure I can, and passages seem to be getting slower rather than faster. I look at bar 48, for example, which my score tells me I was playing at ♩ = 100 back in November. But here I am four or so months later and I'm definitely not even at that pace. And then I panic when I think piano camp is only three months away. It's a constant battle in the mind: I have to keep reminding myself on days like this of the mantra that progress isn't always linear, and keep faith that the breakthroughs will come and that by July the repetitive practice will mean everything is deeply learned and the playing totally secure.

But it is not the kind of 'setback' I needed after a tiring week in which my confidence has already been dented. On Wednesday my lesson with Michael began unpromisingly with his faux weary greeting: 'So, here we are again.' Perhaps not so faux? Did this betray a sense of ennui? Frustration? A hint: *why can't you accept you're never going to be able to pull this off?* I felt a surge of guilt at putting him through all this. Does he feel like a driving instructor with a very slow-learning student? Bracing himself for another week of swerves, agonising seven-point turns and near-misses? Does he feel a sinking heart as Wednesday approaches? At the end of the lesson – in which we seemed to make no progress – he said, not unkindly: 'Perhaps you should take this to another teacher. I'm not sure how much more I can help you.' Is that how piano teachers do it? Fifty ways to leave your student?

That evening Noriko gave her fund-raising concert at Kings Place. The place was full. It was the first time I'd heard her give a full-blown concert in a proper hall, as opposed to the sitting room in Anne Brain's house in the Lot Valley. The sheer power of her playing is what surprised. Nothing about her physique – slender, small-boned, almost china figurine like – prepares you for the big sound that she can draw out of a piano. I don't think I've ever been conscious of the piano itself emitting a little echo, as it did with the final percussive chord she struck at the end of the second movement of Beethoven Op. 109. Months of playing it at a tentative walking speed had left me quite unprepared for the pace and fury with which she attacked the Ballade, particularly the coda – even though I'd seen her give an extremely impressive display during our quick lesson a few days ago. At the end I had virtually to force a conscious decision not to be depressed by her command of the Ballade and just how far away I still am from even the foothills of this piece.

Today, though, things have improved. In the morning one of Richard's chamber-music cluster sends out a group email saying she's had a rotten week – anyone up for a session? I am feeling the same and need some chamber music. So a few of us respond and book to play at our place this evening. Before anybody arrives, I have time for two hours of good solid work on the passage at bar 48 and the coda. And by the time I get up from the piano things are immeasurably better than they were yesterday. Basc camp in view!

There are seven of us in all tonight. Three violins, two violas, one cello and me. Again, with the help of Petrucci Library and a printer, we manage to improvise various permutations of septet – including a Vivaldi four-violin concerto (switching electronic keyboard to a passable harpsichord); Mozart's Sinfonia Concertante; Brahms' clarinet quintet, and finishing with three movements of the Schumann piano quintet. So I end up feeling almost ready for the week ahead and not entirely defeated by the prospect of the Ballade challenges still to come.

Tuesday, 5 April

The day of the British press awards. I've cancelled tomorrow's lesson. Win, lose or draw, it's always a late night of celebrating or drowning. It's a tense event – one of my least favourite of the year. I first went as a nominated young reporter of the year in 1977, when it was at lunchtime, with prime ministers or princes giving speeches which were respectfully listened to, even if they said little. Sometime in the 1990s it moved to the evening and became an aggressive drink-fuelled ritual in which punches were thrown, scores were settled and age-old tensions between tabloid and broadsheet papers broke to the surface. There was once much more of a sense of one industry united on at least one night of the year. Perhaps the shift was precipitated several years back when the former *News of the World* deputy editor Neil 'Wolfman' Wallis jumped on stage and passionately denounced the bias – as he saw it – towards broadsheets and against tabloids. A small thing in itself, but it did bring to the surface a sense of disconnection and resentment – a consciousness of what divided us, rather than what united us as a body of journalists.

This year – phone hacking and WikiLeaks, etc. – we know we are in with a chance of winning the big one. But we also know that a good proportion of Fleet Street journalists hate the work Nick Davies is doing on phone hacking and will do their best in the judging process a) to snub the *Guardian* and b) to reward the *News of the World*. Just to heighten the tension, there are two more arrests of former *NotW* staff in the morning – the former chief reporter and the news editor. Big fish.

For much of the evening, it isn't entirely clear which faction has won. The *NotW* table is at the opposite end of the room at the Savoy Hotel – and each and every time one of their reporters or sections wins an award (four in all) a rousing cheer goes up, the table leaps to its feet and several of them punch the air or send other disobliging signs in the general direction of the *Guardian* table. But right at the end the *Guardian* is, indeed, named newspaper of the year. Half the room applauds, the other half are muted, if not silent. The citation quotes one judge as saying the paper was 'completely unafraid to take on the powers that be'. Another comments: 'What an infuriating paper it is, but it does continue to try to take journalism into the future.' Well, we can live with that.

About thirty of us end the evening in the early hours at the top of Centre Point – the unlovable skyscraper in Charing Cross Road – looking down on the twinkling London streets, drinking champagne and reflecting on a rather amazing year.

Thursday, 7 April

Today I interview for the *Guardian* the great Argentine conductor and pianist Daniel Barenboim, who's in town for a 'cameo concert' at Tate Modern. We meet at Claridge's, Barenboim having arrived straight from the airport in a patchwork jacket and desperate to get up to his room so that he can light a cigar. It's the first thing he mentions to me in the hotel lobby. As if reading his mind, a member of staff shouts down the corridor after him: 'Now then, Maestro' (he really does call him Maestro), 'no smoking now.'

Safely settled into an armchair, Barenboim defiantly produces a double-barrelled leather case, lights a very fat cigar and savours the moment. It's 3 p.m. He isn't due to play his 'pop-up' recital at Tate Modern for four hours. He hasn't yet decided quite what to play, and is not sure of the acoustic that awaits him in the giant Turbine Hall. He looks tired, but up for a conversation. And a long smoke.

As I'm about to learn, a conversation with Barenboim does not take a regular, linear form. If it were a score, it would not resemble a sonata, or indeed anything with a recognisable beginning, middle or end. It is much more like a Sibelius symphony – a multitude of thematic germs, which occasionally fuse into a big theme. So, within five minutes, the thread might go something like this: the shape of the recording industry since the 1980s; the need for new marketing ideas in music, post-internet; the Egyptian and Tunisian revolutions; the Japanese tsunami; the speed of change in the world today; his recent performances in the West Bank; and the nature of musical communication. There is a connection there, and in time it reveals itself, but there are moments, as with Sibelius, where it's not entirely clear where it's all going.

What is immediately apparent, though, is that Barenboim has a lot in common with the other pianists I've interviewed, especially when it comes to the subject of recorded music. I sense that he, too, pinpoints the arrival of the CD as the highpoint of the 'cult of precision'. However, as Barenboim makes clear, he sees this moment as negative for other reasons as well, reasons which I've not heard anybody else voice before today. For example, while he admits that the arrival of the CD was a 'blessing because any technological advance is very positive', he thinks of it as also a 'curse' because poor-quality recordings from the past could now be remastered and made to 'sound almost like contemporary recordings'. 'Therefore all of us artists were not only in competition with our contemporaries, which we had always been and which we always are, but in 1985 and 1990 we were in competition with Furtwängler and Nikisch and all of them.' On top of this was the problem of what he described as 'overabundance', which meant that the public could buy 'a modern recording with the finest orchestra of today at quite a high price' but 'get the same piece played by the Berlin Philharmonic Orchestra for less than half the price'. This, Barenboim implies, was not fair on the contemporary musician.

Barenboim has particularly interesting things to say about the culture of contemporary classical music. The phrase he keeps coming back to is 'ivory tower', and he seems as wary as Alex Ross of a music world which has become perhaps too specialised. For Barenboim, there are two factors creating this 'ivory tower': 'One is that there is no education in the [day-to-day] schools. The second is that the education in the music schools for people who are going to be professionals: it's much more specialised than it used to be. It has become a training ground for music "as a profession". Music, in my view, is not a profession. Music is a way of life – but you need professionalism to exercise it, which is a very different story. Therefore, since the public is made up of so many people who did not really have a music education, you get only the very passionate music lovers who go to the concerts; that's the best part of the society, and they are very exclusive. That's what they want and they spend their time travelling and hearing, away from the rest of the world, away from the human problems, oblivious to development in painting, in many other things. I know I'm exaggerating but I'm trying to make the point. So you get a very kind of specialised audience and you get specialised people who play. Therefore you get a community made up of artists and audience that is an ivory-tower community, because both have lost a great part of the connection between music and everything else.'

Barenboim also seems to suggest that music itself can lead to this 'ivory-tower community', to a world of listeners shutting themselves off from the wider world and all it contains. As he puts it today, 'I'm very much aware of the fact that music gives us the tools to forget so many things that we don't like in the world. How many people come home in the evening, have a favourite drink and listen to a recording, extremely well recorded, very clear, very clean, and they forget everything? They forget that they had a fight at the office, that they fought with their wife or with their girlfriend, or with both, or they had an unpleasant time at the dentist or they went to see their accountant.

'There's nothing wrong with that,' he says, but he warns that we must be aware of music's capacity to let us forget in this way, and remember that music's great value, in his opinion, is that it 'gives us the tools to understand many things about ourselves, about the human being, about society, about how we live, what we live for, etc.'. And then he moves on, true to style, to talk about what the difficulties of life are. He announces one 'fact': 'that we've all, beyond puberty, experienced the difficulties of marrying passion and discipline. When you get passionate about anything, about a woman or the job or about something that you're into and you lose complete sense of discipline. They have to coexist.' And here he comes back to music, which, he says, 'teaches you, basically, that nothing is foreign to the human existence' and that within human existence 'all the different and most opposing elements' – like passion and discipline – 'have to coexist with each other'.

At the end, I tell him about my journey with the Ballade. He pauses and then just chuckles. Why the chuckle? 'I feel like I'd like to fly an aeroplane,' he says. 'I've never heard you play the piano, so I have no comment to make about that, but it's a piece that requires, of course, great pianistic skills and musical thought. But it's the putting together the two things.' This leads him to discuss his 'horror' of pianists 'who divide the technical aspect from the musical aspect'. 'Because once you divide them, you cannot put them again together. For instance, if you take a movement like the last movement of the "Appassionata" of Beethoven, which is continuous movement, or the last movement of the Funeral March of Chopin, and you try to play without any musical content, without any musical expression, just as a "technical" exercise, it's not that difficult – if you can train yourself to do it. But suddenly the difficulty becomes absolutely insurmountable when you try to fill it, having done this work without musicality.'

I try to pin him back down to the specific difficulties of the Ballade. He uses the term 'slippery'. Meaning? 'The G minor Ballade uses so many difficult techniques,' he replies, 'the leaps, the continuous movements, the soft playing, the loud playing, the chords [he mimics playing these different passages in the air, his cigar still in his right hand] – so that you are constantly bombarded with new difficulties and no time to prepare for them because they are suddenly there and you're not ready for it. You just know that you've got to play *filigree*, you know, quietly [fingers make filigree gestures above his head] then you suddenly have to play the big chords' – and here he sings them, puffing out his cheeks, his hands crashing down on the table in front of him.

I ask him when he first played the piece. His answer was the one I'm growing used to hearing from all my interviewees: '13 or 14.'

'It seems to be a piece everyone wants to try as a teenager.'

'Yeah, and then as an adult mostly avoids it!'

In the music room in Blockley there's a large black-and-white portrait of Barenboim, taken by the legendary *Observer* photographer, Jane Bown, in 1969. His large dark, soulful eyes look down on me as I play. Next time I sit down to play I'll remember that a-man-can-dream chuckle.

Friday, 8 April

When I got back from the Barenboim interview yesterday there was an email from Nick Davies:

It's an established *Guardian* tradition that if I leave the country, somebody senior resigns over the phone hacking. So this is just to warn you that I'm heading for California for a week.

Well, he was right: the moment he leaves the country there's a big development on phone hacking. For all their punching of the air and leaping to their feet at the awards on Tuesday, News International is evidently changing its strategy. Or, to put it another way, hoisting a white flag – at least halfway up the mast. The company has apologised to eight victims and set up a compensation fund – which some commentators suggest could be around £20 million – to pay out on all the phone-hacking claims against the company. It's not the end. Not even the beginning of the end. But – after years of denial over the story – the company is finally inching its way to public acceptance of the truth.

Saturday, 9 April

As if to prove Daniel Barenboim's remarks about the 'ivory-tower community' within contemporary classical music, his Turbine Hall recital has provoked wildly conflicting reviews – from the reverential to the contemptuous. Here is the voice of the 'ivory tower' by one Igor Toronyi-Lalic on the Artsdesk website:

> It had all the hallmarks of being an almighty car crash of an event. Barenboim? Chopin? Turbine Hall? You might as well have dumped the piano at the bottom of the Pacific Ocean . . . And why only the slow movement? That made more sense. No doubt Barenboim realised as soon as he stepped into this Jonah's whale of a place that nothing that didn't shift at a snail's pace (dolphins could have learned how to walk in the time he spent on the two waltzes) could make any musical headway in a hall of this size and decided instead to settle on a few choice morsels that wouldn't be flattened. So we got four works in total. Four. Each desperately padded out with chit-chat. The usual Barenboim shtick. A mixture of the worst of Tony Blair and the best of Nicholas Parsons. And the music? His legions of crazed fans massed in the hall stretching out their hands for just one feel of this modern Messiah will no doubt disagree but Barenboim isn't a pianist that can just turn his hand to anything and magic up a masterpiece. Mention his name in pianophile company and it is quickly dismissed. We were also wrong to attend last night's recital.

Fiona Maddocks, online on the *Observer/Guardian* website, by contrast, noticed the crowd of 1,100 who had been attracted to an event with almost no pre-publicity (8,000 people applied for 400 seats, plus overflow), their rapt attention and standing ovation. Evidently no one had told them that they were 'wrong' to attend.

Sunday, 17 April

Lessons with Michael remain difficult. I'm now fairly sure that he's not trying to give me the brush-off, but his mood is not encouraging. Last week he was feeling poorly: he'd had a sore throat, and had even been to see a specialist about it. He quoted the following exchange:

Specialist: I'm sure there's nothing wrong.
Michael: Are you one hundred per cent sure?
Specialist: No, but I'm ninety-nine per cent sure.
Michael: How about an MRI scan?

We dived straight into the coda, and were immediately back to the problem of trying to coordinate the pedal with the LH rather than the RH. Michael had been thinking about this difficulty, and made me play it slower than I've ever played it before. We did this for half an hour. Then he took me back to bar 48 – where the first passage work begins – and I underwent the same meticulous examination. For the past fortnight we've been struggling with my inability to switch a fourth finger for a third on one note in bar 48, which Michael – and all the scores I've consulted – says I have to do.

This of course is how lessons have always been with Michael; he has always insisted that by 'baking in' bad habits you set yourself up for trouble for the future, and so lessons can be very narrowly focused and critical. However, his tone seems somewhat harsher recently. For instance, last week, as I kept making the same mistake, he couldn't resist a little outburst: 'No! You played with your fourth!'

So I tried again.

'No left hand, that's a 5 you're playing, not a 3.'

His eyes were glued to the keys. I began to feel flustered.

'No, Alan. You slipped a 3 instead of a 4.'

He paused at one point and addressed me quite severely. 'Alan. You're just not precise enough. You don't work hard enough at getting everything right. You're just not learning it thoroughly enough, putting the work in.'

I was suddenly 11 years old again, being told off by the fearsome choirmaster at Guildford Cathedral, Barry Rose. I felt flickers of resentment, and even a little shame, at Michael's diagnosis and insistent tone. But the point of being an adult learner ought to be that you *can* accept fair and constructive criticism. I go to him to learn, not to be flattered or charmed or coaxed into playing this piece. But I can taste the bitterness I felt as a teenager at such tickings-off. And how, back then, they made me want to just give up. Still, things weren't much improved by the start of this week's lesson. He sighed as we sat down: 'Am I ready for more Chopin at this hour?'

However, this weekend I think I might have made the breakthrough I've been waiting for after all the frustrations and anxieties. I've just had two days of intensive practice on my beautiful Steinway bathed in spring light, and now feel for the first time that I can 'play' most of the piece. What I mean is that after this weekend I think there's nothing technical, on a bar-by-bar basis, that's beyond me. The LH arpeggios at bar 166 – that is, the return of the second tune – for instance, are now under the hand. And I have begun to play them with a kind of 'ripple' rather than a series of individual picked-out notes. I've also resolved the problem in bar 48 – my struggle in switching a fourth finger for a third on that one note. After two weeks of trying to make the change, my natural instinct was still to play it with the fourth. If I played very slowly and concentrated I could force the third to come down, but then the moment I sped up, the fourth would nick its place on the black key. So today I've taken the disobedient decision that I'm going to ignore Michael and the books and play it with the fourth. It works, so why not? And I can now play most of the coda, though only in eight-bar bursts. The problem of course is going to be knitting all these eight-bar sections, and then all of the other passages, into one. The piano has undoubtedly helped: it's got a *much* lighter touch than the London instrument.

At one point over the weekend practice is interrupted by a very large cock pheasant who walks up to the music room – apparently drawn by the reflected ghost of another large cock pheasant – and squawks repeatedly, aggressively and loudly. Is that going to happen all the time?

After my particularly satisfying practice on Saturday morning, and prompted by thoughts of Charles Rosen, I decided to search online for Josef Hofmann playing the Ballade in the 1930s. To start with I thought I had the wrong link: he begins with a piece of improvising as people talk. But then, without a break, he launches into the first notes. He has brisk, unsentimental tempos, with lots of rubato, beautiful inner voices and shaping of phrases. And it's the fastest waltz I've ever heard. Then the coda is played not so much at breakneck speed, but a convulsive tempo – perhaps too fast: there's no sense of demonic, just a blur of speed. But it is utterly individual. There's also an awful lot of audience-coughing on the recording. With the preamble – about forty seconds – it still comes in at 8:31 – so that's just 7:50 for the Ballade itself. Charles Rosen is right – you would never hear a contemporary recording like this.

Saturday, 23 April

Easter Saturday. We've been down in Blockley since Wednesday, and I've had two visits – from Charlie Bennett, the Chipping Campden wine merchant and a very talented amateur pianist who has organised an amazing music festival in the town, and Tif Loehnis, former literary agent and a decent viola and piano player, both of whom came over to christen the Steinway. We played the 'Goldberg' Variations in the Rheinberger/Reger two-piano version on both occasions.

The papers are reporting some new scientific research which shows, in the *Daily Mail* version, that 'Those childhood music lessons could pay off decades later – even for those who no longer play an instrument – by keeping the mind sharper as people age'.

The lead researcher, Brenda Hanna-Pladdy, PhD, found that musical activity throughout life constitutes a challenging cognitive exercise, essentially making your brain fitter. 'Since studying an instrument requires years of practice and learning,' she says, 'it may create alternate connections in the brain that could compensate for cognitive declines as we get older.'

I look up a summary of the original research. The scientists had studied a group of musicians who had all begun playing an instrument at about 10 years of age. Most of these were pianists, but there were also woodwind players, strings, percussion and brass. These musicians had statistically significant higher scores than a group of non-musicians on tests relating for 'visuospatial memory, naming objects and cognitive flexibility' and the brain's ability to adapt to new information. These are the functions that usually decline with age, exactly the kind of functions that go with Alzheimer's. However, they found that 'the age of acquisition' is also critical; so the effects are diminished if the musician doesn't pick up the instrument at an early age and stick with it.

Yesterday evening, in mellow dusk sunlight, we went down the high street to hear the church choir sing J. H. Maunder's sacred cantata, *Olivet to Calvary*, a work seared in my memory since I recorded it with the Guildford Cathedral Choir for EMI at about the age of 12. At the time I didn't know any of the great Bach, Handel or Haydn choral works, so Maunder – a South London parish church organist who died in 1920 – seemed pretty good to me. I remember a subsequent music teacher's crushing dismissal of both the composer and the work and the instant realisation I wasn't supposed to like Maunder at all.

I hadn't heard it for forty-five years – and had never seen the work performed in the circumstances for which it was written: a small amateur church choir. It certainly isn't the *Messiah*, but it's quite understandable why it was so immensely popular in churches for decades after it was written in 1904. It's tuneful, simple and skilfully written for amateur singers and organist. It lasted just over an hour, with the evening spring light slowly fading on the honeycomb stone of the nave.

Today I looked up the recording I made and found a review in the *Musical Times* from 1966, where the critic Basil Ramsey wrote: 'Here is a perplexing problem. Does this work warrant the preparation that has resulted in such an irresistible performance? Sweeping transformations can be made to music, however questionable its worth; and even poor words take on a superior air in such circumstances. The delusion will work for some and not others.'

It's another illustration of how musical tastes can change at alarming speed – just thirty years can make all the difference. Online, I discover that, in 1922, an American reviewer for the *New Music Review* wrote organists and choristers of the English-speaking world should unite to raise a monument to J. H. Maunder as a great benefactor of the human race in general and of church musicians in particular.

Still online, I was led by a tweet to the website PianoZap, which claims to teach people by watching the depression of keys on a keyboard. 'Unlike the old times, in which you had to use sheet music to play different songs, or take endless boring piano lessons, in today's modern technology, piano video tutorials is the next big thing!' True enough, there is a video tutorial on how to play the Chopin G minor Ballade – illustrated by an 'invisible' pianist at the keys of a white grand piano. Could anyone really learn a piece as complex as the Ballade by watching the depression of keys?

Friday, 29 April

I've been in America for a week in advance of expanding our US operation. Which means a week's missed piano practice. I've been wondering how much information the piece contains; how much data has my brain absorbed in this learning process? So a couple of days ago, I emailed Lauren Stewart, the Goldsmiths College musico-neurologist:

> This may be a silly question, but is there any way of measuring the amount of data in the Chopin Ballade? I can measure an audio file of the music. Or the size of a PDF file of the score. I'm wondering if anyone has found a way of measuring the size of the data that a pianist has to absorb in nine minutes, or fourteen pages, of music.
>
> The thought behind the question is to try to explain what's involved in committing a piece like this to memory, and how it might compare with other forms of data (would it be the same as memorising a fourteen-page poem? Or is there something more complex in having to remember, say, four musical lines at once – with cues for LH, RH, pedals, dynamics, etc.?).

Lauren points me to her Goldsmiths College colleague, Dr Marcus Pearce, who studies music, information and neural dynamics. He emails me back today. His email is occasionally cryptic, given the complexity of what he's trying to tell me, but fascinating too:

> Hello Alan,
> Not a silly question at all, actually a very interesting one although difficult to pin down a precise answer as you've already noticed.
> To make a start on finding an answer, let's imagine a simpler task than

yours, in which you've decided to learn by heart all the pitches of the melody in the right-hand part so that you can recite the note names. This removes two kinds of complexity: first, we remove the motor components of learning a piano performance by only asking you to reproduce the score; second, we simplify the task still further by only requiring you to memorise the pitch of each note in the melody ignoring (for now) harmonic movement, timing, dynamics, articulation and so on.

This transforms the task into something (learning a sequence of pitches) more akin to learning a poem by heart (learning a sequence of words). I know this seems somewhat philistine but bear with me while we use this vestigial version of the Ballade to sketch out an analysis and then we'll see how we might (in theory at least) extend it to the piece in all its complexity.

The question of how much information there is in this melody depends both on the melody itself and the person memorising it. Our melody is fixed, so let's focus on the person. Imagine an individual (let's call her Jenny) with no previous experience of music trying to learn the task in a serial fashion, starting with the first note, then moving to the next like you might try to learn a sequence of numbers (e.g., pi to twenty decimal places).

In information theory, the amount of information present in an event such as a note in this melody (its information content) is related to its probability (specifically, the negative log probability). The higher the probability the lower the information and vice versa. I think the most intuitive way to think about this relationship is as follows. First, if you expect something to happen (i.e. you think it has a high probability) and it does happen (i.e. you are correct) then that event has given you very little new information whereas if something unexpected (i.e. with low subjective probability) happens, that event provides new information about how the world works. To take a musical example, suppose you switch on the radio and find yourself listening to a piece of instrumental music and find yourself trying to guess the composer. The parts that are most probable (least surprising) will tend to be common across styles and composers, while the aspects that are improbable (or unexpected) in a general musical context will be those that are most characteristic of the composer's style and therefore those that carry most information.

Right, back now to Jenny learning this melody. Suppose the melody has a pitch range of three octaves. Then one of thirty-six notes can possibly appear at each position in the melodic sequence. Since Jenny has no previous experience of music (her musical brain is a *tabula rasa*), each note is equiprobable. That is, at each point in the melody, each note has a probability of 1/36.

Aha, you might say, but actually it's not 1/36 because (for example) we know that this is a melody taken from a piano piece so there are tessitura constraints and if we know the key signature there will also be tonal constraints that make some scale degrees more likely than others. Suppose Jenny learns these constraints through experience of music before trying to learn the melody. Some of the pitches in the melody will be more probable than others, they will have less information than the less probable ones, which contain more information. An estimate of the amount of information in the melody for Jenny can be obtained by summing the information for each note in the melody.

Then it should be obvious that different melodies differ in the amount of information they contain: longer melodies will contain more information than shorter melodies, all other things being equal; melodies containing many highly improbable notes will contain more information than melodies of the same length with a greater proportion of highly probable notes.

In this way, we can compute a concrete estimate of the amount of information in the melody for this particular individual. By using sensible constraints based on psychological research, we can justify generalising the estimate to an average western listener.

You will immediately note that there are various things wrong with this analysis, including the following:

1. Jenny's estimates of the probability of pitches is the same at all positions in the sequence, regardless of the preceding context. A leading note, for Jenny, does not lead anywhere. We can address this issue by using what are known as conditional probabilities: i.e. by conditioning the note probabilities on the identity of the notes in the preceding context (such that, for example, the tonic is highly probable after the leading note; or a change of registral direction is highly probable after a melodic leap).

2. We have left out rhythm, metre, dynamics, harmony, articulation, ornaments, etc. Some of these can be introduced into the analysis relatively easily, others would take a bit more work. Moving from melody to full polyphony, in particular, is notoriously difficult.

3. The task Jenny has taken on is somewhat different from yours: she is happy to reproduce the score from memory; you want to actually perform the piece which involves additional issues of procedural motor memory. I don't have a good answer to this one although I can imagine replacing the pitch alphabet we discussed above with a repertoire of movements some of which are more probable (i.e. more familiar) and lower in information than others but this is probably a PhD in itself.

I suspect you're after a concrete number: given some assumptions and a bit of time, I'd be able to compute an estimate of the information content of the Ballade (at least the melody) along with that of some other pieces to put it in context.

Incidentally, I'm writing this in Mallorca, where Chopin spent an unhappy but productive winter with George Sand.

PART FIVE

Saturday, 14 May

It's been a fortnight of not much practice. Last weekend was spent catching up after my trip to New York and this week has been extremely busy. In fact, I haven't played the piano all week. On Monday and Tuesday I was immersed in writing a speech on libel which involved reminding myself of all the intricacies of the changing laws on defamation, privacy, super-injunctions. Then, after giving the speech on Tuesday, I stayed up until two o'clock refreshing myself on the new Defamation bill (whose publication I'd missed when I was in Libya) because I had to appear before a Commons select committee on Wednesday. In all, I've had four days that started with a breakfast meeting and three that ended at 2.30 in the morning. So three seventeen-hour days and no time for any piano. When I got down to Blockley last night, I sat at the keys of the piano and felt completely distant from the Ballade, as though I'd never remember anything about it, not a single note, which was a bit frightening.

However, today I've been feeling my way back in quite successfully, and I'm trying a new experiment, which is to look at my hands as I play. I guess it's another form of memory reinforcement to go along with the visual – so the notes on the page and the shapes of them – and the aural. My experiment isn't in any of the books I've read on music and memory – but it strikes me there's something about looking at the shape of my fingers as they move into position for particular chords or phrases or sequences that should be distinctive and, er, memorable. Of course, it only works in passages where you can remember the music to begin with. A musical chicken and egg.

I take a little time out from practice to restock the fish. Fish Cottage can't be Fish Cottage without fish. When we first moved here I used to go down occasionally to the local fish farm to buy live trout. They never lived twenty years (as on the gravestone), but they did live two or three years. Then a couple of years ago the rules changed and you had to write to an office in Whitehall to get permission to buy the fish. So now whenever I need to restock I have to write off to Whitehall with a Section 30 form. Amazingly enough Whitehall is able to identify the little bit of water that runs through our garden. They claim to know that it's called Leigh Brook, which is more than I ever knew. This time round, permission has been granted for six brown trout up to thirty millimetres in length, so long as the fish are handled into the receiving water and I don't tip the transport water into the brook. When I put them in today, the trout look a little startled to be in a little clear calm stream as opposed to the tank which they had shared with a thousand other fish for the whole of their lives.

As I practise in the piano room later in the afternoon, I see the sun dappling the water and the bullet shape of brown trout nosing up and down the stream looking very curious at their new existence.

This evening, we go to hear the Russian virtuouso Boris Berezovsky play in Chipping Campden church as part of the music festival organised by Charlie Bennett. Sofya Gulyak, another wonderful Russian pianist, had played at lunchtime and was almost perverse in her wish to look anywhere but at the keyboard. In any slow passages she stares up at the wooden roof and stone pillars of the church with an amazing instinctive feel of where the notes are on the keyboard geography. It is an incredibly powerful performance of the Liszt B minor sonata, with a glorious sense of the harmonies, the peace and the power of letting a twelve-foot Steinway grand just echo and resonate, especially this particular Steinway, which had been set up by Jeff Shackell.

Boris Berezovsky is the opposite – more in the tradition of nineteenth-century showman. He begins with arrangements of Schubert songs, but unlike Sofya Gulyak he is almost glued to the sheet music, with Richard, the church organist at Chipping Campden, as his page turner. Though he plays flawlessly and with immense power, it is also clear that this is not music he's necessarily played before, and this brings a rare spontaneity to proceedings.

But even Berezovsky hasn't anticipated the end of 'Am Meer' when, as the last ghostly note dies, there is the distinct sound of another piano playing rather discordantly offstage. Berezovsky breaks into a huge smile and says to the audience, 'Sorry, that's my son,' striding off to have words with the 7-year-old, who is happily whiling away the time on the upright keyboard in the vestry.

It feels very much like live music-making, outside of the so-called 'cult of precision', this atmosphere of not being sure what he would play. We go round to see him in the vestry afterwards and his little son is larking around while Berezovsky enjoys a cigarette in the crisp night air of Chipping Campden, round the back of the church. Does he enjoy playing here? Yes, the acoustic is rich, he says, before pouring praise on Jeff's Steinway – 'Wonderful, wonderful, wonderful.'

Sunday, 15 May

Charlie Bennett, the festival organiser, suggests I might like to interview Boris Berezovsky before he heads out of town this morning. I find Boris having coffee at the Noel Arms, a sixteenth-century coaching inn in the high street (deserted, this Sunday morning). He's in the garden and still chain-smoking as his 7-year-old plays around. We only have a short time before he has to set off back to his base in Brussels. He likes Brussels, he tells me, just as he enjoys playing in Japan more than America; the Japanese seem to appreciate classical music, even if their culture is so different he can't possibly believe they understand it; in America he always has the feeling that there are a lot of men in the audience who would rather be watching a ball game, but have been dragged along by their wives.

In Russia, he says, the G minor Ballade is extremely popular. 'It's one of those pieces of Chopin which is played by children and professional pianists alike,' he tells me. 'There are few pieces which are enjoyed by everyone and it's definitely one of them.' Like so many others, Boris first came to the piece as a teenager. 'But now,' he says, 'I don't play any of the Ballades. For me it's too poetic.'

'Too poetic?'

'Yes, too poetic. I prefer music which has more to do with either dance or song element in it. The pure poetic element is, at the moment, not very close to me.'

But that's not to say Boris doesn't admire the Ballade. On the contrary, 'The Ballade is a piece of extreme Romanticism. It's about feelings which were blown out of proportion. There is a wonderful beauty about this period of art in music and the first Ballade – maybe it's the climax of all this. There are feelings of happiness and sadness and then, you know, the final nails in the coffin, if you want.'

I am struck by this phrase 'nails in the coffin'. What does he mean? Boris says this is a Russian phrase for the Ballade's coda, coined by a teacher to describe the final repeated chords in the passage. So now we have Perahia's bodies rising up from the grave and Boris' nails in the coffin – both describing the same shattering page of music.

Does he find the Ballade difficult? I sort of know what he's going to say and, sure enough, the answer's no. Having seen his performance the night before, I put it to him that he probably doesn't find anything very difficult. 'Almost. There are certain things. I tell you honestly, Ligeti, for me, is very difficult, Ligeti Etudes very difficult – not so much technical but just to get through all these notes and cross-rhythms and whatever. I think a computer would be the best performer, but I still don't give up the hope of playing one day Ligeti Etudes which are extremely, extremely difficult.'

But is there nothing he struggled with in the Ballade? 'The end is the only challenge,' he says. 'For a professional pianist, it shouldn't be a challenge to play this piece but, obviously, the end causes certain problems with the coda, the famous coda.' He has a tip to help me negotiate this. 'The best way around this is pedal. Pedal, as Chopin said, is the soul of the piano. It helps a lot so you don't have to play it too clear. The pedal in Chopin wouldn't hurt and it will help to cover up some things which normally without pedal would come sticking out. It helps to cover up mistakes and other stuff – so just put it on and enjoy. That's a bit of good advice.' I can almost hear Michael shuddering a hundred miles away.

Back in London this evening I go to hear Charles Rosen's recital at the Queen Elizabeth Hall. It's barely three months since I saw him the day after his pacemaker was fitted, and tonight he seems particularly frail. He steps, pale, onto the stage with a walking stick, and grips the side of the piano for stability. This is probably the last time we'll see him on a London stage: the last almost-direct connection with Liszt. His playing is very withdrawn. Much of the finger dexterity is there, but the overall mood is perhaps too introverted to be compelling. It is nonetheless fascinating to see a man with seventy years of study, thought, practice and analysis informing the music. And if I could be guaranteed now to play the piano as well in twenty-five years, I'd settle for that.

Wednesday, 18 May

My first lesson with Michael in a while. He's tired – he's had one of his sleepless nights. 'I'm not sure I'm going to be of much use to you,' he says as he opens the door. I tell him I've been working on the bridge passages, and he asks me to play them. I play and it is markedly better than it's ever been in front of Michael. He picks me up on a few fingerings, but it feels, for the first time, as though the bulk of the hard work – learning every note, making sure every finger is in the right, agreed place – has been done. Now it is about playing it faster – and musically.

On my way into work I think of my mother and carpentry. Once my brother and I hit late teenage years and she found she had more time on her hands, she took up woodwork. (Later she took up electrical rewiring, stone carving, wood lettering, painting and a huge countrywide search for mason's marks – or graffiti – in English churches.) Sometimes I'd play around with her pieces of wood – she would go to auctions and second-hand shops to buy old mahogany wardrobes to dismantle and use for their wood; she once dismantled an old Canadian harmonium for the same purpose. I remember realising as I watched her that the first lesson of carpentry is what a precise skill it is. It's no good measuring to approximately the nearest millimetre. It has to be exact. You have to choose the tenon rather than the bench saw, pick the small enough drill bit, and use the set square and the right grade sandpaper in order to end up with a table that works.

It's clear why this suddenly came to mind. I can now play even the most difficult sections of the Ballade, but I have to remain aware of the weak joints, each fracture, and continue to revisit them until they're mastered – and of course, if I stop focusing on them, they won't just remain weak joints, they'll get weaker. In carpentry each piece you make is built of joints, each one crucial to the integrity of the whole; I need to remember this with the Ballade. There's no room for imprecision. Each dovetail and dowel matters in exact detail.

Friday, 20 May

Despite the breakthrough I felt at Wednesday's lesson, this has been a hard week to practise. Someone once told me that Dennis Stevenson, the former chairman of Pearson and much else (a keen amateur violinist, for instance), divides his life into fifteen-minute chunks. I'm feeling the same, except that the units feel like five-minute parcels. At the moment days start at 8.30 and can carry on to 2 a.m. the following morning. No thinking time, or down time. Just getting stuff done.

This week has been dominated by yet more discussions about the direction of travel for the media business. The enormity of the disruption is so large that it feels as if constant conversation is the only way for colleagues to absorb the implications of what's going on. Seventy of us – journalists, developers and commercial colleagues – disappeared from the building for two days to discuss new ways of working together.

This intense concentration on the future came during the week we opened a small exhibition celebrating the 190th anniversary of the *Guardian*. I enjoyed reading C. P. Scott's centenary essay to the American nation here – less famous than his much more quotable essay on journalism published in 1921 ('comment is free . . .'). In it, he seizes on the new technology of the day:

> The world is shrinking. Space is every day being bridged. Already we can telegraph through the air or the ether, from Penzance to Melbourne and tomorrow we shall be able to talk by the same mechanism. Physical boundaries are disappearing: moral boundaries must speedily follow suit . . . What a change for the world! What a chance for the newspaper! More and more we shall take our pulpit seriously and preach to all the world.

The first bit – on the change/chance – has always seemed to me rather inspiring; that a man who had been editing a paper for nearly fifty years – *fifty years!* – could still be so attuned to the possibilities of technological change. But it seems to me unlikely that people want 'sermons' today – and many people today are wary of any implication of the journalist being on a higher plane, delivering truths or revelations to a passive, accepting congregation beneath them.

Saturday, 21 May

Today saw the 'grand opening' of the music room. Or rather, we invited the people who designed and built it, and assorted neighbours whose lives were disrupted by eight months of hammering, drilling, dumping and excavating, to a modest glass of fizz to toast it. The architect, Ed Tyack, and his architectural partner, Mike Naismith, were there – gently pleased with the realisation of their vision (though Ed said he never gets overly attached to his own buildings: it's always on to the next one). We thanked Henry and his team of builders. Then Beatrice Cranke, a teenager at Chipping Campden School, sang three songs with me at the piano – Weill's 'My Ship', Madeleine Dring's 'Business Girls' and 'Cry Me a River'. One or two people asked about using the room: Blockley is immensely musically active – it currently has a brass band, a ladies choir, a 'blokes choir' and the church choir: not bad for a village of 1,500 people.

Wednesday, 1 June

A lunch appointment cancelled at the last minute, so I take the opportunity to nip over to Archive Bookstore, the extraordinary secret bookseller behind Marylebone station, which has a basement crammed from floor to ceiling with second-hand music – with dozens of unsorted boxes perched precariously on top of each other. The place always reminds me of the antique shop in Orwell's *Nineteen Eighty-Four*, it is so incongruous and out of time. The basement room is (if possible) twice as crowded as I've seen it before – with music, not people. There is, literally, not a square inch of space on which to perch a score or book.

I want to stock up on scores for the music room, so I spend an hour sorting through miscellaneous parcels of chamber music – all wrapped in brown paper. Some bear the imprint of Westminster Music Library – one of the great music-lending libraries (based on a donation of thousands of scores by Edwin Evans, the music critic of the *Daily Mail*, for twelve years, to 1945). But others are from West Ham public library and Plaistow – both very poor areas in the East End of London. Everything about it – the thought of the *Daily Mail* music critic giving his scores to a public collection; the idea of East End amateurs playing chamber music together with scores borrowed from the local library – is from a foreign age. Only this morning I came across an interesting table about how the British use their spare time nowadays: half an hour a day on hobbies and games; two and a half hours of TV. I don't think Arnold Bennett would have been very impressed. Nor Clay Shirky.

This evening it's the Royal Academy Dinner. This is always a very grand evening, with people out in tails or black tie and medals. It's held to coincide with the opening of the great celebration of public taste – the Summer Exhibition. Well, not taste exactly, but an opportunity for the 'ordinary' artists to exhibit in the quasi-religious sepulchre of the RA. And every year there's the same chorus of disapproval for the idea. 'Potting-shed wannabes,' sniffs one critic this year. Another critic considers their contributions 'no more embarrassing than the worst works by the Academicians'. This year there's been added controversy because the exhibition's coordinator, sculptor and painter Christopher Le Brun, has been quoted as describing some of the work being submitted by the public as 'just psychotic'. In an interview in the *Independent*, he was merely patronising. Asked why the Academicians are embarrassed by the exhibition he said: 'They are embarrassed because there is a question of quality . . . For the artists, the context in which their work is shown, namely whom they're hung next to, and where, is also uncontrollable.' He added that many amateur submissions were 'not terribly good' and said: 'There are things amongst them but you have to look hard.' Different art form, same arguments.

At the dinner, I bump into Harrison Birtwistle, the British composer defiantly un-medalled and with a piece of yellow insulation tape wrapped around one arm of his glasses. He pounces on me for the supposed lack of classical music coverage in the *Guardian*. I reel off the names of the people who write regularly for us – including at least two critics who are passionate and knowledgeable about modern music. 'Yes, but they just write reviews,' he says. 'What happened to the essays that people used to write?' He refers to Tom Service's recent review of his violin concerto in Boston – 'A year out of my life and just a small review.'

In the context of all this amateur art, I ask him about the role of amateur music in his life. He doesn't write for 'amateur forces', he says very candidly. 'It just doesn't sound good. Other people manage it better than I do.' He brightens, though, as he describes the role of amateur music-making in the formation of his own musicianship – playing the clarinet in bands and musical groups in and around Accrington in Lancashire. 'I remember playing in *Lilac Time* – do you know what it's about? About the life of Schubert. With, of course, no reference to the possibility that he was gay.'

Thursday, 2 June

I host a little dinner in honour of Nick Davies – attended by some phone-hacking victims and some journalists, MPs and lawyers who have fought a tenacious, and sometimes lonely, fight to get at the truth. I sit next to Hugh Grant, who has surprised many people – perhaps even himself – by the way he has articulated his anger over this cause. Peter Oborne – a *Telegraph* journalist – is there: it's been incredibly important that a significant figure from the right has taken up the cause in the way he has – both in print and TV. The victims – most of whom have not previously met each other – huddle in corners of the room comparing notes on the tales of intimidation, obstruction and dishonesties to which they've been subjected for years. But the real hero of the evening is Nick – one of the most naturally talented reporters I've ever worked with. He's had a few long dark nights of self-doubt during the course of this story, which he's been working away at for three or more years now. It's not remotely over yet (in fact, I have a suspicion it's barely begun) – but this is a night to pause and celebrate what the best of reporters can do. I keep thinking of a book by a *Guardian* colleague, Alison Benjamin, called *A World Without Bees* – which argues that, were anything nasty to happen to bees (and they've been having a rough time of it recently), the planet would be done for. I feel a bit the same about reporters.

Thursday, 9 June

Piano camp is on 21 July, which means I have just forty-odd days to have the Ballade ready for performance. I'm going to have to play it in front of nearly a dozen people who know about the piano, some of whom actually teach the piano – a very exacting audience. I don't know a) how much time I'm going to have in the next few weeks, and b) how much progress I can make in these weeks. Even if I did have much more time, there are still lots of things that feel very insecure: they can sometimes go right and sometimes not. When I play at my best now, I'm surprised at things that come naturally, including arpeggios and runs and scales that would have troubled me even three months ago and would have seemed impossible a year ago. But there's now just not much time left.

Today I get out my metronome, which I haven't used for a long time. Depressingly enough, I can play the waltz at ♩ = 100, which – my markings on my score tell me – is the same speed I was playing the piece at in early December, more than six months ago. By March I had reached 116. So this is a passage which has slowed down just when I need it to be speeding up. I'm going to have to make progress here fast.

I've also hit a new snag with some of the pedalling in bars 150–4 – a fiddly (and difficult to phrase in the right groupings) piece of rising passage work. In yesterday's lesson with Michael, we spent ten minutes looking at this. He thinks I'm using the pedal too much and muddying the textures because of it. He's right, of course. He suggests in an email today that I instead 'persevere with a crochet pedal because it gives greater clarity to the octave bass and helps to bring out the melody in the right hand'. It's what Fleet Street calls a 'reverse ferret'. Back to square one on this particular section then. After the joy of thinking I'd broken the back of the hard work on the Ballade last week, it's another sobering reminder of how much there is left to do.

And at the back of my mind, there's the worry that I might have even less time to prepare than I think, because the temperature on phone hacking is continuing to rise, and rising rapidly. The BBC has begun to focus on the extremely nasty piece of work who did a prison spell before being hired back onto the *NotW* under Andy Coulson. We've covered this story before – it was the issue that led me to try to warn David Cameron about Coulson before the 2010 general election – but, as ever, it sometimes takes an extra gust in the sails from someone else to make a story unignorable.

Most of the people trying to block the proposed Murdoch takeover of BSkyB have given up hope, but interest in other recent developments in the hacking story make it inconceivable, I think, that this is going to be allowed to happen. So I write a leader today which ends:

> With any other company there would be calls for a wholescale clear-out of those at the top – including the board, chairman and chief executive. But News Corp is a very unusual company, dominated by one family and quite unresponsive to normal political and shareholder pressure. The prime minister is a good friend of the chief executive of News International and hired Coulson. Rupert Murdoch supported the Conservatives at the last election, doubtless hoping that some favours would be returned. If all this were happening in Italy *The Times* would be writing thunderous leaders. But do not look to *The Thunderer* for coverage of this particular story. Without the scrutiny of other journalists very little of this would have emerged. That's why media plurality matters – 37 per cent of the press may ignore a story, but there will be others who won't.
>
> It is obvious that the police must now investigate the vast amount of detective material, though it is puzzling why they have deliberately excluded it from Operation Weeting, the third Yard inquiry to look into phone hacking. But what of Mr Hunt's dilemma? On narrow grounds he may be tempted to wave through the BSkyB takeover. But how seedy the coalition government – including the Lib Dems, who were so vocal on this subject before the election – would look if that were to happen without also ordering a public inquiry to examine all the evidence which the police have been sitting on and about which, until recently, they did so little. If Cameron is disinclined to stir this particular hornet's nest (was his own phone ever hacked, incidentally?) then Clegg should force his hand. He will find British public opinion very much on his side.

Friday, 10 June

Michael and I have now been through every single bar of the piece and I've concluded that it's time I tried to find a back-up teacher – I feel in need of a pragmatic outside ear to help me form a realistic sense of what's secure and what isn't as I build up to my piano-camp performance. Lucy Parham is the perfect candidate. We're friends, we've had lessons before, and she plays the Ballade regularly. Now is the time for me to learn from her performer's mentality to the music – how to get round tricky corners, how to finger a particular note for maximum effect and so on. Where Michael, having never performed it, is more concerned with the mechanics of learning and is punctilious in concentrating on details, Lucy goes straight for the larger sweep.

I go round to her flat in the Barbican. Lucy asks me to play the Ballade right the way through for her – something I haven't yet done in eight months of lessons with Michael. She says it's vital to get a sense of the whole piece, and know what a performance of it takes in terms of stamina, concentration and overall shaping. I manage pretty well – at any rate, no shaking, or completely tensing up as I imagined there might be when I had to play it for another set of ears.

Lucy then, in her usual way, darts around the piece, giving me practical tips. At the very start, don't begin with LH little finger and RH thumb, as I am currently. It's the first, dramatic, note of the piece, and needs to arrive with more force. So, as before, she suggests I bunch the thumb behind the third finger on each hand to form a kind of robust hammer. Once you've struck the note you can then switch to 5 in the LH and the thumb in the right. And she's right – it works. Then there's the first phrase. Lucy says mine is shapeless: it's not rising or telling a story. I should think of it as a series of phrases – three in all – each beginning on the E flat. Again, it's effective. It does give a better shape to the whole passage.

She has probably a dozen such insights. The most interesting involves the opening Moderato – from bar 8 onwards. She wants me to play it more softly, and insists that, with the chords in the accompaniment, the first should be louder than the second. I like this sensation of the two chords weighted differently – it sounds a little bit like the human heart, that *lub-dub* of valves shutting and opening. Lucy uses the word *Bebung* to describe this,

© Sven Arnstein

which, I discover later, is a technical term originally used about the clavi-chord – the ability, once a note has been struck, to depress the key to alter the pitch – so, almost vibrato. It is used in relation to Chopin to indicate a quiet repetition of a note, though some musicologists appear to be a bit sniffy about applying the clavichord term to the piano. Whatever it's called, this ability to make the music reference the human heartbeat is brilliantly employed later in the piece (around bar 200) where the motif keeps coming back – with rising excitement and fervour, bordering on terror. By this stage (it happens exactly a hundred bars previously as well) the downward 'sigh' at the end of the phrase is replaced by a rising question. There's anxiety, not resignation. The heartbeat is quickening, a frightening thud rather than a reassuring pulse.

After months of – utterly necessary – concentration on very small segments, darting around the piece with Lucy has been, as I hoped, a change of pace and perspective, and allowed me to appreciate the piece in a completely different way.

I wonder, though, how long this new phase of having lessons from two teachers a week can last. Not long at all, I'm sure.

Sunday, 12 June

I'm now at a dangerous stage. More and more I can play passages without looking at the music and sometimes surprise myself by the way my fingers fly at certain bits of the piece; they do truly seem to have acquired a 'mind of their own', to use an utterly ascientific figure of speech. And while it's slightly wondrous watching the fingers flying around the piano without any kind of conscious control, it's also unnerving. It feels like a confidence trick in some ways – with one part of my body fooling the other that it's in charge. I should feel happy: this is what the whole exercise has been about, nearing the moment where I could play the piece at speed in a way which is beginning to sound plausible. But I have a nagging insecurity about knowing *how* it is that I've arrived at this point. If I can't explain it, then how can I feel relaxed about it?

In the evening my colleague Ian Mayes comes over to Blockley for the night. He's writing the latest volume of the *Guardian* history and he spends three hours taping me on various aspects of the story of the past couple of decades. We first worked together on the launch of *Guardian Weekend* – more than twenty years ago. Before then he'd spent most of his career in Northamptonshire, leaving to work at the BBC quite late in life and pitching up at the *Guardian* in his early 50s. He'd never been to university – and, when he arrived at the *Guardian*, had barely been abroad. But he is a serious autodidact who taught himself Italian and perpetually devours art history.

On Sunday morning he asks to hear the Chopin. He doesn't know the piece, and as I play I realise it's completely different playing to someone who is unfamiliar with the music in question. I am suddenly very conscious of playing the piece as a narrative – telling a story. Playing to music teachers, the emphasis is on getting the notes right. But playing to Ian, I want to show what the music *is* – to convey the conflicting passions and turmoil contained within it. The opening is a clearing of the throat, an announcement that the story is about to begin. The first bridging passage has to be urgent. The second tune, an oasis of calm and beauty – I have to make him feel that sudden change of mood. And then the build-up to the return of the tune in grand, majestic tones. And so on – with added urgency and tension as the coda approaches. I've told him to look out for the madness of the final section – so now I have to signal to him in my playing that this is the moment I was talking about: the winding up of the coil and the sudden, explosive release. The notes at the end are ragged, but I'm not sure he notices, or cares. And nor, much, do I on this occasion. I've played the piece in a new, vivid way. The next time I play it will be for Michael, and I know I will retreat in speed and in expression. But this has been a little moment of release. And I now understand the imperative to really go for it – that the true impact of the piece lies in the sensation of the pianist risking all. Which is something that a lesson doesn't always encourage.

Thursday, 16 June

At yesterday's lesson with Michael, I ask to work on the double page of LH arpeggios – bars 166–92 – where, for twenty-six consecutive bars, the LH is in a repeating pattern of broken chords. Whenever I play this, I find it daunting, exhausting – and potentially injurious. I can usually feel my arm getting tenser and tenser as I keep on with these repetitive patterns (though of course every bar is subtly, or not so subtly, different). I suggest to Michael that there's something missing in my training or technique which means my wrists are insufficiently flexible, and I therefore play with a too-rigid hand, which is why I sometimes find myself seizing up.

Michael doesn't seem very persuaded by this theory. He makes me play some of the passage and, as usual, he alights on fingering as the problem as we get into a discussion about whether I should play a certain note with my third or fourth finger. I'm suspicious of this. Michael's answer to everything seems to be fingering. This problem really doesn't seem to have anything to do with it. But he's right about many things, so maybe he's right about this.

I tell him I'm playing the piece to one or two other teachers. I'm worried it might be a tense moment, but he instantly nods agreement. 'Very good idea,' he says, maybe a bit relieved at the thought that this might release him from the sole responsibility of getting the piece up to scratch.

Then it's off for a taxing day at work, which doesn't end until 11 p.m., after an official black-tie dinner for a much-revered former non-executive director of the Guardian Media Group. I sag home at midnight, knowing I still have two or three hours of work ahead of me. I end up forcing myself to go through until about 2.30 a.m. preparing a script and slides for a series of all-staff briefings in which *Guardian* CEO Andrew Miller and I are going to bring colleagues up to date with *Guardian* finances and current strategy.

I'm then up after four hours' sleep to finish off some of the charts and do the technical rehearsal. Andrew and I then 'perform' in Kings Place's main hall – where we did the Schumannathon last autumn. But the context today is purely corporate, not musical. We do the same ninety-minute presentation four times, each time to about 350 people – it's dense in financial detail and in laying out the route through to a sustainable future.

At about 3 p.m. there's a half-hour pause between presentations. On my way back to my office – my mind set on a quick twenty-three-minute burst of emails – I bump into Peter Milican, the man who built Kings Place and who now runs it, having transformed himself from property developer into concert programmer.

'Fancy seeing Simon?' he asks. 'Rattle. He's downstairs with the OAE.'

Well, yes. That does seem a good use of twenty-three minutes. And so we stand at the back of the rehearsal as Rattle – beaming and commanding in a white linen shirt and trainers – coaxes gorgeous sounds out of the Orchestra of the Age of Enlightenment as they play their way through the Mozart two-piano concerto with the Labèque Sisters performing on reconstructed eighteenth-century forte pianos. I'm struck by the absolute attention to Rattle's instructions – the easy manner in which he tosses off commands about matters of phrasing or bowing and how instantly this body of professional musicians picks up, almost intuitively, on what he wants and gives it back to him.

And then, my watch ticking round to 3.25, I tear myself away.

Friday, 17 June

Up very early to go to Lucy's flat for my second piano lesson of the week. Again Lucy wants me to play the entire piece: 'You have to get used to playing the whole thing.' This morning I feel sluggish after the four hours of sleep and six hours of presenting the day before and Lucy's strong tea doesn't really make much difference. I'm conscious that I'm rushing things and in a couple of places I ground to a temporary halt as the speed–accuracy trade-off bites with severe effects on the latter. Given the day before, I don't think this slight backwards step is too worrying.

Lucy then starts working on the same passage as Michael – the arpeggios in the LH at bar 166 – but her approach is different. Instead of looking at the fingerings, she wants me to move my arms as I go up and down the arpeggios. She wants more fluidity in the joint between the forearm and the wrist. After that she makes me play the same arpeggios but in E major, then F, then F-sharp major – the point being that in each different key the arm has to make different (and sometimes much greater) adjustments to get round the notes. By the time I play in E flat again the passage seems much less problematic. Now she makes me play the first half of each bar in the passage, and then the second half of each bar. We move on to the waltz, where we do the same.

Lucy seems pleased with our progress. Soon, she says, I'll be ready to add real musicality to it all, which is so hard when you're still learning the notes. This would not, I think, please Daniel Barenboim, with his insistence that by the time you've learned the notes, it's too late to inject the musicality. But I think I'm with Lucy on this one. The piece is very gradually revealing itself to me in its possibilities; it's almost the first time in my life where I've so internalised the notes and technical demands of a piece that I can begin to glimpse it in purely musical terms, and with any degree of confidence that I can achieve the sound and meaning for which I'm aiming.

Sunday, 19 June

There's been a lot of rain in Blockley recently, so the sedum roof of the music room has turned a lovely mix of yellow, green and red, with bumble bees swarming all over it. And people have been taking up the offer to use the music room. The singers from the nearby Longborough Opera, for example – several of whom are lodging in the village – have discovered the room and have started to use it. One soprano arrives at 9 a.m. this morning, does half an hour of rather astonishing yoga warm-ups and then launches into her vocal exercises. She pops her head around the door at one point and asks if I could accompany her in some of the pieces she's working on for a scholarship exam. So, for forty minutes, I sight-read my way through some Weber, Gounod and Mozart, thinking: 'This is why you've spent nine months ankle-deep in mud and debt.'

I spend the afternoon on emails and writing a 1,200-word piece on the future of journalism. Then, back in London in the evening, there's a session with the Spider Club. We start with a really clever arrangement of Mozart's 'Jupiter' Symphony, then a plausible rendering of Tchaikovsky's *Sleeping Beauty* waltz. A rather ropey account of the *Meistersinger* overture follows, before a break for some supper. And then the second and fourth movements from Tchaik 5. At the end of every piece (especially the slow movements of the Mozart and the Wagner) there's the usual agreement that virtually all music, played in this fashion, is infinitely more complex than the ear 'hears' in a concert performance or – perhaps especially – in the home.

Saturday, 25 June

I'm on my way back to London after a couple of days in Moscow, where I gave a talk at a conference – *another* – on the future of media. But I wanted to do this one – mainly because I hadn't been to Russia since the fall of communism, and this provided the perfect excuse to meet some movers and shakers and give myself a crash course in how the Putinocracy is faring – and also to protest at the recent harassment of the paper's Moscow correspondent by FSB, the successors to the old KGB. I arrived on Friday, when I began my day by being locked into the RIA Novosti with four or five other journalists for a meeting with President Medvedev. I hadn't asked for any time with the president, so it was rather a surprise to be offered the encounter. The security was awesome – roads closed off, Alsatians prowling around for hours in advance – but the event was pointless: journalists as window dressing. Later on I was to give my talk, and this proved almost as frustrating. I'd originally been told to prepare forty minutes. By the time I arrived in Moscow it was down to twenty minutes. And then three minutes before I spoke the organisers announced that none of the audio or video equipment worked. Halfway through the talk the sound went entirely, so it wasn't clear that anyone heard much of what I'd come to say. I did, though, manage to enter a protest to the relevant minister about the expulsion of the *Guardian*'s Moscow correspondent. He promised to raise it with the president. This seems unlikely.

In the evening we were able to get into the second round of the Tchaikovsky piano competition in the magnificently restored central hall of the Moscow Conservatoire. The last time I was here was in 1983 – the brief rule of Chernenko – for one of the biannual trips the *Guardian* features department used to make to foreign capitals. I remember drinking sweet pink Georgian champagne in the bar with Chris Huhne, then the *Guardian*'s economics editor, now a Cabinet minister.* There's no bar in sight now – but the hall is just as impressive, dominated by fourteen huge murals of the great composers – from Bach to Mahler, via Chopin – and with a crystal-clear acoustic. On the stage there were four Steinways – and one Fazioli for the second round – four pianists and four different Mozart concertos. The hall was packed, with conservatoire students sitting on every available inch of the floor and stairways. The refurbishment evidently didn't stretch to air conditioning, with numerous women fanning away the warm Moscow night.

The announcements were all in Russian, ditto the programme, which made things hard to follow. First up was a Ukrainian who played exactly the right notes in exactly the right order in a way that made the correctness of it all perhaps more memorable than the musicality. And then an American who was the opposite: so individualistic as to border on the quirky – fated, one suspected, to be marked down for that as much as a couple of barely noticeable slips. And then a Russian who was technically all there – but perhaps a little lacking in drama in a concerto, K491, which is full of it. And, finally, another Russian who was more assertive and . . . But by this stage I was simply grateful not to be sitting alongside Barry Douglas, Vladimir Ashkenazy and Peter Donohoe on the jury table having to make the impossibly fine distinctions between fantastically gifted pianists. Particularly in Mozart concertos.

The list of past winners in the back of the programme included several years when the jury refused to award a first prize – Donohoe being one of

---

* Huhne resigned from the Cabinet in February 2012.

them in 1982. Best, but of a mediocre bunch. Imagine how simultaneously elated and deflated one would feel at that.

For all the frustrations over the talk, then, the outing to the conservatoire made this a good trip. But in the airport tonight an email from Anne Brain, the owner of the farmhouse in Lot, reminds me that piano camp is now less than a month away. I've missed four days of practice all told with this trip and the preparation beforehand. And I already know that I'll only have two mornings next week when I can be certain to find practice time before work. Is it going to be enough?

Monday, 27 June

This morning I did have time to practise and I worked on the coda, which still slightly panics me (of course!). I'm using a technique of Lucy's, playing the whole thing in the RH but just the beginning of the bar in the LH – or the end of the bar, not the whole of the bar in any case – to see if it has any effect. I think it does.

At one point, I got stuck on bars 162 through to 175, partly because there's a page turn. I've realised that that's the one thing I've never rehearsed: page turns. This one is particularly confounding in my edition because it begins with a B-flat major scale (though nothing's ever that simple in Chopin: it's complicated by an E natural). Then, as the page turns, which you would naturally do with your left hand, the LH has to crash in with a chord precisely as the scale in the RH changes into some other key that I can't immediately work out. So I don't have a free hand and I haven't yet sorted, let alone memorised, the mid-scale modulation.

At lunchtime, I meet up with Simon Russell Beale, the actor, who is a very keen pianist. We head down to the basement of Kings Place and I show him the concert hall. The staff around are all dead impressed to meet him. We sit down at a grand piano in a small rehearsal room with a couple of sandwiches, and play through a few pieces, including Ravel's *Mother Goose* and the Strauss suite from *Der Rosenkavalier*. He's a fluent, confident sight-reader. I'm impressed. We end playing the beginning and then the conclusion of Brahms' own four-hand version of *A German Requiem*. Simon is a

Brahms nut and seems genuinely transported by the discovery that there's a version of the piece that he can play.

Does he practise much? 'Alas, I haven't practised seriously for years,' he says in a quiet voice, initially not much more than a whisper. 'But I've played all my life. I don't have a piano at home. Luckily, most theatres have pianos. So I tend to use theatre pianos. In New York, for example, I was working in the Brooklyn Academy of Music doing *Twelfth Night* and it became a joke among the security staff at Brooklyn that I'd be there at eight o'clock [in the morning] with my score. Sam Mendes said, "One of the great images of my working life is coming into the rehearsal room and finding you at the piano." It's two hours – I'm sure it's the same for you – it's two hours of absolute joy.'

'You play for *two hours*? That's "not serious"?'

'Well, if it's a ten o'clock rehearsal and I'm there at eight, I can get two hours in. As I say, it's very irregular but I started doing it in New York. I wanted – it's a stupid idea – to learn all the forty-eight Preludes and Fugues of Bach.'

'And can you?'

'No, of course I can't. My memory . . . my memory is terrible.'

We discover that we've both been choirboys, and agree that being trained to sight-read did for our memories. 'It takes me hours to memorise a piece of music, hours, even a song. I mean, a little eight-bar prelude . . .'

If he has no memory, then as an actor how does he . . . ?

'How do I memorise the words? I don't know, it's weird, isn't it? That's fine. Touch wood! But that's never been an issue, isn't it weird?'

Before I have to return upstairs to work, Simon talks about the appeal of classical music to him later in life, which echoes something of my own experience. 'You know the Death of Theatre,' he says, 'which has now been going on for 400 years? It's been dying since it was born really, as we know. Always reaching out for youth and young people, which is great. But I wonder whether there aren't experiences in people's lives that happen later. I don't think I ever went to the theatre in my 20s. I certainly didn't go to any concerts. Perhaps it's just part of growing up – well, you're not growing up, but growing older. I mean, you kind of – I just – need something, I just need something.'

Wednesday, 29 June

'Three weeks to piano camp,' I tell Michael at this morning's lesson, so he suggests I play the whole Ballade to him – my debut with him. It's 8 a.m. and I haven't played properly for five days. But I play it all right-ish. I'm concentrating so much on the notes that I don't imagine it was very musical – as expected, the opposite of playing to my friend Ian – but most of the notes were (with appropriate tempi – i.e. very cautious) in place, except during the coda, which is more than a little ragged. Michael does not do effusion, at least not with me. But at the end of it he raises an eyebrow: 'That hung together much better than I was expecting.' Could be worse, in other words. Not a total train wreck.

He then begins to pick me up on things, of course – too much pedal here, a wrong fingering there, and so on. And, generally, he thinks I'm playing the whole thing too loud. He wants me to take the LH, in particular, down in the big restatements of the second theme. At one point he zeroes in on the beginning. He wants a big wash of pedal over the first two bars, but then spots Lucy's handwritten instructions to the contrary, a kind of pianistic lipstick-on-the-collar moment. I explain her view (that the new pedal should begin on the E flat). He hums and says: 'Well, I don't think I agree, but let's leave it.' He isn't cross – I think – just genuinely interested at someone else's contrary view. It's the first time there's been a direct conflict between my two teachers.

Friday, 1 July

Just back from a forty-eight-hour editorial away day in Oxford. We meet at Nuffield College – partly because it's so much cheaper than any conference hotel (I'm a visiting fellow and get 'mate's rates'), but also because it's small, friendly and well run. Two long days of discussing the future of news, the balance between print and digital – and the more practical stuff to do with budgets and, as ever, managing the dizzying pace of change in the industry. I ask if there's a college piano – and there is – a solid and well-worn Blüthner upright which sits in the annexe to the chapel. So I am able – Russell Beale–style – to keep up my Ballade practice with two early morning workouts of twenty minutes before everyone else is up and about.

On the way back from Oxford, I nip in to see Jeff Shackell at 'Nimrod'. He wants me to try the hundred-year-old piano he was so keen for me to buy last September. It's now restored and unrecognisable from the faded, down-at-heel, literally moth-eaten instrument I saw. He says the Duke and Duchess of York came close to buying it (or having it bought for them) as a wedding gift, but in the end it went elsewhere. I try it and can see what Jeff had done to it – and why he likes these old Hamburg Steinways. It has a full, bloomy tone which is in a way both more rounded and direct than mine. For a few minutes I'm downhearted: should I have held on for this one after all? But, the longer I play on it, the less torn I feel. To my ears it doesn't quite have the touch and subtlety of colouration as my 1978 Steinway. It will make someone very happy I'm sure. Even if it's not a duke.

Sunday, 3 July

Chamber-music weekend at the Fish Cottage music room, with Richard Sennett's B quartet – actually quintet, since Mark doubles up for Richard on cello when the latter's hand tires (he had an injury to it some years back). They've been playing together for four or five years now, and have had the odd musical weekend away at Prussia Cove in Cornwall.

We kick off on Saturday at about 3 p.m., after tea and cake – playing a mixture of piano quintets, piano quartets and piano trios for about three and a half hours, all in a very relaxed way, still surrounded by yet-to-be-unpacked suitcases bursting with music and clothes. We break for a drink and then play a bit more. Richard produces some smoked salmon and Staffordshire oatcakes. We sit on chairs in the sun next to the stream eating, drinking, talking. More playing before supper – and then again after supper.

By now we've moved on to clarinet music as well. I haven't touched the clarinet for six months . . . but the feeling and touch soon come back. We start with Mozart's Kegelstatt Trio: none of us has played it for at least fifteen or twenty years. At the end of it, Susanna, the viola player, says, 'I know I've played that before but I have no memory of it.' For me, there are occasional moments when there is a flash of intuition as to what is about to come. Through distant time and memory something prompts a feeling of how a phrase should, or would, sound; or how a few notes should best be fingered. Something is certainly lodged in some deep well of memory.

The acoustics of the music room really work for mixed ensembles of this sort. It's very intimate, blossomy and warm in sound, but with every note clear. It's a big enough space that you can sit in a circle or a horseshoe, either with or without the piano. It really leads to an unforced quality of sound and a much greater instinct for listening to each other as you play.

We carry on until about 1 a.m., have a leisurely breakfast this morning, and start again at about 10.30, playing right the way through to about 4.30, with only a brief pause for lunch. We get through an awful lot of music. Mozart piano quartets are followed by the Brahms Clarinet Quintet – including the slow movement, which is one we have all avoided in the past because of its tendency to fall apart in the middle. Today we manage it with Mark conducting us to prevent implosion. We're all pretty good sight-readers and very rarely during the course of our twenty-four hours do we break down and have to start again.

I've improved with age as a chamber musician. It's not that I'm better technically, but I'm much more aware of *how* to play chamber music, how to listen and realise the obvious: that your part isn't a solo part. You're listening for when to blend in and when to emerge from the mingled textures of sound. You start to use your eyes as much as your ears. I didn't know when younger that the most precious moments are when you can start having eye contact – either with your friends' eyes or with their instruments. I didn't understand that looking at a string player's bow may give you the most precise sign – within a fraction of a second – of the moment at which they're going to make their instrument sound. With a woodwind instrument you're using your hands, tongue, lips, eyes, arms, ears, fingers, upper body and even feet as ways of producing sound, keeping time, signalling to others and merging into the lines, beats and washes of music around you. My daily twenty minutes is one thing: this weekend of shared music-making has been intense, life-enhancing, restorative.

Back in London tonight there's an email from Nick Davies headed 'Important hacking story', announcing: 'I think this may be the most powerful hacking story so far.' It's the revelation that the *News of the World* hacked into the phone of the missing teenager Milly Dowler in 2002. The Dowler parents were told by the police that some of the messages had been deleted. They're saying this gave them false hope. Nick's been working away at this for some time. He's right: this will be *big*.

PART SIX

Monday, 4 July

A gruelling and dramatic day. Before going to the office to begin work on the Dowler story, I am up at the crack of dawn and across town to St James's Park. There, in a special suite, I have breakfast with Condoleezza Rice. The hotel has bodyguards outside and in reception. A burly American security man accompanies me in the lift up to her room. He knows we're due to talk music. 'Do you play music?' I ask. 'No, sir, I used to play the piano and now I play with logistics and play with arrangements and I play with politics.'

I apologise to Rice for seeing her so early in the morning. 'Early' for her is 5 a.m., she replies crisply – that's when she normally gets up to work out. A few years ago, I read a piece in the *NYT* about Rice and her piano playing while she was Secretary of State, and today's my chance to find out how someone dovetailed the job of running armies and waging wars with life as an amateur pianist.

How did she get started with the piano? She says she's from a family of pianists – 'My mother, grandmother and great-grandmother were all pianists' – and when Rice was 3½ years old and her parents were at work her grandmother began to teach her. She picked things up very quickly, and at the age of 4 told her father 'I need a piano'. 'And my dad said, "Well, I tell you what, when you learn to play 'What a Friend We Have in Jesus' perfectly, we will buy you a piano." So I went to my grandmother's house the next day and I practised for eight hours and when they came home I knew "What a Friend We Have in Jesus" perfectly. My parents never wanted to disappoint me so they went out and they rented a piano because they couldn't really afford to buy one. So that's when my piano career sort of took off, at 4.'

By the age of 10 she was playing 'little concerts' and enrolled at Birmingham Southern Conservatory of Music. It was autumn 1964, just a few months after the Civil Rights Act had been passed, and Rice was the first black student at the conservatory. Four years later the family moved to Denver. Her father became assistant dean of the University of Denver and when the time came Rice enrolled as a music major at the university's Lamont School of Music. It was here that she first played the G minor Ballade, as part of her junior-year recital. She was 18 years old and didn't find it a struggle, at least not in terms of the technical aspects – 'except that infernal last Presto, which is really just . . . the coda is impossible'. What she did find difficult was bringing musicality to her playing of the piece. 'It's just hard to really understand it musically,' she says. 'Actually, you know, it's not so hard to get musical in the parts of the piece that are soft and elegant, everybody can do that, but to be musical in the Presto or musical in the development section, that's hard.' I'm not sure this is precisely what I want to hear now that I have less than three weeks to achieve just this.

I'm, of course, interested in how Rice mastered the Ballade – did she have a particular method of practising? 'I learned it the way I learned every piece, and I still do to this day, which is that I will take a very small section of it, and I'll learn that, particularly in the difficult parts. I'll learn that, and then I'll learn the next very small section, and then I'll learn the bridge between them, so that there's no gap. I tend to practise both hands together. You know, some practise left hand, one, then right hand, but I think that's more difficult than actually learning two. And I try to learn by practising slowly which is, for me, a real challenge because I, very often, before I really know it, I'm playing at speed.' So, not that different from me.

A year after her junior-year recital, Rice had a realisation. 'At the end of my sophomore year I was invited to the Aspen Music Festival School. I go to Aspen and I meet these 12-year-olds, and I'm 17, and I'm working very hard at it, but they're not working very hard at it and they are really good, and I'm sort of OK. And I thought, "You know, I just may not have what it really takes to be at the top of this profession," and I really never wanted to be a piano teacher.' So she went home and told her parents she was changing majors. First she tried English literature ('which I hated'), then State and Local Government and Political Science ('and that was really boring'), until finally settling on International Politics. She then went on to do a Master's at Notre Dame and was playing piano less and less – 'I would play, you know, here and there, I would play Christmas carols or something, but I really didn't play very much after that.' As she entered politics, and then went on to work for George H. W. Bush from 1989 to 1991, the piano was given even less time. However, when she left Washington in 1991 to become provost of Stanford University, things changed.

'One day I was sitting with the dean of the Law School [Paul Brest], who was a violist, and he said, "You know, I have this chamber group and we want to try some of the piano literature. Would you come and play with us?" I said, "You know, Paul, I haven't played serious music in ten years." He said, "No, no, no, come play with us." And I did, and that's how I got back into playing, through chamber music.'

She then played regularly with that group until 2001, when she moved back to Washington as National Security Adviser to George W. Bush. Though she still intended to attend an annual music festival in the summers, there was the possibility that the demands of work were again going to deny her the time to play piano. But a little while later, in 2002, 'My secretary came in and she said, "Yo-Yo Ma is on the phone." And I said, "You mean the cellist?" and she said, "Yeah." We had met at Stanford, he played a concert and I had gone backstage to say hello. And he said, "You play, don't you? I hear you play?" And I said, "Well yeah," and he said, "Well sometime we'll play," and I thought, "Right, sure we will." Well, he called to ask if I would like to play with him. He was receiving the National Medal of the Arts. So we played the second movement of the Brahms D minor violin sonata, which a lot of cellists actually poach. And, after that, I thought, "You know, I don't care how busy I am, I have to play more." And thanks to the same person, Paul Brest, who knew some musicians in Washington, I put together my own chamber group.'

She would play with this group about every six weeks or so, and managed to keep it going even when she became Secretary of State in 2005. 'Generally what I would do is, I'd set a time to play with the quartet, with the chamber group. If they hadn't heard from me for a while, they'd call me, because I think they became really good friends – one of the nice things about chamber music is you become really good friends. I would then get something on the calendar; sometimes it survived the crises and sometimes it didn't. But I really tried to play every few weeks and, when I was going to play, that gave me more incentive to actually practise. So, even if I would drag home at 8.30 or nine o'clock I'd sit down at the piano for maybe half an hour. I got very good at using even fifteen minutes to practise and to get something worked out.'

She even managed to keep up her practice when travelling on state business. 'There was a hotel in Berlin,' she tells me, 'the Adlon, and there was a grand piano in the suite. They started leaving music for me. I guess from an interview, or something, they'd known that I played the Brahms Op. 116 and Op. 118. I arrived one day from a particularly bad trip to the Middle East, you know, just nothing had gone right. I walked into my suite in

Berlin and there, on the piano, was the Brahms, the Henle version, and I opened it and I just played for an hour. I played Brahms and it was just wonderful. I could feel the physical effect, absolutely.'

I wonder if, like me, she feels a difference between the way she practised as a youngster and how she practises as an adult. 'I think about the time that I was a college piano major,' she says, 'and I was practising four or five hours a day but, you know, one hour was kind of reading through whatever I was playing, another hour was reading through what might be coming next and another hour was talking to the person in the practice room next to me, another hour was my boyfriend stopped by and we'd talk. The luxury of having four or five hours a day to practise was something I would give everything for now but I'm a much more efficient practiser because I don't have much time.'

© Getty Images

We speak a little about the benefits of playing the piano, especially in relation to the stresses of the day job. Rice describes playing as a 'release point' from these stresses – vital if you're going to do your job well and stay sane. Rice tried other release points too while in office – 'I also learned to play golf during this time. I would try to watch football. I would try to do things with friends.' But music proved far more effective than any of these other outlets.

'The great thing about struggling with Brahms is that it is transporting, you cannot think about anything else. There are a lot of activities that, while you're doing them, your mind is still wandering and thinking "Oh I've got that problem" or "I need to solve this that way". With the piano you have to be there with it in the moment. So when I was playing, either practising or with my group, I was just right there with the music. And when I finished, I was tired but my mind was clear and I felt, you know, you feel this sense of release because you've not been concentrating on whatever difficulties you had that day. So it was really, it was very important. And I could tell because, when I was practising, the phone would ring, or something, it's like you've been brought out of a deep sleep, you know, you're startled all of a sudden, because you're so far into what you're doing.'

And now that she's left government, what has happened to her piano playing? Does she find she needs it just as much as she did back then? 'The story now,' she replies, 'is that I play a good deal more.'

She's in select company in combining high politics with music: in the serviceable-to-decent category of political pianists you might include Harry Truman, Helmut Schmidt, Ignacy Paderewski and Ehud Barak. Later in the day I see a photograph of Rice sitting next to British Foreign Secretary William Hague, another amateur pianist, at the unveiling of a statue of Ronald Reagan. Hague has said he gave up the instrument – at least for the time being – on being made shadow Foreign Secretary. So I suspect they didn't talk about the piano.

I'm back in the office in time for the two morning conferences – the first a review of the previous day, the second one, unusually for a newspaper, open to all and more forward-looking (though, if there's a really big story like today's breaking, it's often not discussed at this stage). Then there's an hour-and-a-half meeting with various buying directors from advertising agencies. During an interlude I'm at last able to set in motion the editing of the Milly Dowler story. Because Nick doesn't work in the office – he works from home on the south coast – there's less of the usual toing and froing that would happen with an office-based reporter. The main thing the story needs, I think, is a more straightforward structure. Nick's written it slightly discursively, which I'm not convinced is right. The lawyers must see it and, to be on the safe side, at least two desk editors as well as the subs.

I'm then pulled away into a meeting with the design team, before, as coincidence would have it, an International Press Institute lunch with the Culture and Media Secretary, Jeremy Hunt. The lunch, all off the record, is downstairs at Kings Place, attended by a select group of executives and veterans from the media business. Somebody asks Hunt about regulation of the press and phone hacking. He mounts a stout defence of the Press Complaints Commission and the general status quo in relation to regulation. Obviously, no one around the table (a few of whom were gamely batting the usual News International line on regulation) has any idea of what is about to be unleashed in the afternoon.

Immediately after lunch I'm in another design meeting for an hour or so. Meanwhile an odd letter's arrived from the chief constable of Surrey asking us not to use the Dowler story as it will cause distress to her parents. But Nick tells me they know all about it, and are relaxed about the story going ahead. By now it's increasingly difficult to concentrate on the discussions of the future design of the paper. The story is what's called 'a marmalade dropper' in the trade – a piece so transfixing that you let slip the marmalade between the pot and the toast. Otherwise known in some tabloid circles as a 'Fuck me Doris' story. In the end I have to rewrite the piece in gaps between another prolonged meeting, this time with consultants who have been in the *Guardian* looking at internal processes and structures. Nick is sitting in Lewes waiting for my re-draft, and then the lawyers and the news desk will have to look at his revisions. But we get there in the end. At about 4.30, we launch the story on an unsuspecting world.

In the way of newspaper life, I then have to go into yet another meeting, which takes me out of the loop as the story begins to ricochet around the web. By the time the meeting is done – at about 6.30 – it is evident that this is going to be absolutely huge. So many of our other phone-hacking stories have been published to deafening silence elsewhere. This time, every other paper has weighed in, and this whole scandal, which has bubbled away for two years with only periodical breakthroughs into the wider consciousness, has suddenly burst into cacophonous life.

I stay at the office as late as I can, watching the story ripple around the world. But eventually I have to leave for a private dinner in honour of a remarkable little charity which works by donating mobile phones and little spy cameras in conflict situations so that there can be multiple witnesses to brutality, torture, etc. I get home around midnight: the story's just starting to spread in the US. I sense this is the beginning of an extraordinary week.

Tuesday, 5 July

We're waiting to see how News International will react to the story today. I know from experience that they have a history of lashing out when attacked – very aggressively, and sometimes completely dishonestly. But this time there's been a silence – which feels like shock from the *News of the World* rather than the prelude to a counter-attack. In fact, they've started briefing there may be worse to come. We sit around thinking, 'What could be worse than hacking into the voicemail of a murdered teenager?' We don't have long to wait. Other papers, including the *Mail* and *Telegraph*, report that the hacking targets include the relatives of people who had died in the 7/7 al-Qaeda atrocity in London. And the relatives of people who have been murdered in Iraq. As the crisis deepens the silence from Wapping becomes more understandable.

Nick has had a long cup of coffee with Glenn Mulcaire, the private investigator at the heart of the affair. He has no quarrel with anything we've written, and he wants Nick to publish an apology for what he got up to.

In the form he told it to Nick, it would be quite something. But Mulcaire runs it past his lawyer first, who, in a lawyerly way, strips it back to the bare minimum. It's interesting how even the 'villains' of Nick's story turn to him. It shows how fair and accurate his reporting is.

Everyday office life goes on regardless at the *Guardian*. Today there's a heads of department lunch and a meeting with the developers creating our iPad app. But just as I'd found yesterday, it's increasingly hard to concentrate on anything but the Dowler story and its ramifications. The story is now global, and we've media enquiries coming in from all over the world. So in the middle of the afternoon I clear out my diary and focus only on phone hacking – breaking off in late afternoon to write a leader.* By about 8.30 the guts of the story are ready and a few of us dart across town to observe some focus groups who are looking at dummies of a few of the new design things we're thinking of trying in the paper. We sit behind a one-way mirror as *Guardian* readers – some loyalists, some part-time casual readers – pick over the work we've been doing. Eating crisps washed down with warm white wine, I either want to hug the people on the other side of the glass – there are some readers for whom the *Guardian* is as close as they get to a religion – or else break through the mirror and shake them by the shoulders because they seem to be so stubborn or opaque.

A handful of us then end up with a hurried Vietnamese meal off Oxford Street, before once more working until 2 a.m. Every hour you spend away from the news cycle, you have to spend time catching up – fifty emails an hour is not uncommon. But this story is generating much more than that. And it seems to be getting faster and faster too, acquiring international dimensions, business implications, widespread personal consequences, and potential political ructions.

Wednesday, 6 July

There's absolutely no chance of a Wednesday piano lesson today. I have a 7 a.m. start, going over to White City for the *Today* programme. Then

---

* The first, as it turns out, of four consecutive leaders on the subject.

it's into the office to marshal the growing team covering the numerous angles spinning off from the Dowler story. We're following up the leads being thrown up by other papers. Did the *NotW* hack the phones of the parents of two 10-year-old girls murdered by a school caretaker in 2002? It looks like it. There are other reports suggesting senior editors authorised payments to the police. One or two large companies have said they're pulling advertising from next Sunday's *NotW*. The prime minister has condemned the Dowler hacking as a 'truly dreadful act'. NI's CEO, Rebekah Brooks, has finally broken her silence to say she's 'appalled and shocked' by what the *Guardian*'s revealed. Meanwhile I'm giving interviews to American, European and British media outlets, and beginning another leader for tomorrow. In the late afternoon I nip over to the City to do *Jeff Randall Live* on Sky, which is broadcast from the top of the Gherkin. From there, I jump into a taxi and head to ITN's building for *Channel 4 News*.

I get to the studios in Gray's Inn Road thirty minutes early, so head up the road intending to sit down in a Costa to write the other half of the leader. But I notice that a piano shop has just opened next to Costa. I pop in. There are about ten pianos in a space the size of a little front room – among them a Fazioli 278 (the full concert grand), several uprights, and a couple of Schimmel grands. I sit down and try out the Fazioli, and the Schimmels. On each of them I attempt to play the first passage work in the Ballade, which I have been able to play from memory for the last three months, but today I just can't remember which note it starts on. The coda is still there, and I can play a little bit of the waltz, but these mental blocks still remain. I don't know if it's just the adrenaline of the moment, or something still unresolved in my memory. Either way, if things carry on at the rate they are with this story, my Ballade playing is bound to deteriorate. Indeed, it strikes me now that even getting to piano camp is in serious jeopardy. But this little twenty-minute interlude before going live on prime-time national news helps calm me for the interview and, as always, resets the brain.

From the studio I go back to the office and catch up on the emergency debate in the Commons. And it's also looking as if George Osborne's phone was hacked. The BSkyB takeover deal is now hanging by its fingernails and half a billion dollars has been wiped off the Murdochs' stake in News Corp. I polish off another editorial, grab a sandwich and work until 1 a.m. The other papers are unleashing a flood of stories on the other groups of victims, and Rupert Murdoch has now appointed one of his senior directors to oversee an internal investigation. One or two fellow editors call with nice words. Which never happens. Bed at 2 a.m.

Thursday, 7 July

At the office I begin what will be a historic day with a breakfast meeting and then another morning on hacking. The political pressure's building on Cameron. He's now musing over holding a public inquiry into the whole affair. Peter Oborne has written a thundering piece damning him in the *Telegraph*. Its headline: David Cameron is in the sewer because of his News International friends. Labour leader Ed Miliband is piling on the agony. And today there are new allegations of police officers pocketing tens of thousands of pounds from newspapers. *The Times* is reporting that there are several arrests of former executives imminent. More advertisers are pulling out of the *NotW* and the Royal British Legion is dropping the paper as its campaigning partner in disgust at the revelations about the hacking of war heroes' phones.

I break off for a critics' lunch, encouraging them to think about how critics might react to the new digital publishing context. They're much more receptive to the potential of technology than when we last discussed it a couple of years ago. Then it's more TV interviews – including NBC and ITN – and an online discussion with readers, which consists of about 400 questions. At the same time, the head of the British army piles in on *NotW* – 'plumbing the depths' he says – and there's an emergency debate in the Lords.

I'm just coming to the end of the online discussion when Dan Sabbagh, our media editor, barges into my office talking loudly and deliberately into his mobile. He's repeating back the things the caller is telling him.

'What? So you're going to close the *News of the World*?' he says, sitting down and staring straight ahead. 'That's the end of the *News of the World*? This Sunday's the last edition?'

The call goes on for a couple of minutes, whereupon he rushes out of the room, followed by me. He strides through the newsroom waving his arms and yelling, 'It's over! It's over!' Everybody's looking up from their desks in astonishment, at the sight of a journalist marching through the newsroom, literally shouting news. It's one of the most dramatic moments

I can remember as an editor. Dozens of staff swirl back round on their chairs to tweet the fact. Within seconds the world will know. Within two minutes the wires will have confirmed it. But, for an instant, there is just the human shout and the gasped response. There's stupefaction on colleagues' faces that things have come to this. It's a hold-the-front-page, stop-the-presses, stop-the-clocks, stop-everything scoop. The history of newspapers has just been rewritten.

Someone rushes off to 'snap' [publish a one-line summary of] what we know. Then we do what newspapers always do at such moments – huddle together for a conference. Around twenty colleagues gather round a table in the middle of a newsroom – leaning in to hear the questions and commands. Who's going to write what? Who wielded the knife – James or Rupert? Was it the advertising boycott that swung it? Where does it leave Cameron? What happens to the BSkyB bid? What should we do on the web now, what holds for later? Who can do the big magisterial read on the history of the *NotW*? Will the paper be relaunched as the *Sun on Sunday*? Is it just a gambit to save James Murdoch and Rebekah Brooks? What's the mood in the newsroom? Who will go down to the pub to take the temperature? The work's quickly divvied up and people dash off to hit the phones and keyboards or jump into taxis. I clear out my diary and make – and take – a lot of calls, including more from other Fleet Street editors. Then it's time to write another leader.

I'm wanted on *Newsnight* – but first have to fit in a little speech for Richard Norton-Taylor, a friend and colleague retiring after thirty-eight years on the paper, who's having a dinner in Soho. So there's a pit stop for that before I jump into another cab and head to White City for the second time this week. As I head over the A40 flyover it brings back memories of making this same journey in 1997, at the end of the Neil Hamilton trial – the Conservative MP's libel case against the *Guardian* had just collapsed in dramatic ignominy – and I remembered that first taste of the lonely feeling of trying to empty your head of everything before being interrogated live in front of the nation.

Newsnight over, I drop back in on the retirement dinner – by now, really, really, really tired. Home at about midnight, still fielding phone calls from assorted politicians and colleagues. It's now a billion dollars that's been wiped off News Corp shares. The police have announced they're looking at email hacking as well as phones. Emails until about 1.30 waiting for the adrenaline to subside. Realise it won't. Not for days. Or weeks.

Friday, 8 July

This morning is the first time I've touched the piano all week, apart from my little spell in the piano shop. But I don't get far before being interrupted by a call from our political editor, Patrick Wintour, who wants a briefing on the message I'd passed on to David Cameron's office about Andy Coulson and phone hacking before the 2010 election. The news is that the police have informed Coulson he will be arrested this morning, and Patrick thinks the message I passed on is bound to be an issue in the live press conference the PM is holding this morning. I manage to play another fifteen minutes of Ballade before abandoning it.

At the press conference Cameron announces two inquiries into phone hacking and the general culture and ethics of the press. He is indeed then asked if it's true I tried to warn him about Coulson having hired a known criminal then on remand on suspicion of violent crime. The PM dodges the first question; Patrick follows it up. Almost immediately we start getting a lot of calls on it at the office. We draft a statement about the warning. Do we really want to get into a briefing war with Downing Street itself? We make it clear that I had also briefed Gordon Brown, then prime minister, and Nick Clegg back in the spring of 2010. Coulson is arrested – and released after nine hours of questioning.

Rebekah Brooks has told an angry meeting of *NotW* journalists that they'll understand better in a year's time why they've done what they've done. 'Eventually it will come out why things went wrong and who was responsible and that will be another very difficult moment in this company's history. We have more visibility perhaps with what we can see coming than you guys. I am tied by the criminal investigation but I think in a year's time, every single one of you in this room might come up and say, "I see what she saw now."' So the true explanation for the closure is perhaps not what's been revealed this week: there's worse to come.

The working day ends with some serious nastiness from News International journalists, who ring about teatime threatening to run a story linking Nick with the use of crooked private detectives. Nick, who's in York attending his daughter's graduation ceremony, is completely puzzled by it – wholly, one hundred per cent untrue, he says. The threats get more and more pointed – until Nick tracks down the private investigator alleged to be involved and finds he's been rung earlier in the day by an unnamed journalist who, he sensed, was clearly trying to trap him. And then yet more mafioso threats, with a senior executive on one title threatening to work over the *Guardian* – and me – in another News International title. I don't actually believe that the editor of the second title has any knowledge that his column space is being volunteered in this way for a revenge hit. But the very fact of the threat is symptomatic of how one or two NI executives still feel they can use the muscle of the organisation to bully people into doing what they want.

Meanwhile, really lovely emails pour in all day from journalistic colleagues and hundreds of readers, some of whom have read the *Guardian* all their lives and just want to say how pleased they are we saw this story through. It's been a frantic week, and a momentous one. Difficult to work out what it all means yet – but it does feel that we've reached a watershed where the fear that one organisation has exercised over great swathes of public life for two or more generations may finally have been lifted.

Saturday, 9 July

As I step out of the house in Kentish Town our next-door neighbour Gill breaks off from washing her car to say what a great thing the *Guardian* had done. Then Dick, the builder over the road, is punching the air; and then somebody riding past on a bike screeches to a halt to congratulate me; and then somebody walking their dog . . . That's never happened before – and will almost certainly never happen again, so I might as well savour the moment.

We get in the car and drive down to Blockley, where I sleep all afternoon. In Wapping they're preparing the last edition in the *NotW*'s 168-year history. Rupert Murdoch's flying in to handle the crisis personally. In my semi-insomniac way, I always sleep with Radio 5 playing through an earpiece. But tonight I keep hearing my own name on the radio, and so I end up with little sleep.

Sunday, 10 July

This morning we walk down to the village stores to buy the last edition of the *News of the World* – the honey-coloured buildings of sleepy Blockley a million miles from the sleazy intrigues of the hackers and their handlers.

I've managed to steal about two hours of piano practice over the weekend and have been conscious of the music really pouring out of me after all the tension. It almost feels as if I'm treating it as a workout – doing repeated passages on chords, arpeggios, scales, almost obsessively playing different passages repetitively to try to block out the week. And it seems extraordinary to think that only six days previously we'd been sitting in that same music room playing chamber music with little idea that the media world was about to be up-ended in such a spectacular fashion.

I write another editorial this afternoon, and then it's a two-and-a-half-hour journey back to London as I start to get myself back up to speed for the week to come, the car operating as a kind of mobile office as Lindsay drives. I have an hour's break in the evening to play some four-hand stuff with Martin Prendergast, before settling down again for another marathon late-night session. Murdoch's been on television doing a bizarre little walk-about for the throng of press outside his London flat. As he promenades, smiling and arm in arm with Rebekah Brooks, he is asked what his first priority is – his empire tottering, his biggest newspaper closed this morning, or criminal investigations and civil suits crowding in? He points to Brooks and says, 'This one.' Does he have a PR genius in the shadows, or is this all his own work?

Monday, 11 July

Yes, the situation is definitely serious for Murdoch. He's just withdrawn the News Corp bid for the sixty-one per cent of BSkyB he doesn't already own. It's all getting a little surreal. The *Guardian* leads on a story about the *Sun* getting hold of details of the illness of Fraser, the son of Gordon and Sarah Brown. The *Sun* hits back later denying they got access to the actual medical records. Brown says he and Sarah were reduced to tears by the paper's behaviour in confronting them before they had even had official confirmation of the diagnosis. The *Sun* is clearly desperate to prevent any toxic reputational damage spreading from the Sunday title to the daily. Elsewhere, the *NYT* claims five police officers had their phones hacked.

In *Slate*, Christopher Hitchens has written a good piece getting to the heart of the disclosures and what the whole affair is about:

> The most neglected aspect of the entire imbroglio is this. Most of the allegations of shady practice against the Murdoch octopus have come from another newspaper. Under the editorship of Alan Rusbridger, the *Guardian* has been engaged in breaching an old unspoken code of the British press racket – that 'dog does not eat dog'. The prime minister's office showed itself incapable of conducting an investigation; the courts and the prosecutors appeared to have no idea of the state of the law, and the police were too busy collecting their tip-off fees. Admittedly, it isn't usually the job of these institutions to keep the press honest. (Indeed, I could swear that I read somewhere that the whole concept was the other way about.) Still, it's encouraging to record that when the press needed a housecleaning, there was a paper ready to take on the job.
>
> Over the same period, Rusbridger and the *Guardian* formed the London end of the media consortium that tried to impose some element of sorting and priority on the mess that WikiLeaks had become. Now here was serious disclosure – some of it gained by invasion of privacy – on matters of real importance. What strikes the eye about the material in the *News of the World* is its relentless nullity: when cruel things happen to unimportant people, or when sordid things happen to famous people. Prurience and voyeurism supply the only energy. A sort of Gresham's Law begins to drive the news, or rather to drive out actual information by means of huge waves of mawkishness and populism. In this sense, too, a lot hangs on the outcome of the battle between the Murdochian and *Guardian* worldviews.

Tuesday, 12 July

Cameron's getting ready to make another statement. There's been a massive buy-back of News Corp shares and an imminent motion urging Murdoch to drop the BSkyB bid. On top of everything else, the Commons home affairs select committee has been sitting – grilling John Yates and Andy Hayman, two of the police who were so half-hearted in their pursuit of the true extent of the *News of the World* hacking scandal. We discover that only 170 out of 3,800 possible victims have been contacted by the police.

Wednesday, 13 July

Up at 7 a.m., with a TV crew doing a live broadcast to Australia from my sitting room. I then walk around to Michael's house for a piano lesson. It wouldn't be true to say that Michael knows nothing about what has been going on in the outside world – he did say that he'd seen me on *Newsnight*, or the news – but it's plain that the story holds limited interest for him. So we don't waste much time discussing Rupert Murdoch. Neither is it true that my mind is completely devoid of anything musical this morning; but it's not so much a cold start today as a cryogenic one.

I play the entire Ballade through for him, only the second time I've done so. As usual, Michael sits right by the side of the piano as I play – unlike Lucy, who sits back on a sofa – so I'm hyper-conscious of his beady eyes flitting between the keyboard and the score on his knee. Early on, I fluff some arpeggios and I hear him gasp in a completely involuntary way. Given that I've had, by now, nine days of working sixteen hours a day at least, I'm not utterly dismayed or surprised by the mediocre result. Despite the onslaught of new information at present, it seems the procedural memory is holding fairly firm. Michael seems – how would one rank it? – not entirely displeased. At the end, he says something mild – not 'you've got a lot of work to do' or 'that was good' or 'that was terrible', just something understated like 'you can do much of it'. I was OK on the musicality front, he says: it was a musical performance. I suppose that's the most important thing.

Of course, he then gets stuck straight into four or five passages where he feels the wheels have been separated from the chariot. But this time my heart doesn't sink. I find myself back in our strange little piano bubble, and *needing it*, as we discuss why I am still playing such and such a finger, and why my left hand still hasn't got the right notes in such and such a chord, and why I'm not using syncopated pedalling in the right place. Soon he's leaping up, pushing me aside, demonstrating how to do it, and then pulling me back and demanding I copy him. There's nothing I can do except concentrate completely and fully on what's going on. For an hour, I can think of nothing else. But by nine o'clock, I'm back into the routine that will doubtless end at two o'clock tomorrow. And piano camp is – assuming I make it – now just eight days away.

Later News Corp finally withdraws its BSkyB bid ahead of another Commons debate on the proposed deal. The Dowlers have met with the prime minister. And the government has named Lord Justice Leveson – a former criminal silk and high-court judge with a no-nonsense reputation – as the man to head the two inquiries it's now set up into the whole saga. Gordon Brown has made a blistering attack on Murdoch and News International.

Thursday, 14 July

It's been another extraordinary day. Yesterday, Tom Crone, the legal manager at NI, quit. Today, Neil 'Wolfman' Wallis, former deputy editor of the *News of the World* under Andy Coulson, and former editor of the *People*, was arrested. The jaw-dropping moment is the revelation that Scotland Yard had hired Wallis. After the *Guardian* story of July 2009 revealed the huge pay-off to stop the original case (which proved the 'lone rotten apple' theory at the *NotW* was untrue), you'd have thought any policeman would want to give Wallis a wide berth. And yet, we now discover that, secretly, he was taken on to advise Sir Paul Stephenson, the commissioner, his assistant commissioner, John Yates, and the head of press at Scotland Yard – for £1,000 a day. Why? The only reason the Yard can come up with is that they thought it would give them better access to Number 10.

I feel particularly gobsmacked by this because Stephenson and Yates both came to see me (while advised by Wallis, I now learn), telling me that I shouldn't be running the hacking stories by Nick Davies and that we were over-egging them. I can't understand why they thought it was appropriate to hire him and why they didn't think it was appropriate to tell me that they had taken him on as an adviser. I think it makes their positions very, very difficult. I ping off a letter to Stephenson asking why he didn't think it appropriate to tell me who was advising the Yard when he came in to see me.

There's a headline in the US magazine *Adweek* today: 'The Ben Bradlee of Phone Hacking'. Who could complain about being compared to the hero of Watergate? But then the piece continues:

> If you had to pick a man for this role from Central Casting, you almost certainly wouldn't pick Rusbridger. Ben Bradlee, the *Washington Post* editor who ran that other legendary investigation once upon a time, was a man who looked the part – the kind of man who, his own reporters once said, would 'grind his cigarettes out in a demitasse cup during a formal dinner party'. Rusbridger, 57, is different – he looks more like Harry Potter's lonely uncle than the kind of man capable of bringing down Rupert Murdoch.

In *All the President's Men*, Bradlee was played by Jason Robards. This role sounds more like one for Charles Hawtrey.

Meanwhile, Rupert Murdoch has given an interview to the *Wall Street Journal* (part of his empire), in which he says that News Corp has so far handled the crisis 'extremely well in every way possible', making only 'minor mistakes'. Has he got any clue what is going on? There have been some extraordinary photographs of him around London – typically in a baseball cap and shorts clambering in or out of plush chauffeur-driven limos.

Friday, 15 July

So the end of another incredible week. On Sunday night, I thought things were peaking, but I had no idea of the pace of events to come. Once again the story has changed by the hour. I can't remember a story like it when things have moved so fast. Each day there have been four or five developments that would, at any other time, have led the news and lasted a week in themselves. On Monday, it was revealed that Royal Protection Officers had been selling information about the people they were supposed to be looking after. But then, within two hours, it turned out that Prince Charles and Camilla had been hacked. And then, it turned out, every member of the royal family, bar the Queen, had been hacked – and that's probably only because she hasn't got a mobile phone. So that was three amazing stories by lunchtime. But, mentioning them to the media editor at six o'clock in the evening, he looked at me blankly and said dismissively, 'Oh yeah, now that seems so long ago, doesn't it?' There had been three equally jaw-slackening developments during the course of the afternoon.

Now Downing Street is about to release all the prime minister's contacts with editors, proprietors and, I suppose, relevant parties, both before and since he's become PM. And today Rebekah Brooks stepped down, which always looked inevitable. It is said that, within the NI building, she had gone from a feared figure to someone for whom many colleagues had developed disdain. I think the sight of somebody closing down a highly profitable paper, with no good reason advanced, and getting rid of the staff while keeping their own job, was a difficult one to stomach. Perhaps she's simply been taking the heat on behalf of the Murdochs. Rupert Murdoch met the Dowlers today – pronouncing himself 'humbled and shaken'. A bit different from the 'minor mistakes' tone of a day ago. Are his advisers finally getting a grip?

The Times has published a critical editorial about NI's handling of the whole affair. Good for its editor, James Harding. *The Times* has done well this week. Then, this evening, Les Hinton, chief executive of Dow Jones and the man who was at the NI wheel at the time of the *NotW* hacking, also quits. Murdoch is parachuting in a company man from Sky Italia to clean up the mess. It's corporate meltdown.

About three weeks ago I'd thought this was precisely the time I'd be going into my last-minute preparations for piano camp. Fat chance.

Saturday, 16 July

So Murdoch does have a PR adviser after all. Today a personal full-page apology from the great man himself was printed in every national newspaper. I think I'll have this framed alongside the July 2009 *News of the World* editorial accusing the *Guardian* of deliberately making it all up. It's almost exactly two years from one to the other. Should we keep the money from the adverts? The general consensus on the staff is that we should give it to charity.

Marvellous *Telegraph* leader today – ends by comparing the Cameron misjudgement in getting in too deep with the Murdochs with something out of *The Godfather*:

> In October 2009 Mr Wallis was engaged as Sir Paul's personal adviser – an appointment the commissioner failed to acknowledge publicly until he was forced to this week. Mr Wallis also advised John Yates, the police officer previously in charge of the Met's investigation into phone hacking. Even in Palermo, this would raise eyebrows . . .
>
> This is the United Kingdom we are talking about, not one of those southern European countries whose corruption Britons have traditionally found so amusing. It will be a long time before we can make any more jokes at the expense of Italy or Greece. After the revelations of the past week, the whole world has learned the shameful truth about modern Britain: that its leading politicians and policemen have been lining up to have their palms greased and images burnished by executives of a media empire guilty of deeply criminal – and morally repugnant – invasions of personal privacy.

Exhausted by the week but unable to let go, I take the iPad to supper in a country pub near Blockley to keep an eye on what the Sunday papers have got. As the meal arrives, I see they're running with a story that Stephenson failed to declare an £11k stay at a luxury health spa, whose PR adviser was – yes – Neil Wallis. That surely cooks Stephenson's goose.

Sunday, 17 July

And on it goes. Brooks has been arrested. I decide to give up on the weekend, leaving Blockley and driving straight back to the office. Within an hour or so Stephenson's live on TV announcing that he, too, is resigning. He is gracious enough to imply he's glad that I ignored the advice he gave me in the autumn of 2009 to lay off the story. It's another very late night as we heave tomorrow's paper around to take in the new developments, with one or two colleagues also having to drop what they were doing and rush into the office. It's now hard to keep up with the tally of resignations and arrests at all levels of the police and News Corporation. Everything gives the appearance of the wagons being circled around Rebekah and James.

It's very doubtful whether I can now escape for piano camp, which is just four days away. And even if I do get there, who knows what state my playing is going to be in? On Tuesday James and Rupert Murdoch appear before the Commons committee. If that lights another fire under events, I'll definitely have to cancel. If it draws a line for the moment, I'll go and make as good a fist of it as I can.

Monday, 18 July

More evidence of the international interest in the story this morning: a Norwegian journalist flies in unannounced and tells the people at the front desk that he won't leave the building until I've given him an interview (I don't). Then this afternoon news comes in that Sean Hoare, one of the *NotW* reporters involved in the hacking, and the whistleblower who claimed Coulson knew what was happening, has been found dead. That's all the story has been lacking, but Nick's convinced Sean was finished off by years of too much drink and drugs, not by someone trying to silence him. I spoke to him barely a week ago – intrigued by a story in the *New York Times* in which he revealed that the paper could not only hack phones, but track them, too. That capability – of being able to locate any individual at any point in time and listen into everything going on in their lives – is a capability the Stasi would have envied.

He sounded a nice man, and Nick writes a lovely tribute to him for tomorrow's paper:

> He made no secret of his massive ingestion of drugs. He told me how he used to start the day with 'a rock star's breakfast' – a line of cocaine and a Jack Daniel's – usually in the company of a journalist who now occupies a senior position at the *Sun*. He reckoned he was using three grammes of cocaine a day, spending about £1,000 a week. Plus endless alcohol. Looking back, he could see it had done him enormous damage. But at the time, as he recalled, most of his colleagues were doing it, too . . .
>
> It must have scared the rest of Fleet Street when he started talking – he had bought, sold and snorted cocaine with some of the most powerful names in tabloid journalism. One retains a senior position on the *Daily Mirror*. 'I last saw him in Little Havana,' he recalled, 'at three in the morning, on his hands and knees. He had lost his cocaine wrap. I said to him, "This is not really the behaviour we expect of a senior journalist from a great Labour paper." He said, "Have you got any fucking drugs?"'
>
> And the voicemail hacking was all part of the great game. The idea that it was a secret, or the work of some 'rogue reporter', had him rocking in his chair: 'Everyone was doing it. Everybody got a bit carried away with this power that they had. No one came close to catching us.' He would hack messages and delete them so the competition could not hear them, or hack messages and swap them with mates on other papers.
>
> In the end, his body would not take it any more. He said he started to have fits, that his liver was in such a terrible state that a doctor told him he must be dead. And, as his health collapsed, he was sacked by the *News of the World* – by his old friend Coulson.

The thing many people don't get about Nick is that he does actually like and respect many tabloid journalists. He often insists it was the former reporters in the *News of the World* who drove his story – they wanted the truth to be told. In the original coverage of the phone-hacking story he wouldn't name any junior reporters because he felt it was unfair to single out people who were simply working under instruction.

Today's resignation: John Yates. Cameron's cut short his African trip to rush back for another Commons debate. News Corp shares drop by another five per cent.

Tuesday, 19 July

I have a dream about piano camp. I play the Ballade so badly that the teacher refuses to teach me. 'I'm sorry,' he says in front of the whole class, 'but I expect a certain degree of preparation and there's simply no point in continuing.' He closes the music and ends the masterclass.

The day, as predicted, is dominated by the Select Committee for Culture, Media and Sport. The session begins with an inquisition of two cops at the heart of the three original half-hearted investigations into the hacking. The MPs are dripping with disbelief. Then the Murdochs are up on the stand. (Is it only two years ago that MPs stepped back from forcing Brooks to come and give evidence – some of them frightened by the thought of the revenge that the stable of newspapers might exact on them?)

The first twenty minutes are among the most extraordinary things I've ever seen on television, as Tom Watson, the Labour MP who's been the most tenacious pursuer of the story, exerts an almost mesmeric hold on Rupert Murdoch, who looks completely out of it. There are interminable pauses in his responses. His son keeps trying to intervene on his behalf, only to be gently rebuffed by Watson. Is it an act? Is this really the most feared newspaper publisher in history – the man whom *Vanity Fair* editor Graydon Carter once described to me as 'the man who, every day of his life, causes grown men to adopt the foetal position'? But when Watson stops, the questioning sometimes loses its focus and the Murdochs visibly relax and gain in confidence. James, in particular, quite effectively mixes amnesia with corporate legalese. Then it is all derailed by some idiot with a foam pie attacking the older Murdoch just as Louise Mensch, a Tory MP, is beginning to develop an interesting line of questioning.

In the evening Nick and I go out for a meal, which we very rarely do, maybe once or twice a year, and we plot what he is going to do with the next bit of the story. He wants to go off to New York to look at the American end of things. We end up drinking with a few colleagues, including a

Guardian film crew that's recorded some of the events of the past two days.

Nick's very mellow. He's not been sleeping well recently, winding himself up with all these stories. Mainly, it is just lovely to see him alone at this moment of achievement after all that he's been through. It's been really tough for him at times. We've been together professionally since July 1979, so that's thirty-two years. Laurence Topham, the *Guardian* video producer, asks whether we had ever written a story together: we remember that in 1981 we jointly covered the trial of the Yorkshire Ripper. One did the morning shift, one the afternoon. A full broadsheet page a day of court reporting.

Back at home, I feel a tiny bit deflated by the day. Knowing as much about the story as I do now, it was a bit frustrating to watch the very patchy efforts of the MPs to land a blow on the evidently much-coached performances of the Murdochs and, later, Rebekah Brooks. But then listening to the midnight bulletins on radio, I realise it is one of those occasions where you have to see the bigger picture – this amazing moment in public life where the most powerful media mogul of this, or any other, age was finally called to answer to Parliament itself, and sat there – however pre-cooked the soundbite – and admitted this was the humblest day of his life. That's the big picture. Everything else is detail.

Wednesday, 20 July

Today's make-or-break time for piano camp. If I'm going to go, then I need to leave tomorrow. It all depends on whether the story accelerates again after yesterday's select committee hearing, or finally shows signs of slowing down.

In any case, I make time for a lesson with Michael this morning. It's essentially a dress rehearsal for piano camp, but it doesn't go well. I am now *very* tired, and it shows. Michael is not the sort to draw a veil over any failings. 'Hmm, quite a lot of wrong notes,' he observes, accurately enough. For a moment I think, 'There's no danger, is there, Michael, of you going into the motivational-speaking business?' For five minutes – as he sifts through my fingerings for explanations of the less sound passages – I feel mildly irritated. But this is just another symptom of my tiredness. He's being patient and kind in trying to stick a bit of last-minute Elastoplast on my playing.

I then chase into morning conference. Conferences have been incredibly full – fifty to seventy colleagues a day for the last few days. After the Murdochs, today's the day that Cameron has to face the music before the select committee. It's quite extraordinary watching him perform – so polished and yet so slippery. He squirms (but barely perceptibly) when repeatedly asked if he has ever discussed the BSkyB deal with the News International executives during the twenty-six meetings he's now owned up to; he has to be asked eight or nine times before it's completely certain that, yes, he is admitting he has, indeed, discussed the deal. It's another example of how, as the story unpeels, the detail is worse than we imagined or wrote. I had always thought there was simply an unspoken understanding about what Murdoch wanted in respect of BSkyB – and I had always believed that Cameron would be too cautious ever to discuss the matter with his close friends at the top of News Corp or News International. Yet here's the prime minister effectively confessing that they did discuss the deal – though (of course!) it was all innocent and above board.

In the middle of the afternoon the legendary former *Sunday Times* editor Harry Evans appears in my office unannounced. He's been in the select committee hearing and is, at 82, really quite emotional about seeing it all. He says he particularly treasures the fact that it was a brilliant piece of reporting that exposed rotten journalistic practices. He sits down, a little moist in the eye, and compares Nick's dogged pursuit of the story with the reporting of Emily Hobhouse, the *Manchester Guardian* reporter who exposed the existence of British concentration camps during the Boer War. 'And I know my *Guardian* history,' he winks. And he does: his connection with the paper goes back sixty years. 'It's up there with anything the *Guardian* has done.'

By the end of the day it seems that things are working in favour of my escape to the Lot Valley. There's a definite feeling tonight that, for the moment, the heat has gone slightly out of the story – and MPs are now all leaving to go on their holidays. So the piano camp wins, after all.

PART SEVEN

Thursday, 21 July

—•◂•▸•◦•—

Up at 6.30 and set off for St Pancras International to meet Martin Prendergast, who is also going to Lot this year. My suitcase of music is so heavy that when Martin and I get to Gare du Nord the taxi driver asks: '*C'est un cadavre?*'

A surge of relief as I sink into the seat on Eurostar, and a bigger surge once ensconced on the TGV heading south from Paris. I can't escape the story entirely – the phone keeps ringing, emails keep stacking up – but I begin to get a palpable sense of easing away from it all. I have been through many periods of editing on adrenaline – but this is the longest stretch I can remember where the sheer journalistic buzz drives you on through sleeplessness and exhaustion. I doze a bit, try to read and remember the self-same journey in July 2009 – almost exactly two years to the day – when I had to delay my departure for piano camp for 24 hours in order to give evidence to the Commons select committee on culture. On phone hacking again, needless to say. It's been a two-year chunk of my life: eighteen months of fairly lonely pursuit, with no one else much interested; six months of gradual crescendo, and then three weeks of total mayhem. Nick Davies had been told at one stage that Rebekah Brooks had predicted to colleagues that the story was going to end with 'Alan Rusbridger on his knees, begging for mercy'. 'They would have destroyed us,' he said on a *Guardian* podcast last week. 'If they could have done, they would have shut down the *Guardian*.' The past ten days have been like moving from a hushed and deserted street into the raucous uproar of a nightclub in full swing. One moment, silence: the next, pandemonium.

Each year I stay at the same bed and breakfast on the edge of Prayssac, run by Ruud and Geri, a lovely Dutch couple. It's an unpretentious bungalow, with their enormous St Bernard in the garden, about a mile from Anne's house, where the piano course is based. As we draw up outside it today, I get a call to say that James Murdoch's evidence to Parliament has been directly challenged by his former lawyer and a *NotW* editor. So I have to rush upstairs and write an instant leader on the rickety bedside table – again, echoing 2009, when I had to do exactly the same thing. Perhaps the story will refuse to leave me alone this week.

Friday, 22 July

Piano camp at last. Each year the set-up is more or less the same. Every morning, from breakfast to lunch, there's a block of masterclasses in which a handful of the 'students' present their chosen pieces to an audience made up of the other students and that year's teacher, usually a concert pianist or professor from one of the main conservatoires. Over the course of the week each student will have three of these sessions. After the student plays the piece, which is very much a serious performance, the teacher spends forty-five minutes giving advice and working through some of the problems, as the other students look on and glean what might be relevant to their own progress. It's all held in the large stone-flagged main room of Anne's house, on the little vineyard-dotted hill above the village.

According to the schedule, pinned up on a noticeboard in the kitchen, my first of these masterclasses is to take place this morning – I'm fourth on. So just twenty-four hours after leaving London I find myself doing my after-breakfast practice, but this time in an old garage round the back of the farmhouse, where, in amongst all the discarded mattresses and lawn-mowers, saws, benches and bits of garden hose, there's a grand piano, an upright and a ping-pong table. Today will be the first time I have played the entire Ballade in front of an audience of more than one. It had been my aim to have the Ballade mastered by now, but even though I've made giant leaps in recent months, things are still shaky, and the events of the last two weeks, the exhaustion and lack of practice, will surely have made things shakier. At the end of the week, the students give a concert, when they give the definitive performance of their chosen piece or pieces. It was of course there that Gary played it last year – is there any chance that I'll reach my goal of playing it as well as he did exactly twelve months later? I've got a week to make it happen.

At 9.30 we gather for the first 'parade'. This year we have Jenny, a Suzuki music teacher; Jimmy, a retired Cambridge philosophy don; Charlie Bennett, the Chipping Campden wine merchant; Howard, a senior drinks company marketing executive; Patricia, a retired shopkeeper from Yorkshire; Fiona, a psychotherapist from Wiltshire; David, a London hand surgeon; Martin . . . and me. Gary and Wendy are on another course this year, so I shall miss the chance to compare Ballade notes with him. Our hostess Anne plays – both piano and flute – but generally chooses not to, busying herself with the background organisation until after supper, when she joins in the fun.

Our tutor is William Fong, the 40-something head of keyboards at the specialist Purcell School and a professor at the Royal Academy. His CV says he has won piano competitions in many countries, including the Busoni, Cleveland and Concurso Internacional de Piano in Spain. He comes across as mild-mannered, intelligent and thoughtful: it's immediately clear we're in good hands for the week. Improbably enough, given his rather studious demeanour, he is as passionate about fast cars as he is about cycling. He has driven down from London in a vintage Porsche ('Got it for £5k: it was either that or a Mondeo. In two years I won't have to pay any road tax it's so old.')

Jenny, the music teacher, is up first with a Bach prelude and fugue. William's gently encouraging. 'Piano playing is very easy in a way,' he tells her. 'All the keys are there, you just press them down in the right order. They even come up on their own. We don't have a sense of the difficulty other instrumentalists have when they have to link notes. So we need to emulate that a little bit. The left hand, for instance, doesn't feel like staccato, more like bowing.' The key to the prelude is the left hand: this, he says, is the case with most pieces. 'I'm told that landscape painters find skies and the background most difficult. After that everything falls into place. Always, as pianists, we should work from the LH upwards.'

It's rare to find really good pianists who are this articulate and sympathetic and responsive as teachers. It's going to be a good week.

Next it's the retired shopkeeper Patricia, with whom I've been on courses before. She's in her early 70s and claims never to have had a proper lesson. Due to her domestic circumstances she rarely gets the chance to practise and is quite unconfident about her abilities. But she has more natural talent than most of the people on the course, which makes one wonder how good she could have been with tuition and the freedom to practise. Today she plays the first movement of the Grieg piano concerto. William's verdict: 'You do a lot of the difficult stuff really well. And some of the easy things less well.'

Then, after a break for coffee, it's the surgeon, David, with the Chopin Barcarolle. William asks him: 'How much time do you get to practise?'

'An hour a day.'

'Are you efficient?'

'Not very.'

'But you are in the rest of your life? An hour a day is good. Two is better. You have to be extremely efficient with an hour. That means spending more time working out how fingering works.'

Then it's me. This is it – the moment I've been building up to all year. There have been numerous times when, as I've sat alone practising at the piano over the past months, I've imagined it: finally sitting down and performing to an audience. But this feels strange and a bit anticlimactic, the 'build-up' having stopped dead in its tracks at the beginning of the month. My body is still buzzing with adrenaline and my mind is halfway across Europe – a bit wired, still distracted – and I'm not at all settled for this moment . . . *now* . . . sitting in front of the keys, the room hushed and all eyes turned towards me.

The first two pages start fine. It's not especially musical – I'm struggling to get the feel of the piano straight off – but all the notes are in place. But then the squashed flies at the end of the second page fall apart and I can feel my body tense a little for what lies ahead. The first bit of passage work is very ragged and I'm suddenly horribly conscious that the nerves have kicked in. Not a kick so much as an electric jolt. Shaking nerves – as in the right foot trembling uncontrollably. It's ultimately disconcerting – firstly because I can't now guarantee that any of the pedalling is going to work as it should and, secondly, because when I last suffered from this sort of attack of nerves five or more years ago, the trembling spread to the hands. If that happens today I'm finished. Forty-eight hours ago I had been in charge of a national newspaper and weathering one of the biggest international media storms in a generation. Now I'm consciously quivering – struggling to control nerves in front of an audience of eight. And I'm thinking about this as I play – the contrast between the nerves required to see the Murdoch story through and my present state of jelly. I retrieve from somewhere in my brain a piece of advice (*From Lucy?* I'm trying to remember who told me at the same time as playing) that the best way to deal with a trembling foot is to dig the heel into the ground. So I dig away at the stone flags. And it seems to help a bit. But by now I've lost any sense of whether my pedalling is working at all. How can my brain be processing all these things in parallel – thinking of my heel grinding into the floor; wondering who gave me that advice; thinking about Murdoch; trying to anticipate the trouble on the next page; making sure the fingers still kept on playing?

Then I'm into the section with the big chords – some of them are there and some of them are mysteriously missing. Just not there at all. In one bar I even improvise something with the LH while concentrating on the RH. It's all turning into a car crash. After a year of practice. A very public nightmare. The passage with the rising scales is flashing past – very erratically. I feet hot and flushed. I'm still only halfway through. I remember Barenboim talking about how the Ballade keeps hurtling at you.

Suddenly it is the waltz. In some part of my mind I can see Barenboim tracing delicate movements in the air with his fingers in the smoke-filled bedroom at Claridge's. I manage to slam on the brakes and, for the first time, believe I might be able to get it all under control again. But the brakes fail on the next page and I'm skidding down a steep hill. By the time we're into the broken chords, though, I've managed to regain a small semblance of control again. God knows where that came from, but I no longer feel as if I'm at the wheel of a two-ton lorry hurtling down a steep slope. This modicum of confidence lasts all of two pages and then . . . the coda.

The first ten or so bars are actually good. I play what Chopin wrote. I don't rush them; the notes are crisp and the pedalling just as Michael would have ordered. But then disaster strikes: I simply can't remember what note the next section starts on and the piece grinds to a halt. I can feel blood pulsing through my temples. The mind has shut down altogether. A second passes, maybe two. How can I recover? How is it possible to get going again? Somehow – perhaps I looked at the music, the whole thing's now a blur – I find the note and, at the third attempt, the music starts again. But this is, let's face it, a catastrophe. The coda, which I've been able to play in the privacy of my own room for weeks now, has well and truly risen up to bite me with a vengeance. Was there ever such musical hubris?

The coda begins to pull impatiently, mindlessly ahead of me again. I somehow get to the top of the ascending patterns at bar 233 only to then fluff the journey back down the keyboard. I then have two attempts at the chromatic scale back up the piano before making a total Horlicks of the scales coming down – even playing the wrong note altogether in the LH. The G minor scales are awful. And to round it off I mess up the crashing octaves at the end. There's a ghastly silence at the end and then polite clapping. Nine months' work and I've fucked it up. (Something else to add to Rupert Murdoch's charge sheet.)

Out of the corner of my eye I see William striding towards the piano. 'That will be very good,' he says brightly – a rather masterly use of the predictive future tense, relieving himself of the need to pass comment on the excruciating few minutes he's just had to sit through. He takes me to the final page in the score and asks a direct question: 'How much time a day do you spend playing scales?'

'Er, none,' I mumble.

He sits down at the stool and plays scales for two minutes, going through endless permutations of majors, melodic and harmonic minors in numerous keys.

'That's how I begin every day,' he says. I suddenly feel the inner rebellious 15-year-old in me rising. He asks me to play four octaves of G minor with the LH. I fumble my way up and down.

'If you could scrounge five minutes to ten minutes a day to do scales it would help enormously because what you want to do musically and your musical ideas are in advance of what you can do technically. I'm not here to do quick fixes. What I can do this week is to sow some seeds for the long term.'

And then he asks me to play him the beginning. He peers at the score to check whether I intend to start on the third finger (as per Lucy's fingering). He suggests the second finger would be better. And then he wants me to start with my hands in my lap and drop onto the keys. He asks me to drop my fists on the piano instead of striking a C. He's trying to explain how the weight of the arm and the hand should relate to the keyboard – something other piano teachers have tried to implant in me before. I always struggle, never quite clear what's meant by the phrase beloved of pianists – 'arm weight'. He wants the whole of the first line played as one phrase reaching up to the top G. We discuss the weighting of the following F sharp and the meaning of the pause that follows – and what weight to give the subsequent F sharp. And then how to play the C which introduces the little sigh at the end of the Largo section. Again he thinks I'm playing it without subtlety. He asks me to rest my hand on his and shows the touch he wants. I'm still not getting it, though. I notice he's playing it with his fourth finger rather than the third I've been using. Should I switch? 'The finger's not the problem,' he tells me, picking up a pencil and using it to play the note with infinite delicacy. I try not to feel crushed by this demonstration that an HB pencil has more musicality than I could conjure up today. We then move on to the Moderato, which he says he always feels is a waltz – even though written in six beats. He wants me to play it faster, and for it to feel in three beats. I'm not convinced I agree with that, but I try it and it gives a movement and life that was doubtless lacking in my earlier, much slower version.

There's encouraging applause at the end of the session – there always is at the Lot – but I sense that, in my peer group's eyes as well as William's, I'm just another amateur who's bitten off more than he can chew.

Piano-camp afternoons are dedicated to private practice, but today I know I have to rest, hoping to find the energy later in the week to catch up. It's overcast and threatening rain. Phone calls keep coming in from the office, staving off sleep.

In the evening William plays us a recital: Chopin Polonaise-Fantaisie, Debussy *Estampes* and Ravel *Gaspard de la Nuit*. He's very keen on sitting low at the piano – so keen that none of the stools in the house was squat enough for him to play on, and Anne had to ask the tuner to bring a saw with him. He duly cuts three centimetres off each leg of the main piano stool to enable William to get the right angle to the keyboard. His stool is now almost as low as Glenn Gould's famous chair, which was barely fourteen inches off the ground. He plays beautifully.

Saturday, 23 July

Martin plays the third movement of the 'Moonlight' Sonata incredibly crisply, followed by Jimmy with the Brahms Handel Variations, a monster of a piece. Each year on the piano camp the students bring more and more ambitious pieces. William tells Martin to think of Beethoven sonatas as reductions of orchestral scores. 'Think in instrumental colours. Think of up bows and down bows in phrases, for instance.' He wants Jimmy to be more conscious of harmonic structures – 'Western tonality is based on how far western composers take us away from it.' The wine dealer Charlie follows them with Haydn's great F minor variations, then Jenny ends the morning with a very tender account of Chopin's Nocturne No. 20 in C-sharp minor, Op. posth.

My plan is to grab a few minutes each day to discover the piano histories of some of my colleagues on the course – when did they start playing? Did they leave the instrument and come back to it as I have? What does it mean to them? During an interlude today, I set the iPad down in front of Fiona

Ballantyne Dykes, the psychotherapist with whom I've shared maybe four or five courses now.

I started piano when I was about 5. When I went to senior school, I had a really good teacher. She took me up to Grade 8 at 16 and then, after that, for the next two years, I didn't really do anything. She had left so I was sort of passed around people, and I didn't know what to do next. Then I left school and I didn't play for twenty-five years.

I brought up a family and then, of course, when the children started piano lessons, I managed to play the odd, you know . . . but I forgot more and more and more. By the time I got back to wanting to play again, I had to go right back to scratch.

I'm 52 now. So it must be ten years ago that I started . . . I went with one of the kids' piano teachers, I found out he did lessons with adults, as a group, so I went with a friend for a bit of a laugh. That seemed less self-indulgent really. We did Sticky Toffee and silly little pieces. I got better quite quickly. When I caught up to where I had been I didn't want to share a lesson any more. It became the one thing I could do which wasn't for anybody else, a guilty pleasure.

When I decided to go for the Associated Board of the Royal Schools of Music Diploma it was about confidence really. The teacher suddenly made me think it wasn't out of my reach and then it became a wonderful focus because it meant I had to practise, so it sort of gained its own status in my life. It meant I could do it without feeling that I shouldn't be playing the piano.

I did the diploma, in 2003. I think I had been playing again for about four years. You have to play a complete programme as if you are giving a performance. And you have to dress as if you're giving a performance. It was much more scary than childbirth, but not as painful!

Then you have to do a twenty-minute viva on your music and you have to do programme notes and really research the background and then you have this bloody sight-reading. I don't know whether they were being kind to me but they gave me a waltz and there's something about a waltz that you know you can just keep it going. I think I'm prouder of that than most things I've done in my adult life. In the run-up I was probably practising an hour and a half a day. In the evening, late, after the children were in bed . . . with a job as a counsellor, kids, family, playing, usually between ten and eleven at night. It's still what I do.

I had a sort of crisis a couple of years ago and thought I don't know why I do this, it's too much time, and I'm not getting any better, I'm still terrified of playing, so what's the point? Then the thought of giving it up felt like a bereavement, I felt really, really sad. So that gave me a new impetus and I tried to think about it differently. It doesn't really matter if I never reach anybody's standard, but I still want to be good.

Music has definitely been an emotional prop. And it de-stresses as well. I'm in a nicer mood if I get my piano practice in. I think it's a physical thing as well as an emotional thing. There's something very soothing about . . . Do you ever have moods when you think, 'It's got to be Bach,' or something?

I used to belong to a piano group which met once a month and I did a masterclass when one or two Lot regulars were in the audience. One of them got hold of me afterwards and said was I interested in joining this course and I was amazed. It's been far more than I ever imagined because it's become the important focus for music, thinking about what you're going to play, hearing other people playing, widening your repertoire, extending your ambition for what you might be able to manage, and then having the best teaching you'd ever dreamed of.

In the afternoon, I finally start to knuckle down to some practice, and at last have the luxury of hours, rather than minutes, for the first time in weeks. I can feel the pressure of work very gradually receding. Then this evening we go off for dinner at a local restaurant, returning to play Armagnac-oiled Mozart 41 and Tchaikovsky's *Sleeping Beauty* in eight-hand arrangements till midnight.

Sunday, 24 July

Breakfast on the farmhouse terrace with the sound of William playing the Schubert Wanderer-Fantasia. The weather is strange this year. Normally there are clear blue skies every day and a particular kind of parched heat. But, so far, not a minute of sun and everyone in jumpers or cardigans.

At the morning's parade, Thelma – the wife of Colin, a retired BBC HR manager who helps Anne with the administration – plays Beethoven Op.

28. 'You all have very good music ideas,' William says at the end, 'but your technique lets you down.'

As with us all.

He turns to the group.

'Who has more than fifteen minutes to practise a day?'

Two hands go up. William looks genuinely thrown by this and gazes up at the ceiling for about ten seconds, wondering what he could possibly say.

'Because of your working lives?'

We nod.

'You have got to put in the hours. The piano, of all instruments, is the most athletic. At some point in your life you have to spend maybe two hours a day and you would see a huge difference in what you were able to do. If I have a concert coming up I can do three hours a day. But when I was 13 or 14 I was doing five or six hours a day. That means I have got money in the bank. When doing Young Musician of the Year I was working seven or eight hours a day. So my fingers really did work very well, and that helps later in life.'

We all look chastised.

'There's no reason any of you can't feel the sense that your technique is growing all the time, no matter if you're 10 or 80 or even 90. It will certainly improve. Now, if you've only got fifteen minutes a day, you have to be extremely well organised. If I had fifteen minutes a day and I was working on the Chopin G minor Ballade I'd split my time into three portions. The first five minutes I'd maybe focus on the last page. That would also be my warm-up. The next five minutes I'd work really hard at the scales. You have to be really warmed up for that, so the first five minutes would also be your warm-up.'

He then embarks on an encomium on the benefits of playing scales, the myriad approaches to practising them, and the importance of practising them with the right weight, never too 'lightly'. Eventually, he catches himself: 'Sorry, I can spend hours talking about scales. And then,' he finishes off, 'for the final five minutes, try another part of the Ballade.

'At the weekend I assume you can rehearse for longer – perhaps ninety minutes. Divide it into fifteen-minute sections. Quarter of an hour means you really focus your mind. For example, you could just try maybe the first two pages. And then for the next fifteen minutes do the whole coda, or whatever. Once that fifteen minutes is finished move on. Don't be tempted to spend an extra couple of minutes on it. That's how it focuses the mind – you only have fifteen minutes to achieve that amount of work.

'And then spend fifteen minutes of each weekend session on at least one complete performance so you get to know how everything fits together. We too often forget how things are put together. You choose a good tempo, but if you come to a section where you are not comfortable then do an artistic rallentando, and then pick up the tempo again. So you're still practising that section but in the context of the large scale, so you can feel how everything fits in.

'The golden rule for practice is one step at a time, so that it's digestible. It's the same for 10-year-olds as it is for 47-year-olds. Piano is like programming with a computer. You have to put the information in right. I have some bad habits I learned when I was young and I have to work to overcome.'

It's then time for my second masterclass. Straight to business – no play-through performance today. William starts by looking at the '*Bebung*' chords in the first section (the heartbeat effect). But then he stops everything to talk about hand position. He asks everyone what they were taught about the ideal hand position – whether it's as if grasping an apple or grasping an egg in the hand. The crucial thing, he says, is to remember the facet that distinguishes humans from animals – the ability of thumb and finger to be opposite each other and to come together. 'Imagine that position – thumb and finger pinched together – as you place your hand on the keys. But with the rest of the hand low on the keys. Then play down to the bed of the note' – i.e. sinking the note until it can depress no further.

We spend ten minutes just trying to get the sound he's after from this technique. Then we move on to the LH at bar 24. He is very keen on movements into and away from the piano as he pushes into a phrase and then pulls away from it. Next we look at the squashed flies, the eighteen notes which I'm dividing 6-8-4.

'Why not just make it 6-6-6?' he asks. 'Then practise it by pausing on the first of each six.' We do that, before he suggests pausing on the second note in each six-note cluster. And then to try the pause on the third. And so on. 'The point is that the brain is engaged with the different variants – a much better practising technique than simple dotted rhythms.'

We skip to the start of the coda. Again, he wants that low hand position in the RH, but with the thumb and finger position a little higher – i.e. dropping the forearms, rather than playing 'from above', and with a movement into the keys, lifting away at the end of each phrase.

William finishes off by looking at the LH at the start of the coda. How do I practise it? he enquires. 'Er, by just playing it a bit slower?' No, he wants me to play the first note twice, with a dotted rhythm and then jump down and hold the lower note. This is to build up spatial awareness so that I get confident about where to land. And once I've mastered that, he wants me to practise the same in reverse, so that it's a dotted note followed by a leap *up*.

This is all such a fundamental change to the way I've been doing things. It took me back to tennis or golf lessons ten or more years ago in which I was told everything I'd ever been taught about how to serve/drive was 'wrong' and to start again from scratch. I do try the new techniques in my afternoon practice, but it's an awful lot to take on board, and though I make progress with it I'm not quite able to grasp every new element William has introduced. But I am learning useful new things about how to practise. And at least in today's session I was not a tangle of nerves. So things are getting back on track.

Though I know Martin Prendergast well from London, I decide to make him my next interviewee. I've never quite discovered his full 'piano history', and so I ask him how it all started – and how he fits it into his job as head of corporate development at the National Theatre.

My dad was a jazz pianist and a jazz organist in the 1960s, which was fantastic, you know, so much fun. I had a record of jazz nursery rhymes. I've always had a piano in my life, always played.

When I was 16 the local music centre had a harpsichord that no one played so I took it home in the holidays. Other kids were outside playing football and sniffing glue and I'm trying to play the Preludes and Fugues, or trying to, at least. I did the grades but I stopped playing, really, and having lessons when I was 17.

When I was 27, I decided I needed another creative outlet. I found a teacher, from a list in Brixton Library. I was attracted to Elizabeth Werry because she also taught harpsichord; she had been a Baroque specialist. We did lots of Bach. She was brilliant and she got me up to Grade 8 with distinction when I was 29. It's not an easy thing to do, and I was so pleased.

When you're a grown-up and you take piano lessons you're so committed to it in a way that you're not when you're a child. It's your money, and you're paying for the lessons. It's a totally different experience, even though, for most of the time, I was playing on a crappy electric keyboard on a wobbly stand on headphones. Actually, when you're trying to get back up to Grade 8 standard it doesn't really matter.

Next I decided to go for the performing diploma and it was really hard.

Elizabeth persuaded me to focus on my repertoire and she made me play a bit more in public, like little soirées; I got a massive kick out of the big concerts.

I practise before I go to work. The alarm goes off at 5.30, and I try to play from 6.30 to 9.30, because I start at ten. At weekends I practise about three or four hours a day. I try never to play scales or exercises on the piano, because of the neighbours, so I do my exercises on the Clavinova.

I get several things out of playing the piano. I think you become better at listening to music through playing it, you know, and it feels fantastic. I think it expresses aspects of being alive that are very difficult to articulate. Listening to music, making music, definitely enhances life.

On the other hand, it's very challenging. On paper, playing the piano is a nightmare. It's expensive, you can never do it, it eats time, it gobbles time, the better you get, the worse you realise you are, it's a curse. Why does anybody do it?

If you haven't played for a few days it's like keeping fit. If you go to the gym three or four times a week, then you go for a week without going . . . it's a similar sort of thing, but for your brain.

I had a slight epiphany moment when I was playing in recital. I'd focused on, absolutely rooted mentally on the quality of the sound, so I forgot that there was an audience. It was amazingly liberating, because I wasn't fretting about playing the wrong note; I was just listening to the music. I think you have to go through trying and trying and trying and not doing it well, to realise what playing the piano properly is like.

The day ends at midnight with Beethoven 5 for eight hands.

Monday, 25 July

At this morning's parade, Martin begins the day with Chopin's Nocturne No. 17 in B, Op. 62, No. 1. The piece starts with a grand spread chord which resolves to a much quieter one – William spends ten minutes coaxing Martin to make a beautiful sound with the second chord.

'Do you have a pet cat?' he asks Martin.

'Yes,' says a startled Martin. 'Charlie.'

'Ah, I suspect you stroke him like this.' William makes languorous, tender stroking gestures with his right hand. 'Well do that with a piano. It's a sensitive instrument. If you stroked Charlie like that' – he makes a prodding gesture, parodying Martin's keyboard style – 'he'd run away. Think of making a lovely sound. Think of a vat of warm chocolate and putting your hands in it. Suppress the notes on the beat, nourish the ones off the beat.'

It's still grey outside. We break for coffee and biscuits and survey the vine-dotted landscape under glowering skies. Next it's Jimmy's Brahms Handel Variations again, then Charlie Bennett plays Schubert's Impromptu Op. 90, No. 1, and Jenny Macmillan follows up with Kapustin's Sonatina. 'How many of you use metronome to steady pulse?' asks William during Jenny's session. A few hands go up. William wrinkles his nose in disapproval. 'The worst thing you can do is to have clicks every four. It gives you a crutch – you're not developing your own sense of rhythm. Sinatra had an inner sense of long meter – he'll seem to be out of time and then, bang, he's right there on the beat. Which is, actually, not so different from what we should be doing with Chopin. The pulse goes on and on, with absolute flexibility above it.'

In past years there'd be a break now for swimming or canoeing. But it's too cold for that – and anyway, there's too much practice to cram in. I'm now back in the rhythm of piano camp, and doing at least ninety minutes' practice a day. I'm also trying to follow the rules William set out on Sunday morning – including spending no more than a quarter of an hour on any one section or problem. My practice here is much more relaxed than when I'm back home. I've realised that when I have only twenty minutes in the mornings, I am impatient for progress – and press to play faster before I can play slowly, desperate to convince myself that I'm making discernible improvement. But, with over ninety minutes to play with, it's much easier to ease into practice, never forcing it. Here's how I'm approaching my practice sessions at the moment:

Ten minutes on G minor scales.

Ten minutes on the last two pages, making sure I have the exact shape of the final octaves in my mind.

Five minutes on the long downward runs at bars 246–50. Taking it slowly.

Five minutes on the upward run at bar 130. I used to think I could play this, but it is one of several passages that seems to have become a little less secure this week under proper scrutiny.

Fifteen minutes on the leap of death in the coda. Breaking it down into individual leaps. Two notes, then three, then four. Then a different rhythm but starting on a different note.

Five minutes on the two bars before the coda.

Fifteen minutes on the LH in the arpeggio section, with different rhythms. 1–23456; 12–3456; 123–456, etc.

Ten minutes on the RH in the same passage and two hands together.

Ten minutes on LH octaves and chords, 149–58.

Ten minutes both hands on the same section. Again, taking things very slowly.

Five minutes on the waltz. Very slow, once more.

And then, finally, I'll play the entire piece through just to remind myself of the overall architecture.

In the evening we play Dvořák Slavonic Dances for eight hands and two movements of Tchaikovsky 5. We've been joined by Liz Warde – a remarkable woman who combines teaching and nursing with bringing up five children in a pretty tough part of Manchester while still playing the piano every night. She is going to join us for the rest of the camp, and during a break from playing I ask her to tell me quite how she manages to squeeze the piano into her amazingly complex life:

I have five children, three girls, two boys. When I first met you I had two jobs, I did three and a half days' nursing and I did two days' teaching. I was going from night duty to school without a break, when a concert was on. It just got a bit much.

I was brought up in Hampshire but we moved further and further north. My dad, he was a maths teacher. I was about 9, I think, or maybe 10 when we moved to Manchester. I started piano at nearly 14, and then I did Grade 4 and Grade 7 and in less than three years. I was really interested and I just played all the time, but after that I didn't do that much. Yeah, I got interested in going out. I continued doing scales which is really odd. I sort of quite like scales, I didn't play pieces. Then I got married, at the age of 21 and, then, at 22, had a child, and I didn't touch a piano for about . . . I had fifteen years of having children.

I don't know if you know Wilmslow? Well, I've been there for thirty years. I started teaching about 1990, I think, for real. I did that and then did nursing and, when I qualified, that's how I met Anne [Brain].

The hospital was called Christie's. Anne was operating. She was digging out this massive tumour, and music came up and then, I think a question was asked, it must have been the twelve-note system or something and I said something and Anne just looked at me. She just carried on with the operation and at the end she called me into the back room, and said, 'Come and see my tumour,' you know, that she had just dug out, and then she was firing questions. About music. So she told me about this place. And I said I couldn't possibly because I wouldn't be up to standard, and she said, 'Oh no you sound right.'

I only really started properly practising when I came here. I did musicals for school and, when I did that, I had to practise a hell of a lot for a week to learn something. But, since I met Anne, I've been seriously practising, first of all without a teacher, and now with a teacher. I've had him for about four years now. He was mad keen on exercises, which suits me.

Well, when I was on nights, you couldn't actually practise, but, and it's partly why, you know, partly why I did give up nursing and stuck to one job, it was either the nursing or teaching. All the time, it was always after midnight. I got a digital piano because of that so that I can do it at one o'clock, two o'clock, in the morning, it doesn't matter.

I don't mind doing performances for kids, you know, I'll play for kids. And I don't mind doing it for parents but to play for anyone who actually knows what it's all about, it's terrifying, I just won't do it. Yeah! So much so that when you look at the keyboard you don't even recognise it, and you think, 'Where the hell is C?'

The most frightening situation I've been in was, I think, in hospital. There have been a couple of times when things have gone wrong and you look and you think you've got to do something immediately, like a resus or something, but I can't remember ever being scared at school.

Why do I like playing? I enjoy sitting down, getting prepared, doing the exercises, and doing the piano piece. I enjoy every single bit of it and it's a problem when I have to get up each time. I don't play for anybody, there's no reason to do it, except here, so this is like a motivation but I don't even need this motivation to go and play really because I absolutely love it.

I can practise for about one and a half hours and I might actually do that about four, maybe even five times a week. But I enjoy it. It's not like wasted, I just love doing it. Probably do it all wrong.

This course means everything to me; it's inspiration isn't it? I always take home things that I actually use, even if it's a really very practical thing. I keep meaning to do what I hear from William – chop some inches off the piano stool. Everybody has different things, so I think it's so practical, you always take something back, and it influences you for the rest of the year, well years, actually.

We end the day with midnight swimming in Anne's pool just outside the main music room. Work now at last seems very far away indeed. There are still one or two calls from the office – and I continue to check the headlines in every break. On past form war will break out, a reporter will disappear off the radar or a giant writ will land and suddenly I'll be hooked back in. But for the moment all is peace and quiet – or else it's so bad they're keeping it from me.

Tuesday, 26 July

The nerdiest piano camp ever. This morning Thelma gives up her session so William can give us an entire lesson on scales – he wants to give us the essential building blocks of technique that he thinks we're all lacking. The Fong way to play scales takes us from how to sit ('I sit forward on the piano stool. If you sit right back on the stool you lose that ability to move'); tempo ('Choose a tempo where you can keep the pulse and not hesitate. If you go too fast then you are simply practising being hesitant'); what we should be doing with our thumbs ('Off the keyboard when I'm not using them. It's easier to play legato like this'); the importance of thinking in terms of groups of notes ('Like we group letters when we read a book'); the need to vary practice rhythms, and the necessity of regular practice ('Three scales each week'). I sense that scales are to William what fingering is to Michael. I fail them both.

When that's over it's time for my third masterclass. Again, I don't play it through: we plunge straight in. William isn't convinced I've secured the joins between each passage so urges me to concentrate on establishing a relationship between the different sections. He also wants me to play with my left hand lighter on the keys. 'Allow arms to lead and fingers to follow,' he says. 'Lightness gives a sense of velocity without having to play as fast.' Good tip – but I have a feeling there's a week of lessons simply on that point. He also spots that I'm struggling with the big A/E major section today. He insists the key here is to learn the LH from memory. 'It's the only thing holding you back.'

Does he have any tips as to how to get it learned?

'Looking at the score away from the piano is important.'

In the evening another concert from William himself. Word has spread locally about the eccentric Brits in the house at the top of the hill who meet for their piano courses, and thirty or so locals turn up – some expat Brits (including the clarinettist Janet Hilton, who has a house nearby), but mostly French neighbours. We're all treated to a big programme – Prokofiev's third sonata; a Mozart adagio; a Schubert Wanderer-Fantasia crackling with energy, but shot through with moments of great delicacy; and rounded off with the Chopin B minor scherzo. I see our landlady, Geri, across the room, looking transported – there is a transfixing intimacy to a concert on this scale, no one more than twenty feet from anyone else. We're all in a horseshoe around the piano, feeling the sound, but also the physical impact of the instrument's percussive power. William is a really fine pianist – thoughtful, technically complete, powerful. Not for the first time I wonder about the minute distinctions between the world-famous concert pianists and the ones who are merely excellent.

Wednesday, 27 July

I grab William for a few minutes over coffee this morning. He's used to teaching professionals, and youngsters about to turn professional, so I'm keen to ask him what it's been like teaching amateurs for a week. 'I don't feel as if I've changed my teaching style at all,' he says. 'I think the only difference is that by the time very talented students are 14 or 15 they hopefully have the technical tools they need to express their musical ideas coherently and with a relative amount of ease. Most of what I've done here is actually to do with building technique, helping you to find the right technical solutions to project the music as best as you possibly can.'

But what's he made of the difference brought about by the age of the students? At the Royal Academy, his work is surely for the most part with people in their teens and early 20s. 'What's interesting is that all the pianists here already have a pretty well-formed intellect, and it's interesting to see how that's brought to bear upon grappling with musical problems. Also, because you've all had a rich and varied human experience, you're able to see the music in those terms as well, and invest your interpretations with that human experience. I think you probably could tell the difference between the playing of a 14-year-old and a 50-year-old, if both had the same technical equipment.'

I also want to ask him about some of the things I've been discussing with other pianists. Where, for instance, does he stand on the question of the recording boom of the twentieth century? What effect did he think it has had on classical piano? He seems of a similar mind to the others I've spoken to – 'Quite a lot of things have become much more homogeneous.' But he doesn't think this is down to the rise of recorded music alone. He mentions the 'advent of big brass instruments', particularly from orchestras in the United States. 'That meant that everything else had to be inflated, so you have pianos that are very, very powerful but sometimes lack the wonderful transparency of the recordings you hear from the 1920s and 30s.' When you listen back to these earlier recordings, by the likes of, say, Rachmaninov, 'they sound very individual, but that's after they've understood the essence of the music, what makes it work, and assimilated that in their own way. Too often today you get a brilliant pre-performed package on which the musicality, for want of a better word, is projected on top, rather than the other way round, where the brilliance emerges from what's required in the music.'

During the week I've learned a thing or two about William. He has a quick, puckish sense of humour which occasionally breaks out in puns. Away from the keyboards, he's a fanatical cyclist – he's appeared in serious lycra on a couple of afternoons to go off touring the Lot Valley. I've also learned a little about his family. His mother was French and his grandfather a Chinese immigrant who arrived in Liverpool at the turn of the century. Having spoken to Noriko Ogawa about the trend of young Asian pianists excelling at the Ballade online, and the culture of these children being pushed, I wonder if William had felt similar pressure. 'I was pushed pretty hard, mainly by my father,' he says, and he believes the 'huge burst' of music playing in China is to do with the family unit. 'Each family, up until now, has had one child, who is expected to reflect the best of the family and to prioritise that. The parents have a huge amount to do with it and they do push hard. I mean, they're tennis parents.'

Just before the morning parade begins, I ask him about his own experience with the G minor Ballade. He says he's played it, and yes, as a teenager, for its emotional appeal at that age. But to him the piece has remained compelling ever since: 'It's always interesting and, even if you don't understand that immediately, it strikes a note almost subconsciously.'

Finally, I ask William about setting myself a reasonable target. After the disaster of my performance on Friday, I know that I need to have a deadline by which to finally master the Ballade and play it to an audience. My thought is to arrange this for December – I have to accept that work goes on at a relentless pace and I won't be able to always practise as I'd like to, no matter how strong my fantasy – but a further six months seems doable, and at the same time not *too* generous. December will mark eighteen months since I first set myself the challenge. It doesn't possess the same pleasing symmetry of returning triumphantly to the spot where I conceived of the project a year before, but given the year I've had, it would be an achievement nonetheless. But does William think I'll have it done by the end of the year?

'Of course you will. There's no question about it. You can play it now. If you want to play it better within the next few months try to organise the little practice time that you have in the way that I suggested, so you really use it efficiently. But, equally important, is that you should try and force yourself from now on, even if it's slightly under tempo, to perform the Ballade once a day in its entirety, waltz and all. The value of performing is that it exposes the parts that you aren't sure about. I don't know whether you've got any pets at home, perform to your pets, you know, perform to your teddy bears, it doesn't matter. You need to have a sense that, when you sit down to play, it's a concert, not practising, so you get used to the sense that "I have to play this and I have to play it in its entirety at the best possible level, with somebody listening".'

Confidence bolstered, I head to the morning masterclass, where Fiona plays Granados' *Escenas románticas*, followed by Martin's wonderfully graceful account of the first movement of the 'Moonlight' Sonata. Jimmy and Charlie then round off the morning with different accounts of the Brahms Handel Variations.

We're already nearing the end of the week. This evening's the big event – the last night of piano camp, with each student supposedly giving their definitive account of the piece they've been working on. This was supposed to be my moment: I'd sit where Gary had sat a year earlier and play the piece as well as he had. That's not going to happen, but I'm still determined for the Ballade to be as good as it can be tonight. Or, at the very least, not quite the disaster of five days previously. Tonight I can't blame Rupert Murdoch. He's been out of my mind for a good few days now. Sort of. The test is to see how much my brain and fingers have absorbed with nothing else to distract them.

In the afternoon I have a twenty-minute rehearsal slot on the grand piano and run through the whole piece. With no audience and no nerves much of it's there and I'm privately pleased with the clear progress I've made this week on the areas I've concentrated on. But there is definitely still a whack-a-mole feeling to it all – just as I tidy up one corner of the piece another bit starts falling apart. For instance, I've never had a problem with the chromatic run on the penultimate page, but this afternoon at the grand it was all over the place. The little introduction to the waltz – secure for weeks – is now a mash of wrong notes. And so on.

Just before going on in the evening, I get a phone message out of the blue from Julian Assange's 'PA' wanting a meeting. I haven't heard from Assange for over six months now and had sort of assumed we'd never meet again. Why the sudden call? I decide not to call him back until tomorrow. I just need a clear mind tonight. I have a flashback again to that memory from school, of playing the Mozart clarinet quintet in front of an audience of hundreds of pupils and parents; just minutes before going on a junior boy rushes up and tells me a master wants to see me. I sent a message back saying this was impossible and duly walked on stage. All the way through the piece my mind was whirring away: *What could I possibly have done wrong that demands this urgent meeting?* In the middle of the lingering long notes in the slow movement it came to me: *I have an illicit toaster under an armchair in a shared room. Perhaps I've inadvertently left it on?* So I spent two more movements wondering if I would soon discover I had set fire to the school. When I stepped off the stage I discovered this was, indeed, the cause of the summons. I had come close to arson. So, tonight, if I am going to play the Ballade with anything approaching competence, it's probably best that I put Julian Assange from my mind.

At the concert, there's an end-of-term feeling, everyone a bit dressed up and most rising to the occasion with decent performances. I start quite confidently – feeling much less nervous than five days earlier. At bar 6 the C minor chord doesn't speak, which has never happened before, but otherwise, the first section goes fine. I play it faster, as William has suggested – more like a waltz – and skim pretty well over the G minor arpeggios. In fact, it's not going badly. I'm relaxing. And the room feels attentive inasmuch as I'm allowing anything to penetrate my square-metre total exclusion zone of concentration. The second melody doesn't quite sing as I'd have liked it to, but so far so good: it could be a lot worse. All this I'm thinking as I'm playing – a quiet running commentary in some far-off recess of the mind.

I'm into the big chords and – wham – suddenly I'm playing a whole load of wrong chords. Chords from nowhere, not chords at all, just horrible clusters of noise. *What on earth is happening?* The same running commentary. I keep pushing it back: I can't allow an inkling of conscious thought to jump in and bring further disruption. I need to regain seamless connection between some unconscious sphere of my brain and my fingers; and quickly I manage it – the fingers recover and revert to playing the right notes. But then – at the complicated octave scales at 119 – just at the end of the big chords – the wrong notes again: a sudden squall. Commentary: *How can I stop it capsizing the whole thing?* But already I'm in the waltz, there's no pause or moment to recover equilibrium, the notes just keep coming. Or not coming, in the case of a few LH plonks. Still, I gradually recover and the next three pages are more or less right. At the first performance this week, I'd become totally destabilised by my errors. Tonight I'm taking them in my stride, never feeling overwhelmed or shaky.

But there are more errors to come. At bar 206 for some reason I landed on a B flat. Voice in head: *I've played it correctly as a D hundreds of times. So why the B flat all of a sudden?*

Then I'm dragged into the coda. I set off at a steadyish pace. (Voice: *Who has told me in recent weeks that it's more effective to play things slowly but right?*) The fingers are dropping in the correct places: the sound's pretty good. But then suddenly another out-of-the-blue storm: a fistful of wrong notes from nowhere. Again, no warning, and in a place which wasn't covered in 6B pencil circling – so not a 'fracture' I've ever fretted over before. This time I'm a little thrown. A few bars later and another cluster of weird-sounding notes, and then another. Now I'm flustered. And my consciousness is breaking in – frantically trying to find a moment where both hands might reset themselves. I find one, but the downwards tumble of chords 240–2 is a mess nonetheless. My brain has started to behave like my computer sometimes does when there are too many programmes open: there's a time lag between input and action; that feeling of tapping in text, only to see nothing on screen, and then a rush of letters as some hidden buffering process catches up.

Voice: *Now you're in trouble. The chromatic scale coming up's going to sink you.* But it's OK. And then there's applause and I realise it's all over. Back in my seat, I can feel my cheeks flushed and my pulse racing. That was full of errors and inexplicable misplayings. But I feel oddly more confident, not less. OK, I'm still way off where I want to be – but tonight was a bit of a breakthrough. For the first time I have played the Ballade to an audience and didn't feel completely intimidated by it. Progress.

Thursday, 28 July

So piano camp is over for another year. There are the usual farewells and swaps of email addresses and phone numbers. I pull William aside for a moment, and ask him the same question as yesterday (I want to know if my fairly rough rendition has affected his assessment): 'Will I be able to play the Ballade by December?'

'You can play it already,' he says again. 'You just want to get better.'

It's official then. I *can* play Chopin's first Ballade. Almost. Sort of. Nearly. Sometimes.

As the train nears Paris the phone calls begin once more and emails start building up again. And I book to meet Assange.

PART EIGHT

Friday, 5 August

Drive down to Blockley in the evening. As we drive out along the M40 I know that Nick Davies is heading for an assignment in Maida Vale to have a drink with a man in the movies, one George Clooney. I'm sure it won't go to his head.

I've been back from piano camp for a week now, and tomorrow head off for Italy, but it's been an intense seven days, and I came back to earth with a bang. Within twenty-four hours of being back in London, I received a call from the Hertfordshire police, who thought I may have been the last person to speak to Sean Hoare. This wasn't the case – I'm pretty sure he had dinner with someone from the *NYT* after speaking to me that day. But I send them my notes of our discussion, in which he revealed that, for a few hundred quid, the *NotW* could track a person as well as hack them.

The climax of the working week was Thursday and my mystery meeting with Assange, whom I hadn't seen since November. Such was the secrecy that there was no word of the venue until half an hour before. It turned out to be an anonymous block of meeting rooms in the City, behind Liverpool Street, apparently rented by a supporter.

I walked into the room and was immediately conscious that, in a corner, there was a figure wearing what looked like a pair of dark glasses. He was filming me on a camera linked to the glasses. I suggested to Julian we turn off the filming while we established why we were there. He replied brusquely that it's now his policy to film all contacts with the media. I was tempted to leave. Instead, I flipped open my iPad and said I'd keep a record, too. Assange nodded.

He gave no initial clue as to why he'd called the meeting. There was a rather rambling little speech about Kazakhstan, and then he began what appeared to be a form of interview about English libel and media law. He said this was because he hadn't had the chance to get this onto film at the time we were working together – no idea why. Since my position has always been that we will support him in his legal fights with the media, I felt happy talking to him about this. The silent third man kept on filming, occasionally moving around the room for a different angle.

We discussed why we had gone to the *New York Times*, and why we had felt that the First Amendment protection would help with the story. Then he wanted examples of media law working against us in Britain in the past. He moved on to some quite detailed questioning about the reasons for particular redactions in the documents we published last year. After about forty minutes he began to warm up slightly – up to this point he had been very matter-of-fact and inquisitorial – and talked about how we might work together again. The *Guardian* was his natural partner, he said. We should, as it were, bury the hatchet. But the material he wanted to work on next didn't seem immediately explosive, or sensational; it was related to material already in our possession, to do with Afghanistan. At the end we spent about twenty minutes discussing what he thought was happening with his extradition proceedings, both in Sweden and in America.

The overall tone was tense but civil, and slightly more friendly towards the end. We will never be best friends, but he appears to want WikiLeaks and the *Guardian* back working together. The silent man showed me his dark glasses once we'd finished: fancy goggle-style viewfinders that allow you to move the camera without moving your head. Every meeting I've ever had with Assange has been strange – this was about six out of ten – but if he truly wants to rebuild bridges, that's fine by me.

Meanwhile, Nick Davies has set off for Los Angeles. Clooney is not alone in wanting to talk about the film rights: there are now several bids to make the film of the hacking affair and Nick's agents want to get him around town to meet interested people. I revisit Ben Bradlee's autobiography to see what he says about the making of *All the President's Men*. Initially, he refused to allow the film-makers to use the name of the *Washington Post* or their names 'out of a sense that what privacy we had was not long for this world'. He tells the story of Dustin Hoffman hanging around the newsroom to get the atmosphere and how they ended up watching a 'jumper' – someone threatening to throw themselves off a building.

Everyone in the crowd was fixated on the jumper until they realised Hoffman was alongside them. 'Then all eyes left the poor jumper to focus on the dashing young actor. Jumper is forgotten (he didn't jump).' A perfect example of the Heisenberg principle, named after the German physicist who discovered that the act of measuring, even observing subatomic particles actually changed the composition of the subatomic particles.

As intense a week as it's been, we did manage to get to Blockley last weekend. On the Saturday evening, we'd been invited to see a performance of *Siegfried* at the Longborough Opera, a private opera house built by a couple behind their home. We've never yet made it to Longborough before, despite it being only ten minutes away. This is partly because Lindsay has a slight allergy at the sight of a certain sort of Englishman dressed up in a dinner jacket in mid-afternoon as part of a corporate entertainment package that happens to include opera, but could equally well be polo or boat races. So it was with slightly heavy hearts that we set off for *Siegfried* at 3 p.m. on a sunny Saturday after-noon – and a further sinking feeling when we see so many of the black-tied brigade as we arrive at the house, a comfortable, but hardly baronial, house on the edge of the village. But the feeling didn't last long. It was replaced instead by total admiration for what Martin and Lizzie Graham – the opera's organisers – have achieved here, just three miles from where we live.

Martin Graham was born in Longborough. The first thing he said on being introduced to me was 'Blockley – pretty rough village when I was growing up'. He started life as a builder, made a fortune as a developer and then decided to build his own opera house on the site of chicken sheds in his grounds – with the intention of staging the first Ring cycle in a private opera house anywhere in the world. As he was telling me about his dream over drinks in the first interval, he caught my sceptical eye – a look that must be very familiar. 'You are looking at an extremely conceited man,' he said.

The barn-like structure of their 'opera house' (with discarded seating from the Royal Opera House) sits 600 and is fronted by a mock-classical portico, topped by a statue of Wagner made by the nearby Whichford Pottery. Which builder put up the shed? 'I did a fair amount myself,' Graham said before fixing me with an old-fashioned look. 'A man must build.' This made me feel a bit feeble, having built not a single brick or plank of my own music room.

How does he stage Wagner operas? He launched into a diatribe against the excesses of professional opera houses – he described one particular piece of staging at the Royal Opera House that (he heard) cost £250,000! 'In Wagner you just want to keep it simple.' So he kept production costs to a minimum. There's a fifty-something piece orchestra. The singers accept lowish fees because it's great to get these parts on their CVs. They lodge out with locals, whose reward is in tickets (some have been using the music room for warm-up sessions). And his masterstroke was finding Anthony

Negus – a Wagnerite in his early 60s who had worked as an assistant to the great Wagner conductor Reginald Goodall, as well as Charles Mackerras and Pierre Boulez. In the end, it was as engrossing an evening of opera as I've enjoyed anywhere.

Sunday, 21 August

Back in Italy, in the same old farmhouse on the La Foce estate, looking out over the baked landscape. And, just as a year ago, I'm doing hour-long practice in the cavernous room with the upright Yamaha and the ping-pong table. I've been splitting these hours up in exactly the way William suggested: scales, followed by fifteen-minute sections on different passages, followed by playing the whole piece through.

I've been paying particular attention to the big E/A major tune, since William pinpointed it as the weakest link and hinted that I will never really play the Ballade until I have memorised this chunk. When he told me this, I had already memorised most of the coda and the waltz and some of the runs and scales on pages 2 and 3, and I really thought that loading my brain with another passage would be impossible – there wasn't enough room, I'd *over*load, and then start to forget the other passages. But of course William was right that I *had* to learn this section. The passage is indeed very problematical – and it's where I felt most flustered when I tried to play it on piano camp.

Over the past two weeks in Italy, I'm not sure I consciously set out to memorise this section, but I have played it more often than anything else, and very slowly, repeatedly, left hand on its own and then right hand on its own, the beginnings of bars and then the ends of bars; playing it without the music and not playing the next chord until I could work out what the following one should be. I tried to listen and force myself to think of the harmonic patterns. And the result is that today, as the holiday comes to an end, I can almost play this section by memory. It has become lodged somewhere in the grey matter. My brain keeps surprising me.

But it's very, very slow still. I've just tried playing the passage and I can do it at ♩ = 60, which, according to my score, is what I was playing it at in January. So anybody sitting outside the room and listening to the piano practice might think I haven't got any better at all. But of course the difference is that I can now play it at the same speed from memory as I did when I was reading it.

I've also spent a lot of time on holiday going over the diary I've kept of the last year – all the written notes, recorded interviews, bookmarked websites, etc. – and pulling them together into something more concrete. If I'd known a year ago quite how intensive the news agenda was going to be, would I have embarked on learning this staggeringly difficult piece? Probably not. A judicious internal voice would have told me to shelve it for later in life when the helter-skelter existence of handling massive news stories was but a distant memory. But Chopin has kept me sane throughout all this. Without Op. 23 the year could easily have become slightly obsessive, or – more accurately – even more obsessive. Of course, without the torrent of news I might even have managed to learn the piece within the twelve months I originally set myself. But the longer time frame has also allowed me to go deeper and deeper into understanding the piano and the piece, giving me more time for encounters with proper pianists, brain scientists and the like. I can't think of anything else in my non-working life I have sunk into with quite so much focus.

Naturally, while we're in Italy, there's another huge story – the riots playing out on the streets of several English cities. I'm in touch with the office – but there's a strong team in place doing a brilliant job of covering a fast and difficult chain of events. One young reporter, Paul Lewis, has been putting in extraordinary hours combining traditional reporting skills with the crowdsourcing capabilities of Twitter. I'm tempted to fly back, but the tone of voice of my colleagues suggests they're having a whale of a time without me and, really, there's no need.

Saturday, 10 September

I've now been back in the office for a few days, and the barometer of editorial stress is rising. The high point this week came on Tuesday, when WikiLeaks published its entire cache of diplomatic cables – to unanimous condemnation by all its main former media partners and with Assange trying to shift responsibility onto the *Guardian*. Is this the same Assange who, only six weeks ago, sat down with me asking that we should work together again? He's popped up in various places, including a conference in Germany, insisting he's known 'for about two months' (i.e. the beginning of July) this is all the *Guardian*'s fault. Now he's busy on Twitter saying the *Guardian* should never be trusted with anything and must be shunned by all right-thinking people. Deep sigh. Is it worth the time and effort to engage in an argument over this? There are Assange-worshippers scattered around the world who will believe anything he tells them. There are as many, if not more, Assange-haters who would love to see a mud-fight between two former collaborators. And, in the middle, a larger number of Assange-agnostics who may be divining a pattern, seeing a man who eventually insists on falling out with everyone.. I'm tempted to publish a transcript of our 4 August meeting (thank you to the man in dark glasses, whose mystery presence prompted me to keep my own record) – in which, with as much warmth as he could summon, Assange told me: 'The *Guardian* is a natural ally which is why, of course, we engaged in this deal with the *Guardian* in the first place . . . I want to try and work if possible a way to engage with the *Guardian* again.' But, in the end, life seems too short to engage in a he-said-she-said shouting match with the odd one. So we'll let it pass.

I've been able to keep my daily practice up, and on Monday I have an evening one-to-one lesson with William Fong in the basement of Kings Place on a very nice Steinway D. It's very cold down there and I've come straight from a day's work. William suggests I play the whole piece to him to begin with. I try it quite slowly and deliberately and play much better than I think he'd heard me before – it's of course much less stressful playing to one person than to nine or ten.

He starts by looking at the G minor scales towards the end of the piece. I can honestly say 'yes' when he interrogates me as to whether I've been playing my scales. But, years of teaching the piano doubtless encourages scepticism about such assurances. He duly asks me to play an octave of G minor, but very quickly. I oblige. 'You can play it perfectly quickly' – so why wasn't I playing them quickly in the Ballade? 'Just imagine they're easy, and work backwards, i.e. play the last octave and then two octaves but with a real speedy flourish. Make sure you can make the last octave arrive in the right place and then worry about the rest.'

The section that still falls apart a bit is the big A major/E major section. I made giant strides with this in Italy, but I've reached a tricky intermediate stage with it now: I'm in that uncertain territory between memorising the notes and reading them. William says he's been in this place himself thousands of times with pieces when he hadn't quite learned them. He advises me to start playing with the music on a piano seat next to the piano instead of on the piano itself. There's a psychological difference between having it in front of you so that you can look up at any moment, and on the seat beside you where you can't read it. It's a kind of safety blanket.

For the rest of our lesson, we move around the piece, looking at various small problems in detail. At one point, when we're looking at bar 14 – he wants me to stop completely on a D before playing the following C sharp with a dramatic emphasis – William says quite emphatically, 'Look, Alan, you've got to think of yourself as a great pianist.' So, having earlier advised me to think of how music would be if it was easy, he now demands that I think about how I would play things if I was a superlative pianist. 'Stop thinking of yourself as a quite good pianist who sometimes plays out of a hobby and suddenly think of yourself as a great pianist.' I'll try . . .

At the end of the lesson he says he's impressed, especially with the coda and the left hand, which he feels is now much more secure. He says that in general, it's all much more coherent and assured than it had been in Lot, so all that Italian practice has come to something.

I think I've got through the phase of being obsessed with fingerings and notes. There are just a few bars now – literally only half a dozen – where I have anxieties about what the notes are or the fingering. And so there's more thought going into the sound I'm making, as though I've moved through some sort of barrier of learning into a more expressive phase. This weekend I've been at Fish Cottage and musing on something William told me on Monday – that I make a big noise when I play. This was not, I think, intended entirely as a compliment. He said it was because I was pressing my fingers so heavily into the keys. Essentially, he was saying that if I can be more nimble with my fingers instead of pressing deeply into the keys then I'll find a lot of passages in the Ballade much easier. This comes back to something I've always struggled to understand – the difference between arm weight and finger weight and hand weight and shoulder weight (all expressions that piano teachers use). In the past I've told Michael that I just don't understand this use of the phrase 'weight' in relation to arms or shoulders and he says he struggled for a long time to understand it too. Eventually he had to imagine there was nothing between his shoulders and his fingers so that his hands were almost detached from his body. In his head, the signals went from the shoulders down to the fingers and the arms were just a conduit, they weren't part of the playing mechanism, as it were.

Down at Blockley today I've been trying this – just thinking of the fingers – and it does make a very different sound, less heavy and less percussive. But I'm still miles away from being able to play it confidently in public. I'll be lucky if I can do it before my new end-of-year deadline.

Saturday, 24 September

The hacking affair has been marked throughout by strange behaviour from the police. This began with their original decision to pour ice-cold water all over our July 2009 revelations about the hush money paid to cover up a legal case which disproved News International's 'one rogue reporter' theory. Editors can't be conspiracy theorists, so for a long time I did my best to find an innocent reason for Scotland Yard's apparent collusion with a gargantuan media company. The latest piece of strange behaviour came last Wednesday afternoon, when out of the blue, a couple of cops turn up in reception at the *Guardian* carrying a very big black file which is, it turns out, a production order on our reporter Amelia Hill, trying to get at all her notebooks, emails, tapes and so forth, in order to try to discover the source of the various *Guardian* stories relating to Operation Weeting, the fourth and latest police inquiry into phone hacking.

We sit around in the office slightly dumbfounded by this latest move. As we read the production-order document, it becomes clear that not only is it an application under the Police and Criminal Evidence Act (PACE), but it's also throwing the Official Secrets Act at Amelia for unauthorised contact with a policeman. If every reporter who spoke to a copper without permission was locked up, the country's newsrooms would be very empty places indeed.

Section 5 of the Official Secrets Act is so rarely used our lawyer has to turn to a textbook in the middle of the meeting to see exactly what it's about. We realise there's going to be a bit of a firestorm ahead. But we have a good legal team ready for the fight and so we go out, all guns blazing, with various interviews in America and in the UK. I go on the *Today* programme and other radio and TV criticising the police behaviour. British national papers are often slow to support each other (see hacking, *passim*) but over this there's a gradual ripple of support, beginning with the *Daily Mirror* on the Saturday, then the *Sunday Times* (a News International title) and the *Telegraph* and *Independent* on the Monday. By Tuesday, the *Daily Mail* and their bullish correspondent Richard Littlejohn are onside. Which is the first time, I think, Richard Littlejohn has ever supported the *Guardian* on anything. Only the *Sun* can't bring itself to say anything at all.

It must be evident to the police that they've made a stupid PR mistake, if nothing else. The only mystery is whether this is the last gasp of the dying regime – rudderless since the resignation of Paul Stephenson – or whether it is the new man, Bernard Hogan-Howe, trying to stamp his authority on relations between police and reporters. If the former, then it might just about be understandable, though unbelievably stupid. If the latter, then it's worrying because it would indicate that we have a new commissioner with a very authoritarian view of how the press should behave.

The rest of this week includes a flying trip to Birmingham, a visit from the *NYT*'s media correspondent, David Carr, and a big debate at Banqueting House in Whitehall chaired by Harry Evans. After the ninety-minute televised discussion, news breaks that the police have withdrawn their production order. It's a warm evening and suddenly the pavement outside is full of reporters ringing their news desks and filing copy about the police climbdown. All of which means that I'm back on the *Today* programme on Wednesday morning instead of at my piano lesson with Michael.

Just as the excitement over the Official Secrets Act dies down on Wednesday, we learn that Julian Assange's autobiography is to be published the next day, serialised in the *Independent*. It seems a complicated and messy saga in which Assange, once more, has fallen out with almost everybody he was involved with. The long and the short of it is that his publishers, Canongate, have decided to publish the book anyway, despite the fact that Assange has not given his consent and has, indeed, tried to block it.

The book arrives early on Thursday morning. A skim through the early chapters is quite interesting: they're revealing about his childhood, upbringing and his early hacking days. As anticipated, the last chapter is a rather bitter rant in which he condemns all, or most, of the media players he worked with this time last year. He's particularly vituperative about Bill Keller of the *New York Times*, but has a sideswipe at me explaining that his loss of temper back in November – the eight-hour marathon meeting in which he'd barged into my office and insisted that I personally extract a front-page apology out of the *NYT* – was down to being confronted with 'a lily-livered git . . . with eyes like marbles on a pogo stick'. He has a certain gift as a phrase-maker.

Through all this – threatened arrests and a publishing *coup de théâtre* – I do manage to squeeze in three mornings of twenty-minute practice. I'm beginning each session in the William Fong method, practising my scales, and as a result I can now play the scales at the end of the Ballade much more fluently and quickly. But all my concentration at the moment is on the middle section with the big E/A chords and especially the runs at the end of them. This whole passage is still, for me, the hardest in the piece. But I've been making definite progress. I play it right through today, not particularly carefully but trying to capture the spirit of the piece. It's quite untidy in places but not far off being at the sort of level now where I could imagine playing it in a relaxed performance, if there is such a thing.

Saturday, 1 October

Another slightly-too-packed week. Liverpool on Monday for the Labour Party conference, which involved a *Guardian* party that went on to about one o'clock in the morning, too many lunches, coffees and several snatched meetings/meals with assorted politicians and aides. The following day, a Guardian Media Group board meeting and a dinner for advertisers around a sometimes quite heated discussion between the legendary Watergate reporter, Carl Bernstein, and Nick Davies. On Thursday evening we host a debate on phone hacking at the Royal Institution: Bernstein again – all First Amendment, no regulation – and Sylvie Kauffmann, the former editor of *Le Monde*, with a completely different opinion from the point of view of French regulation, puzzled by the British tabloids. The French, for better or worse, have no tabloids, so they – like the Americans – can't understand the British debate at all. It's a puzzle we don't solve: the country with the least regulation and the country with the toughest privacy laws are, in some ways, much more restrained in the boundaries of what they consider acceptable than the UK, with its unreconstructed libel laws and its medium-grade regulation.

On the way back to Blockley at the end of the week I have dinner in Oxford at the invitation of Eric Clarke, the music professor. I guess he must be about the same age as me, and he talks about how the study of music has changed during the time he's been involved. He says music is now a much more relaxed discipline in which you can study world music, pop, music from a historical or practical point of view, improvisation, electronic music, and so on – altogether a much more flexible discipline than thirty or so years ago. He also talks about the degree of allusion involved in playing the piano; that the piano is considered the most romantic of instruments, and yet it is the most inexpressive. Once you hit the note, there is nothing you can do with it; you can't alter it or bend it; the note starts dying the moment the hammer has struck the string – you can't grow it, it dies. He's also interesting on the way in which pianists talk about the act of touching the key. In physical terms, by the time the note sounds, the hammer has, of course, already struck the key. So the art of stroking or touching or caressing the key is not easily explainable in physical terms because of the mechanics of the piano.

Anyway, it's been good to be down in Blockley at the end of such a week, especially with the Indian summer weather. I've mustered three mornings of practice during the week. In these, I've tried to remember that the flip side of memorisation is that there's a danger of then only focusing on velocity. But sometimes you have to take a step backwards, and go back to reading the piece carefully and playing it much, much, much more slowly, almost as slowly as when you were originally learning it – just to keep bolstering the memory.

This morning I sat down and tried a speed test, playing the Ballade as fast as I could. Admittedly, I had to sacrifice a bit of accuracy on one or two little passages, but it was ninety per cent there. I did it in 10:17, as fast as some of the slower commercial recordings. It was what athletes call my 'pb', or personal best. All that was missing was the silver foil recovery blanket and the glucose drink.

Friday, 14 October

It seems like we're in the middle of a festival of press inquiries – parliamentary, police and judicial. Last week and this week it's been the Leveson Inquiry, the judge-led public inquiry looking into the standards, ethics and practices of the British press, ordered up by David Cameron after the Dowler story. Last

Thursday, I had to give evidence to it for the first time – or, at least, address a seminar on why a free press is necessary in a democratic society. In fact, this was the first time in living memory that every British editor turned up to be in the same room at the same time to talk about the future of the British press. There was a slightly forced atmosphere of bonhomie, which was punctured only by a magnificently coruscating account of working on the *Daily Star* by a young man, Richard Peppiatt, who denounced the tabloid culture and was in turn promptly denounced by every tabloid editor in the room.

The inquiry's QC, Robert Jay, was in the front row and, at one point, he turned round to me – I had never met him before – and said, 'I much enjoyed your review of Daniel Barenboim's recital a couple of years ago.' This was the one in which Barenboim played the last three Beethoven sonatas in one sitting. Jay says he has at least a dozen recordings of those three sonatas, so whatever type of QC he might prove himself to be in the course of this inquiry, he at least has very good musical taste.

This Tuesday, there's a Lords committee on the future of investigative journalism: I'm down to give evidence with Ian Hislop, the editor of *Private Eye*. It's the second time we've done this double act. The parliamentarians are rather star-struck by him and he obliges with a very fluent performance, alternating between outrage at the UK's media laws and some good gags. We agree about much – though Hislop, editing a fortnightly satire magazine and not very involved in webby things, wrinkles his nose at anything digital. The parliamentarians are earnest, serious and, in the best sense, well meaning. Whether anything they say will make any difference is another matter.

The week, though, was dominated by the Defence Secretary Liam Fox and his strange friendship with his former business colleague and adviser, a man called Adam Werritty – another *Guardian* scoop, broken by one of our young new reporters, Rupert Neate, who has been pursuing this story since last June. Werritty and Fox, it turns out, kept on meeting up in different contexts and different corners of the globe, with the former handing out business cards claiming to be Fox's adviser. Fox finally resigned on Monday, which I think surprised nobody – except Fox himself, who gave every appearance of simply wanting to tough it out.

So yet another taxing few days, and my tiredness has crept into my piano practice. I've been playing with fingers which can't quite remember what they're supposed to be doing, playing unevenly and allowing mistakes to slip past without correcting them. However, at the same time I realise

I'm enjoying the piano very much at this stage. The news agenda may be throwing every possible obstacle between me and Chopin, but I've managed to keep going at the edges. If I were training for a marathon I'd be able to argue that the resultant wash of endorphins, adrenaline, serotonin and dopamine was good, in return, for my work life. I don't know quite what mix of chemicals are stimulated by having to get my fingers round Op. 23 – but I can feel the benefit at the office. Editing, total editing and nothing but editing would send anyone a bit dotty.

And surely that applies to any job. Martin Kettle, a *Guardian* leader writer and keen music lover, comes to see me later to give me feedback on a lunch he's had with M or C (I always forget which is which) – the director general of MI5, Jonathan Evans. They spent an interesting lunch discussing al-Qaeda and Russia – and then ended up discussing Telemann. The news somehow makes me feel a little bit more reassured about the nation's security. A total non sequitur, I know.

I'm now at the stage where I feel more relaxed about the big question of whether I will be able to play this piece. As a result piano lessons with Michael are now richer. Which is not to say he's stopped picking me up on every minor mistake. This week – 8 a.m. on the Thursday, as Leveson had done for my usual Wednesday slot – he was extremely unforgiving about making me play a small section repeatedly, slowly, until I had the patterns mastered to his satisfaction. I'm going to be in New York next week, and he's going to be in New York the following week, so there will now be two weeks without a lesson.

Sunday, 16 October

A weekend in Blockley, and beautiful sparkling weather. Yesterday we drove across to Cheltenham in gorgeous golden autumnal sun to debate on the aftermath of phone hacking with James Harding, editor of *The Times*, and others at the *Times*-sponsored literary festival debate.

This morning, Jessica Lough, a friend from the village, came round to the music room with her flute, which she has taken up again after a gap of decades, and we played some Gluck and some Mozart and some Handel sonatas. I then played her the Ballade, mindful of William's instruction during piano camp to perform it to anybody I find – even a dog. This took a little bit of courage, because she used to be a concert agent and has represented many famous pianists, including Radu Lupu. She sat on the sofa staring out into the garden as I played.

But performing, even to one friend, frays the nerves, which is doubtless why William recommends doing it often. I immediately start making errors which simply don't occur to me when I'm playing on my own. Around bar 146, the whole piece starts falling apart for about ten bars and I'm really wrestling with it to try to get it back in control – extremely difficult when you've established a particular tempo in a passage. It's like a slamming on the brakes with a runaway train. And it's a difficult thing to regain the tempo once you've lost it. There are bits I'm pleased with but, overall, I'm plunged back into the feeling of nervy playing and being rather frightened of the piece, which I don't feel now when I play it alone.

Afterwards, Jessica's review consisted of two words: 'brutal' (as in 'What a difficult piece'), and 'brave' (as in 'Are you crazy?'). An honest assessment. She tells me a story about working for Radu Lupu when he was playing the Brahms Second Piano Concerto for the first time. He was then married to Elizabeth Wilson, the cellist, and about five days before he was supposed to play the piece, she rang Jessica and said, 'I'm just warning you that I'm not sure Radu is going to be able to perform this and you might want to get a stand-in.' She explained this was because she hadn't heard Lupu practising at all: he still hadn't yet played the piece, five days away from performing it. But then, two days later, she rang up and said, 'It's OK, it's going to be all right, he can play it.' What he'd been doing was just learning the piece by looking at it and getting it into his mind; his technique could do the rest. Now obviously that's not true of my technique, or most people's for that matter. Jessica's point is that it's always possible to keep in touch with, and even make progress on, a piece of music even if you're away from the instrument. Which is good news, as I'm about to go to America for a week.

After Jessica leaves I stay at the piano for a little Ballade work. I start with my scales and try to listen to myself properly as I play them – my new policy is to be a completely honest listener. I realise I've been fooling myself in imagining that I could play a B-flat major scale. In fact, in all the scales I'm finding problems coming down in the left hand, which is a fairly basic technical fault – but with B flat I wasn't even sure which finger

I should be starting with in the LH. It's quite a sobering moment to realise that, at the age of 57 and with modest pretensions, you've never really known how to play a B-flat major scale. And there's another realisation: if I'm going to meet my aim of performing the piece around the beginning of December, then I've got about six weeks – and I'm suddenly conscious that I've yet to find a venue or invite anyone. I must be in some state of denial.

This evening there's more music, back in London with one of Richard's chamber groups – my first such get-together since early July, as Richard's been in NY. It's the usual story with the ever-eclectic Richard: a random mix of players, including three violins, two violas and two cellos. But we scrape together sheet music somehow, including a version of the Mozart Clarinet Concerto for clarinet and string quartet. Playing this really was reaching into the mists of memory for me. I played the first movement with an orchestra at school . . . help . . . forty years ago. The third movement I never properly learned back then, and I hadn't touched the clarinet since early July – over three months ago – the day before we broke the Milly Dowler story. To make it worse, I'm playing off the full score. But I know the first movement so well that, even across four decades of neglect, the fingers somehow match up with the notes in approximately the right place. Another half-understood aspect of memory.

Tuesday, 18 October

Back to New York. A third of our readership is in North America. There are maybe 10 million people in the US and Canada who come to the *Guardian* every month. Given that we've barely spent a dollar on marketing that's quite interesting – however we really have to double the North American readership before we get on the major advertisers' schedules. There's a definite appetite for what we do, which is different from what either the *New York Times* or the web competition does. The British journalism tradition is distinct from the American. In many ways it's the reverse. We have impartial broadcasters and a polemical press. They have the impartial *NYT* and Fox News.

We've now opened a small newsroom in New York with the instruction to behave like a start-up. They have no legacy print edition to worry about: they can organise themselves, and behave, as a true digital news organisation. But it all needs setting up – the core editorial and technology staff, a publisher, the marketing and press.

On the plane over, I watch an advance copy of a new film, *Pianomania* – a documentary with, on the face of it, the most unpromising leading man and subject matter: a mild-mannered piano tuner with some difficult clients. It's a portrait of Stefan Knüpfer, a Hamburg-based tuner, as he ricochets between Alfred Brendel, Till Felner, Pierre-Laurent Aimard and others – equipped with nothing more menacing than a tuning fork and a disarming smile. His clients are 'generally dissatisfied', despite all his attempts to pick, manipulate, tune and voice instruments for them. Aimard is shown performing with an orchestra and one of Knüpfer's inventions – a series of glass shutters, which sit like sails on top of the piano, reflecting the sound away from the orchestra and towards the audience. Good for playing with strings – but rejected when he tries it for Aimard's solo Bach recordings. Frau Knüpfer bakes him a compensatory cheese-cake to cheer him up. It's never going to break box office records, but it's a totally original glimpse into an unknown world.

And then, since I'm going to have a cup of coffee with her in New York, I read a book by the woman who has just become my opposite number at the *New York Times*, Jill Abramson. Her escape from editing, it seems, is her dog. When we do meet a couple of days later we end up discussing what all editors obsess about these days – the economic model of newspapers. No mention of dogs or pianos.

Monday, 31 October

Back in London for over a week now, and it's been extremely busy. Last Thursday morning I had a call from Giles Fraser, the canon at St Paul's Cathedral, who I knew had been agonising about his position given the mood amongst his colleagues to evict the Occupy London protestors camped out in the cathedral precincts. He calls to say he's resigned, has slipped out of the house early to avoid the inevitable press attention, and is in semi-hiding in the Tate Modern café. I tell him to jump in a cab and I'll interview him myself – I could just fit it in before heading across town for lunch with the MI6 chief, Sir John Sawyer. Giles arrives twenty minutes later looking unshaven and in a pair of jeans and black sweatshirt. We talk for an hour about his reasons for quitting. He borrows a shirt and razor off me in order to make himself semi-presentable for a photograph and I dash off to lunch, filing the best quotes from the back of a cab, just like a proper reporter. Back in the office by three, file by five.

Today's similarly hectic, but also another one of those days when editing a paper – actually, simply being a journalist – is just one of the most interesting jobs in the world, if only because of the people who swim through your life and the things you discuss. In the morning Martin McGuinness, the former IRA and Sinn Fein leader and now Northern Ireland's Deputy First Minister, comes for a cup of coffee. He's just unsuccessfully stood for president in the South and we spend three-quarters of an hour discussing policing, security and the politics of Northern Ireland. As I show him out, I tell him that the next person in – for lunch – is the Archbishop of Canterbury, Dr Rowan Williams. His face brightens and he says what a nice man Williams is and would I send him his regards, which I do. 'Martin McGuinness says he really likes you,' I add. Rowan – beset, as ever, by endless ecclesiastical divisions over gender and sexuality – allows a bushy eyebrow to arch a bit and remarks drily, 'Well at least that's one.'

The Leveson Inquiry is very preoccupied by these encounters between media and politicians, police, etc. The *Guardian* tradition is usually to throw them open – either (with morning conference) to any member of staff or (with lunch, breakfast, etc.) to a sizeable group. There are about a dozen of us round the table in my office for sandwiches with the archbishop. We talk about the St Paul's protests and about finance, the City, inequality and poverty. Today he seems more confident and more at ease with himself. Colleagues, even the more militant atheist ones, are impressed and moved by the genuine intelligence, capacity for listening; and the thoughtful speech patterns and sheer piety of the man.

No sooner have we cleared up from Rowan than Dick Costolo, the chief executive officer of Twitter over from San Francisco with a couple of colleagues, arrives to talk about how the *Guardian* is using Twitter – in his view more imaginatively and more progressively than any other newspaper in the world. We've actually been collaborating with Twitter over 2.5 million tweets they gave us at the time of the English riots, which we're analysing to see what was going on in those days on social media. Two or three years ago Twitter was a minority obsession of a small group of us on the paper. Now there's barely a single reporter who could do his job effectively without it. Another little symptom of the tornado of change buffeting the news business.

In the evening I arrive late for a drink with a bunch of old university friends who hadn't met together for thirty-five years – sparked by an email out of the blue from David Toynbee, whom I last saw as an undergraduate, a keen amateur pianist who is now an educational administrator. We're with Robert White, a keen viola player, Mike Tooby, who has enjoyed a curatorial career in the arts, and Philip Feeney, a composer of ballet scores and a pianist with ballet companies. We meet in the snug of an underground bar off Holborn in central London. There's a noisy office party (they look like City laywers) in swing and nothing to eat but crisps and peanuts. Not so very different from the evenings we used to spend together in the public bar of the Merton Arms round the back of Magdalene in Cambridge, only tonight we're not going to play darts. We're missing only Richard Morrison, now music critic for *The Times*, who was the other member of our group back then. I'm again embarrassed by my poor memory tonight and struck by the ability of other people to remember more about my life than I can. David remembers going to an Arsenal–Derby game with me at Highbury; I have no memory of it at all. And Philip remembers the little activist operetta that I had written as part of the protest in Cambridge in the mid-1970s to save the picturesque Kite area. This started to come back to me: while on strike at the *Cambridge Evening News*, I wrote a musical, including all the song numbers, words and orchestrations, which we performed in a little local hall to raise money for the campaign. 'Not that it did any good,' said Philip. Though we did save quite a few blocks of Victorian terraces from demolition and submersion in 1970s' concrete. Maybe the little musical played a minuscule part.

In the middle of the drink we have an amnesty of scores. David Toynbee returns to me a score of Ravel's Pavane which I hadn't seen since the mid-1970s. I've discovered I have an old Brahms score of his with which I reciprocated, and then I return to Philip a full score of Verdi's *Falstaff*, which I had been nursing in assorted suitcases and bookshelves since circa 1976. I see the Pavane score cost 28p. I also note that it has absolutely no fingering or marks on it at all, which casts me back to the way I used to just muddle through pieces with no preparation at all. There's a little legend stamped on the bottom of the front page which reads 'This copy may be sold in the British Empire only'. Yes, it was that long ago.

Saturday, 5 November

Another full-on week, and again the St Paul's occupation is involved. At about three o'clock on Tuesday afternoon, I get a call suggesting I do an interview with the Bishop of London, who's just that day reversed the decision taken by the dean and chapter to try to clear the protest camp, the decision which had led to the resignation of Giles Fraser last week. I jump in a cab and go to see the bishop in his seventeenth-century palace just opposite St Paul's, which is rather confusingly called the Old Deanery. For the second time in a week I'm doing a rushed clerical interview. I've got a ninety-minute window to transcribe the highlights of a one-hour interview and write a coherent 1,200-word account. I pay for it later – working past midnight because there are two days of board meetings coming up and need to prepare. So I turn up at Wednesday's lesson with Michael Shak – my first for two weeks – really quite unready.

The first thing he asks was what my schedule is running up to the (still unarranged) performance: he was always of the school that needed to practise continually in the weeks and days before a performance, and even in the green room seconds before you go on stage. I play the piece all the way through to him with maybe eighty-five to ninety per cent accuracy. He looked pleasantly surprised at the end – his eyebrows went up and he said, 'Quite good, Alan,' which I took to mean 'really quite good' rather than quite ('moderately') good. I need a moment to recover.

We then spend the lesson concentrating on the middle four pages which I now think of as the meat of the piece in terms of difficulty. When I play the big E major/A major section in isolation this time, I come unstuck. I still need visual prompts to remind myself what comes next even at a slow tempo – I still haven't quite memorised it. But, as I sit there repeating the LH chords, it suddenly strikes me that there may be a solution to the fingering, which could be the key to this whole section. I explain it to Michael. We are possibly the only two people awake in the western world to whom this would be a remotely interesting conversation. Michael is intensely engaged. I try to show how, if I think of the second finger as the anchor on which the hand is going to pivot through this section, then you can leave the second finger in place all the way through, using it as a fixed point for knowing exactly where the hand position should be. It's important because the hand is making a series of arcs up and down the piano, with an ever-changing sequence of chord progressions. Having one finger as a pivot helps 'feel' the geography, given that the eyes are going to be fixed on the large chords and octave runs in the RH. It seems like an experiment that might keep me engaged for at least a week in any case.

I'm being thrown by the very different touch of my two practice pianos in London and Blockley. The Steinway is feather-light, the Fazioli workhorse heavy – and it's becoming increasingly difficult to make the adjustment between the two. A German technician had a look at the Fazioli a year or so ago and stuck lead weights underneath the keys to make them easier to depress. But now they're not rebounding quite as perkily as they should. I've been in touch with Jeff Shackell, who says he can take the whole action apart and re-weight each key (with lead bored into the wood, rather than stuck underneath). If my passion was for classic cars rather than classic pianos, then there would be no surprise in finding problems with a 10-year-old or 30-year-old BMW or Audi. But I'm still in the foothills of under-standing what's entailed in owning a finely set-up instrument.

This week I lose my nerve and ring Terry Lewis, the London dealer for Fazioli. He calls back after checking with the *fons et origo* – Paolo Fazioli himself. This is like speaking to Mr Dyson about a broken vacuum cleaner. He says he could sort it out easily enough if I ship it back to the factory in Sacile, near Venice. So that's what I've done. (It's also an excuse to go out and see the factory, something I've long promised myself.) The piano is taken away this morning and the equivalent of a 'courtesy car' arrives – a six-foot Kawai. It feels as if it's had a long life being mistreated in the public bar of a cheap hotel. The sound is submerged, as if the piano were under-water. If it were a courtesy car, then its clutch and brakes are burned to a frazzle. It's truly horrible.

Saturday, 12 November

The hacking story continues to bubble away. As in a cauldron. Last week, there were, very unusually, legal papers released to the House of Commons culture committee, which were astonishing in that they revealed that the editor and lawyer at the *News of the World* knew about the pattern of the illegality within the paper back in 2008. This makes the aggressive rubbishing of the *Guardian* by News International back in 2009 all the more remarkable. It had nothing to do with the truth – usually at least a passing concern of a reputable news company – and everything to do with closing down the story. Secondly, the police admitted that the number of hacking targets was now edging up to 6,000 which was double the number that even we gave in our first account in 2009, but absolutely miles away from the 'handful' that the police originally came out with in response to our piece. Then, this week, on *Newsnight* and in the *Guardian*, another private detective, Duncan Webb, revealed how he had been keeping various people in public life, including MPs, the Attorney General and the lawyers who were suing News International, under surveillance. News International came out immediately and admitted the story and said it was 'inappropriate' behaviour. It all simply reinforces the feeling of a very thuggish and sinister company which kept watch on anybody it wanted to. Just because it could.

On Thursday James Murdoch again gave evidence to the House of Commons, a marathon two-and-a-half-hour session in which his choice was between appearing competent and in charge of his company – or incompetent and ignorant of anything that was going on underneath his own nose. He chose the latter path, a course which involved him not remembering very much at all and pleading that his colleagues had kept him in total ignorance, a strategy which is apparently known by lawyers as 'confession and avoidance'. You confess the facts happened but you avoid any responsibility for them.

I had to write a leader and do a podcast on the Murdoch appearance as soon as it concluded, and then trimmed down a piece for the Comment pages before going across town to give the Orwell Lecture, in memory of the great man, in front of an audience which included the legendary Marxist historian, now well into his 90s, Eric Hobsbawm, which was slightly intimidating. My old and dear friend Lisa Jardine, who has just recovered from a chemotherapy course, was also there – which was the opposite. Also in the audience was George Orwell's son, Richard, who was only 5 when his father died and who was brought up by Orwell's sister. He turns out to be what his father might have called an amiable cove: after his father's death he'd subsequently spent a life in agricultural machinery and in renting holiday cottages in the west of Scotland.

The week was the usual hamster wheel, and only let up very slightly yesterday, when I sneaked in a visit to Brixton to look at a youth project in which a group of volunteers edit and publish a magazine about young street life, culture and music in South London. But the early mornings have mercifully been free enough to make solid progress on the Ballade, despite the scourge of the courtesy piano. As well as being muffled, its action is dreadfully sluggish – which means I'm going to have to play slowly in the run-up to the concert, which I've realised I'm unable to put off booking any longer if I'm to do it this calendar year. So in the middle of the week I take a deep breath and reserve a space for the evening of 13 December, at the Arts Club 1901, an art nouveau former teachers' house in a side street near Waterloo Station, barely half a mile from the Royal Festival Hall.

At Wednesday's lesson with Michael we work from the middle to the coda, which we haven't looked at for a long time, and Michael – I think – notices progress. He says at the end, 'That was one of the best sessions we've had for a long time.' But he wants to look again at my pedalling in the coda. I confess that I don't think I am ever going to master this, not in time for the concert anyway. But he asks me to try it nonetheless. He just stares at my feet, and then bursts out laughing: 'You've actually got it, Alan. You don't realise you've got it, but you've got it.' Quite a lot else is wrong, I suspect, but the pedalling is right.

But the end of the week has been so hectic that today, Saturday, is the first time I've been able to sit down with the Ballade in forty-eight hours – and tomorrow I've booked a lesson with the concert pianist William Howard. I heard him play the Ballade at Kings Place a few weeks ago, and I know he will be frighteningly aware of everything that's still wrong.

Sunday, 13 November

I come back early to London for my lesson with William, who's primarily a chamber musician. I drive across to his place in Earls Court – a basement flat, with a Boston grand piano. He rhapsodises about the G minor Ballade, which he thinks the greatest of Chopin's four Ballades. He's played it since he was 17, thinks it's one of the most fascinating joining points between the Classical era and the Romantic era – a simply revolutionary piece. He doesn't play it every year and he puts it occasionally away for a year or two and then comes back and plays it again.

Eventually, I know I can no longer delay playing it to him. He sits across the sitting room in sight of my hands.

I'm immediately aware of nerves. In the first passage work, my hands tense up horribly and the whole section is a Horlicks. But the rest is – with rough edges – mostly there, and I manage not to panic when the occasional bit goes wrong. Not a disaster of a performance – but still nothing like what I hear in my head and think I should play.

William strides across the room, saying he thought I'd got inside the piece musically, which is generally code for 'but technically, it's rubbish'. He immediately starts talking about my hands. The position of my hands is good; I have a good technique; sometimes I am capable of making a very beautiful noise . . . but he saw a terrible tension there – I was so desperate to control the notes, I was making life much more difficult for myself. This I am completely willing to believe, because a) other people have told me that in the past, and b) playing to him today, I really felt the tension, certainly when things seized up at the start. Indeed, after playing I felt a real muscular burn in my hands.

So he starts addressing this by making me play the second grand statement of the second tune with the aim of loosening me up. He tries to make me imagine that, if I took the piano away from underneath the hands, my fingers would just fall onto my knees, i.e. that I was just letting the hand drop naturally onto the keys, which is also what William Fong had told me to do. It all comes back to this concept of arm weight which I've found so difficult to grasp. He insists that, by putting too much effort into the fingers, the sound comes out more percussively than it should. Paradoxically, it also means that I don't make as full a sound. He makes me play the octaves with the triplets in this section and observes that my hand position is also very fixed. He wanted to make me feel more 'floppy' and relaxed about the notes.

Next, he asks me to play the coda – in particular, the trapeze of death. Again, he says, I'm playing with a very rigid hand position. For the leap, he wants me to imagine a frog sitting completely silently until it's seen the fly and then moves.

At the end, he asks me how I feel I am progressing in the overall mastery of the piece. I tell him there are some days when I feel I have ninety per cent of the notes under my fingers now. He smiles sympathetically and says that, in his experience, when you've got ninety per cent of the notes under your fingers, you're about forty per cent there. From now on, he says, it's all about building confidence and security into the whole piece.

As we pack up I tell him how my moments of error seem to happen when there's a gap between the unconscious and the conscious. My aim is to get to the point where the notes play themselves, as it were, without the conscious breaking through. William tells me that is absolutely how a professional pianist operates – they need to be in control of that gap. Really, he says, being a professional means that you can turn in a decent performance in the worst circumstances. So, whether you were jet-lagged, or have flu, or really don't like the piano, or aren't feeling great, you can still play the piece impressively. That is what marks a professional from an amateur.

This evening, it's time for another session with the Spider Club, at Bryan Youl's house. I arrived to find Bryan and my brother Richard playing Bruckner 4. We work through the Beethoven septet, followed by three overtures – *A Midsummer Night's Dream*, the Brahms *Tragic Overture* and *Don Giovanni*.

Later we get to discussing the Ballade. Bryan recalls hearing Arturo Michelangeli play it, when the great man was maybe in his early 70s. Bryan sits down and plays part of it to indicate how Michelangeli had played the piece that night, suddenly hesitating over a simple bit before the coda. Bryan says it was obvious to him, as a neuroscientist, that Michelangeli couldn't quite work out what was supposed to happen next. It was just a split second of hesitation, but Bryan had never seen this from him before. In fact it was the last time he ever saw Michelangeli play, and he speculates that there was some crisis of confidence that night as he tried to process all the notes in the Chopin Ballade, which, soon afterwards, led him to withdraw from the concert stage.

Saturday, 26 November

Life seems to be dominated by Leveson-related stuff at the moment. Yesterday, this takes the form of breakfast with *Times* editor James Harding and *FT* editor Lionel Barber – the second we've had to see what common ground there is between us on the future shape of regulation. I then had lunch with Tony Gallagher, the *Telegraph* editor, in which we covered the same turf. All four of us are pretty much on the same page, with one or two marginal differences over where to draw the line over the private lives of footballers, etc. The question is how much our views coincide with the editors of the tabloids and mid-market papers.

Earlier in the week, on Tuesday, I have to attend two award ceremonies in one evening. At the first, the *Guardian* Public Service Awards at the Intercontinental Hotel, I host the beginning of the evening and introduce the main speaker, the radio presenter Nicky Campbell. I then walk up Piccadilly to the Sheraton Park Lane for the Foreign Press Awards, where Nick Davies wins not only the main reporting award, but also Journalist of the Year. There's then a third event – again Leveson-related – a Victims of Hacking party going on in Shaftesbury Avenue. We find Hugh Grant, Steve Coogan and several of the MPs who have been pursuing the issue – and lots of the lawyers. I have a long chat with Coogan, who has, that day, given evidence to the inquiry. He sometimes comes across in interviews as rather obsessed about the issue, but tonight he's relaxed, intelligent, perceptive – past caring, really, what the tabloids could do to him, feeling they had outed every secret he had in his cupboard. Grant said the same sort of thing. 'Actually, I don't work very much at the moment but that's by choice, but I could work anywhere in the world, if I wanted to, and it wouldn't be affected by the tabloids giving me a nice write-up. In fact, I would pay a lot of money never to have my name in any tabloid paper in any context ever again, and a lot of actors feel the same.' It's a good-natured evening with little huddles of lawyers and victims, and the MPs talking about arcane issues, such as the difference between the statutory and non-statutory basis for regulation. I get home at about 1 a.m., with an hour of work still to do before I could go to sleep. The next day's papers get wind of the party and one or two try to make out something sinister or improper in the gathering.

Then on Wednesday the *Sun* goes into attack-dog mode over a vaguely humorous sketch we'd published on the inquiry that morning: they claimed we'd made an erroneous claim about the paper. The *Sun* style is to wear down the opponent by bombarding them with aggressive, sneering calls and emails. The emails are actually pretty funny, since the paper's executive accidentally attaches a string of internal *Sun* emails showing minimal levels of concern inside the NI. The next morning a package arrives at the office by courier containing a roll of lavatory paper, attached to a note from the same *Sun* executive suggesting I use it to 'wipe the arse' of the *Guardian* journalist who'd written Wednesday's piece. A marvellous demonstration of how News International has turned over a new leaf and wants to put its 'nasty party' past behind it. I put it in a taxi to Tom Mockridge, the supposed new broom at the head of NI.

It seems that all this Leveson focus is taking a toll on the Chopin. I think I might actually be regressing – this morning I couldn't play the coda at all. Sausage fingers. The crucial thing is not to panic. There's only two weeks until the concert now, but I have a two-hour lesson with Michael scheduled for tomorrow, so hopefully I can get things back on track then.

Monday, 28 November

Round to Michael's yesterday morning for my lesson, and I manage another half-hour practice this morning. After Saturday's blip, things are now more secure. There's a tense moment, though. At one point I suggest a 'cheat' by which I would play an octave in the LH rather than attempt a big leap to a single note. Michael freezes and is motionless for about three seconds, and then says drily: 'Why don't we just play what he's written?'

Throughout the day, I've been keeping half an eye on Leveson. Today's main witnesses are Charlotte Church and Anne Diamond, neither of whom I have had much interest in over the years, but both of whom speak power-fully and self-confidently . . . and devastatingly when detailing how the press had treated them. It dawns on me that my image of many of the 'celebrity' witnesses has been wholly and unfairly mediated by others. I did at one point think of Sienna Miller, if I thought of her at all, as a bit rackety, air-headed and candles-both-endsy. Yet here she is, articulate, intelligent, firm and rather impressive. Just like Max Mosley last week – previously scorned as one-dimensionally mad and depraved.

This afternoon I was off to Buckingham Palace for a spectacularly ill-timed reception to celebrate the media. I imagine it had been fixed by well-meaning advisers a year or two ago, before phone hacking exploded into life. As it is, it's coincided with the height of the Leveson Inquiry, and many of the guests quietly say they feel slightly sheepish about admitting to being a journalist in the current climate, much as, a couple of years ago, bankers kept a bit quiet about what they did. A meeting of one estate in crisis with another looking pretty confident.

We are separated into various pens, colour-coded by badges. I end up in a little group which is introduced to the Queen. Our pen includes the editor of *Cosmopolitan*, who makes a little speech about how hard it is for many young women today. The Queen mutters something in agreement about how hard it is for the young to get a job. She has no reaction at all on being introduced to someone from the *Guardian*. Total silence. I suggest she might read our racing pages. Polite laugh. Has her life been affected by the internet? All those who work for her (she gestures around) but not herself. She has many other things to do. Not even Twitter? She laughs, pulls a face and moves on.

In the next room are several people from the newspaper group which hacked into most, if not all, members of her family and their staff – all beams and earnest handshakes and nervous laughs. Suddenly I find myself speaking to Kate Middleton, one on one, no flunkies or hangers-on. She claims not to read any of the papers. Is *anything* about her life the same? I asked. 'Well, I'm cooking for him tonight,' she says, pointing to William.

My friend and *Observer* columnist Henry Porter meanwhile has eyes only for the paintings. 'There's a Canaletto, and a Rubens and a Vermeer.' He knows them all, but has never seen them in the flesh. A bit like the family which owns them. A royal keeper of the pictures introduces us to Rembrandt's 1660s picture of a shipbuilder and his wife, and is wonderfully eloquent about the narrative that led Rembrandt to portray the scene. And then, via a chat with the *Daily Mail* gossip columnist Richard Kay, and the former *Sunday People* editor Bill Hagerty, I head out into the deep-gravelled court-yard in search of a pub.

My final pianist interview – with the British-Australian pianist Stephen Hough, 50, who is, among many other things, a visiting professor at the

Royal Academy of Music and something of a polymath – a writer, poet, painter, thoughtful blogger, amateur theologian and composer. We meet in his mews house in North London. His partner, Dennis, is downstairs writing Christmas cards. Both of them are wearing Crocs, the most comfortable shoe in the world, but which I'm banned by my daughters from wearing on grounds of fashion crime. Upstairs there's an electronic keyboard – his two concert instruments are in a separate studio nearby (one used to be a Fazioli but he recently sold it). Otherwise the only clue to his life is in the prints of composers on his wall. He sits in a wicker chair, the score of the Ballade across his knees, and speaks in precise tones that occasionally hint at his Cheshire roots.

Stephen, as an extremely gifted youngster, first played the G minor Ballade when he was 12. He mastered it very quickly and was soon able to play it at concerts. 'I think it's just an astonishing piece,' he says. 'I love pieces which work with the brain and the soul at the same time. That seems to me what great music is.' The first Ballade, he thinks, is the epitome of this. 'It's not a piece that just spills over in a kind of indulgent sentimental Romanticism. It's so controlled and that's what gives it such power.' According to Stephen, this duality means the Ballade becomes a particularly exciting piece to play or listen to, as 'everyone who plays it really plays it differently, at least you hope they do, because, like a great play . . . an actor can take it in all sorts of directions'.

But there have been times when he didn't play the piece at all. In fact, for a time he abandoned classical music entirely. This was in his early teens, he says. 'In that period I was listening to pop music most of the time, I just felt no interest in classical at all.' So what brought him back into the classical fold? 'Funnily enough, it was a Brendel recital in Liverpool. I remember he played Beethoven Op. 109 and 110 and the Schubert G major sonata – maybe the other way round actually: the first off was the Schubert. I then became fascinated with that period and that style and I wanted to be serious.'

And did he come back to Chopin at the same time? No. That came a little later, when he listened to a recording of Josef Hofmann playing the fourth Ballade. 'It's a rather extraordinary performance,' he says. 'He sounds desperately angry in it. I think he was drinking. It was at the end of his real performing career, it's from the Carnegie Hall. It's well worth rooting out. It's one of the craziest performances of anything I've ever heard. But there is a point at which he slams the whole flat of his hand in the bass and creates this roar of sound. But it's got some amazing things in it and it actually awakened me, I think, to the dramatic quality of Chopin. It's extremely powerful emotionally and disturbing.'

Does he agree with Murray Perahia that the Ballades tell stories? He does, but doesn't have his own. 'Well, I don't know, it always sounds a bit fanciful to superimpose a sort of plan on the piece.' He sketches out a plan for me, though: as the piece goes on, the 'first subject' is trying to get away and break into this more joyful 'second subject', but it can't – the bleakness keeps returning: 'it's back to that every time' – until you reach the coda.

'It seems to me that the second subject is some sort of unobtainable happiness happening somewhere else, perhaps. I don't think it's Chopin experiencing that. I think the experience is in the bleak, tragic first subject, this kind of heartbeat that you get [he sings it, stressing that the second note should be slightly softer than the first always, so that it really does feel like a heartbeat], which keeps coming back. So you try to get away from it by the second subject and, no, it's back to that every time, until you have the final coda which is the sort of terrifying moment where there's no hope. I think there is a real despair about that in the way there is with the fourth Ballade, it's the same psychology, in a way. The waltz, I don't know. It's a wonderful moment, it's a necessary moment of light relief, well, not light relief, but a fast music which is not part of the tragic story, in a way.'

When he speaks about the coda, Stephen touches on something new for me, saying: 'When you watch someone playing it, it's not just what you're listening to, it's what you're seeing.' In the coda, the pianist's action is particularly dramatic, quickly going from the bottom of the piano to the top, then round the bottom and back up again. 'It's like shredding, ripping up a love letter or something. You know there's something – physically it looks dramatic.'

Stephen then talks about the theme of exile in Chopin. 'I mean, Chopin is as much French as he is Polish racially and, certainly, culturally,' he says. In his opinion, Chopin loved Paris and wouldn't have gone back to Warsaw 'if you'd paid him to – he didn't even go to visit his family'. He suggests that Chopin actually liked the *image* of being a Polish exile in Paris. 'If he had had a PR working for him,' he adds, he'd have told them: '"That's what I want to be seen as, please. Can you make sure the newspapers get this right?"' In fact, he thinks 'there's a lot of artifice about Chopin as a person', and confesses that whenever he reads his letters or any biographies he likes the man less. 'I think Chopin is someone it is best just to stick with the music.'

I ask him later how he manages to keep the coda under control. 'I think the point is that it can be too fast and if one can keep that in mind it's probably useful. It's in two, but I think it can help if you think of it in four because that will slow you down a little bit.' So that's something to try. He also gives me the now familiar (but none less essential) advice of breaking any passage that remains problematic into small pieces. As he puts it, 'I think the worst thing is to come to this and say, "Ah, this is a difficult coda." It's not. It's a coda with a few really difficult moments, a few quite difficult moments and some very easy moments.'

He speaks so confidently about the Ballade, I doubt there is anything in it that he finds really hard to play. He agrees. Or rather, there's nothing he struggles with technically. He does, though, think that the dual identity of the Ballade – its masterful entwining of both 'the brain and the soul', premeditated design and the illusion of immediate and intense expression – makes the piece, and in fact much of Chopin, a challenge. As he puts it today, 'I think the problem of playing his music generally is the combination of the improvisation quality with form. You need to feel that the piece is being improvised as it's written and yet you also need to know what's going on structurally so that the piece makes sense, that it hangs together. That's the sort of intellectual problem of playing it.'

Before I leave, Stephen gives me some encouraging final words for my performance. The Ballade, he said, 'needs to have the passion of fire and not just a feeling that you are going for the notes. So when you've done all of the practice, when all of it's done and you're actually in front of the audience, I think, *go for it*, and don't worry if notes come astray because perhaps that's part of the excitement, perhaps this coda is never more exciting than when a few notes are missed.'

'Well that has the potential of making my coda very exciting,' I tell him. 'Mine too.'

Saturday, 3 December

This evening we go to Kings Place to hear Imogen Cooper playing Mozart's 'Jeunehomme' Concerto with the Academy of St Martin in the Fields. She plays it just beautifully with such a soft delicate sound. My eyes are fixed on her hands, which seem to move on an entirely horizontal plane, with very little vertical effort at all. But how?

I catch up with her afterwards and she tells me she's about to start relearning the first Ballade, having recently performed the fourth. 'I played it to Rubinstein once. It was around 1967, I was in my late teens. I played it to him and then he played it to me, which was pretty nice, I must say. I played to him a few times.' She let out a full-throated chuckle at the memory. 'He was a wicked old man, he really was.'

Later we have a chance to sit down at a piano with my score. She starts running her fingers over the piece, musing out loud as she reacquaints herself with the piece. She breaks off from playing at bar 36, pondering why Chopin had written two appearances of the same little figure so differently in the piece – moving towards a tied note here, but not in the agitato restatement (bars 40–3). And she doesn't like my pedal markings in this section (two per bar, three beats each): she prefers Chopin's own marks, which show a clear break between the two pedals, so the ear hears the tied note more clearly. She then comes to the big horn call in bar 56, telling me: 'I came to the conclusion two days ago that the way to make these really sound like horns is to concentrate on the Ds and not worry about the right hand.'

At the second theme, she stops again and wrinkles her nose. 'Too loud. You hear it played really softly so rarely. People think "big tune" and they're off. I've always had a block with the arrival of this tune. Maybe it's the fourths.' Next, she's pointing accusingly at a little 'breath mark' between the octave B-flat leap in bar 71. 'Ah, I don't agree with that mark. Who put that in? I think it goes on.' When she reaches bar 80, she sees that I've marked a sudden change of tone to pianissimo. She giggles. 'That's what Alfred [Brendel] used to call "a little dog peeing up a tree".'

'It's all different markings,' she mutters to herself at one point, 'I must get this edition.' She next breaks off at the little odd-sounding upward rising figure at 130. 'Do you know what this is? The third act of *Tristan*. Exactly the same chords.' Her fingers ripple their way up to the top. 'Or do I mean the second act?' She breaks off again at the trill on 179. 'I find that really hard. Do you find that hard?' I confess that I don't even attempt a trill – just a turn.

And so on. It's a fascinating little glimpse of a serious pianist thinking her way back into a piece – querying, prodding, experimenting, testing, still finding surprises and variation. And proof perhaps of Stephen Hough's theory that the complexity of the Ballade allows infinite reinterpretations.

Sunday, 4 December

A lesson with Lucy today, with nine days to go before the concert. I play it through pretty reasonably: one or two little shaky passages; one moment where I have a complete memory lapse of about a second and a half, which is very unsettling. But, overall, I'm learning not to be too thrown by rackety sections and to retain some kind of control. She takes me briskly through the whole piece with a few final 'performance and projection' tips: play up the drama of this passage here, exaggerate here; make the loud things louder, the soft things softer.

She then plays me the American virtuoso Earl Wild's recording of the Ballade, made when he was 90 – most eccentric but rather beautiful. Lucy said it sounds like an old man playing it for the last time, as though he didn't care how it was *supposed* to be played but just wanted to live and revel in the moment of each note for a final time, even at the cost of occasionally losing the structure. It was, she says, like watching a Hollywood film of the 1940s. Nobody would play the piece like that today – it was a kind of period piece. It gives me confidence to play the piece the way I hear it. I'll never play it 'correctly'. But I have lived with it for nearly eighteen months and there are things that speak to me now which I don't find in many professional performances. The only value I can bring to the piece is my response to it. There's no point in aping the 'true' way.

Just before I leave, I stick a tape recorder under her nose. Does she think I've accomplished my mission?

LP: I think you should give yourself a major pat on the back for a huge achievement because it's not easy to do what you've done, it's not even your day job and—

AR: Are you officially telling me I can play it?

LP: I'm officially telling you, you can play this piece, very well, technically, confidently, and you've achieved what you set out to do. So you need to have the confidence to go ahead and play that in public because you *can* do it. I've heard it here. You can do it.

Well, it doesn't get much clearer than that. So that's three teachers certifying that I have – more or less, with due qualifications – achieved what I set out to do. Now I just have to do it in public.

Tuesday, 6 December

Up at crack of dawn yesterday to fly to Venice with younger daughter Lizzie and the Fazioli dealer Terry Lewis. The plan is to go to see my Fazioli back where it was made – in the Sacile factory about an hour north of the city and talk about the reconditioning of the piano. We're met by the great man in the modernist reception that's been grafted onto the more functional factory space. He shoots out a hand and offers just one word: 'Fazioli,' as you would say 'Steinway' or 'Bechstein'. He has unkept grey hair, but everything else is just so – monogrammed shirts, wool jacket, silk red tie, rimless glasses and, to round it all off, a Fazioli watch.

His parents grew their own furniture-making business on the adjoining site. Paolo himself was both a pianist and an engineer. Out of this combination – furniture, engineering and piano-playing – grew the ambition to make the finest piano on earth. Some people think he's done just that – they rhapsodise about the best instruments that emerge from this building, set in its own parkland within view (though not today, all misty and closed in) of the Dolomites. Others wonder if the very fact that so much of a Fazioli is hand-built means that it can never match the uniform predictability of a Steinway. And then there's the formidable scale of the Steinway operations in Hamburg and New York versus the forty-odd staff in Sacile, who manage to produce just over two pianos a week. But the Fazioli certainly has a cult status among those who aspire to the best and who love the idea of true craftsmanship in musical instruments, of which the handmade tradition in this factory is one of the last examples in the world.

Before we sit down together to look at my piano, Terry offers a tour of the factory, which is all fed by natural light from slits in the high ceiling. The tour begins by looking at where the inner rims are constructed. These are strips of veneer-grade mahogany joined together with warm glue and then pressed into a piano-shaped mould. Fazioli, says Terry, pioneered a technique involving passing an electric current through the glue to allow the air bubbles to escape while the frame sets solid, thus making a 'harder' and therefore more resonant outer frame. To one side stand dozens of up-ended inner rims – the concert grands long, giraffe-like and elegant; the smaller grands like generously built tenors or squat, overweight basses. Then we're taken to the spraying room, where ghostly shapes move on conveyor belts through a haze of black polyester.

On to the polishing room (and the realisation that the sequence of Terry's journey bore little relation to the sequence of actually building a piano), where a masked figure in green overalls is sanding down a shell already bearing the distinctive gold FAZIOLI logo. Nearby are two middle-aged women standing on each side of a table polishing piano legs, dwarfed by giant aluminium air vents. There's also a half-assembled piano, with no keyboard, but already strung. Another workman is bending over it, adding hinges, sockets and locks. Then we move to look at the soundboards, where another worker – short, bearded, jeans and trainers – is matching strips of quarter-sawn red spruce, each around a centimetre thick, before gluing them together manually. In a nearby room we find scores of soundboards stacked along one wall. They stay there for three years, waiting patiently to be chosen, whereupon they are mounted on the individually built frames. On top of that is placed a hornbeam, mahogany and boxwood bridge, hand-carved ready for the stringing.

We then meet the man who makes each string individually, before passing them on to a colleague who strings the instrument. 'It takes half a day,' says Terry proudly. 'At Yahama, it takes twenty minutes.' This becomes a bit of a theme. The Fazioli keyboard is German-made, but to a Fazioli recipe which mixes ceramic and plastic. Lesser makers simply use plastic. And so on.

At one table we find Daniel, a portly man in a fawn jumper, applying a measuring gauge to individual parts of the German Renner-made actions, tossing rejects into a cardboard box. He pulls out a discarded wippen – the spring-loaded heart of the key mechanism, a finely engineered assemblage of wood, screws, felt, wire and leather. 'Too stiff,' he sighs. He has written '*guasto*' (no good) on the side. Does he play the piano? 'Only a motorbike,' he said. And then, holding a guilty finger to his lips, he utters a forbidden word: 'Yamaha.'

In the next room is a monster Fazioli concert grand – the very one, it transpires, which I'd seen on stage at the Moscow Conservatoire, where it was being used for the Tchaikovsky piano competition. It's back for an overhaul. I slide over in a beaten-up old office chair on wheels to try it. The first note of the Ballade booms out of it like an enormous sonorous cathedral bell. I become uncomfortably aware that half the factory floor can hear me and feel too inhibited to play – or, indeed, remember – much of the piece. If only I could wish them away for ten minutes while I let loose on this gargantuan construction of wood and iron. Instead, we come across a Dutch-born technician fine-tuning a 212 – explaining how only on a Fazioli do they tune the 'non-speaking' bit of the string – that is, the bit of a string beyond the pin on which it's stretched. Finally we met Claudio Valent, the head technician, who's patiently shaving and pricking hammers to equalise the 'voicing' of an action, a job that can take two days. He leads us into a showroom full of pianos. An American woman's trying out a concert grand. We stand and listen to five minutes of her Chopin before Claudio turns to the instrument behind me. 'This is your piano.'

So it is: I hadn't recognised it in the row of gleaming beasts under the showroom lights. I feel a little warm tug at being reunited, especially now I know what it took to make a piano like this. Claudio is puzzled by my use of language as I begin to describe my problems with the piano. What do I mean, 'it is too *heavy*'? He has weighed the down pressure on each key. His instrument said it was roughly fifty grams, which is what it should be. I tell him about the different technicians who have tried various things to ease the action, including the man who'd glued lead weight beneath the keys. Claudio shudders.

'Maybe you mean "difficult" rather than "heavy"?' he asks. I wonder if he is being a little defensive about one of his babies. I throw in Imogen Cooper and Lucy Parham as expert witnesses who have also said it's too heavy, and who know what they're talking about, even if I am struggling to describe it. Eventually he peels back some sticky tape on twenty or so blobs of lead and positions these on the keys, somewhere between the lid and the string. It's slow work. Each blob takes around a minute to ready and position. He won't be hurried. This is the pace of the hand, not the machine. Try again, he suggests. Yes, that's definitely lighter, but still stiff.

Claudio evidently feels we are getting somewhere. Paolo Fazioli himself then wanders over to join in. It feels like the moment the senior registrar defers to the consultant. In this case a consultant with a Nobel Prize in medicine. It is the pianistic equivalent of the laying on of hands. None of us would be here without the mild-mannered dapper figure currently running his fingers up and down my keyboard. This is his DNA. Fazioli and Claudio are soon in earnest discussion, in Italian. As Fazioli runs his fingers over my keys – his keys! – concentrating intently, Claudio is shifting his weights around them, trying further weights along the shank. They both agree: the piano does need the lead weights. It's just a case of deciding on the precise weight, the exact location of each one, and then drilling them in individually. In the end they settle for forty-eight grams. Once those are inserted, they insist, the whole action will have to be taken apart, cleaned, lubricated and regulated. I can expect the piano back within about two months. Nothing about Fazioli is hurried.

'It's quite often the other way round these days,' says Fazioli, swivelling to me on the elegant (Fazioli-designed) piano stool. 'The young conservatoire pianists develop such strength, they want heavy actions.'

Dealing with clients must be the least enviable bit of his job.

He leaves us to attend some conference of Italian business people and Terry takes us next door to the gorgeous little concert hall Fazioli has built adjoining the showroom, which features a beautiful ten-foot concert grand. Here I play the Ballade to an audience of two. Lucy told me she recently played a really fine Fazioli in a London concert. 'Normally I can't wait for a concert to end,' she said. 'But this was such a beautiful instrument I just wanted it to go on for ever.' I had the same feeling today. If Claudio can work a fraction of the magic of this giant on my own more modest piano, I promise never to complain about a piano again. Ever.

Lizzie and I work out that if we get up an hour early we can snatch maybe thirty-five minutes for breakfast in Venice en route to the airport. It is a beautifully crisp sunny day and in the end we manage thirty-seven minutes in a tiny café down a side street two minutes from St Mark's. Never did a coffee and pastry taste sweeter.

Monday, 12 December

This is it – the night before the performance.

And the climax to my little journey in amateur piano playing has coincided with the climax to a remarkable story for a group of amateur singers. Gareth Malone, a young conductor so baby-faced that even hard-nosed tabloid hacks feel an urge to mother him, has been training a choir of army wives to sing as part of a TV show. This follows on from an earlier series in which he marched into socially deprived areas and persuaded people who had never given music-making a thought to sing. There's always something incredibly touching about people who have the gift and commitment to surface the universal latent talent for music-making, whether it's in the slums of Venezuela or Berlin, where Simon Rattle found the poor Turkish immigrants who performed as dancers in *Rhythm Is It*, his film of *The Rite of Spring*.

In this case, Malone has been working with women who have never sung before, and who are quite low on self-confidence, living together in barracks, with their husbands quite often abroad in war zones with all the insecurity that brings. In a very short period he's given them a recognition of the musicality that, in his view, lurks inside everybody. He's also given them that general sense of confidence that comes from the growing awareness of the capability to be creative and perform. It has been a very, very moving programme and, last night, the army wives' record became the Christmas number one.

I had to stay down in Blockley today since I'd promised to address the Blockley Discussion Group – a local village forum – this evening. So at shortish notice I've called an away day for eight senior editors to come down and spend the day in the music room discussing strategy, with a delicious lunch cooked by a neighbour in the middle. It was just as well there's no Wi-Fi or phone signal in the music room: it meant we concentrated on the conversation and not the mini Twitter flurry about the newly raised uncertainty as to whether it was indeed *News of the World* journalists who deleted Milly Dowler's voice messages back in 2002. This was hardly the most critical bit of our story – most newspapers in July thought, rightly, that it was far less significant than the fact of the voicemail hacking. And, moreover, no one has actually denied the deletion angle, either in July or in the five months since. Neither the police nor Glenn Mulcaire thought the story was wrong when originally published. But we should, of course, have attributed it to our (very good) sources rather than stated it as a fact. If we'd added three words – 'reliable sources say' – our story would still be right, as opposed to an accurate account of what many of the players involved in the events believed at the time. The main duty now is to clarify and correct the original story – including all its web versions. The irony is that the emerging truth about the *NotW*'s behaviour over Milly Dowler is, if anything, worse than what we originally wrote – though not all of it is yet in the public realm, or is yet writable, for legal reasons. When the full truth comes out it will do no favours either to the police or to News International. But this glitch does give assorted parties the opportunity to give us a bit of a kicking, which I'm sure they will duly do. Doubtless just in time for the concert. We drive back late to London, getting home well after midnight.

Am I feeling confident?

Well, on Wednesday I had my final preparatory lesson with Michael. As usual, he perched by my right shoulder. It was 8.15, but, on one cup of coffee and a bowl of cereal as fuel, I played it well enough to surprise him. His eyebrows definitely went up at the end and he said, 'That really is the best you've played it.' A lesson with Michael isn't, necessarily, something to boost pre-match confidence and, naturally, he went on to point out that there were wrong notes here and there – he couldn't help himself in pointing out that, in the A major section, I was using some 'cock-eyed fingerings'. That made me feel better, actually – otherwise I'd have felt a bit uneasy at his praise.

There were, as I played to him, a couple of those moments where the mind just plays tricks that it has never played before, but I'm now getting quite good at ignoring individual aberrations. They creep up from nowhere and there's little I can do about them, but more importantly I now have enough memory of the piece that I can recover quickly, no matter what errors are randomly thrown into it.

At the end of the lesson, just as with Lucy, I stuck a tape recorder under his nose to get his verdict. He chose his words very carefully, but, in his own way, he was saying, yes, I could pretty much play the piece.

That's the best version of the piece that I've actually heard you play. I mean, it's been a . . . it's a wonderful project, at times hair-raising. There are many times I would have liked to have discouraged you from pursuing it. In the last few weeks, I've begun to relax about it and feel that, you know, you've pretty much realised your ambition. Obviously, it's not note perfect, by any means, you know, but it's terribly musical playing and you've met so many of the technical demands with, what I thought, was a ridiculously minimal amount of time to practise.

I think I can settle for that at this stage.

Tuesday, 13 December

So this is the big day, the final test. I didn't get to bed till well after 1.30 a.m. and I'm tired, and all day long a little too full of low-level adrenaline to feel completely calm about tonight. A few journalists have decided to keep going on the deleted emails angle: most have already moved on. The parents of Milly Dowler are still, through their lawyer, insisting that the essence of the story was right: that they did indeed have discussions with the police about *News of the World* journalists deleting messages, and that this knowledge – together with the hacking and apparently deleted messages – was behind their false hope that she was still alive. Meanwhile News International is still pointedly declining the opportunity to deny that its journalists did in fact delete the voice messages. The whole matter would be resolved if the *Guardian* were allowed to simply come out and say what we knew then and what we know now. But we're hampered by having to protect sources, and moreover contempt-of-court rules mean we can't make this knowledge public. The police seem remarkably eager – for reasons only known to them – to exonerate NI's private detective, Glenn Mulcaire. But when Nick Davies sat down with him for two hours the day after our Milly Dowler story in July 'to clear up the record' it didn't occur to him to deny the deleted-messages angle.*

We plan how we'll write about it today; also what we'll say to Leveson and how we'll handle press enquiries. Meanwhile I also keep half an eye on the hearings (where assorted News International lawyers are having a sweaty time), while also planning a session for 300 staff to tell them about new ways of producing the paper and new shift patterns. So there's no brain space to think about music. The plan is to leave the office by 5 p.m., giving me ninety minutes to try the piano at the venue, the Arts Club 1901. I also want to set up a projector and screen for the talk I plan to give before I play. I'll speak for about forty minutes beforehand, so the audience – a few family, colleagues and friends – can have some context. They need to understand what on earth I'm doing standing up in public to play an impossible bit of Chopin. The real point is not that I can play it to concert standard: it's been part of a much

---

* The matter was still unresolved when, in May 2012, the police conceded they would never get to the bottom of what happened but confirmed the Dowlers' account, in which senior police officers had discussed the *NotW* habit of deleting messages and agreeing that Mrs Dowler's fears were reasonable.

broader experiment in how to use your time, how to relish – and revel in – being an amateur. If one person leaves the room tonight intent on re-learning an instrument, that wouldn't be a bad result. It's just as well they're all mates. No one in their right mind wants to come out on a dark December night to hear a ten-minute amateur performance of one Chopin piece.

Of course nothing quite goes to plan. At 4 p.m. the fire alarm goes off. Almost certainly a false alarm, but it means the whole building has to be evacuated floor by floor. It also means standing on a freezing pavement in the streets of King's Cross for forty-five minutes before being allowed back in. My fingers are quietly turning blue and none of it is doing much good for the concert nerves. But I do keep my 5 p.m. appointment with the taxi and get down to the venue. There's an agitated spasm of emails in the cab as I head south. A News International executive – the one with the penchant for sending scatological notes – has popped up in front of a House of Lords committee to launch an excitable, if carefully scripted, personal attack on me. Then another email: a former NI executive has apparently penned a piece for some website saying I should resign. So there's something coordinated brewing. I decide against clicking on the link and realise I'm never going to clear my mind sufficiently if I keep on reading emails, texts and tweets. So by the time I get south of the river I steel myself and turn all electronic devices off until after the concert. The team back at the office know what I'm doing and where I am. For 364.98 days in the year I'm on call. But for the next couple of hours they'll have to jump in a cab and haul me out if anything genuinely serious happens.

The Arts Club 1901 – velvet chairs and red flock wallpaper – will hold just over three dozen, packed six across with an aisle down the middle. At the moment I don't feel nervous, but I do feel buzzy, tired, my mind still racing around all the angles of the phone-hacking saga and the eddies, tempests and storms around it. I sit down at the 7′ 6″ Steinway C to try to distract myself. It has a big fine baritone voice in the lower and middle notes. The touch is heavy compared with the Blockley piano, but manageable. My friend Martin Prendergast, who can't make it tonight, pops in and I play it through for him. This works as a dress rehearsal. At bar 51 – the first bit of complicated passage work – I hit a mental roadblock. My right hand has suddenly decided to invent its own fingering for the bar. I'm in a hopeless tangle of third and fourth fingers, throwing the following five or six bars into disarray. As has tended to be the case recently, I recover – but it all jangles the nerves a bit.

Martin is naturally ebullient and rippling with enthusiasm – and he bounds over full of encouraging words. But he works in the theatre and I suspect he has perfected the art Alan Bennett describes for dealing with suspicious actors in his essay 'Going Round': 'Whatever you thought, even if you slept through the whole of the second act, you have to go in there saying it was all marvellous. Marvellous. It was *MARVELLOUS*.'

Once Martin's gone I keep repeating the passage. I suppose it's never been the most secure, but quite why an entirely new fingering has emerged from nowhere in the past twenty minutes is extremely disconcerting – anything might happen in the concert. The truth is that, with ninety minutes to go, I still have no idea whether I can play the Ballade in a performance. I can play ninety per cent of the notes right when relaxed and on my own, but this is a different proposition entirely. William Howard was right in his definition of a professional pianist: they are sure of getting the piece in a triple lock and virtually certain of producing a reasonable performance, no matter what medical, meteorological, technical or psychological obstacles crop up on the night. I am not. I think back to the books on musical memory I've skimmed through, with their list of how the greatest pianists had a quadruple or quin-tuple method of making sure it would be right on the night – auditory, visual, muscle, structural, harmonic, you name it. Too late now.

Soon enough the room is humming with people – including no fewer than four of my teachers. There are the three other members of the Spider Club and two violinists from our quartet, Charlotte and Clive. The teachers – Michael, William Fong, Lucy and Noriko – have all been introduced to each other and are sharing good-natured jokes about the Sisyphean endeavour in which they've separately been involved. I can't delay it any longer.

So I begin my talk, explaining how I came to be playing the Ballade; how hard it is; how mediocre I am; and what kind of journey I've been on over the past sixteen months trying to coax the piece into my fingers and brain on twenty minutes a day. As I talk, I gradually relax. I'm among friends, I realise. They want me to succeed. The majority of them aren't musicians: they won't be listening out for every slipped note. Isabella and Lizzie are in the front row, Lindsay further back. None – except the teachers – has ever heard me play the whole piece before, though Lindsay and the girls have, of course, heard endless muffled repetitions of individual passages through walls and ceilings. Last Christmas Lizzie even wrote out a page of the coda on manuscript paper and framed it for me. It hangs in the music room.

Finally, before actually sitting down at the piano, I play the audience two audio clips from my interviews over the past year. First, there's Emanuel Ax wishing me well, warning that I'm not going to play it like Pollini – before cheerfully adding that nor is he ever going to manage that standard. And then it's Murray Perahia's Bronx tones chastising all those who claim to hear errors in Horowitz's YouTube performance of the Ballade. 'There's all these idiots writing in, "Oh there's so many mistakes." I don't hear them, I really don't hear them . . . As far as I'm concerned it's a perfect performance. I don't hear those wrong notes that everybody hears . . . All these nuts, you know, they write into YouTube, they say, "I can play better than that," so I say, "Well, post it then, let's hear it."'

Subliminal message not too subtly delivered, there's a small pause as I approach the piano. Suddenly I think this is crazy. What mad vanity was this, to imagine that I could pull off a plausible version of the piece – and to do so in the most testing possible conditions, in front of a packed room, and half a dozen professional pianists? From somewhere I remember hearing the British pianist David Owen Norris tell a roomful of astonished American critics how, in a similar moment, he seriously contemplated attacking himself with a fire axe in the green room rather than walk out on stage.

But, by the time I sit down at the keyboard, I'm strangely calm. There's no way on earth I am about to play a perfect performance of the Ballade, but I understand that I want to tell a story and I want to share with friends the result of the private expedition I've been on. I take a deep breath and bring the joint thumbs-and-first-finger of each hand down on the first octave C. Suddenly I'm blind to the audience. My conscious world has shrunk to a very intimate space bounded by the span of the keyboard. And within that tiny dot of concentration there's an inner circle of unconscious from which the notes are beginning to well. I have instantly snapped into what I think athletes call the zone – relaxed, distilled, heightened, oblivious, intense all at once.

The first few pages are not too bad. I'm conscious of taking my time, not rushing, having reminded myself that this is an occasion for telling a story, not for showing a teacher what progress I've made since last week. If this is the Matterhorn, I'm walking confidently along a ridge with a sheer drop on either side. It's impossible to savour the moment – certainly not to enjoy the view – but at the same time there's a sensation of something like awe. The slow second subject sings its way to the back of the room. The big chords are mostly where they should be, the octaves more or less as written; the waltz could be a lot worse.

Then, about halfway through, I'm conscious of burn in my forearms. So I'm not as relaxed as I feel – and the very thought of the burn makes me tense a little more, conscious of all the tumbling, rushing passages to come. The music isn't flowing as naturally as I'd like and there have been too many wrong notes along the way. But this is a survival course as well as a narrative . . . and so far I'm still alive. And something is coming back from the audience. They want me to do it. I can sense them sitting there intensely – and, probably, tensely – silently urging me on.

I'm two bars away from the coda and the big beast of a Steinway has just unleashed a deep organ-like D to mark the two bars marked 'il più forte possibile' – as loud as possible. My hands, though still tense, wrench everything they can out of the instrument. The first bar is marked appassionato – rushing forward. The second poco ritenuto – slowing down. The effect is like the winding of a spring which will explode with the next note – the first chord of the coda. I've played this link maybe 200 times in the past sixteen months. But tonight it's precisely here that my mind goes blank. I just can't remember how the coda begins. Totally ridiculous. I know it so well. I do. It's there in my brain even now, just at the front above my eyebrows – but I can't retrieve it. And somewhere else in my brain – creeping down the back of my neck now – there's a fleeting instinct of panic. Which is going to win? Should I stop, regain composure and restart? Or linger for a fraction of a second and see if the fingers ignore the momentarily frozen brain and find the notes for themselves?

In the end, the hesitation lasts maybe three-quarters of a second – none of the non-musicians later said they noticed a thing – but it feels like several heartbeats have passed. And then, just as suddenly, something unblocks. Not with a snap, but a sort of surge, like a sluice gate opening. For a few bars I'm still flustered and thinking back: *How could that have happened?* The coda has bitten back after all, at the very moment when it's vital that the brain keeps discipline over the fingers – the exact spot all those pianists have talked of when they describe the fear of losing control as the relentless fury of the notes drives them forwards. I suspect there are little sprays of wrong notes as I struggle to wrestle the bucking beast back into control. But my overall sense of calm up to this point hasn't been completely torn away: there are no shakes in the arms or feet and I haven't missed a beat (I think) since that first chasm of hesitation.

By the last two pages, the niggling fear of complete capsizing has receded. I'm into the final torrents – snaking chromatically to the top of the keyboard, then cascading all the way down. Then up again in octaves. Up even further in more or less coordinated tenths. Finally – the most dramatic ending to any piano piece I know – the jagged octaves that begin in dissonance from opposite ends of the piano, slowing down as each is hammered out, before they converge and crash chromatically and ever more furiously back down to earth.

Suddenly it's over. My hands have ended as they began – with thumbs and fingers joined in intoning a unison note of despair (yes, Stephen Hough was right: it *is* despair). There's a moment of silence and then everyone's on their feet and the girls are rushing towards me for a bear hug of congratulation (theirs) and utter relief (mine). I can't remember ever feeling such an instant, immediately physical surge of release.

We adjourn to the little bar upstairs for drink. People say nice things. The teachers are warm – possibly a little pleasantly surprised that the technical wheels largely remained attached to the pianistic chariot. 'I wish you had spent more time playing scales,' says William, shaking his head a little sadly. 'If you really gave up work and played for five hours a day, you really could achieve something.' They all use the word 'musical', which is the best word of all. For Lindsay and the girls, all those disjointed snatches suddenly made some sort of coherent sense. They're smiling with recognition: '*So that's what it was all about.*' Michael looks relieved. He, of all people, knows how much worse it could have been. My chamber-music friends bubble with enthusiasm: they know something of the terror and slog involved. Richard, my big brother, says he wishes my mum had been alive to see it. We agree none of this would have happened without her quiet ambition and insistence.*

I don't switch on my phone until after 10 p.m. I've been out of contact for five hours – the only such gap, plane journeys apart, in the past year. A rivulet of emails floods onto the screen. Some of them bear the legend 'urgent'. But, as I scroll down them, I see that even the allegedly pressing ones have managed to resolve themselves during my little period off-air. I seem to have missed nothing of any great significance apart from a little baiting from current or former News International executives, all of which will keep for another day, or be comfortably ignored. Read them, or go home, order up a Chinese takeaway and savour the moment? No contest.

---

* My favourite reaction to hearing the Ballade came some weeks later when I repeated the talk and recital at the Chipping Campden literary and music festival, near Blockley. In the bar afterwards a physically imposing amateur pianist leaned over conspiratorially and uttered just two words: 'Big balls.'

EPILOGUE

So I managed it, even if it's taken months longer than I budgeted. I fooled myself I could lick it within a year, which would have taken me to August. At one stage I even thought I'd beat the builders and have it done by spring. And I still, even in an empty house and with a full night's sleep, have not played the G minor Ballade with every note perfectly in place. But I have, over sixteen months of snatched private moments and lessons, learned a great and very difficult masterpiece of the piano repertoire and can – in the professional view of at least three proper pianists – play it. Sort of.

When I embarked on the project, I had no way of knowing that these sixteen months would be the most intensive of my working life. There were two major stories – WikiLeaks and phone hacking – which not only made global headlines for weeks on end, but were deeply controversial in some quarters and involved immensely powerful adversaries and, in the case of phone hacking, several time-consuming inquiries. They bookended a year which saw revolutions, wars and revolts in the Middle East, a devastating tsunami, several English urban centres in flames, and the near-collapse of the European financial system. All this piled in on top of trying to negotiate the digital revolution, the most profound challenge – technical, economic and journalistic – that the press has seen in generations, if not ever. A job that was routinely twelve to fourteen hours a day Monday to Friday regularly expanded beyond that and ate deeply into the sixth and seventh days.

And now, at the end of this journey, I know the answer to two questions. Is there time? And, is it too late? Yes, there's time – no matter how frantically busy one's life. There's always enough time in a week to nibble out the odd twenty minutes here and there if one wants to make it a priority. Of course, our children were grown up by the time I embarked on this odyssey, even if the demands of work had expanded exponentially. But then I think of my fellow piano camper, Liz Warde, who frequently worked a day shift as a teacher and a night shift as a nurse in order to make ends meet as she brought up five kids . . . and still she carved out time to play the piano. Ask Liz: yes, there is time. And more than that, by making time, life improves: under the great pressure and stress of the year, I've discovered the value of having a small escape valve – something so absorbing, so different, so rebalancing.

And the answer to the second question seems to be equally encouraging. Back in the summer of 2010 I had no idea of just how capable a 56-year-old brain was of learning new tricks. In the course of the past year and a half I have asked mine to develop attributes it had never previously displayed. Could I really train that sponge of grey matter – already full to overflowing, it often seemed – to not only learn 264 bars of immensely complicated musical notation, but also to memorise great swathes of the piece? It had been decades since I had consciously memorised anything beyond a street address or phone number and the skill of memorising a single bar of music was one I had always assumed beyond me. My brain would doubtless have more quickly absorbed the vast complexity of the data contained in Op. 23 forty or more years ago – along with French, chemistry, algebra, the future pluperfect of a first conjugation Latin verb and the finer details of the war of Spanish succession. But back then I was lacking either the will or the motivation to memorise music. So it's heartening to know that, quite well into middle age, the brain is plastic enough to blast open hitherto unused neural pathways and adapt to new and complicated tasks. So, no, it's not too late.

And I've learned my mother was right – right to make me play; right in the pleasure music would give me; right that music ability is both a social ice-breaker and the forger of deep and lasting friendships. During the time it took me to learn the piece, I've had engrossing conversations with proper pianists and with neuroscientists, played with a 90-year-old and with a 16-year-old, with a world-famous actor as well as a primary-school teacher, with a science professor as well as a cardinal. I've at last learned how to practise, and I can finally play scales. I've also immersed myself in a single work of art more deeply than ever before. I became fascinated by the Ballades, these four masterpieces of western classical music. Listening to them in concerts now, I sit there spellbound by their greatness: they are a gift handed down through time like the pyramids, a Shakespeare tragedy, a ravishing Monet or a Norman cathedral.

And I've enjoyed thinking about the parallels between music and digital media, and the ways in which technology is transforming ideas about who can create, distribute and respond. I think back to Claus Moser and his memories of how common *Hausmusik* was in the Berlin he fled in 1936. I jump to Clay Shirky focusing on the 100 million hours amateurs have devoted to creating Wikipedia since it was launched in 2001. The blogger – able, for the first time in history, freely to publish and distribute his or her thoughts – has more in common than they might think with Moser's chamber-music companions in pre-war Germany. The young Korean or Japanese pianists, posting their versions of the G minor Ballade on YouTube to an audience of thousands, is in some ways a throwback to an earlier age, only with mass distribution. EMI may be struggling with the drastic disruption to all the existing business models of the music business, just as most newspaper companies are wrestling to come to terms with the very similar revolution in information. The world needs professional musicians and journalists – but we should celebrate this rebirth of an amateur tradition, alongside the professional world.

George Bernard Shaw, quoting Wagner, wrote in the early 1890s: 'the masterpieces of music are kept alive, not at the theatres and concert-halls but at the pianofortes of lovers of music'. With initiatives such as the online Petrucci Library project – the service created by countless people who have freely devoted their time to uploading more than 170,000 scores so that anyone can have free access to any work no longer in copyright – the masterpieces have as strong a chance as ever. After ordering one batch in a bound performers edition from a man named Theo Wyatt, I received an email from one of his daughters to tell me a little bit about him. He was, she said, 91, with failing eyesight and physically frail.

> He pioneered the production of music at home in his living room when he retired early from the Civil Service at 55. His purpose is to make sheet music as widely available as possible at the lowest feasible prices because of the pleasure he has derived from amateur chamber music-making.

I'm sure Theo is glad to have lived long enough to see the connection between GBS, Wagner and Wikipedia's Jimmy Wales.

So what next? Having squirrelled away this little bite of daily time and acquired (or discovered) these new skills, how best to make use of them? Well, two or three years ago there were all sorts of great piano pieces which I would have loved to play but which were on a mental shelf marked 'never going to happen'. They included the last three Beethoven and the last three

Schubert sonatas; the first two movements of Schumann's Fantasie op. 17; the same composer's *Etudes symphoniques* and Chopin's Polonaise-Fantaisie. But say I tried one a year for the next ten years, embarking on the project in the same way I have the Ballade? I'd still be some way short of my three score years and ten and I'd have moved from someone who always regretted letting the piano drop out of his life to someone who'd conquered nearly a dozen of the greatest, most challenging and wonderful pieces known to man or woman. Well, I say 'conquered' . . .

No time? Too late?

Play it again.

SCORE AND COMMENTARY

Dédiée à Mr le Baron de Stockhausen

BALLADE
Opus 23
1835

*) Deutsche Erstausgabe: *Lento.*
   German first edition: *Lento.*
**) Deutsche Erstausgabe:
   German first edition:

© 1986 by Wiener Urtext Edition, Musikverlag Ges. m. b. H. & Co., K. G., Wien
Wiener Urtext Edition No. 50 100

Das widerrechtliche Kopieren von Noten ist gesetzlich verboten und kann privat- und strafrechtlich verfolgt werden.
Unauthorised copying of music is forbidden by law, and may result in criminal or civil action.

Introduction

The very beginning is like how 'The Rime of the Ancient Mariner' starts. He stops one in three, he grabs the guy by his shirt and says, 'You're going to listen to this story.' For me, that's the same thing when he hits that C. It means 'stop and listen to what I'm going to tell you'. **Ax**

'A sigh.'
Perahia

The beginning is the enslavement, the sadness about losing, about Poland being under the grip of three powers. **Perahia**

Theme A

This descent is very important to the rest of the piece . . . you have it here in terms of *sighs*. When you have these very obvious descending lines, it tells you something of the emotional mood, the sadness. **Perahia**

The tragic first subject has this kind of heartbeat and, quite importantly, the second note should be slightly softer than the first always, so that it really does feel like a heartbeat, which keeps coming back. **Hough**

(take your time)

We hear another voice in the bass . . . it's more than just a counterpoint, it's a real sort of melody that's combining with it, going in the opposite direction. **Perahia**

Chopin's tendency to write these little *roulades* of his, written in his little notes, always sparks off a reaction that these must be extraordinarily fast. I can remember as a kid seeing these things on the page and I couldn't imagine what you'd have to do to play them. They could all be written out easier. In fact, it's not faster but it's a psychological thing. If they were written in big notes, you wouldn't have that. **O'Hora**

First moment of blind panic at squashed flies on the page. Lots of time with Michael working out how to divvy up the 18 notes. 6+6+6? Or 6+8+4?

Now we have the transition phrase. It takes these sighs and speeds them up . . . it's double the speed. And also the whole phrase is in a descending direction. So, in a way, it condenses all of the material of the first thirty or so bars and puts them in two four-bar statements. **Perahia**

All of this stuff . . . It's completely not melodic and yet we don't hear it as just decoration. We hear it melodically. It almost isn't a melody in the outer sections at all, it's just piano figuration. And yet, Chopin has the genius that, unlike, say, Mendelssohn, or even Weber, where you have melody and then you have decoration or something, in Chopin the decoration is the melody. They've become one in some strange kind of way. **Hough**

Passage work links theme A and theme B.

Pencilled in metronome times and dates: evidence of attempts to start slowly and build up speed. Managed 20 notches in 3 weeks, then abandoned.

Chopin's passage work never sounds like filler of any sort. If you played any passage of Chopin in a very slow tempo, like the part leading up to the second theme, adagio, you would find that you can make it incredibly beautiful and melodic and it would make a lot of sense. It's all melodic and all beautiful and all elegant . . . and all not mindless passage work. The only other composer I can think of who does that all the time is Mozart. **Ax**

Horribly confusing changing patterns. Fingerings need meticulous planning and learning. So much going on so fast in both hands. Need to memorise, not look at score. Almost give up at this point.

Arpeggios! Last seriously attempted c. 1970. All the fingerings seem 'wrong'. And LH horn calls enter at unpredictable moments. Seriously tricky.

Suddenly, there's hope but the hope is in turbulence, the hope is in martial activity, war. **Perahia**

Horn call (in fourths) introduces theme B.

Theme B

The second subject is even harmonised in fourths, which is
something really quite extraordinary. **Hough**

This is very personal . . . it's a feeling of love, maybe love to this
Polish girl, maybe love to Poland, but it's still love. **Perahia**

It seems to me that the second subject is some sort of unobtainable
happiness happening somewhere else, perhaps. I don't think it's
Chopin experiencing that. **Hough**

It's the first pianissimo in the piece. It's always been piano until then, so,
when it comes, I think there is a kind of a gasp of a new colour. It's
miraculous, of course, beginning on that fourth, that comes out of that
horn call that has itself come before, of course, in the middle of those G
minor arpeggios. How it melts and adjusts and then, finally, it becomes
the beginning of the new subject. That's one of those master strokes that
only a genius can do. **Hough**

First appearance of theme B is perfectly playable – though getting tune
floating above bass takes time. At least two lessons with Michael taken up
with working out the pedalling of bars 73–75. RH seems to be in three
broad beats, suggesting three pedals. But LH seems to be in two. What's
known as a 'hemiola'. Michael is delighted at the challenge. He suggests
pedalling with RH, even though counterintuitive. And then five changes
of pedal in 75.

Speeded-up echo of theme A.

Gentleness of theme B ends abruptly with a falling ninth. This becomes an important interval.

Theme A reappears, but much bleaker and edgier.

Lucy has written '*Bebung*': she wants the effect of the second note echoing the first, like a heartbeat. Michael is less fussed.

Split octaves between hands, or play in RH? Michael wants the former, Lucy suggests the latter. One hand helps when it comes to turning the page. Mundane, but true.

Return of theme B.

The textbooks will tell you it's an A major. I don't think it's an A major . . . I think it's an E. **Perahia**

Murray says it's in E major as opposed to A major? Is that what he said? Wow! Wow! Interesting! **Ax**

When you come to that climax, here, it is fortissimo but, it should not be bashed and it should not be hurried, it should open up something with a very relaxed, large sound. It is certainly A major, for me. **Brendel**

It's an ecstatic moment. It's a moment of radiant outpouring. I don't see it as triumphant nor as majestic. Maybe this will stick in your mind and you'll never be able to hear it again, but it's the moment in *The Sound of Music* where Julie Andrews just runs up the hill and The Hills Are Alive'. It's that kind of moment of sheer exuberance. **Hough**

This page is covered in pencil because it's so *hard*. The coda is terrifying, but this is murderous in its own way. There's no short cut to memorising the LH chords – just no escape. Every bar is subtly different. RH octaves not easy either. No good looking at score. Nightmare.

These three octave runs are so difficult for me. Firstly, what are they? My pencilled scribble suggests 'B minor apart from E sharp'. As if that helps. Next, how does one finger such a scale in octaves? The RH thumb plays every note. The upper line ought (to anyone with a technique) be reasonably simple – a mix of 3-4-5. But I'm not used to a thumb-3 stretch over an octave, so it's going to be a mix of 4 and 5. Each of the three scales harder than the previous one. Needless to say, all needs memorising.

The second theme comes back fortissimo fervently hoping that this love can flourish, but it's going to constantly go higher and higher and higher with all of these octave runs to a triple fortissimo. So this ascent is this yearning to cut the yoke of the sadness that started the piece, of the descents that started the piece. That's a very pivotal moment. Besides the virtuosity that's needed you need the passion for these octaves – you know, to brave this ascent, it's very strong. **Perahia**

Each of these three octave scales is not quite a conventional scale. So each needs learning and memorising. And fingering. The LH needs to play itself.

Very fiddly repeated pattern of 16 notes. But the pattern doesn't fall on the same beat. Nor do the LH chords. Part music, part maths.

— Waltz

> There are one or two performances where this comes off well. For me, one of the shortcomings of the performances is that they often get too fast. It is much more demanding to play things two or four degrees slower, and with all the clarity and with all the necessary rhythm, than just to dash away. **Brendel**

This, for me, is the present exile in Paris, in the society of Paris, with all the fineries, the bourgeois sophistication. Strauss uses these kinds of waltzes for vulgarity in the *Rosenkavalier*, and Mahler too. I think it's a cynical thing. **Perahia**

> Everybody plays the waltz so fast that you actually can't hear what is going on. The right hand and left hand are basically echoes of each other and you should be able to hear that. **Rosen**

More 'sighs'.

More pencilled and dated metronome marks to help structure practice (and convince myself I'm making progress?). The RH is not too tricky, but the LH involves huge leaps and awkward middle voices – and keeps changing subtly. Do you look at RH or LH to judge the jumps? Either. But not the score. Which means this, too, has to be memorised.

We spend at least three lessons on these four bars. RH and LH seem to work to patterns – at times the same, at times different. Pedal to emphasise these patterns (if so, which hand?) or one pedal per beat?

I have pencilled in F-sharp minor melodic, with a chromatic leading note to the dominant – this must have come from Michael. As if that would help me. Followed by falling and rising arpeggios which another teacher – Lucy – has deemed must be legato. All coordinated with LH fanfares.

More fanfares in LH.

The sort of simple figure that comes back to bite you. Repeated four times. Michael wants it legato. I think 'legato can wait' and learn the wrong fingering. But wrong fingering doesn't give legato. So have to unpick fingering and try 124/135/245, which is not at all intuitive. And quite a lot of wasted time.

Surely one of the nastiest page turns in all piano music. This is where you wish you'd practised your B-flat major scales harder at school – though even then it's complicated by an E natural. And then, precisely on the turn, the LH has a big spread chord and the RH switches into E-flat minor. Another scale I never learned.

Third statement of theme B.

You've had this sort of climax of the waltz section,
and I think this is the top point in the phrase, and
maybe the fortissimo is for this B flat where it ends,
but, to me, after that, it subsides a little bit, and
suddenly this arpeggio, I think, is rolling in a mezzo
forte and the theme in a semi forte. It's actually quite
expressive and it's just warm. **Hough**

Twenty-six bars of broken chords in the LH, each
slightly different, with a minimum stretch of a ninth or
tenth – sometimes much more. To begin with this gives
me severe RSI-like pains. I have to slow down and learn
how to keep the LH light and fluid.

Six notes in LH against five notes in the RH. Hardish,
but worse to come.

Lucy suggests switching 3 to 1 (thumb), purely to get the
hand into position for the octave fanfare. Chances are in
performance the eye will be so concentrated on the
tricky arpeggios in the LH that the RH could badly
mis-hit.

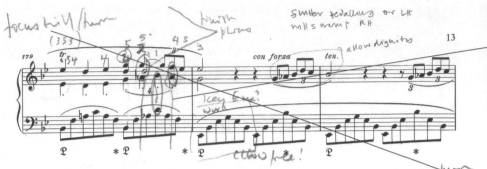

Six notes in the LH. That's the easy bit. In the middle are four notes, all played with the RH thumb. Only the first and third notes – the B flat – coincide with any of the six. The other two have to fall between the LH notes. And then, further to complicate things, the outer notes in the RH also fall between the LH, with a tied triplet at the end to make life even twistier. Michael's pencil lines sort of indicate how the notes should fall. I think it means you have to imagine eight or nine staggered moments in time, depending on how you count them.

'Focus trill/turn' scribbles a teacher. Two different fingerings suggested – 4/5/4 or 3/5/3. Both are v difficult: the first because the fourth and fifth fingers are weak; the second because it's awkward to stretch an octave with thumb and third finger.

Echoes of (speeded up) theme A again.

Switching of fingers on a note (e.g. replacing a fourth finger with a thumb without resounding it) is so-called 'legato fingering' – done to create a smoother line. Don't remember learning this as a teenager. But watch any professional pianist's hands and they will be using this technique constantly.

A sudden drop of a ninth heralds return of theme A at original speed and in original key. Ninth anticipates the frenzied RH ninths at start of coda.

Theme A returns.

You get this minor ninth fall which happens so much, and then back again – 'There's no escape. We thought there was but, actually, no' . . . And this is the third time this comes. It's like the three chances you have and, I'm afraid, if you blow it on the third one, there's not ever going to be a fourth. I think you really feel a sense of that. **Hough**

Descending pattern of falling sighs in original statement of theme A replaced by ascending phrases.

The two bars before the coda are as loud as possible. That really is such an incredible cry of despair. It's absolutely heart-rending if you do it with great passion, great loudness, and not too fast. You kind of try not to think about the coda at this point. You try not to think of the coda as being the signal for the starter's gun, you know, that you're off to the races. I think maybe the Presto shouldn't be too presto. **Ax**

The minor ninth comes back here in these outer voices, I think that minor ninth is a very important moment from the first time it occurs. **Hough**

Coda

The coda is hell for every pianist. You breathe in, and then off you go and then, if you're too excited, you blow up. So every pianist is so scared right from the beginning. It's notorious. **Ogawa**

The strength of the piece is really in this coda. The amount of virtuosity needed for it is huge. Much of the practice that one does has to go into these various difficulties of the coda, but it's not for a virtuoso showpiece, it's for the intensification of these emotions that have been kept down through the piece. They rise a little bit at different points and then there's just an explosion at the end. **Perahia**

Huge leaps LH. Manic energy in RH. Rhythms all feel wrong. Complex pedalling decisions. Welcome to the first four bars of the coda.

I don't think I ever played the coda accurately. You know, it's a very, very hard thing . . . this one has such dramatic extremes. It's incredibly hard to do it really presto and loud and powerful and without too much pedal. **Ax**

The tremendous brilliancy of a coda is very much like a fast cabaletta from an Italian opera. **Rosen**

The coda is the nearest you get in Chopin where you actually need to feel a player at the edge of their powers. That's not at all common with Chopin because of dignity and *souplesse* and everything in the aristocratic sense of the music. **O'Hora**

The hardest moment is when you leap down the octave. Once you're down the octave, it's not so difficult. Important here to keep a loose wrist so that you don't become tense, that the thumb is also free. The thumb can often get tight more than the other fingers because it's the odd finger out, it's not shaped like the others, it's in a different position, it's thick, it's heavy, it's cumbersome. **Hough**

Death-defying leaps in RH. Manageable slow, but increasingly dangerous as speed picks up. 14 bars of this to survive. All has to be memorised. Too much flurrying around in both hands to look anywhere but at the keys.

Next eight bars need memorising too. Chords and patterns not at all obvious. Hands, wrists and arms by now feeling burn.

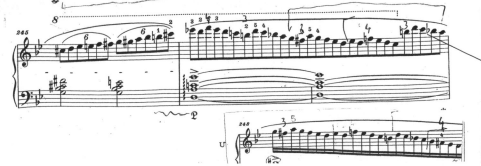

The coda can be too fast and if one can keep that in mind it's probably useful. It's in two, but I think it can help if you think it in four because that will slow you down a little bit. If it's just an easy-going two I think the danger is that it will be too fast. **Hough**

The chromatic scale is not really very difficult. We all learn chromatic scales. What's difficult about it is you begin in a strong part of the piano, go to the weaker part of the piano, but you need to make a crescendo. The danger here is that you start too loud and so you can't actually make a crescendo as you get to the smaller strings which have less resonance. If you crescendo with the left hand, it will give the illusion that the right hand is making an even bigger crescendo. **Hough**

The mood is, 'this can't go on any longer, revolution . . . the furies of hell will be unleashed on this' . . . It's just ultimate destruction. There's no rescue for anybody, these trumpets are very important . . . under the final ascent . . . these trumpets announce the doom. **Perahia**

The coda is not comfortable and I think it's supposed to maybe sound not so comfortable. It's not supposed to sound as though you're playing with ease. There's a struggle going on and the release of the struggle is that low D. That's when you can really think in terms of half bars or bars but before that I think you're really thinking in quarter-note segments and sometimes even eighth notes. **Ax**

An 18-note pattern of sorts – repeated once and then breaking off after 13 notes and changing into a very rapid descending G minor scale. Extraordinary sweep in five bars from the very heights of the piano to the very depths.

*) Siehe Anmerkungen zur Interpretation.
  See Remarks on Interpretation.

UT 50100

It's like shredding, ripping up a love letter, or something. You know there's something, physically it looks dramatic and I think these pauses are, you know, very important that they have their space. **Hough**

I can't help but be reminded of the idea of the tombs opening up, you know, at the end of the world, and everybody in horror and then the end of the regime of everything . . . everything. **Perahia**

A cruel moment. These two scales have to sound equal, don't they? But the second one is much harder than the first because it's in tenths rather than in an octave, so I think you have to be conscious that you don't have too much of a smile on your face as you do this brilliant G minor scale going up and then find that, when you get to the second one, it sounds very tentative and nervous. Do the first scale in the manner in which you will be able to do the tenths because otherwise it will sound like the tenths aren't as strong as the first one. **Hough**

This, to me, is almost like shaking someone by the shoulders, even on the page, but when you watch someone playing it, it's not just what you're listening to, it's what you're seeing, seeing on the page, seeing on the piano. Also, I think it's quite important in a performance that there's accelerando, that these bars are actually the right length, often they're doubled in length. **Hough**

Totally terrifying . . . that violent dissonance, coming together, I don't know, it's scary. **Ax**

Once you've got the accelerando of this chromatic scale going, it's just, you know, there's nothing more to say, I just have to finish this, it's too much, then it finishes. I don't think it ends and then it's a kind of big dramatic pompous ending. I think it ends. It's over. It's finished. **Hough**

ACKNOWLEDGEMENTS

The book wouldn't have been possible without the help of many friends, colleagues, family and strangers. Some helped with the music, some with the thinking, some with practical help, instruction, organisation, ideas, moral support, listening and encouragement – recently and/or over many years. Special thanks to Lindsay Mackie, Isabella Rusbridger and Lizzie Rusbridger. The customary apology is for prolonged absences from a writer who has been silently toiling in another room. For my family, this was true: but they had the additional burden of the writer as a very noisy, repetitive and insistent presence. I hope it hasn't put them off Chopin for ever. Particular thanks to Alex Bowler, my editor at Jonathan Cape. It's common to read complaints that old-fashioned editing and attention to detail have disappeared from publishing houses. Alex is the living proof that it ain't so. In no particular order, additional and sincere thanks go to Lucy Parham, Alfred Brendel, Richard Sennett, Keren Levy, Irene Brendel, Michael Shak, Mark Prescott, Martin Prendergast, Gary, Clive Coen, Susanna Eastburn, Charlotte Higgins, Rodrigo Braga, Ronan O'Hora, Anne Brain, Helen Walmsley-Johnson, Emanuel Ax, Murray Perahia, Ninette Perahia, Peter Beaumont, Ian Black, Derek Bourgeois, Isabel Sutton, Emma Kraemer, Pamela Merritt, William Fong, Ruthie Rogers, William Howard, Richard Goode, Marcus Pearce, Shehani Fernando, Ray Dolan, John Sloboda, Eric Clarke, Peter Milican, Terry Lewis, Jeff Shackell, Nicholas Wroe, Lauren Stewart, Georgina Henry, Ian Mayes, Colin and Thelma East, Noriko Ogawa, Philip Smith, Wendy Gonsalkorale, Fiona Ballantyne Dykes, Henry Goodrick Clarke and the Blockley builders (especially Phil, Stewart, John), Imogen Cooper, Marcus Pearce, Paolo Fazioli, Charlie and Vicky Bennett, Gill Diamond, Richard Rusbridger, Stuart Wattenbach, Lucy Heller, Deborah Siepmann, James Pollock, Howard Southern, Christabel Gairdner, Jenny Macmillan, David Evans, Eddie Miles, Liz Warde, Sheila Fitzsimons, Dennis Chang, Stephen Hough, Angela and Frank Rose, Irving Wardle, Michael Kimmelman, Alex

ACKNOWLEDGEMENTS

Ross, Sarah Miller, Patricia Hewitt, Ed Tyack, Condoleezza Rice, Claus and Mary Moser, Henry and Liz Porter, Francesco Cioncoloni, Simon Russell Beale, Dan Franklin, the other Dan Franklin, Claire Conrad, Tif Loehnis, Boris Berezovsky, Charles Rosen, Joe Mercuri, Jean Bourgeois, Kathleen Dunn Davies, Kat Vipers, Suzie K, James Rhodes, Marilyn Anderson, Robert Hahn, Aygün Lausch, Universal Editions, Melissa Denes, Judy Grahame, Jessica Lough, Lynn Nesbit, Richard McMahon, Clay Shirky, Malcolm Singer, Ruth Nye, Paul Chadwick, Philip Feeney, G. H. Rusbridger, Ronald Harwood, Robert Harris, Gail Rebuck, Rosamand Annett, Sue Birtwistle, Bryan Youl, Imogen Tilden, Mark Porter, Richard Morrison, Anna Tilbrook, Tracy Lees, Rebecca Folland and Piers Thorogood. From the *Guardian*: Paul Johnson, Ian Katz, Kath Viner, Sheila Fitzsimons and the main players in WikiLeaks and phone hacking: Nick Davies, David Leigh, Amelia Hill, the Media Guardian team, Dan Roberts, Harold Frayman, Gill Phillips . . . plus assorted lawyers, police, subjects of hacking, MPs and colleagues from other newspapers. You know who you are.

FURTHER READING

Memory and Piano Performance, Roger Chaffin, Gabriela Imreh and Mary Crawford. Psychology Press, 2002

Men with Sheds, Gordon Thorburn. New Holland Publishers, 2002

Modern Man in Search of a Soul, Carl Jung. Routledge, 2005

Piano: The making of a concert grand, James Barron. Times Books, 2006

Ballads Without Words: Chopin and the Tradition of the Instrumental Ballade, James Parakilas. Amadeus Press, 1992

Chopin and the G Minor Ballade, David Björling. Lulea Tekniska University, 2002

A Walk on the Wild Side, Earl Wild. Ivory Classic Foundation, 2011

Chopin: The Four Ballades, Jim Samson. Cambridge University Press, 1992

The Music of Chopin, Jim Samson. OUP, 1994

Music in London 1890–94, George Bernard Shaw. Constable, 1934

How to Play Chopin? Part 5: Chopin's Ballades, Regina Smendzianka. At www.chopin.org

Notebooks and Conversations, Sviatoslav Richter. Faber and Faber, 2001

City Boy, Edmund White. Bloomsbury, 2009

Pianists at Play, Dean Elder. Kahn and Averill, 1986

The Craftsman, Richard Sennett. Penguin, 2008

Piano for Pleasure, Charles Cooke, foreword by Michael Kimmelman. Skyhorse, 2011

I Found My Horn, Jasper Rees. Weidenfeld & Nicolson, 2008

Chopin: The Man and His Music, James Huneker. Charles Scribner's Sons, 1921

INDEX

Abdul-Ahad, Ghaith 184–5, 188,
  189, 191–2, 193, 194–6
Abraham, Gerald 160
Abramson, Jill 320
Ackroyd, Clive 81
Adie, Kate 194
Adrià, Ferran 176–7
Adweek 268
Aimard, Pierre-Laurent 320
Al Jazeera 80, 190
Alberti group 61
Aldeburgh, Suffolk: Red House 30
All the President's Men (film) 268,
  306
Andrew, Prince 70
Archive Bookstore, London 230–31
Arrau, Claudio 171, 181
Arts Club 1901 326, 344, 345–9
Ashkenazy, Vladimir 242
Aspen Music Festival School,
  Colorado 252
Assange, Julian 27, 28, 69, 70,
    80–81, 88–90, 92, 93–4, 97,
    107, 120, 125, 127, 128, 158,
    165, 300, 302, 305–6, 309–10
  autobiography 313–14
Attenborough, David 179, 180
Australia 98, 99–100
Australian Broadcasting

Corporation 99
Ax, Emanuel 185–8, 346–7, 357,
  363, 369, 381, 383, 385, 387

Bach, Johann Sebastian 79, 132,
  161
  Double Violin Concerto 178
  'Goldberg' Variations 215
Ballade No. 1 in G minor, Op. 23
    (Chopin) 1–2, 61–3, 93, 94,
    120, 121, 128, 130, 143–4, 150,
    153–4, 159, 160, 161, 164,
    166–9, 173–4, 177, 178, 185–6,
    211, 225–6, 334, 335, 336
  score and commentaries 13–22,
    356–87
Barak, Ehud 255
Barber, Lionel 329
Barenboim, Daniel 66, 76, 122,
    208–11, 212–13, 240, 283, 316
Bayes, Thomas 115
BBC 190, 233
  Newsnight 261, 325
  Today 47, 108, 258, 312, 313
  Young Musician of the Year 51
Beale, Simon Russell 243–4
Beaumont, Peter 190, 191, 192, 193,
  195
Bechstein pianos 32, 66, 84, 205

Beethoven, Ludwig van 122, 124,
 159, 160–61
  Cello Sonata Op. 5 No. 2 205
  piano sonatas 6, 50, 132, 206,
   211, 286, 299, 316, 353–4
  symphonies 152
Bell, Emily 145
Bellini, Vincenzo 23, 161
Benjamin, Alison: *A World Without
 Bees* 232
Benjamin, George 137–8
Bennett, Alan: 'Going Round' 346
Bennett, Arnold: *How to Live on
 24 Hours a Day* 44–6
Bennett, Charlie 215, 224, 225, 281,
 286, 293, 299
Berezovsky, Boris 224–6
Berg, Alban: Violin Concerto 143
Berg design agency 56
Berger, Karol 167
Berlin, Isaiah 126
Berlusconi, Silvio 110, 195
Bernstein, Carl 314
Bernstein, Simon 201
Billington, Michael 52–3
Birmingham Southern
 Conservatory of Music, Alabama
 251
Birtwistle, Harrison 231
Biss, Jonathan 42
Black, Ian 189, 190, 193, 195
Blair, Tony 69, 151
Blair, Cherie 142
Blair, Leo 142
Blockley, Gloucestershire 28, 29,
 30–31, 128–9, 229, 264, 307
  Discussion Group 342
  see also Fish Cottage

Bolívar (Simón) Orchestra 72–3
Bosch, Hieronymus: *The Garden of
 Earthly Delights* 177
Boulder, Colorado 56
Boulez, Pierre 308
Bourgeois, Derek 132, 133
Bourgeois, Jean 132–3
Bradlee, Ben 268, 306
Brahms, Johannes 121, 159, 253–4,
 255
  Clarinet Quintet 128, 207,
   247
  A German Requiem 243–4
  Handel Variations 286, 299
  Op. 117 intermezzo 129
  piano quartet 53
  Second Piano Concerto 318
Brain, Anne 7, 75, 206, 243, 279,
 280, 285, 288, 294–5, 296
Brendel, Alfred 12, 75–6, 126, 145,
 320, 332, 335, 369, 373
Brendel, Irene 12
Brest, Paul 252–3
British Press Awards 207–8
Britten, Benjamin 30, 85
Brixton: youth project 326
Brody, Adrien 61
Brooke, Heather 70, 80, 89, 93
Brooks, Rebekah 69, 259, 261, 262,
 264, 269, 271, 273, 274, 279
Brown, Fraser 265
Brown, Gordon 262, 265, 267
Brown, Jane 211
Brown, Sarah 265
Browne-Wilkinson, Nicholas 180
BSkyB 100, 179, 234, 259, 261, 264,
 266, 267, 275
Burns, John F. 80, 89

Bush, George H. W. 252
Bush, George W. 253

Cambridge Evening News 3, 322
Cameron, David 32, 40, 151, 234,
  260, 262, 266, 267, 269, 270,
  272–3, 275, 315
Camilla, Duchess of Cornwall 269
Campbell, Nicky 329
Canberra 99–100
Canongate (publishers) 313
Caroll, Walter 183
Carr, David 313
Carreno (Teresa) Youth Orchestra
  of Venezuela 72, 73
Carter, Graydon 273
Casals, Pablo 79
Charles, Prince of Wales 269
Chipping Campden: festivals
  224–5, 349n
Chopin, Frédéric 3, 13, 23, 87, 94,
  III, 121–2, 124, 152–3, 161, 167,
  220, 226, 333
  Ballades 2, 4, 55, 154, 332–3, *see
    also* Ballade No. 1
  Nocturnes 3, 135, 286, 292–3
  Polonaise-Fantaisie 173, 354
Chua, Amy: *Battle Hymn of the
  Tiger Mother* 154–5
Church, Charlotte 330
Cioncoloni, Francesco 22–3, 26
Clarke, Eric 314–15
Clarke, Henry Goodrick 31, 33, 34,
  41, 229
Clegg, Nick 234, 262
Clooney, George 305, 306
Coen, Clive III, 127, 178, 346
Condy, Oliver 64, 65

Conservative Conference,
  Birmingham 70
Coogan, Steve 329
Cooke, Charles: *Playing the Piano
  for Pleasure* 23, 54, 57, 176, 203
Cooper, Imogen 138, 334–5, 340
Cooper, Robert 189
Cork, Mr (music teacher) 132
Corke, William 181, 183
Cosmopolitan 331
Costolo, Dick 321–2
Coulson, Andy 40, 151, 234, 262,
  267, 271, 272
Cranke, Beatrice 229
Crone, Tom 267
Crowley, P. J. 102
Curzon, Clifford 166
Czerny, Carl 140, 159
  School of Velocity 71

Daily Mail 215, 230–31, 257, 313,
  331
Daily Mirror 272, 313
Daily Star 316
Daily Telegraph 37, 54, 190, 232,
  257, 260, 270, 313, 329
Dalrymple, Mrs 30
Danemann pianos 30, 130
Davies, Nick 28, 40, 55, 80, 142,
  151, 207, 211–12, 232, 247–8, 255,
  256, 257–8, 262–3, 268, 271–2,
  273–4, 275, 279, 305, 306, 314,
  329, 344
Debussy, Claude 42, 49
  'Clair de Lune' 131
  'Homage à Rameau' 181
Delhi 52, 54
Denver, Colorado: University 251–2

Derham, Katie 64, 65–6
Diamond, Anne 330
Dispatches (Channel 4) 68–9
Dixon, Jeremy 64, 67
Dolan, Ray 111–19, 122, 145, 146, 148, 152, 178
Donohoe, Peter 242–3
Douglas, Barry 242
Dowler, Bob and Sally 248, 256, 267, 269, 344
Dowler, Milly 248, 251, 255, 258, 259, 315, 342
Dowling, Tim 204
DreamWorks 165, 171
Dudamel, Gustavo 72
Dunn Davies, Miss 131–2
El-Dursi, Abdulmajeed Ramadan 191
Dykes, Fiona Ballantyne 1, 286–8, 299

Eastburn, Susanna 127, 178, 247
Edmondson, Ian 141
Elizabeth II, Queen 331
Ellsberg, Daniel 70
Evans, Edwin 230
Evans, Harry 275, 313
Evans, Jonathan 317

Fazioli, Paolo 324, 337–8, 340
Fazioli pianos 47, 74, 75–6, 181, 259, 324, 337–41
Feeney, Philip 3–4, 134, 135, 322
Felner, Till 320
Fidler, Roger 56
Financial Times 37, 329

Fish Cottage, Blockley 28–30, 41, 47, 176, 223–4
music room 30–31, 68, 71, 72, 92, 96, 103, *110*, 110–11, 129, 130, 149, 171, 184, 205, *229*, 229, 240–41, 246–7
Fisher, Edwin 66
Fleisher, Leon 149
Fong, William 281–2, 284–5, 286, 288, 289–91, 292–3, 296–9, 301, 302, 308, 310–11, 314, 318, 327, 346, 349
Foreign Press Awards 329
Foucault, Michel 126
Fox, Edward 64, 65
Fox, Liam, MP 316
Foyle, Michael 64, 65, 66
Franck, César: Prelude, Chorale and Fugue 87
Fraser, Giles 320–21, 323
Frayman, Harold 70
'Freelance 09' (tweeter) 107

al-Gaddafi, Muammar 191, 193, 195
Gaddafi, al-Saadi 191
Gaddafi, Saif al-Islam 185, 191, 195
Gallagher, Tony 329
Gibson, Janine 204
Gieseking, Walter 122
Goldsmith, Jack 157
Goodall, Reginald 308
Goode, Richard 42, 173–5, 185
Goodyear, Stewart 143
Gould, Glenn 285
Graham, Lizzie 307
Graham, Martin 307

Grant, Hugh 176, 232, 329
Granta 7
Green, Gill 81
Greenwood, Colin 205
Grieg, Edvard: *Holberg Suite* 132
Guardian 5, 37–39, 42, 56, 63, 172,
    228, 237, 242, 261, 275, 314,
    316, 319–20
  and British Press Awards
    207–8
  and *News of the World* phone
    hacking scandal 8, 40, 41,
    255–8, 260–61, 263, 264–5,
    267, 270, 312–13
  staff and correspondents 47,
    52–3, 72, 83, 96, 127, 141, 173,
    204–5, 213, 231, 237, 239, 242,
    274, 317, *see also* Abdul-Ahad,
    Ghaith; Davies, Nick
  and WikiLeaks 8, 27–8, 39, 70,
    88–90, 93, 96–7, 107, 149,
    157, 165, 171, 313, *see also*
    Assange, Julian
Guardian Media Group 96, 97,
    239, 314
Guardian Public Service Awards
    329
Guardian Weekend 237
Gulyak, Sofya 224

Habermas, Jürgen 126
Hagerty, Bill 331
Hague, William 255
Haitink, Bernard 84
Hamelin, Marc-André 101
Hamilton, Neil 261
Hanna-Pladdy, Brenda 215
Harding, Daniel 188

Harding, James 269, 317, 329
Harding, Luke 128
Hare, David 76
Harwood, Ronnie 93, 193
Hausmusik 84–5, 353
Hayman, Andy 266
Heisenberg principle 306–7
Hesketh-Harvey, Kit 64, 66
Hess, Nyra 165
Hewitt, Angela 114–15
Higgins, Charlotte 127, 178, 346
Hill, Amelia 312
Hilton, Janet 297
Hindu (newspaper) 54
Hinton, Les 269
Hislop, Ian 316
Hitchens, Christopher 265
'HM' 114
Hoare, Sean 40, 55, 271–2, 305
Hobbs, Jerry R. 44
Hobhouse, Emily 275
Hobsbawm, Eric 325–6
Hoffman, Dustin 306
Hofmann, Josef 159–60, 215,
    332–3
Hogan-Howe, Bernard 313
Horowitz, Vladimir 66, 169, 170,
    177, 180, 347
Hough, Stephen 331–4, 335, 349,
    357, 361, 365, 369, 377, 381, 383,
    385, 387
House of Commons Select
    Committee for Culture, Media
    and Sport 273, 275, 279
Howard, William 326, 327–8, 346
Huhne, Chris 242
Hunt, Jeremy 234, 256
Hurst, George 152

Independent 37, 231, 313
Ingram, Mathew 158
Ingrams, Richard 64, 66, 68
International Press Institute: lunch 256
Ismail, Mohammed 191, 192, 194, 195

Jacobson, Julian 65
Janáček, Leoš: Sinfonietta 139, 142
Jardine, Lisa 326
Jarvis, Jeff 173
Jay, Robert, QC 316
Jenkins, Simon 102–3
Johnson, Alan, MP 41
Jung, Carl 5, 45

Kaplan, Benjamin 152
Katz, Ian 80, 96, 128
Katz, Mark 162
Kauffmann, Sylvie 314
Kawai piano 324
Kay, Richard 331
Keller, Bill 40, 90, 102, 157, 195, 313
Kentish Town 47–8
Kentner, Louis 87, 95, 97–8
    Piano 94–5, 97
Kettle, Martin 317
Khan, Jemima 176
Kimmelman, Michael 178–9, 200–4
Kings Place concert hall 42, 63–4, 243
    concerts 64–7, 200, 206, 334
Kissin, Evgeny 76
Knox, Alex 136
Knüpfer, Stefan 320

Labèque Sisters 239
Labour Party Conferences 57, 59–60, 314
Laplace, Pierre-Simon 115
Le Brun, Christopher 231
Leeds International Piano Competition 152
Leigh, David 28, 69–70, 80, 81, 90
Leveson, Lord Justice 267
Leveson Inquiry 8, 267, 315–16, 321, 329, 330–31
Lewis, Paul 309
Lewis, Terry 183, 324, 337–8, 340
Libya 188, 189–96
Ligeti, György 226
Lill, John 81
Liszt, Franz 87, 123, 158, 159
    Réminiscences de Don Juan 159
    Totentanz 143
Littlejohn, Richard 313
Locker, Frederick 58
Locker, Jane 58
Locker-Lampson, J. 58, 82
Loehnis, Tif 215
Longborough Opera 240–41, 307–8
Lot Music summer piano courses 1–2, 7, 75, 120, 136, 151, 233, 243, 279, 280–302
Lough, Jessica 317–18
Lupu, Radu 318

Ma, Yo-Yo 253
McBurney, Simon 47
McCabe, Eamonn 47
McEwan, Ian 111, 115
McGuinness, Martin 321
Mackerras, Charles 308
Macmillan, Jenny 281–2, 286, 293

McMullan, Paul 55
Maddocks, Fiona 213
Mallory, George 44
Malone, Gareth 341–2
Marlboro Music festival, Vermont 175
Mascolo, George 88, 90, 107
Maunder, J. H. 216
  Olivet to Calvary 216
Mayes, Ian 237–8
Medvedev, Dmitri 241, 242
Mendelssohn, Felix 186
Mendes, Sam 244
Mensch, Louise, MP 273
Menuhin (Yehudi) School 171, 175, 179, 181–3
Michelangeli, Arturo 328
Mickiewicz, Adam 13
Middleton, Kate 331
Milhaud, Darius: Scaramouche 145
Miliband, David 180
Miliband, Ed 59, 260
Miliband, Louise 180
Milican, Peter 64, 239
Millar, Stuart 80
Miller, Andrew 239
Miller, Sienna 330–31
Mockridge, Tom 330
Monde, Le 90, 92, 93, 96, 176
Morrison, Richard 134–5, 151, 322
  Moscow Conservatoire 242
  Tchaikovsky piano competition 242–3
Moser, Lord Claus 64, 66, 83–8, 94, 95, 97, 179, 180, 353
Mosley, Max 331
Mozart, W. A.
  Clarinet concerto 319

Clarinet quintet and trio 127–8, 133
Concerto for Two Pianos 239
Fantasy in C Minor, K475 132, 133, 136
'Jupiter' Symphony 241
Kegelstatt Trio 246–7
Magic Flute overture 151
Piano Concerto No. 24, K491 242
Piano Sonata No. 16 in C Major 6, 133
Requiem 140
Sinfonia Concertante 178, 207
Sonata for Two Pianos 87
Mulcaire, Glenn 257–8, 342, 344
Murdoch, James 261, 271, 273, 274, 279–80, 325
Murdoch, Rupert 100, 234, 259, 261, 263, 264, 266, 268, 269, 270, 273, 274
Murray, Tai 142–3
Musical Times 216

Naismith, Mike 229
National Youth Orchestra (NYO) 41–2, 64, 139–40, 142
Neate, Rupert 316
Negus, Anthony 307–8
New Music Review 216
New Yorker 161
New York Times (NYT) 28, 38, 40–41, 70, 80–81, 88, 89, 90, 92, 93, 96, 101–2, 107, 176, 178, 195, 202, 251, 265, 271, 305, 306, 313, 319, 320

News Corporation 100, 142, 234, 259–60, 261, 264, 266, 267, 268, 271, 273
News International 40, 41, 68–9, 212, 234, 256, 257, 259, 262, 263, 267, 269, 275, 312, 313, 325, 329, 343, 344, 345
News of the World (*NotW*) 40, 55, 68–9, 100, 141, 151, 176, 179, 184, 207–8, 234, 247–8, 251, 257–67 *passim*, 271–2, 342, 344
Norris, David Owen 347
Norton-Taylor, Richard 261
NotW see News of the World
Nye, Ruth 171, 181, 182–3
NYO *see* National Youth Orchestra
NYT see New York Times

Oborne, Peter 232, 260
Observer 38, 204, 211, 213, 331
O'Connor, Cardinal Cormac Murphy 64, 65
Official Secrets Act 312
Ogawa, Noriko 151, 152–6, 185, 200, 206, 298, 346, 381
O'Hora, Hannah 120
O'Hora, Ronan 120–25, 144, 149, 153, 154, 359, 383
Oliver, Christian 138–9
Olle (Andrew) Lecture 100
Orchestra of the Age of Enlightenment 239
Origo, Antonio, Marchese of Val d'Orcia 11
Origo, Iris, Marchesa of Val d'Orcia 11
Orwell, George 326
    Nineteen Eighty-Four 230

Orwell, Richard 326
Orwell Lecture 325–6
Osborne, George 259

Paderewski, Ignacy 255
País, El 90, 92, 93, 96, 176, 177
Parham, Lucy 41–2, 43, 50–51, 63, 77, 99, 109, 144–5, 235–6, 239–40, 243, 245, 266, 336–7, 340, 346, 367, 375
Pearce, Dr Marcus 217–20
Peppiatt, Richard 316
Perahia, Murray 8, 76, 165–70, 173, 174–5, 180, 183, 193, 226, 333, 347, 357, 359, 361, 363, 365, 369, 371, 373, 381, 385, 387
Perahia, Ninette 165, 180
Perkins, Sue 64, 65
Perlemuter, Vlado 4, 132
Petrucci International Music Score Library Project 140, 150, 178, 207, 353
Phang, Rosalind 183
Philip, Robert 162
Pianist, The 61, 93
Pianist Magazine 32, 67
Pianomania 320
PianoZap (website) 216–17
Piatigorsky, Gregor 177
Picasso, Pablo: *Guernica* 177
Pickard, David 64, 65
Pienza, Italy 11
Pizarro, Artur 99, 117
Polanski, Roman: *The Pianist* 61, 193
Pollini, Maurizio 178, 186, 188
Poon, Tiffany 143
Porter, Henry 31, 93, 331
Porter, Liz 93

Porter, Mark 141
Prendergast, Martin 42, 67, 145, 264, 279, 281, 286, 291–3, 299, 345–6
Prescott, Mark 127, 138, 246, 247
Press Complaints Commission 41, 256
Price, Adam, MP 69
Private Eye 316
Putin, Vladimir 110, 241

Radiohead 204–5
Radley College, Oxfordshire 139, 140
Ram, Mariam 54
Ram, Narasimhan 54
Ramsey, Basil 216
Rattle, Simon 72, 239
  Rhythm Is It 342
Rice, Condoleezza 251–5
Rice, Mr (music teacher) 85–6
Robards, Jason 268
Robinson, Jennifer 88, 89
Rose, Barry 131, 214
Rosen, Charles 158–61, 166, 215, 226, 373, 383
Rosenthal, Moriz 158–9
Ross, Alex 161–5, 175, 187, 209
  The Rest Is Noise 161
Royal Academy Dinner 231
Royal British Legion 260
Royal Protection Officers 269
Rubinstein, Arthur 159, 335
Rusbridger, Barbara vii, 54, 131, 132, 136, 227, 352
Rusbridger, Charlie 139
Rusbridger, George 4, 30, 32, 130, 132, 135

Rusbridger, Isabella 4, 6, 13, 128–9, 135, 156–7, 346, 349
Rusbridger, Lindsay 4, 12, 13, 128, 135, 142, 307, 346, 349
Rusbridger, Lizzie 4, 6, 13, 128–9, 135, 156–7, 337, 341, 346, 349
Rusbridger, Richard 139, 205, 227, 328, 349
Rushout, James 29

Saatchi, M&C 76
Sabbagh, Dan 260
St Paul's Cathedral: occupation 320–21, 323
Saint-Saëns, Camille: *Variations on a Theme of Beethoven* 145
Salisbury, Peter 75–6
Sand, George 220
Sarkozy, Nicolas 195
Sassens, Saskia 126, 205
Sawyer, Sir John 321
Schimmel pianos 63, 74–5, 259
Schmidt, Helmut 255
Schubert, Franz 160–61, 170, 232
  Die schöne Müllerin 136–7
  G flat Impromptu 75
  sonatas 76, 354
  Tänze 6
  Winterreise 136–7
Schumann, Robert 153, 161
  Canonic Etudes 42, 67
  Dichterliebe 127, 136–7
  Etudes symphoniques 65, 354
  Fantasie Op. 17 6–7, 65, 135, 354
  Kinderscenen 42, 64–7, 132, 182
  piano quartet 53
  piano quintet 207

Scott, C. P. 37, 61, 228
Scott, Mark 99
Scott Trust 38, 96
Sennett, Richard 126–8, 173, 178, 205, 206, 246, 319
Serkin, Rudolf 159
Service, Tom 231
Shackell, Anna 74
Shackell, Jeff/Shackell Pianos 32–4, 57–9, 63, 73–4, 81–2, 129, 199, 224, 225, 246, 324
Shak, Michael 6, 51, 77–9, 87, 91–2, 93, 97–8, 103, 104, 108–9, 136, 142, 152, 157, 161, 171, 175, 179, 206, 213–14, 227, 233, 235, 238, 245, 266–7, 274–5, 311, 317, 323–4, 326, 330, 343, 346, 349, 365, 367, 375
Shaw, George Bernard 83, 111, 353
Shirky, Clay: *Cognitive Surplus* 52, 85, 353
Sibelius, Jean 209
Singer, Malcolm 181
Slate magazine 265
Slough, Andrew 44
Smendzianka, Regina: *How to Play Chopin* 55
Snow, Jon 49
Somaiya, Raavi 80
Sontag, Susan 126
'Spider Club' 205, 241, 328, 346
Spiegel, Der 28, 70, 81, 88, 90, 92, 93, 96, 107, 176
Spielberg, Steven 165, 171
Steinway pianos 32–4, 57–9, 63, 73–4, 75, 81–2, 129, 158, 160, 166, 205, 246, 310, 324, 337, 345

Stephens, Mark 88, 89
Stephenson, Sir Paul 267–8, 270, 271, 313
Stevenson, Dennis 228
Stewart, Lauren 145–9, 152, 217
Strauss, Richard: *Elektra* 120
Su, Szuyu 'Rachel' 143–4
Sun 265, 272, 313, 330
Sunday People 331
Sunday Times 275, 313
Surrey Advertiser 135
'Suzie K' 150–51, 155
Swami, Praveen 54
Szpilman, Wladyslaw 61, 93

Takemitsu, Toru 152
Taseer, Salman 142
Tchaikovsky, Peter I.
   eight-hand arrangements of symphonies 140
   Fifth Symphony 72, 73, 137–8, 241
Tilbrook, Anna 151–2
Times, The 7, 37, 102, 135, 234, 260, 269, 317, 322
Tooby, Mike 322
Topham, Laurence 274
Toronyi-Lalic, Igor 212
Toynbee, David 322
Trelawny, Petroc 66
Truman, Harry, US President 255
Turing, Alan 115
Twitter/tweets 100, 130, 138–9, 143, 150, 164, 165, 321–2
Tyack, Ed 30, 229

Uchida, Mitsuko 47, 189

Val d'Orcia, Italy: La Foce estate
  11, 12, 308
Valent, Claudio 339–41
Van Cliburn competition, Fort
  Worth, Texas 202–3
Vanity Fair 273
Viñoly, Rafael 178, 200
Vulliamy, Ed 72–3, 204

Wagner, Richard 159, 307–8, 353
  Meistersinger 138, 205, 241
Waldman, Michael 137
Walker, Sarah 64, 66
Wall Street Journal 41, 268
Wallis, Neil 'Wolfman' 207, 267,
  268, 270
Wang Wang 187
Wang, Yuja 187
Warde, Liz 294–6, 351–2
Wardle, Irving 7
Washington Post 89, 90, 268, 306
Watson, Frank 181–2, 183
Watson, Tom, MP 69, 273
Wearing, Clive 114
Webb, Duncan 325
Werritty, Adam 316
Werry, Elizabeth 291

White, Edmund: *City Boy* 126
White, Robert 135, 322
WikiLeaks 8, 27–8, 69–70, 79,
  93–4, 96–7, 101–2, 108,
  109–10, 120, 125, 127, 128
  see also Assange, Julian;
  Guardian
Wild, Earl 336
Willeby, Charles 111
William, Prince 331
Williams, Conrad 64, 65n, 67
Williams, Dr Rowan, Archbishop
  of Canterbury 321
Wilson, Elizabeth 318
Wintour, Patrick 262
Wright, Josh 130
Wu, Enloc 133, 134, 136
Wyatt, Theo 353

Yamaha pianos 11, 32, 47, 75,
  338
Yates, John 266, 267–8, 270, 272
Youl, Bryan 205, 328
YouTube 95, 101, 143, 169, 170, 347,
  353

Zhou, Annie 143